The Information-Literate Historian

A Guide to Research for History Students

Second Edition

Jenny L. Presnell
Miami University (Ohio)

New York   Oxford
OXFORD UNIVERSITY PRESS

Oxford University Press is a department of the University of Oxford.
It furthers the University's objective of excellence in research, scholarship,
and education by publishing worldwide.

Oxford   New York
Auckland   Cape Town   Dar es Salaam   Hong Kong   Karachi
Kuala Lumpur   Madrid   Melbourne   Mexico City   Nairobi
New Delhi   Shanghai   Taipei   Toronto

With offices in
Argentina   Austria   Brazil   Chile   Czech Republic   France   Greece
Guatemala   Hungary   Italy   Japan   Poland   Portugal   Singapore
South Korea   Switzerland   Thailand   Turkey   Ukraine   Vietnam

For titles covered by Section 112 of the US Higher Education Opportunity
Act, please visit www.oup.com/us/he for the latest information about pricing
and alternate formats.

Published by Oxford University Press.
198 Madison Avenue, New York, New York 10016
http://www.oup.com

Library of Congress Cataloging-in-Publication Data
Presnell, Jenny L.
   The information-literate historian : a guide to research for history students /
Jenny L. Presnell.
      p. cm.
   ISBN 978-0-19-992604-6
   1. History—Research—Textbooks.   2. History—Methodology—Textbooks
   I. Title.
   D16.2.P715 2012
   907.2—dc23
                              2012022555

9 8 7 6 5 4 3 2
Printed in the United States of America
on acid-free paper

The Information-Literate Historian

For my parents,

Joseph (1921–1994) and Carmen (1930–1998) Presnell,

and, of course, Ellie, Gem, and Poco,

Contents

Preface

The creation of this book grew out of my experience teaching a course on historical research in the History Department of Miami University (Ohio). The purpose of the class was to prepare students in basic research techniques for their capstone history courses so that their faculty could concentrate on working with them on the intricacies of the subject matter and more in-depth research skills. However, most of the texts I looked at did not really teach students how to search in databases and how to think historically while performing those searches. None of the books did an adequate job of integrating the Internet into research either as a resource or as a presentation method. In my everyday role as a reference librarian, I also found students struggling to learn how to appropriately use the Internet for research. So, I decided to write the book I wish I had to teach the course.

This volume would not exist without the help of a number of associates, colleagues, and friends inside and outside of academia. Before I even had a book contract, Dean Judith Sessions and then Provost Ronald Crutcher granted me a 13-week leave to research and begin working on the text. Allan Winkler, of the history faculty at Miami University, encouraged me to undertake the project, even when I had doubts that anyone might use such a text. Cecelia Cancellaro of Idea Architects helped me to prepare a prospectus, refine chapters, and present my ideas to a publisher. For the first edition, Susan Ferber at Oxford University Press, more than an editor, kindly tolerated a first-time author who had so many questions and an often "less than polished text." She was kind and patient and shaped the text into a useable resource for many levels of researchers. Her guidance was invaluable. Lisa Grzan and Andrew Pachuta reshaped my text and made the book sound even better. So much had changed since the first edition, a second edition was needed. This second edition was guided by Charles Cavaliere and Lauren Aylward.

Along the way, many individuals read the original, the revised manuscript, and the second edition, offering their critical advice and knowledge in their particular areas of expertise. Thanks to Stacy Brinkman, Chastity Dittmann, Charlotte Goldy, Ken Grabach, Arianne Hartsell-Gundy, Michael Howser, Sylvia Hu, Cindy Jasper-Parisey, Laura Reeves, Lisa McLaughlin, John Millard, Nancy Moeckel, Theresa Mudrock, Melissa Norris, Steven Norris, Carla Pestana, Sven Eric Rose, Lisa Santucci, Robert Schmidt, Helen Sheumaker, Aaron Shrimplin, Amy Stander, Masha Stepanova, Rachel Vacek, Rob Withers, David Wolcott, Susan Wortman, William A. Wortman, Frances Yates, Jen-chien Yu, Judith P. Zinsser, and the readers for Oxford University Press, including: Eric Josef Carolson, Gustavus Adolphus College; Kathryn A. Edwards, University of South Carolina; Thomas Humphrey, Cleveland State University; Christina M. Jiminez, University of Colorado-Colorado Springs; Jonathan D. Sassi, College of Staten Island and the Graduate Center. Thanks too to Matt Edwards, a student in History 206 who allowed me to use his excellent research paper. Special thanks to Michael Howser and Jon Cameron for preparation of the images for the book, to Karen Clift and the Acquisitions Staff for all of those RUSH book orders, and to the Information Services Department in King Library at Miami University (Ohio). University libraries are open and staffed most days of the year (many holidays included), so my original 13-week leave meant extra duty for all of the librarians in my department. Thank you. While I have benefited from the input of many, decisions about the content and style are mine alone.

If you are an undergraduate student beginning your first major history research project, this book was designed for you. It contains research tips, explanations of how historians use sources of all types regardless of format (electronic, paper, or original manuscript). It will help you plan your research thoughtfully and logically. It is my belief that research, the foundation of any historical paper, project, or website, is central. In fact, for me it is more interesting than writing or presenting the findings. And if you have good skills, that research can actually be fun!

New to This Edition

Chapter 1
- Expands/further clarifies how to define and refine a thesis question
- Discussion of periodization of history and how it varies by country
- Expanded directions for note-taking and using citation software such as Refworks or Zotero
- Short discussion on academic integrity

Chapter 2
- Updated sources
- Discussion of transition from print to online reference materials
- New section on using the Internet as a reference source
- Coverage of statistics moved to new chapter 10

Chapter 3
- Discussion of electronic books, especially Google Books
- Coverage of how to use a discovery layer tool, a federated search engine that aggregates a search between the catalog and many online databases

Chapter 4
- Updated search techniques
- New coverage of Google Scholar and how it is and is not useful
- Discussion of different forms of access, the print journal to the electronic article
- How to manipulate the new interface for *Historical Abstracts* and *America: History and Life*

Chapter 5

- New section on how to read a book or journal article
- Expanded discussion of using book reviews

Chapter 6

- Discussion of electronic/online primary sources—how to find and use them
- Expanded list of web resources, especially newspapers
- Added sections on genealogy in historical research and material culture (especially architecture)
- New box on how to visit/use an archive

Chapter 7

- Updated discussion of search engines and how addresses are dynamically generated
- Google Scholar vs. Google web searching is discussed here
- Updated discussion of the deep web
- Inclusion of chart that compares search engines to article databases

Chapter 8

- Added categories to better understand the forms of maps and their purposes
- Lots of updates to sources
- Alternate online programs to ARCGIS, which can be complex, for map creation

Chapter 9

- Enriched section on the historical use of the photograph for social change
- Additional questions for interpreting artwork
- Greatly enlarged section dealing with newsreels, documentaries, and television and media in general
- Additional video sources
- Short discussion of Flickr and YouTube

Chapter 10: New Chapter on Statistics

- Provides coverage on how to search for and critically use statistics
- How to locate online sources of data

- Includes discussion of social surveys, opinion polls, consumer data, as well as a basic compilations of statistics

Chapter 11

- Increased coverage on writing papers
- Discussion of presentations—poster and oral—how to create posters
- Discussion of blogs and wikis and how they can be used to present research
- New types of presentation software aside from *PowerPoint*

The Information-Literate Historian

Introduction: What It Means to Be a Historian

Every day, history influences our lives. Unresolved issues and ill-resolved circumstances create turbulence and conflict, as well as unexpected opportunities for change in our world. As a student of history, you will be asked to assess the events of the past and their effects on the lives of people and nations past and present through a research paper or perhaps an oral presentation, a poster, or a website.

For instance, if you decide to research the decline of the Ottoman Empire and the division and domination of the Middle East by European colonial powers in the late eighteenth and nineteenth centuries, you will need to locate appropriate secondary works, such as books and journal articles written on this topic by other historians. You must also locate primary sources such as British, German, and French government documents, as well as government documents from such countries as Egypt, letters and diaries of individuals involved in the process, and images. Weaving ideas and evidence that you have found in these resources into an argument, you will be able to present your own interpretation of these events.

Whether you are using secondary works like books, journals, and magazines or primary sources like government documents, oral testimonies, letters, and diaries or the vast array of research material available through the Internet, this book will guide you through your research by giving you information and advice about how to locate, evaluate, and utilize the wide variety of sources available for historical research. In addition, you will learn strategies for focusing your thesis, organizing your research, and presenting your material effectively, convincingly, and professionally.

In the following chapters, you will learn:

- questions to ask before, during, and after your research process, as well as questions to ask of your sources and their authors

- search strategies that can be used in both electronic and print indexes and how to figure out what types of sources are appropriate for particular research questions
- how to find and use books, journals, and primary sources quickly and efficiently, as well as how to select the best ones for your topic
- how historians practice their craft and the nature of historical discourse and narrative
- how to find, use, and evaluate media (images, speeches, maps)
- guidelines for presenting your historical research in different formats: paper, oral presentation, and website

Chapter 1 discusses how historians do research and how scholarly information is published and disseminated. Chapter 2 provides an overview of reference resources, which will provide background and factual information to guide you in learning more about your topic before beginning your research. Chapters 3 and 4 provide search techniques for finding books and journal articles and advice on how to use each in your research. Chapter 5 suggests techniques for evaluating your sources. Not only will you need to find appropriate sources that complement and enhance your research topic, but you must also learn to identify quality research. Chapter 6 discusses the use of primary sources and strategies for finding those sources. Chapter 7 focuses on the Internet, how to use it in your research and how to search efficiently through its wealth of good and marginal material. Chapter 8 discusses maps and their use in historical research. Learning to "read" a map is an important part of understanding certain parts of history. Chapter 9 looks at the uses of multimedia in historical research and suggests ways of integrating these forms into your research, as well as techniques for evaluating these resources. Chapter 10 addresses the use of statistics and data in historical research. Finally, Chapter 11 explores multiple ways of presenting your historical research, distinguishing among the research paper, the oral presentation, and the website as presentation formats.

Technology has ushered in significant changes to the study and practice of history. These changes compel the student of history to think about historical research more creatively and to become comfortable using both traditional and newer sources and methods. This book offers insights into the most effective search strategies and provides concrete suggestions and guidelines for research-related questions and concerns. Because of the quantity, questionable quality, and increased availability of both primary and secondary sources, history students must be more sophisticated than ever before about their research methods. Yet today, as in the past, practicing history can be fun; and this book will show you how to enjoy what you do as you conduct your research more effectively.

1 Historians and the Research Process: Getting Started

WHAT YOU WILL LEARN IN THIS CHAPTER
- how scholarly information is communicated
- how to develop a topic and build an argument
- how to begin organizing your project and to take notes
- how to document your research

How Scholarly Information Is Communicated

The research process you are about to participate in is the result of a process of discourse and writing even older than Herodotus, the Greek scholar credited as the father of history. Today, part of the discourse (the discussion and exchange of ideas) of historians' research processes includes presenting research at conferences, talking about topics on listservs and blogs, and writing journal articles and books. At conferences, other scholars interested in the same topic ask questions and discuss alternative interpretations. Similar activities occur online on listservs and blogs, although in a much less formal manner. In journal articles and books, a very formal written exchange or discussion takes place as the authors of these articles cite other historians' interpretations (secondary works), primary sources, and the author. Prior to publication, these printed works have been reviewed or "refereed" by other expert scholars knowledgeable about aspects of the subject. These experts have offered suggestions for improvement and ensure that the publisher of the material is printing responsible, accurate, viable historical research. Indeed, even this book was read by anonymous reviewers, among other readers, who helped the author focus and express her thoughts.

With the advent of the Internet and technology enabling scholars and nonscholars alike to easily self-publish their work, this model of scholarly communication may slowly change to include forms other than the most common formats, the journal and the book. With its multimedia and hyper-linked format and the capacity for jumping around within a text, as well as to other pages and websites, the Internet offers new opportunities for historical scholarship and discourse. However, often, the checks and balances used for quality control are not yet in place, making material more challenging to use effectively.

What Historians Do and How They Do It

Simply put, historians gather clues and evidence from the past in order to understand and reconstruct an image of a particular person, place, event, or time period. Then, using that image, historians interpret its meaning, not only for the past but also for the present. In other words, historians are interested in determining the significance of the past for the people who actually experienced it, in light of how history continues to affect modern society. Historians strive to make meaningful connections between the past and the present.

The study of history is not unbiased, despite the best attempts and intentions of historians. History is not merely a collection of facts and dates but, rather, the unfolding and telling of a story from the past, which always involves a degree of judgment and interpretation. Each historian's past and present influence the questions he or she will ask about the topics of history under consideration. Each historian brings a unique perspective.

Formal and informal methods of practicing history have philosophical viewpoints and methodological patterns, which can be described as fitting into particular schools of historical study. Schools of history are fundamental ways in which historians approach historical questions. For instance, the Annales school, founded in 1929 in France, was a reaction to the traditional way of studying history through the analysis of biography, documents, and events. The historians of the Annales school instead embraced quantitative methodologies of studying history (using statistics) and incorporated material culture and social interpretations (the history of poverty and childhood, for instance) into their studies, which led to the growth of social history after World War II.[1] Other examples of schools of history include the Empiricists, the Marxists, and the Progressives. In addition to schools of history, there are methodologies of practice in history, such as microhistory, which involves looking at one small event and extrapolating information from it to make broad statements about regions or groups of peoples; women's history, which uses gender as a framework for looking at events or issues; and oral history, which relies on interviews and verbal testimonies of individuals who experienced an event.[2] If you continue on to advanced study, additional categories and their distinctions will become clearer. For your purposes as a beginning researcher, it is important to know that these philosophies and methodologies influence historians' writings and research questions. See the bibliography at the end of the chapter if you wish to read more about the various schools of history.

Historians also must consider time and how that time is divided by the cultures that are part of a particular period. Periodization is the practice of dividing time into meaningful segments, the Gilded Age or medieval Europe, for example. Agreement on divisions of time is problematic and varies according to the view of the participants and of the historians that interpret the period. See Box 1.1 for a further examination of periodization and its problems for researchers.

Historians build their arguments, their discourse, and their conclusions upon primary sources. Primary sources are the evidence that individuals, governments, organizations, and cultures or societies leave behind. Some examples of primary sources are a letter from a soldier written home to his sweetheart from the battlefield, a newspaper advertisement offering a reward for a runaway slave, a map detailing the layout of a village from twelfth-century China, a taped interview with a Holocaust survivor, and a battle-axe used in the Battle of Hastings. (Chapter 6 describes, in greater detail, the nature of primary sources and how to find them.) Interpreting these remnants and artifacts can be challenging, requiring imagination, as well as collaboration and discussion with other historians. Individual historians do not work in a vacuum. In fact, one of the central activities of historians is to engage in debate and discourse with other historians about the interpretation of the evidence they have collected.

Secondary works are the interpretations of a topic by other historians that draw on primary sources and other interpretive works to build an argument about a historical idea. Secondary works include books, such as *Pride, Faith, and Fear: Islam in Sub-Saharan Africa* published in 2003; journal articles, such as "The Body as Attire: The Shifting Meanings of Footbinding in Seventeenth-Century China" published in the *Journal of Women's History* in 1997; Internet sites, such as *Heritage: Civilization and the Jews* (http://www.pbs.org/wnet/heritage/) built to accompany the PBS series; and video series, such as *The Century* by ABC News and newscaster Peter Jennings on

Box 1.1 Periodization

Time is essential to historical research. How researchers divide it and define it influences every historical argument. Professor of Modern History at King's College London and author of *History in Practice*, Ludmilla Jordanova states, "Periodization is about managing time, the ways we imagine and conceptualize it and the amounts of it that we study in any given project" (124). Periodization differs by geographic region or culture; medieval is a European history concept that has no meaning to Chinese historians. Sometimes "modern history" is considered as beginning with the fall of the Roman Empire or, alternatively, the invention of the printing press in Europe. A Marxist approach to history would divide history into eras of slavery, feudalism, and capitalism (Lewis). Pre-Columbian history, before the 1492 arrival of Columbus in the "new" world, uses one culture's sense of time to periodize another's history. Periodization changes because different groups/regions have different ways of thinking about the changes in their culture or region. Periodization also changes depending on the field of study. Baroque style (1600–late 1700s) has meaning for art historians, but when Baroque style was popular, historians tend to describe the time as Early Modern (approximately 1500–1800). While these periods overlap, they are not identical. It is crucial to use the best descriptive terminology when looking for resources. As you begin your research you need to think about how you will place your topic in time, how others have periodized your topic, and how you can translate that periodization into actual search terms for the catalogs, indexes, and databases you will use. Jordanova's categories of types of periodization will help you think about searching:

- *Division by rulers, dynasties, or governmental administrations.* For example reigns of monarchs, terms of presidents, reigns of families. In British history, the interregnum defines the era between the monarchies of Charles I and Charles II, when Oliver Cromwell ruled. Using the interregnum as a designation implies that the normal state of government for Britain was a monarchy. The alternative is to refer to this time period as the Commonwealth (Jordanova, 107).

- *Events.* The birth of Christ (B.C. or A.D.), the French Revolution, or the Great Depression (Jordanova, 109–110).

- *Description of time.* Ancient, Medieval, Modern, pre-Columbian, Roaring Twenties, Swinging Sixties. Pre-Columbian defines the evolution of culture based on the perception of the conquerors (Jordanova, 113–119).

- *Type of government.* Communist Russia, Carolingian (the Holy Roman Empire), or Napoleonic France (Jordanova, 119–121).

- *Social and cultural style.* Baroque, Romantic Era. Sometimes these periods are hard to distinguish when they begin and end. Material culture and styles often overlap as fashion and social trends change (Jordanova, 120).

- *Metaphors or Themes.* The golden age of..., the Age of Revolution, the Gilded Age. These periods have very loose boundaries, often defined by the individual researcher (Jordanova, 121–122).

Lewis, Bernard. *The Periodization of History.* Mortimer and Raymond Sackler Institute of Advanced Studies and The Dayan Center for Middle Eastern and African Studies. Tel Aviv University delivered Jan 7, 2008. Full talk available on Youtube http://www.youtube.com/watch?v=OS7-ZRFwVxM.

Jordanova, Ludmilla. *History in Practice.* 2d ed. London: HodderArnold, 2006.

Rosenberg, Daniel, and Anthony Grafton. *Cartographies of Time: A History of the Timeline.* New York: Princeton Architectural Press, 2010.

the history of the twentieth century.[3] Historians carefully study the work of their peers as they conduct their research in order to see interrelationships among these works and sometimes among the work of scholars in other disciplines. They also regularly present their findings for other scholars to debate in journal articles, books, letters to the editors of scholarly journals, e-mails on listservs, and conference papers.

Historians make clear where they are drawing on the work of others by citing these sources in notes, which appear at the bottom of the page or end of the chapter or work. Deciding what to footnote can be complex. A discussion later in this chapter will offer a bit more clarification. However, if you know that you are using an idea or words that are not your own, be safe and document your work with a footnote or endnote. Claiming someone's

---

Box 1.2 Early History Journals

Although other historical journals existed, the earliest, truly modern scholarly historical journal was the *Historische Zeitschrift* founded in 1859 in Germany. It was the first to have the markings of rigorous scholarship and discourse that are recognized in modern historical journals, articles with clear documentation on a single thesis and approved by other historical scholars. Its support or patronage came from the Prussian monarch Maximillian, even though Germany had a highly developed university system. Quickly following this journal were the *Revue Historique* (1876), the *English Historical Review* (1886), and the *American Historical Review* (1886). Each of the major European nations and the United States copied the *Historische Zeitschrift* in professionalizing historical research and writing.

Source: Margaret F. Dalton, *The Origin and Development of Scholarly Historical Periodicals* (Tuscaloosa: University of Alabama Press, 1986), 3–4, 238.

Box 1.3 Academic Integrity

Plagiarism is a constant problem on college campuses. The ease of copying and pasting text, images, and other digital information into a paper or project can be tempting and inadvertent. You must be vigilant in ethically using and documenting other scholars' ideas and works. Students can purchase papers through paper mills or use other students' papers, kept on file by campus clubs and organizations for reuse. Ethically all of these scenarios, claiming someone else's work as your own, are instances of cheating. It may seem easy in the short run when you are crunched for time, but in the long run, you lose out on developing thinking and writing skills your future employers will expect you to have. Software such as *Turnitin* allows your professor to scan or upload an electronic copy of your paper to identify potentially plagiarized passages or inconsistencies in your syntax. Many colleges have honor codes that address academic integrity and plagiarism. Violations of that code can lead to expulsion.

ideas as your own and falsifying evidence is intellectual theft and fraud. Historians properly document their sources.

Practicing History in the Electronic Age: Tips for the Information-Literate Historian

The advent of the computer, along with the accompanying new ways of keeping track of research notes, has had a major impact on the way historians practice their craft. Some historians have likened this electronic revolution to the invention of the printing press. Historian Jeffrey Barlow outlines some of the challenges and advantages to historical evidence in the electronic age in his essay "Historical Research and Electronic Evidence: Problems and Promises."[4] Among the advantages the electronic age brings to the study of history, Barlow lists the following:

- Online access means more people can have access to historians' evidence, both primary and secondary, more easily. For example, many primary sources are freely available online. Many universities make their dissertations available electronically, although some may restrict access. Many journals can be delivered to your desktop through such services as *JSTOR* and the *History Cooperative*. Increasingly universities are also making the "intellectual" works of their faculty available online through an institutional repository or scholarly commons. These digital collections allow you free access to published, pre-published, and not-yet-published works by the faculty of that institution.

- Electronic discussion groups allow for the creation of a broader, more dynamic community. Instead of waiting for the next newsletter of a professional organization or research group, you can read a posting on a listserv or a blog and respond to it immediately. A paper placed on the Internet can have a public bulletin board attached for posting comments. Electronic book reviews such as those on *H-Net* can be written and posted more quickly than book reviews in paper journals.

- On the Internet everyone is equal. Because anyone can publish ideas, more and different ideas can be heard. Because of the lengthy and rigorous review process that print materials must go through, sometimes the publishing process can retard the dissemination of new ideas that are considered radical, controversial, or too offbeat. The

Internet facilitates new and sometimes radical discussions that can have a positive impact on the study of history.

Despite these powerful advantages, the electronic age also poses some challenges to gathering historical evidence, as Barlow points out:

- Historic electronic documents can be unreliable, impermanent, and lacking in authority depending on who has prepared and posted them. They can be easily altered or outright manufactured. Libraries, by virtue of the fact that they have knowledgeable librarians who select and organize materials, have the ability to filter out unreliable material. Through peer review, publishers offer a degree of reliability by having other historians assess the scholarly quality of their work. However, most websites do not have these checks and balances. Also, web pages may disappear, whereas printed and electronic books and journals made available by publishers usually remain accessible in a library.

- Assembling, scanning, and creating an electronic collection are easy enough tasks for anyone to do, regardless of their subject expertise. Such collections can lack the organization and selectivity that a professional scholar and editor would provide in a printed collection. For instance, editors of a collection of letters will often decide which ones are significant and which are less relevant, as well as provide notes about their authors and the context in which they were written.

- Errors can easily and rapidly be picked up and repeated. Barlow cites the *Protocols of the Elders of Zion,* a document fabricated by the Russian secret police from a Russian novel that was purported to be evidence that Jews were plotting to take over the world. It was published throughout the twentieth century and continues to surface today on the Internet as a primary source document. No scholar would include it in a published work as evidence that Jews were trying to colonize other nations, but an uninformed researcher might inadvertently do so if he or she believed certain websites.

- The Internet readily archives documents that are the result of plagiarism or intentionally present biased viewpoints.

While your research will not necessarily conform to a "school" of history, it will take place within the existing narrative and discourse of other historians' research. Selecting a viable topic that not only interests you but also adds to the historical literature is challenging and essential for a successful project.

Beginning Your Research

Where Do Viable and Interesting Topics Come From?

Whether writing a paper, creating an oral presentation, or planning an academic website, your topic selection is crucial. Keep a strong focus. Too much material covering too many ideas will dilute your argument and your readers' ability to follow it, resulting in jumbled facts and ideas. Even if you are creating a website and not attempting to lead your audience to a single conclusion, they should still be able to make sense of your argument and understand the significance of the material you are presenting. Far too often, topics are chosen based on the large amount of secondary works available. Overabundance of sources can lead to an unfocused project. Quantity and quality are not necessarily equivalent. However, having an appropriate number of focused sources for the length of your project is important. You cannot easily and adequately write a 25-page paper based on two books, nor can you manage to incorporate 50 sources into an eight- to ten-page paper.

When selecting a topic, it is best to begin with an idea that you are interested in and that exemplifies a larger phenomenon. For instance, you may be following the current debates on the changing family in twenty-first-century America and want to explore what families were like in a different place and time. Before making a decision about any topic, it is always a good idea to look at a subject encyclopedia article. This type of encyclopedia and other reference resources, discussed in greater depth in chapter 2, are tertiary sources and compiled by summarizing existing research. If you are researching family life in ancient Rome, then an article such as "Motherhood, Roman" in the *Encyclopedia of Women in the Ancient World*[5] will acquaint you with the terminology of your topic, provide background information, and help you focus your thoughts, as well as provide a bibliography for further reading.

Once you have selected a topic, do some preliminary searching in your library's online catalog (see chapter 3) and one of the appropriate online periodical indexes (see chapter 4). Check the availability of resources and the specific focused nature of some of these works you find. Before you are too set on your topic, this is a way to determine that it is viable and that there is sufficient and existing scholarship. Your professor will be asking you to write a paper or complete a project on a topic that is unique, so you must get to know the existing literature.

Developing a Question and Formulating an Argument

Having a viable topic, one that will have primary sources and secondary works to draw upon, is essential but not really the end point of your work. Many students stop at this stage of their research and write a paper or report on a topic. Historical research involves formulating a unique research question and developing an argument by building on others' research and your primary evidence. As author and historian Jim Cullen states, "good questions have the power to turn meaningless *information* into *meaningful* answers."[6] The sample questions below are not yet refined enough to be considered paper topics or arguments, but they represent a strong starting point.

RESEARCH QUESTIONS	NOT RESEARCH QUESTIONS
How did Slaves preserve African Cultures in their everyday lives?	*Slave Trade*
Why did Christianity spread from Byzantium to Russia?	*Russian Orthodox Church Origins*
What were medical practices in Islamic medicine from the eighth to the tenth centuries and how did they change?	*Islamic Civilization and Science*
What were the lives of Indian women in the seventeenth and eighteenth centuries in British-influenced India like?	*Women and Imperialism*

Selecting and refining your question and argument are critical and constant processes throughout your research. An underdeveloped question does not usually lead to an effective paper. Jim Cullen in *Essaying the Past* suggests criteria for identifying a good question. A "good question"[7]

- "is answerable in more than one legitimate way." Asking open-ended questions allows for multiple interpretations.
- "resonates beyond its immediate subject and invites consideration of broader historical issues." Historical questions connect to other historical questions. A question has context, meaning, and relevancy.
- "opens windows not only on the past, but on the present as well." While you must be cautious about connecting the past to meaningful lessons for the present, there can be a certain universality to questions that remain the same over time, even if the answers may not.
- "is answerable." You must have enough data to draw conclusions.

Additionally, historians Henry J. Steffens and Mary Jane Dickerson suggest asking yourself the following basic questions to help you to more effectively focus your thesis or topic and your research process.[8]

1. *"What is this piece about?"* What is your central argument? You may have many issues to discuss, but if you have to boil your argument down to two sentences, what is it that you really want to convey to your audience?

2. *"Why am I writing this?"* Later, this book talks about intentional and unintentional biases and the fact that all historians have subconscious motives and influences when they approach their research. You have a reason for selecting a topic. Understanding that reason is important and can help strengthen your research project.

3. *"Who am I writing this for?"* Who is your audience, aside from the professor who has assigned this project? If, for example, your project is a website, many people will see it. How will you take into account differences in gender, age, educational or knowledge level, and attitudes? You do not have to please everyone. In fact, trying to do so will result in a very ineffective project.

The Blueprint: Concept Maps, Storyboarding, and Outlines

Effectively presenting your research requires some preplanning. Chapter 11 will help you craft the final product, whether you have chosen a paper, presentation, or website. Early in your research you will want to outline your major areas of interest and points of argument. Regardless of your final format, you will still conceptualize your topic in sections or subcategories from which you will make logical links from one section to the next. Do not be afraid to draw organizational diagrams, maps, or charts to clarify those associations before beginning your research. Using the background information you have consulted in chapter 2, divide your research questions into concepts or sections and brainstorm ideas associated with those categories and subcategories. Drawing a concept map (sometimes called a mind map), storyboarding your narrative, or doing a formal outline are all useful methods. To create a concept map, place your central idea in a box and then divide that idea into aspects or concepts in attached boxes and then further connect subconcepts to those ideas. (See figure 1.1.) In this process, there is no hierarchy of ideas. The point is just to try to make associations/relationships between ideas. You will use these categories to organize your notes. This process is a bit looser than the traditional outline process, which

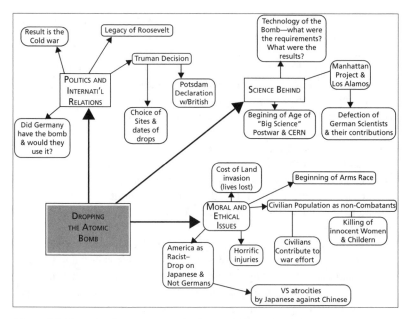

Figure 1.1 Example of a concept map for the very broad topic of the Atomic Bomb. Take your broad topic and begin to divide up the ideas and make relationships.

can also be used as an organizational tool. To outline a topic, select the main ideas, label them with a Roman numeral (I, II) and then list the categories underneath by letters and then numbers). Many word processing programs such as *Microsoft Word* have an outlining feature included. Storyboarding, which is often used to pre-visualize and plan the scenes of a motion picture, exhibit, or website, is another technique you may wish to use. Record your ideas on cards or post-it notes and arrange (and rearrange) them in the order you think your story or narrative will progress. Choose one of these methods to organize your ideas. You can draw them on paper or use one of several pieces of software. See DiRT: Digital Research Tools wiki and the section on brainstorming (https://digitalresearchtools.pbworks.com/w/page/17801672/FrontPage).

The way you arrange your evidence will create different associations and thus present different analyses and perhaps even lead to different conclusions.[9] For instance, as Laurel Thatcher Ulrich researched the diary of Martha Ballard, a midwife in eighteenth-century Maine, she was able to assemble additional primary sources in such a way as to make that diary, previously judged trivial and colloquial, become a rich and exemplary source for the study of women's history. In her presentation of Ballard's diary, she utilized survey maps, tax records, court testimony, an eighteenth-century text on midwifery, as well as secondary sources including a history of Augusta, Maine, to present and interpret Ballard's life and role as a prominent member of her community. The resulting book, entitled *A Midwife's Tale: The Life of Martha Ballard, Based on Her Diary, 1785–1812*, weaves a wide variety of primary source evidence into an amazing piece of history (for more detail, see http://dohistory.org).[10] Current interest in women's history led producers to turn the story of this diary into a PBS program. Not only did the eighteenth century speak to the twentieth century, but this piece of history was translated from a traditional form, a printed book, to a more popular form, a television documentary, and to an enhanced piece of scholarship on a website.

In researching and analyzing *A Midwife's Tale*, Ulrich had to gather and organize a large amount of information from both secondary and primary sources and carefully distinguish her ideas from those presented in these other sources. It is important for you to do the same in your research. No matter how intricately you plan out your research question, your organization will inevitably change, grow, collapse, and transform as you learn more about your topic. Do not become overly attached to keeping exactly the same scheme that you originally outlined. You may even get as far as the construction of the website or the writing of the paper and find that part of your argument is lacking and that you need to come up with more supporting primary evidence or secondary works for a particular section. As you begin writing your paper or planning your presentation, you may discover new questions that need to be explored. This is a normal part of writing history. Researching and writing history is an evolutionary process that will be challenging at first. The way to get beyond these "difficulties" is to read, research, write, and reorganize and to not be afraid of what you might perceive as wasted time. It is probably not, even though some of the sources you have consulted may not appear in your references list.

Taking Notes

Once you have established your categories and subcategories, you must create a system to keep track of notes from your secondary works and primary sources. Carefully documenting the source and origins of the ideas you present is crucial. A simple method for doing this is to assemble a series of index cards coded to reflect the categories and subcategories you have identified. You may want to standardize the appearance of your notecard by placing the identifying information in the same place on each card. For example, information indicating the source on the upper left, perhaps the author's last name and title keyword (Smith, Historiography, for example) or a code that links to a source list (A for source A in a separate source listing). Then, as you take specific notes, mark the cards by title of the subcategory to which they belong, for instance, Russian Revolution—causes, and the source of the information, usually the author's last name and date. A number of books exist to provide instruction on note-taking using paper notecards. Turabian's *A Manual for Writers of Research Papers, Theses, and Dissertations* is excellent for understanding how to take notes, both on note cards and on copies of the actual articles.[11] Software also exists for note-taking. Some historians have used a program called *Scribe* (http://chnm.gmu.edu/tools/scribe/) that can be found on the website of the Center for History and New Media at George Mason University. This free software will allow you to manage not only traditional notes but also digital images. For a list of other note-taking software see DiRT: Digital Research Tools (https://digitalresearchtools.pbworks.com/w/page/17801672/FrontPage) and the section Take Notes.

Knowing what ideas and information to record for future use is essential for accurately presenting your own ideas and for not inadvertently committing plagiarism, taking someone else's words or ideas and claiming them for your own. Whether you are writing a paper or creating a website or presentation, you must be true to your sources. Blatant plagiarism can lead to a failing grade and even expulsion from school. Many schools have honor codes that explicitly prohibit plagiarism. When taking notes, you can save yourself much agony if you distinguish among what you perceive as general knowledge, a paraphrase, or a direct quote. Put one idea on the note card, differentiating the author's idea, your interpretation, and the supporting evidence. Be careful to summarize the author's ideas in your own words. You will need to be able to clearly distinguish your own interpretation from that of your sources. Paraphrases and direct quotes need to be attributed to their original authors and require documentation, usually in the form of a footnote or reference or some sort of website documentation. Knowing what is general knowledge and what needs to be documented can be difficult. The following guidelines will help.[12]

- *General knowledge.* What seems to be commonly known about your topic. It may be hard to tell at first because you may not know much about your topic. However, if you keep reading the same facts and assumptions over and over, that would be general knowledge. For instance, that the Great Wall of China was built in the third century B.C.E. or that John Wilkes Booth assassinated Abraham Lincoln.

- *Paraphrasing.* Taking an author's ideas and describing them in your own words. Usually you will want to make the author's ideas more succinct and focus them in a way that relates to your thesis. (This is not, however, twisting the author's words to suit your purpose.) Using the original syntax of the author and plugging in the synonym of your choice is not really paraphrasing, and although it is not really a direct quote, it is not good writing practice. Either summarize in your own words an author's meaning or use the author's own words as a direct quote.

- *Quoting.* Using the author's exact words. Sometimes an author says something so eloquently that you want to keep the exact spirit of the original language. Perhaps you disagree with the author and need to carefully reflect his or her view to present your counter view. You may also be unable to paraphrase the text in any other way, so directly quoting the author is your only way to convey the idea.

Two of these cases, paraphrasing and quoting, require proper documentation or footnotes or endnotes as they are not your words and ideas but a reflection of others'. With so much content available digitally it is easy to inadvertently plagiarize by copying and pasting text into your notes and then transferring those exact words to your paper. Be careful. If you are unsure if your piece of information needs a footnote, it is always best to document your source with a footnote or a hyperlink with the source or a location. While you do not want to overburden your audience with notes, it is better to err on the side of caution rather than making someone else's ideas look like your own.

Creating Bibliographies and Documenting Sources

There are a number of ways and formats for providing documentation for your sources, both primary and secondary. The *Chicago Manual of Style* and its derivative, *A Manual for Writers of Term Papers, Theses, and Dissertations* (commonly known by the name of its author, Turabian), are generally the preferred citation guides for historians. These books will show you what information you need and how to construct bibliographies and footnotes/endnotes for any source you will use for your project. On

Box 1.4 History of Documentation and Historical Scandals

Originally, history and scholarship were evaluated based solely on the author's reputation. Prior to the middle of the nineteenth century, footnotes as a commonly used and standardized format did not even exist. There were attempts to provide scholarly works with some form of documentation in the eighteenth century, but the primary purpose of the authors was often to teach political or moral lessons, not to interpret the past. Scandals, from questionable sources to outright plagiarism, have rocked the historical community and brought renewed attention to historical documentation. Both Stephen Ambrose and Doris Kearns Goodwin, historical scholars, have been accused of using passages in their works that are nearly identical to those written by other scholars. Debate has also raged for a number of years over the authenticity of Alex Haley's famous saga *Roots*. Journalist Phillip Nobile wrote an article in the *Village Voice* and produced a documentary for the BBC that examined Haley's alleged plagiarism of portions of Harold Courlander's *The African*. Courlander sued Haley, but the case was settled out of court. A more recent case of potential academic fraud has surfaced with Michael Bellesiles and his examination of American gun ownership in *Arming America: The Origins of a National Gun Culture*. The controversy centers on the existence, or nonexistence, of some probate records Bellesiles claimed to use as his primary evidence. Columbia University found sufficient evidence of fraud to rescind the prestigious Bancroft Prize that the author had been awarded.

For more information see:

Grafton, Anthony. "Birth of the Footnote." *Lingua Franca* (November 1997): 59–66. See also his longer work, *The Footnote, a Curious History* (Boston: Harvard University Press, 1997).

"Writing History." January 28, 2002, *Newshour with Jim Lehrer*. Transcript, http://www.pbs.org/newshour/bb/law/jan-june02/history_1–28.html (accessed September 26, 2011).

Kirkpatrick, David. "Historian Says Borrowing Was Wider than Known." *New York Times*, February 23, 2002, 10A:5.

Kirkpatrick, David D. "As Historian's Fame Grows, So Do Questions on Methods." *New York Times*, January 11, 2002, A1:5. For a fuller examination of the recent scandals, see Jon Wiener, *Historians in Trouble: Plagiarism, Fraud, and Politics in the Ivory Tower* (New York: New Press, 2005).

Nobile, Philip. "Uncovering Roots." *Village Voice*, February 23, 1993, 31–38; and the BBC documentary *The Roots of Alex Haley*.

Courlander, Harold. *The African* (Boston: Little, Brown, 1960).

"How the Bellesiles Story Developed." *HNN (History News Network)*, http:// hnn.us/articles/691.html (accessed September 26, 2011).

rare occasions, your professors or teachers may allow you to use Modern Language Association (MLA) or American Psychological Association (APA) style.

Software programs, both free and subscription, exist to help you organize your sources, create bibliographies, and even automatically insert references into a *Microsoft Word* document. *Zotero* (http://www.zotero.org) is a free bibliographic citation manager that allows you to organize your references in folders, create mini notes and produce bibliographies in several formats. Produced by the same organization as *Scribe* (Roy Rosenzweig Center for History and New Media), *Zotero* is a plug-in that works with the Internet browser Firefox. After loading *Zotero*, which can be done on any computer, you can click on a special icon and download the bibliographic information from online catalogs, indexes, and websites. Your citation and other data are stored in your account at *Zotero*, not on your computer. You can attach .pdfs of journal articles, as well as copies of images to your record. Other features include inserting citations within your paper and collaborating with other researchers by sharing your bibliographies online. The *Zotero* website has excellent tutorials and directions for using the software. *Mendeley* (http://www.mendeley.com) is a competing free program. Refworks and Endnote are similar, but require a purchase. Easybib (http://www.easybib.com/) is a common choice for formatting quick citations, but is limited in the formats it covers and does not store your citations. For a list of competing software, see *DiRT: Digital Research Tools* wiki and the section on "Manage bibliographic information" (https:// digitalresearchtools.pbworks.com/w/page/17801672/FrontPage).

You may also encounter these citation styles in some of the indexes and databases you use for your research. Sometimes the database you use will format your bibliography for you. Look for citations with URLs at the bottom of the record or as a formatting feature in the database. Whether using Zotero or any other resources that create bibliographic citations, be careful and check the output. If the data that the database draws from is faulty or input improperly, your citations will be incorrect.

The Changing Nature of Historical Research and What Remains the Same

Historians are gradually changing and expanding their methods of research to take advantage of materials available on the Internet, but the discipline is still grounded in the principle of discussion and discourse based on primary evidence and attribution of those sources. You must learn to practice these techniques of discussion and discourse, while navigating between a traditional print world and the newer electronic frontier. The following chapters will help you understand and utilize standard and new sources and technologies to conduct your research effectively and to present your findings.

FOR FURTHER READING

Study of History and Information

Barlow, Jeffrey G. "Historical Research and Electronic Evidence: Problems and Promises." In *Writing, Teaching, and Researching History in the Electronic Age*: *Historians and Computers*, ed. Dennis A. Trinkle, 194–225. Armonk, NY: M. E. Sharpe, 1998.
  How the Internet has changed historical research practices.
Brown, John Seely, and Paul Duguid. *The Social Life of Information.* Boston: Harvard Business School Press, 2000.
  Simply, how information travels in the age of the Internet.
Burke, Peter, ed. *New Perspectives on Historical Writing.* 2nd ed. University Park: Pennsylvania State University Press, 2001.
  Contains essays that examine the shift to newer ways of "doing" history. Chapters include "History from Below," "On Microhistory," "History of Reading," "Oral History."
Dalton, Margaret Stieg. *The Origin and Development of Scholarly Historical Periodicals.* Tuscaloosa: University of Alabama Press, 1986.
  History of scholarly communication in historical periodicals.
Fischer, David Hackett. *Historians' Fallacies: Toward a Logic of Historical Thought.* New York: Harper and Row, 1970.
  Classic text that systematically points out problems in historical reasoning. Topics include fallacies of "question framing," "generalization," "false analogy," and "factual significance."

Gilderhus, Mark T. *History and Historians: A Historiographical Introduction*, 7th ed. Upper Saddle River, NJ: Prentice Hall, 2010.

Succinct discussion of historians and their craft, including the role of Western philosophical thinking.

Gleick, James. *The Information: A History, a Theory, a Flood*. New York: Pantheon Books, 2011.

How information "technology" has changed over the years.

Grafton, Anthony. *The Footnote, a Curious History*, rev. ed. Cambridge, MA: Harvard University Press, 1997.

History of the use of footnotes in the discipline of history.

Green, Anna, and Kathleen Troup, eds. *Houses of History: A Critical Reader in Twentieth-Century History and Theory*. New York: New York University Press, 1999.

Basic discussion of the schools of history.

Marwick, Arthur. *The New Nature of History: Knowledge, Evidence, Language*. Chicago: Lyceum Books, 2001.

In-depth discussion of the evolution of history as a discipline. Focus is on Western thought.

Munslow, Alun. *The Routledge Companion to Historical Studies*. London: Routledge, 2000.

More up-to-date than the *Dictionary of Concepts in History*. Will also give definitions and discussions of ideas commonly discussed by historians.

Myers, Robin, and Michael Harris, eds. *Fakes and Frauds: Varieties of Deception in Print and Manuscript*. Detroit: Omnigraphics, 1989.

Cites cases of forgery from the fifteenth to the twentieth centuries.

Ritter, Harry. *Dictionary of Concepts in History*. Westport, CT: Greenwood, 1986.

Dictionary that defines major schools and methodologies of historical study and research.

Tosh, John. *The Pursuit of History: Aims, Methods and New Directions in the Study of Modern History*. 5th ed. New York: Longman, 2010.

Ways of thinking about topics and sources.

Winks, Robin W., ed. *The Historian as Detective: Essays on Evidence*. New York: Harper and Row, 1969.

Classic set of essays by renowned historians that provide concrete examples of how to use and interpret primary source evidence.

Woolf, D. R., ed. *A Global Encyclopedia of Historical Writing*. New York: Garland, 1998.

Focus is on major historians and their writings. Many historians have influenced schools of history and trends in historical scholarship.

Wright, Alex. *Glut: Mastering Information through the Ages*. Washington, DC: Joseph Henry Press, 2007.

History of information.

How to Do Research

Barzun, Jacques, and Henry F. Graff. *The Modern Researcher.* 6th ed. Belmont, CA: Wadsworth/Thompson, 2004.

The standard for designing and writing simple to complex research projects in all humanities disciplines.

Henige, David. *Historical Evidence and Argument.* Madison: University of Wisconsin Press, 2005.

Highlights how evidence should be used and can be misused in historical writing.

Marius, Richard, and Melvin E. Page. *A Short Guide to Writing about History.* 7th ed. New York: Longman, 2010.

Discusses writing techniques, using evidence, and other methods for writing history papers.

McDowell, W. H. *Historical Research: A Guide.* London: Longman, 2002.

Background about the nature of the discipline of history.

Steffens, Henry J., and Mary Jane Dickerson. *Writers Guide: History.* Lexington, MA: D. C. Heath, 1987.

Older guide but good for focusing questions when beginning a project.

Storey, William Kelleher. *Writing History: A Guide for Students.* 3rd ed. New York: Oxford University Press, 2009.

Excellent guide for writing a paper. See especially the chapter "Building an Argument."

Weidenborner, Stephen, and Domenick Caruso. *Writing Research Papers: A Guide to the Research Process.* 6th ed. Boston: Bedford/St. Martins, 2001.

Step-by-step guide, from designing a research topic to creating a paper.

Style Manuals and Citation Guides

The Chicago Manual of Style. 16th ed. Chicago: University of Chicago Press, 2010.

David Warlich's Landmark Project. *Son of Citation Machine*, http://citationmachine. net (accessed September 6, 2011).

Put the essentials of your citation in the form provided and you will receive a citation in APA and MLA formats.

Gibaldi, Joseph. *MLA Handbook for Writers of Research Papers.* New York: Modern Language Association of America, 2009.

Harvard Law Review Association. *The Bluebook: A Uniform System of Citation.* Cambridge, MA: Harvard Law Review Association, 1991.

Mills, Elizabeth Shown. *Evidence Explained: Citing History Sources from Artifacts to Cyberspace.* Baltimore, Md: Genealogical Pub. Co, 2007.

Not based on any particular format, this guide attempts to help researchers format different and difficult to cite primary source citations, for example, artwork or probate records.

Publication Manual of the American Psychological Association. 5th ed. Washington, DC: American Psychological Association, 2001.

Turabian, Kate L. *A Manual for Writers of Research Papers, Theses, and Dissertations.* 7th ed. Revised by Wayne C. Booth, Gregory G. Colomb, and Joseph M. Williams. Chicago: University of Chicago Press, 2007.

Turabian, Kate L. *Student's Guide to Writing College Papers.* 4th ed. Revised by Gregory G. Colomb and Joseph M. Williams. Chicago: University of Chicago Press, 2008.

NOTES

1. Many books will outline these and other schools. This definition comes from Martha Howell and Walther Prevenier, *From Reliable Sources: An Introduction to Historical Methods* (Ithaca, NY: Cornell University Press, 2001), 110–112. Some other examples include Anna Green and Kathleen Troup, eds., *House of History: A Critical Reader in Twentieth-Century History and Theory* (New York: New York University Press, 1999); Arthur Marwick, *The New Nature of History: Knowledge, Evidence, Language* (Chicago: Lyceum Books, 2001); Norman J. Wilson, *History in Crisis: Recent Directions in Historiography*, 2nd ed. (Upper Saddle River, NJ: Pearson, Prentice Hall, 2008); and Harry Ritter, *Dictionary of Concepts in History* (Westport, CT: Greenwood Press, 1986).

2. Peter Burke, ed., *New Perspectives on Historical Writing* (University Park: Pennsylvania State University Press, 2001).

3. Charlotte A. Quinn and Frederick Quinn, *Pride, Faith, and Fear: Islam in Sub-Saharan Africa* (New York: Oxford University Press, 2003); Dorothy Ko, "The Body as Attire: The Shifting Meanings of Footbinding in Seventeenth-Century China," *Journal of Women's History* 8 (Winter 1997): 8–27; Public Broadcasting Service, *Heritage: Civilization and the Jews*, http://www.pbs.org/wnet/heritage/ (accessed September 26, 2011); *The Century: Decades of Change*, Peter Jennings, prod. ABC News in association with the History Channel (Princeton, NJ: Films for the Humanities and Sciences, 1999), videocassettes.

4. Jeffrey G. Barlow, "Historical Research and Electronic Evidence: Problems and Promises," in *Writing, Teaching, and Researching History in the Electronic Age: Historians and Computers*, ed. Dennis A. Trinkle (Armonk, NY: M. E. Sharpe, 1998), 206–215.

5. Joyce E. Salisbury, *Encyclopedia of Women in the Ancient World* (Santa Barbara, CA: ABC-CLIO, Inc., 2001), s.v. Motherhood, Roman.

6. Jim Cullen, *Essaying the Past: How to Read, Write, and Think about History* (Oxford: Wiley/Blackwell, 2009), 30.

7. Ibid., 30–34.

8. Henry J. Steffens and Mary Jane Dickerson, *Writers Guide: History* (Lexington, MA: D. C. Heath & Co., 1987), 6–14.

9. W. H. McDowell, *Historical Research: A Guide* (London: Longman, 2002), 10.

10. Laurel Thatcher Ulrich, *A Midwife's Tale: The Life of Martha Ballard, Based on Her Diary, 1785–1812* (New York: Knopf, 1990); Film Study Center at Harvard University and Center for History and the New Media at George Mason University, *DoHistory*, http://dohistory.org/ (accessed September 26, 2011). At dohistory.org, Ulrich discusses how puzzling the diary has been for many researchers, past and present. Some saw it as trivia or a source of genealogical history, while others in the later twentieth century found it only marginally useful for information on midwifery. See the book introduction, 8.

11. Kate L. Turabian, *A Manual for Writers of Research Papers, Theses, and Dissertations*, 7th ed., revised by Wayne C. Booth, Gregory G. Colomb, and Joseph M. Williams (Chicago: University of Chicago Press, 2007); Kate L. Turabian, *Student's Guide to Writing College Papers*, 4th ed., revised by Gregory G. Colomb and Joseph M. Williams (Chicago: University of Chicago Press, 2008).

12. Stephen Weidenborner and Domenick Caruso, "Quoting, Paraphrasing, and Summarizing," in *Writing Research Papers: A Guide to the Process*, 6th ed. (Boston: Bedford/St. Martins, 2001), 122–144; and Turabian, *A Manual for Writers of Research Papers, Theses, and Dissertations*, 36–47.

2

Reference Resources

WHAT YOU WILL LEARN IN THIS CHAPTER

- types of reference resources
- how to locate reference resources
- ways to find and use definitions, background information, and supporting material for your research
- specific reference titles, in print and online

What Are Reference Resources and When Are They Useful?

In chapter 1, you selected a topic and began to do some preliminary research, filling out a vague outline/categories of points that you might want to discuss in your argument. You formulated an argument, which may change as your research progresses. Understanding some basic background information about your topic helps you to consider how and where to begin your search for information and to formulate your search strategy, as well as to design the structure of your paper, project, presentation, or website. Consulting some of the reference resources listed in this chapter will provide you with a broader perspective and make your search for resources more efficient. You will use this chapter's resources in several ways. Initially, you will want to consult encyclopedias and multivolume general histories to ground your topic in historical research and to become familiar with its scope and the terms associated with it. Then, you will want to browse through some of the bibliographies that will lead you to other secondary sources. Each type of resource has a function. Depending on the needs of your research, you may or may not need to consult the other types of resources listed in this chapter.

These resources can be some of the most useful but underused tools in a researcher's repertoire, saving time as well as opening up new avenues of knowledge. However useful, these types of materials are not the foundation of a research project in the manner that primary sources, such as letters or diaries, are.

Reference resources are considered tertiary (third-level) source materials, generally in the format of a book or website, that provide background information and a succinct overview and analysis of a subject or concept. "Tertiary sources" means that these resources have been compiled from secondary sources. Unlike a secondary source book or journal article, reference resources are not intended to be read in their entirety but to be consulted to clarify terms and concepts associated with your topic and to provide basic facts, statistics, and referrals to authoritative secondary sources. For instance, the article on steelmaking in the *Dictionary of the Middle Ages* would help you understand the level of technical knowledge of blacksmiths making armor in the fourteenth century, as well as the form in which steel was transported (*stahlkuchen* or steel cake or bundles or garb) and the market conditions in the Rhineland.[1] From the article in the encyclopedia, you can gain knowledge about the history, process, and place of steelmaking, as well as keywords to search in a database. The article also suggests resources for further reading. Similarly, *International Historical Statistics: Europe 1750–2000* provides statistics on the social and economic fabric of European nations by including tables with such data as passenger traffic on railways by country and by year in the nineteenth century.[2] Statistics will be covered in depth in chapter 10.

You cannot construct an entire research project by stringing together encyclopedia articles, citing statistics, and adding some definitions from a dictionary, some quotes from a book review, and a chronology of events. To build your research paper or website in this way is to act merely as a reporter, not a researcher. To assemble summary information and facts without an underlying thesis or purpose is not contributing to scholarship, only repackaging information.

By definition, reference resources typically provide the following:

- summary information
- definitions
- associative and synonymous terms to make searching easier
- names of individuals associated with an event
- dates and places

- facts
- maps
- timelines
- bibliographies and sources for further reading
- biographical information
- addresses and locations

How to Find Reference Resources

Finding useful reference resources can be challenging. Literally thousands of print, online, and website sources exist that provide reference information. Generally, print reference resources are easy to find and understand. Internet reference resources often try to be all things to all researchers by creating a full virtual library, including reference resources such as encyclopedic information and fact-based information, as well as full texts of primary resources and sometimes even journal-like essays written by the author of the page or provided by the sponsoring organization. While many reference resources exist, and because they are so numerous, it is impossible to have a comprehensive list of sources for history. If you become familiar with the *types* of reference sources available, you can use your library's catalog to locate other relevant ones and search the Internet for others. Throughout this chapter you will find a list of selected reference resources that will be useful during your research process. Your librarian will also be able to suggest many titles, as well as strategies, for using these resources and ways of finding others.

Types of Reference Resources

You will use different types of reference resources to support different research needs at various stages of your research. At the beginning of your research, encyclopedias are often most useful to get your bearings on a subject. When you have a narrower topic with some specific terms, multivolume general histories will help you set your topic in a broader historical context, while biographical resources will help you investigate individuals' roles in history. As your research progresses and you integrate primary sources and more complex secondary works, you will want to use dictionaries and chronologies to understand the meanings of specific words and terms in the time of their origin and through their evolution, as well as the climate in which your events occurred. There are many types of reference resources that can assist you in constructing a research question. Below are the major types of reference resources useful to historians.

Encyclopedias

Encyclopedias can be one of the most useful resources for a beginning, as well as an advanced, researcher. Very quickly, such works provide a broad overview of a topic, as well as the essential facts, keywords, principal participants, and often a bibliography. Use the keywords and the names of principal participants as search terms (see chapter 3 for search techniques) and the bibliography as a basis for beginning your reading. Two types of encyclopedias exist, one general and one specialized (sometimes called "subject encyclopedias"). General encyclopedias, such as the *Encyclopaedia Britannica*, the *World Book Encyclopedia*, or the online *Wikipedia*, attempt to encompass and define the vast amount of human knowledge. Subject encyclopedias like the *Encyclopedia of North American Indians* or *The Encyclopedia of African History and Culture* provide focused, in-depth knowledge on some aspect of a subject, place, or time period. They use terminology that specialists, in this case historians, use to converse about a topic, providing vocabulary to use in your search strategy in online catalogs and periodical indexes described in chapters 3 and 4. Many times the entries will provide at their conclusion a bibliography of articles for further reading. These materials are often standard sources with which to begin your research. For the level of research you are doing, subject encyclopedias are the more appropriate type to use. Their articles are written and signed by professional historians and contain very specific subject matter that will more fully address your research topic than general encyclopedias.

Articles in subject encyclopedias are formatted in two ways. Sometimes you will find their articles arranged alphabetically like a dictionary. These entries are often, but not always, short and definition-like. For instance, *The Modern Encyclopedia of Russian and Soviet History* is arranged in this manner, with entries like "Kizil-Koba Culture," a series of settlements in the Crimea from the sixth to the ninth centuries B.C.E. Other subject encyclopedias are collections of lengthy subject-oriented entries that read like journal articles. "The Aristocracy of Inherited Wealth," a signed article by Ronald Story in the *Encyclopedia of American Social History*, is an example of this type of entry in such a subject encyclopedia. Conceptually, these two types of encyclopedias contribute to your knowledge about your subject in different ways. The alphabetic encyclopedia sets the context of a topic by defining a person, place, or concept. The topically arranged encyclopedia provides a broad, sweeping analysis that contextualizes and analyzes many aspects of a given subject. Each has signed articles, which means that someone with knowledge of the subject wrote the entry or article, which helps you evaluate the quality and accuracy of the information presented. Some subject encyclopedias focus on a culture (*The Encyclopedia of Islam*), a region or country (*The Encyclopedia of Latin American History and Culture*), a subject specialty or type of history (*St. James Encyclopedia of Labor History Worldwide*), or a time period (*Dictionary of the Middle Ages*).[3]

Often, online encyclopedias do not follow the patterns of print encyclopedias because of the Internet's ability to provide unique hypertext access that a static print source cannot. Some electronic encyclopedias are free to the public and are labors of love by individual scholars or academic societies, while other online resources require subscriptions and are often electronic copies of printed encyclopedias. Judging the quality of online electronic encyclopedias is problematic because it can be difficult to tell the origins of the information and the abilities of the author writing the entry. Those collections developed by commercial publishers and requiring subscriptions have some authority built in through stringent publication and editorial policies and practices. The online version of the *Catholic Encyclopedia* (http://www.newadvent.org/cathen/) is a copy of the published 1914 edition, which would exclude all of the reforms of Vatican I and II and the teachings of John Paul II. An encyclopedia of US Civil War battlefield medicine created by a Civil War reenactor may or may not contain correct information. You will need to verify some of the content in other reference resources or encyclopedias.

The Internet and electronic publication of texts have allowed several major publishers to develop cross-searching capabilities among their many fee-based reference publications. Because they are online, these collections can be updated more frequently than new editions of books can be printed. For example, Oxford University Press has collected many of its *Oxford Companion* books in *Oxford Reference Online*. Not strictly history-related, these sources provide basic definitions and background information about a given topic. ABC-CLIO, a major publisher of history books, issues many of its reference publications as e-books. While there is as yet no mechanism to search in the text of all e-books from all the publishers owned by your library, your library may have electronic access to individual titles. Gale, another large publisher of reference materials, offers the *Gale Virtual*

Box 2.1 Wikipedia

Established in 2001 as a communal, multilingual encyclopedia, *Wikipedia* (http://www.wikipedia.org/) allows anyone to create and edit an article about a topic of their choosing. A huge endeavor that includes separate *Wikipedias* in numerous languages such as German, Japanese, Afrikaans, and Arabic, and over 3.6 million articles, *Wikipedia* would seem to be the fount of knowledge. Simple to search, the encyclopedia almost always produces results. However, there are some drawbacks to this online encyclopedia as an information resource. *Wikipedia* has "pillars" or principles which state that authors should write from a neutral point of view, that content is free and can be edited by anyone, and that editors should respect each other. Articles should provide verifiable sources to validate content. The style of the content mirrors encyclopedias and almanacs, not research articles. Because anyone can edit an article, turf and ideological wars have been conducted within certain articles. The entry for "global warming" had been under constant flux as individuals who disagree on the effects and even the premise of the phenomenon altered it. Another article suggested that one of US Senator Robert Kennedy's former assistants might have been connected to a conspiracy to assassinate the senator. The ability of the collective authors to clearly explain the topic varies widely as well, sometimes emphasizing topics of lesser importance. The Mexican American War article emphasizes small skirmishes over major battles. A major concern, the overall accuracy of *Wikipedia* has been debated since its inception. A study by the magazine *Nature*, however, found that *Wikipedia* was only slightly less accurate for selected science topics than the *Encyclopedia Britannica*, finding 162 factual errors, omissions, or misleading statements in *Wikipedia* compared to 123 in the *Encyclopedia Britannica*. However, *Wikipedia* can be useful to ferret out little known facts and references to primary sources. For instance the article on streaking, running naked in pubic, highlights specific occurrences in the 1970s and provides citations. You can follow the sources. The topic of streaking is hard to research in conventional databases. Still, the reliability of the information will remain an issue. As a researcher, you must use *Wikipedia* appropriately and remain cautious about the contents.

Sources: Jim Giles, "Internet Encyclopedias Go Head to Head," *Nature*, December 15, 2005, 900–901; "Criticism of Wikipedia," http://en.wikipedia.org/wiki/Criticism_of_Wikipedia (accessed November 15, 2011); "Wikipedia," http://en.wikipedia.org/wiki/Wikipedia (accessed November 15, 2011); Lucky Homan Rector, "Comparison of Wikipedia and Other Encyclopedias for Accuracy, Breadth and Depth in Historical Articles," *Reference Services Review* 36(1) (2008): 7–22.

Reference Library, a service that aggregates many of its reference products. Your librarian can tell you if your college or school has subscriptions to these electronic resources. Below is a selected list of encyclopedias. New titles are published daily, so this is merely an attempt to list the best at the time of the publication of this book.[4] Consult with your librarian for new titles related to your subject.

Selected Encyclopedias

NORTH AMERICA

Dictionary of American History. Stanley I. Kutler, ed. 3d ed. New York: Scribner's, 2003. 10 vols. Also available online through *Gale Virtual Reference Library*.

Encyclopedia of American Cultural and Intellectual History. Mary Kupiec Cayton and Peter W. Williams, eds. New York: Scribner's/Gale, 2001. 3 vols.

Encyclopedia of American Social History. Mary Kupiec Cayton, Elliot J. Gorn, and Peter W. Williams, eds. New York: Scribner's, 1993. 3 vols.

Palgrave Encyclopedia of World Economic History since 1750. Graham Bannock and R. E. Baxter. Basingstoke: Palgrave Macmillan, 2010.

Encyclopedia of Chicago. http://encyclopedia.chicagohistory.org. (accessed July 21, 2011).

New Encyclopedia of Southern Culture. rev. ed. Charles Reagan Wilson, gen. ed. Chapel Hill: University of North Carolina Press, 2006. 15 vols.

Encyclopedia of Women in American History. Joyce Appleby, Eileen K. Cheng, and Joanne Goodwin, eds. New York: M. E. Sharpe, 2002. 3 vols.

Canadian Encyclopedia: Year 2000 Edition. Toronto: McClelland & Stewart, 1999. 3 vols. (also online http://canadianencyclopedia.com, accessed July 21, 2011).

Encyclopedia of American Foreign Policy. Alexander DeConde, Richard Dean Burns, and Fredrik Logevall. New York: Scribner, 2002. 3 vols. Also available online through *Gale Virtual Reference Library*.

The Princeton Encyclopedia of American Political History. Michael Kazin, Rebecca Edwards, and Adam Rothman. Princeton: Princeton University Press, 2010.

LATIN AMERICA

Encyclopedia of Latin American History and Culture. Jay Kinsbruner, ed. Detroit: Scribner's, 2008. 5 vols. Also available online through *Gale Virtual Reference Library*.

MIDDLE EAST

Civilizations of the Ancient Near East. Jack M. Sasson et al., eds. New York: Scribner's, 1995. 8 vols.

Encyclopedia of the Modern Middle East & North Africa. Philip Mattar, ed. 2d ed. Detroit: Macmillan, 2004. 4 vols.

EUROPE

Critical Dictionary of the French Revolution. François Furet and Mona Ozouf, eds. Cambridge, MA: Harvard University Press, 1989.

Dictionary of Modern Italian History. Frank J. Coppa, ed. Westport, CT: Greenwood, 1985.

Encyclopedia of European Social History: From 1350 to 2000. Peter N. Stearns, ed. Detroit: Scribner's/Gale, 2001. 6 vols. Also available online through *Gale Virtual Reference Library*.

Encyclopedia of the Third Reich. Christian Zentner and Friedemann Bedurftig, eds. Amy Hackett, trans. New York: Macmillan, 1991. 2 vols.

Modern Encyclopedia of Russian, Soviet, and Eurasian History. Joseph Wieczynski and George N. Rhyne, eds. Gulf Breeze, FL: Academic International, 1976–2000. 60 vols., 2 vol. suppl. Edward J. Lazzerini and George N. Rhyne, eds. 1995. Former title: *The Modern Encyclopedia of Russian and Soviet History*.

Encyclopedia of Russian History. James R. Millar, ed. New York: Macmillan, 2004, 4 vols. Also available online through *Gale Virtual Reference Library*.

Modern Germany: An Encyclopedia of History, People, and Culture, 1871–1990. Dieter K. Buse and Jürgen C. Doerr, eds. New York: Garland, 1998.

Europe 1450 to 1789: Encyclopedia of the Early Modern World. Jonathan Dewald, ed. New York: Scribner's, 2004. 6 vols.

Europe 1789 to 1914: Encyclopedia of the Age of Industry and Empire.
John M. Merriman and J. M. Winter. Detroit: Charles Scribner's Sons,
2006. 5 vols.

Europe since 1914: Encyclopedia of the Age of War and Reconstruction.
John M. Merriman and J. M. Winter. Detroit: Charles Scribner's Sons/
Thomson Gale, 2006. 5 vols.

AFRICA

*Africana: The Encyclopedia of the African and African-American
Experience.* Kwame Anthony Appiah and Henry Louis Gates Jr., eds. 2d
ed. New York: Oxford University Press, 2005.

Encyclopedia of African History and Culture, rev. ed. R. Hunt Davis, ed.
(orig. ed. Willie F. Page, ed.) New York: Facts on File, 2005. 5 vols.

New Encyclopedia of Africa. John Middleton, ed. New York: Charles
Scribner's Sons, 2008. 5 vols.

ASIA

Encyclopedia of Asian History. Ainslie T. Embree, ed. New York: Scribner's,
1988. 4 vols.

Kodansha Encyclopedia of Japan. Tokyo: Kodansha, 1983. 9 vols. and
suppl.

Encyclopedia of Modern Asia. David Levinson and Karen Christensen, eds.
New York: Scribner's, 2002. 6 vols.

Encyclopedia of Modern China. David Pong, ed. Detroit: Charles Scribner's
Sons/Gale, Cengage Learning, 2009. 4 vols.

AUSTRALIA

Australians: A Historical Library. Broadway, N. S. W., Australia: Fairfax,
Syme, and Weldon Associates 1987. 11 vols.

WORLD, REGIONAL, CULTURAL, OR TOPICAL

Encyclopedia Judaica. 2d ed. New York: Macmillan, 2006. 20 vols. Also
available online.

The Encyclopaedia of Islam. New ed. E. Van Donzel, B. Lewis, and Ch.
Pellat, eds. Leiden: Brill, 1954– . 11 vols. Also available online.

ehNet:Encyclopedia of Economic and Business History. http://www.eh.net/
encyclopedia/ (accessed July 25, 2011).

Handbook of North American Indians. William C. Sturtevant, ed. Washington, DC: Smithsonian Institution, 1978– .

The Palgrave Encyclopedia of World Economic History since 1750. Graham Bannock and R. E. Baxter. Basingstoke: Palgrave Macmillan, 2010.

Encyclopedia of Race and Racism. John H. Moore. Detroit: Macmillan Reference USA/Thomson Gale, 2008. 3 vols. Also available through *Gale Virtual Reference Library.*

The Oxford Encyclopedia of Latinos and Latinas in the United States. Suzanne Oboler and Deena J. González, eds. New York: Oxford University Press, 2005. 4 vols. Also available online.

Encyclopedia of African American History, 1619–1895: From the Colonial Period to the Age of Frederick Douglass. Paul Finkelman, ed. New York: Oxford University Press, 2006. 3 vols. Also available online.

Asian American History and Culture: An Encyclopedia. Huping Ling and Allan W. Austin. Armonk, NY: M. E. Sharpe, 2010. 2 vols.

Macmillan Encyclopedia of World Slavery. Paul Finkelman and Joseph Calder Miller. New York: Macmillan Reference USA, Simon & Schuster Macmillan, 1998. 2 vols.

BY TIME PERIOD

Civilization of the Ancient Mediterranean: Greece and Rome. Michael Grant and Rachel Kitzinger, eds. New York: Scribner's, 1988. 3 vols.

Brill's New Pauly Encyclopaedia of the Ancient World. Hubert Cancik and Helmut Schneider, eds. Boston: Brill, 2002–2010. 15 vols.

Oxford Classical Dictionary. 3d ed. rev. Simon Hornblower and Anthony Spawforth, eds. Oxford: Oxford University Press, 2003. Also available at *Oxford Reference Online.*

Dictionary of the Middle Ages. Joseph R. Strayer, ed. New York: Scribner's, 1982–1989. 12 vols. and suppl. New York: Scribner's, 2003.

Encyclopedia of the Renaissance. Paul F. Grendler, ed. New York: Scribner's, 1999. 6 vols.

Brill's New Pauly: Encyclopaedia of the Ancient World Classical Tradition. Manfred Landfester, Hubert Cancik, and Helmuth Schneider, eds. Leiden: Brill, 2006. 6 vols.

Oxford Encyclopedia of the Reformation. Hans J. Hillerbrand, ed. New York: Oxford University Press, 1996. 4 vols.

ORB: The Online Reference Book for Medieval Studies. http://www.the-orb. net/encyclo.html (accessed December 31, 2011).

Bibliographies

Bibliographies can provide a collection of resources on your topic and save some of the lengthy searching in other databases and catalogs. In the field of history, they are often a combination encyclopedia, bibliography, and guidebook offer an overview of the literature that exists about a broad topic, such as the US Confederacy or the Renaissance, and include references to standard texts. Sometimes they offer a how-to-do-research feature on the subject, with an overview of past and current scholarship, as well as the locations of other secondary and major primary source collections. Some bibliographies, like *The American Historical Association's Guide to Historical Literature*, break history into periods and broad topics and devote a chapter to each of these.[5] The chapter contains a short two-to-three-page discussion of the topic and its scholarship followed by a lengthy bibliography of classic and current secondary and primary resources.

Bibliographies can focus on a more specific subject, cover a more restrictive time frame, or attempt to be nearly comprehensive. For instance, when issued annually as a printed book, *The Eighteenth Century: A Current Bibliography* attempts to index everything published on the eighteenth century in all disciplines for that year. Some bibliographies collect sources on a very focused subject and are issued only once, for instance, *China During the Cultural Revolution 1966–1976*, gathers together a large portion of the English-language literature on the Cultural Revolution.[6] Although these types of bibliographies are valuable, be careful not to rely totally on their contents as the literature they index can become dated.

Selected Bibliographies

SELECTED GENERAL BIBLIOGRAPHIES OF RESOURCES, INCLUDING HISTORY

New Walford Guide to Reference Resources. Vol. 1, *Science and Technology*; Vol. 2, *Social and Historical Sciences, Philosophy, and Religion*; and Vol. 3, *Generalia, Language and Literature, the Arts.* 8th ed. London: Facet, 2005–2008. Previous title *Walford's Guide to Reference Materials*, published by the Library Association.

Guide to Reference Books. Robert Balay, ed. 11th ed. Chicago: American Library Association, 1996. Also available online through subscription http://guidetoreference.org.

SELECTED HISTORY-SPECIFIC BIBLIOGRAPHIES

Oxford Bibliographies Online. Oxford University Press. http://www.oxford-bibliographiesonline.com/. A subscription is required to access essays

and suggested resources around specific topics in larger themes (Atlantic History, Classics, Medieval Studies, Islamic Studies, Latin American Studies, etc.). A combination bibliography and encyclopedia.
The American Historical Association's Guide to Historical Literature. Mary Beth Norton, ed. 3d ed. New York: Oxford University Press, 1995. 2 vols.
Handbook for Research in American History: A Guide to Bibliographies and Other Reference Works. Francis Paul Prucha, ed. 2d ed. Lincoln: University of Nebraska Press, 1994.
A Bibliography of British History, 1914–1989. Keith Robbins, comp. and ed. Oxford: Clarendon, 1996.
A Bibliography of English History to 1485. E. B. Graves, comp. Oxford: Clarendon, 1975.
Bibliography of British History: Tudor Period, 1485–1603. Conyers Read, comp. 2d ed. Totowa, NJ: Rowman and Littlefield, 1978.
Bibliography of British History: Stuart History, 1603–1714. G. D. Davies and M. F. Keeler, comps. 2d ed. Oxford: Clarendon, 1970.
Bibliography of British History: The Eighteenth Century, 1714–1789. S. Pargellis and D. J. Medley, comps. Oxford: Clarendon, 1951.
Bibliography of British History, 1789–1851. L. M. Brown and I. R. Christie, comps. Oxford: Clarendon, 1977.
Bibliography of British History, 1851–1914. H. J. Hanham, comp. Oxford: Clarendon, 1976.
The Eighteenth Century: A Current Bibliography. New York: AMS Press, 1978– Annual.
Reference Sources in History: An Introductory Guide. 2d ed. Ronald H. Fritze, Brian E. Coutts, and Louis Vyhnanek, comps. Santa Barbara, CA: ABC-CLIO, 2004. Also available online through ABC-CLIO. Also available online through *Gale Virtual Reference Library.*
The Labyrinth: Resources for Medieval Studies. http://labyrinth.george-town.edu (accessed July 24, 2011).
Stanford University Library Guides. http://library.stanford.edu/depts/hasrg/index.html (accessed July 24, 2011). Stanford libraries maintain an excellent list of history-related web guides that also include reference-like resources.

Multivolume General Histories

Sometimes you may need information that establishes a broader historical and theoretical context for your historical research. Whereas encyclopedias generally provide shorter summary bits of information, multivolume general histories provide sweeping, synthesizing scholarly narrative and analysis of topics, nations, regions, and eras. These types of sources examine the standard, accepted historical thought, including interpretations by many of the major, prominent historians past and present, but do not include current, cutting-edge historical theory. Below is a list of the major sets.

Selected Multivolume General Histories

New Cambridge Medieval History. Rosamund McKitterick, ed. London: Cambridge University Press, 1995– .

New Cambridge Modern History. 2d ed. G. R. Elton, ed. London: Cambridge University Press, 1990– .

Cambridge Ancient History. 3d ed. London: Cambridge University Press, 1970–2006.

Cambridge History of . . . and *New Cambridge History of . . .*: Cambridge University Press has a large number of histories that begin with these titles. Searching your library's catalog with these titles will bring a list of results.

Longman Companion to. . . . Chris Cook and John Stevenson, gen. eds. (Longman Companions to History Series). London: Longman.

General History of Africa. London: Longman, 1981–1993. 8 vols. Also known as *UNESCO History of Africa.*

History of Humanity. S. J. De Laet, ed. London: Routledge, 1994–2000.

Oxford Very Short Introductions. Small volumes on a vast array of subjects including Ancient Greece, Global Economic History, Islam, The Aztecs, etc. Search your library's catalog with the phrase "oxford very short introduction."

Africa. Toyin Falola. Durham, NC: Carolina Academic Press, 2000– .

Series Overviews

These two new series combine historiography with an overview of a place, era, or technique of analysis. They are slightly different from the sources above but can be used in the same manner.

Writing . . . History. Stefan Berger, Heike Feldner, Kevin Passmore, eds. London: Hodder Arnold, 2004– . Series so far includes *Writing Gender History* (Laura Lee Downs, ed.), *Writing Medieval History* (Nancy Parnter, ed.), *Writing Early Modern History* (Garthine Walker, ed.), *Writing Post Colonial History* (Rochona Majumdar, ed.).

Palgrave Advances in . . . New York: Palgrave/Macmillan, 2005– . Critical commentary on recent scholarship.

Biographical Resources

Much of history is told through the lives of individuals. Understanding and interpreting their actions and philosophies helps you to understand how they participated in and shaped the world and events around them. Until relatively recently history was written through the study of the lives of predominantly white male leaders and a few women, such as the Egyptian ruler Cleopatra and the British queen Victoria. Biographical information is collected in a number of ways. Often, these characteristics are the points around which a biographical dictionary is organized.

- *Profession/avocation.* It is helpful to know why a person is important, which usually implies a profession, for instance, author, politician, physicist, etc. However, a profession does not always equate with employment. Individuals can also be important for nonemployment activities in which they engage, for instance, reformers (civil rights, suffrage, or temperance).

- *Nationality or region.* Countries want to be able to identify their significant citizens. National identities are formed, in part, by identifying the people who "belong" to a particular country. Sometimes dictionaries are organized by regions as well.

- *Gender, ethnicity, or race.* Famous women, as well as African Americans and other minorities, are often grouped together in biographical dictionaries. Many of the individuals in these groups have experienced similar struggles and likewise have been left out of many of the standard biographical sources.

- *Dates lived/flourished.* It is useful to know who was living at the same time and in the same era. For this reason, certain biographical dictionaries are organized to group together information about people who lived in a particular era.

Knowing how biographical information is organized will help you search for it. For instance, if you wanted information on John Singleton Copley, an American painter, you might look for information in *The American National Biography* as you know his nationality to be American.[7] You would find approximately three pages of information describing his life, followed by a short bibliography telling you where his papers are located and suggesting two book-length biographies you might wish to read for further information. Because Copley is a painter, you could also look for information in an encyclopedia on painters or American painting, such as *Grove Dictionary of Art*.

From Renaissance to Impressionism: Styles and Movements in Western Art 1400–1900.[8] This assumes you know the approximate date your artist lived.

Biographical resources come in several formats: (1) *indexes* to biographical dictionaries and full-length biographies, (2) biographical dictionaries, and (3) full-length biographical books or monographs found through your library's online catalog. The most common way to locate information on an individual is to look for a biographical dictionary by country of origin. Your search results would give you both biographical dictionaries to the country, as well as full-length biographies about the people who were citizens of that country. The subject heading to use in your library's online catalog is "[country]–Biography–Dictionaries (France–Biography–Dictionaries)." Also, you can look for a biographical directory by profession, for example, chemists or perhaps, more broadly, scientists or a bit more specifically, female scientists in the nineteenth century.

While not strictly a *type* of reference resource, another good source of biographical information is obituaries. Published in newspapers, journals, and magazines upon an individual's death, these articles highlight the facts and relationships of the person's life and, when appropriate, list major works and accomplishments. See chapter 4 for periodical and newspaper indexes. These indexes include references to obituaries. Some of the indexes and dictionaries listed below also include references to obituaries.

The possibilities, as well as your search strategies, for finding biographical information are nearly endless. The sources listed here attempt to be very broad in their coverage.

Selected Biographical Resources

DICTIONARIES AND COMPREHENSIVE RESOURCES

American National Biography. John A. Garraty and Mark C. Carnes, eds. New York: Oxford University Press, 1999 and suppl. 2002– . 24 vols. Also available through online subscription. Individuals who influenced American history but were not necessarily of American birth or citizenship. To be included in the print version, individuals must have died by 1996.

Oxford Dictionary of National Biography. H. C. G. Matthew and Brian Harrison, eds. London: Oxford University Press, 2004. 60 vols. Also available through online subscription. Individuals who influenced British history but were not necessarily of British birth or citizenship. Good for locating figures in British colonies. To be included in the print version, individuals must have died by 2001.

Notable American Women 1607–1950. Edward T. James, ed. Cambridge, MA: Harvard University Press, 1971. *Notable American Women: The Modern Period.* Barbara Sicherman et al., eds. Cambridge, MA: Harvard University Press, 1980. *Notable American Women: A Biographical Dictionary Completing the Twentieth Century.* Susan Ware, ed. Cambridge MA: Harvard University Press, 2004. Also available online through *Biography in Context.*

Dictionary of Literary Biography. Detroit: Gale, 1978–. Also available online in *Literature Resource Center.* The term "literary" refers to individuals who write. The focus of the series is primarily on fiction writers of many formats (poetry, drama, novels, etc.) but also includes other types of writers such as historians.

Current Biography. New York: H. W. Wilson, 1940–. Three- to four-page biographies of contemporary individuals who are important and influential in all areas of life (politics, sports, entertainment, science, etc.). Coverage is international, so you could find, for example, a biography of Pol Pot during the Vietnam era. Also available online through *Biography Reference Bank.*

Contemporary Authors. Detroit: Gale Research, 1967–. Also available online in *Biography in Context.* Short biographies that include bibliographies for all types of writers, including nonfiction.

Biography in Context. Farmington Hills, MI: Gale Group, 2004. Online subscription. A collection of biographical dictionaries and other biographical resources. Individuals included may be historical or more contemporary.

The following "Who's Who" sources provide basic biographical data on prominent American and British individuals, living and deceased. Many countries issue biographical sources titled *Who's Who.* While they tend to list living people only, a resource that was published 50 years ago would contain historical biographies.

Who's Who. London: A&C Black, 1849–.

Who Was Who. London: A&C Black, 1897–.

Who's Who in America. Chicago: Marquis Who's Who, Inc., 1899–. Also available online by subscription.

Who Was Who in America. Chicago: Marquis Who's Who, Inc., 1607–. Also available online by subscription.

Dictionnaire de Biographie Française. Paris: Letouzey et Ané, 1930–. Similar to the *American National Biography* and the *Oxford Dictionary of National Biography* but in French, and parts are much older. Still in progress.

Neue Deutsche Biographie. Herausgegeben von der Historischen Kommission bei der Bayerischen Akademie der Wissenschaften. Berlin: Duncker & Humblot, 1953–. Similar to the *American National Biography* and the *Oxford Dictionary of National Biography* but in German, and parts are much older. Still in progress. An online version of this (and two biographical publications from Austria and Switzerland) can be found at Biographie-Portal, http://www.biographie-portal.eu/en/ (accessed November 15, 2011).

A&E Biography. http://www.biography.com/ (accessed July 25, 2011)).

Dizionario Biografico Degli Italiani. Alberto M. Ghisalberti, ed. Rome: Istituto Della Enciclopedia Italiana, 1960– [in progress]. Italian biographical dictionary.

Dictionary of National Biography. S. P. Sen, ed. Calcutta: Institute of Historical Studies, 1972–1974. For India. Would be a bit dated.

Australian Dictionary of Biography. Melbourne: Melbourne University Press, 1966–2000. Also available online at http://adb.anu.edu.au/ (accessed April 12, 2012).

Dictionary of Canadian Biography. Toronto: University of Toronto Press, 1966–. http://www.biographi.ca/EN/ (accessed January 9, 2006).

INDEXES TO OTHER BIOGRAPHICAL RESOURCES

Biography and Master Genealogy Index. Detroit: Gale Research, 1975–. Also available online through subscription. Indexes biographical dictionaries.

Personal Name Index to The New York Times Index. Succasunna, NJ: Roxbury Data Interface, 1976–. Also available through the *New York Times Historical* online, if your library subscribes to that database. Indexes a large number of years by individuals' names. Refers to the print newspaper index.

Biography Index. New York: H. W. Wilson, 1946–. Also available online. Indexes selected journal, magazine, and newspaper articles and interviews.

Chronologies

Chronologies can serve a number of purposes for your research. Sometimes as you read your primary sources, you will find allusions to other contemporary events. Chronologies can help you place primary sources in their contemporary context because they list events in order of the date they occurred and suggest the cultural influences that potentially impacted the individuals and groups you are analyzing. Sometimes these reference sources will categorize social, scientific, and political events in separate lists. For example, for someone studying the period between 1750 and 1850, it could be relevant and potentially important to know that Ludwig van Beethoven (1770–1827), the German composer, was a contemporary of Napoleon (1769–1821), Shaka the Zulu king (1787–1828), Jane Austen (1775–1817), and Thomas Jefferson (1743–1826), and that Joseph Priestly (1733–1804) isolated oxygen in 1774.

Selected Chronologies

The American Chronicle: Year by Year through the Twentieth Century. Lois Gordon and Alan Gordon, eds. New Haven, CT: Yale University Press, 1999.

American Decades. Detroit : Gale Research, 1994– . Also available through *Gale Virtual Reference Library.*

American Eras. Detroit: Gale Research, 1997– . Also available through *Gale Virtual Reference Library.*

World Eras. Detroit: Gale Research, 2001– . Also available through *Gale Virtual Reference Library.*

Chronology of World History. H. E. L. Mellersh and Neville Williams, eds. Santa Barbara, CA: ABC-CLIO, 1999. 4 vols.

Day by Day: The Forties. New York: Facts on File. Also Fifties, Sixties, Seventies, Eighties, and Nineties.

Handbook of British Chronology. E. B. Fryde, D. E. Greenway, S. Porter, and I. Roy, eds. 3d ed. London: Royal Historical Society, 1996.

Hyperhistory Online. http://www.hyperhistory.com/online_n2/History_n2/a.html (accessed November 15, 2011).

The Timetables of History. Bernard Grun. New York: Simon & Schuster, 2005.

Web Chronology Project. http://www.thenagain.info/WebChron/ (accessed November 15, 2011).

BBC History Timelines. http:// http://www.bbc.co.uk/history/interactive/timelines/ (accessed November 15, 2011).

Dictionaries, Etymologies, and Word Origins

Words and language are central to historical research. If a word or phrase is central to your topic, look it up in one of these dictionaries. Meanings

---

Box 2.2 Oxford English Dictionary

The *Oxford English Dictionary* (*OED*) is considered the authority on the changes in uses of English words. The *OED* developed from an 1859 proposal by the Philological Society of London to take words from quotes from significant works dated 1250–1858. Samuel Johnson (1709–1784), author of the first substantial dictionary (*Dictionary of the English Language*, 1755), included in his definitions a sentence that used the word. The editors of the *OED* established a system whereby the general public sent subeditors 4 by 6 cards that contained prospective words used in the context of a sentence with a citation. The whole process nearly became unmanageable, with the first edition of the dictionary not completely published until 1928. A similar project begun in Germany in 1852 by Jacob (1785–1863) and Wilhelm (1786–1859) Grimm, the *Deutsches Wörterbuch*, was not completed until 1960. In many cases, slang or cant, "the vulgar tongue," is left out of these dictionaries. So despite their comprehensiveness—the *OED* has over 475,000 words—you still may not find the word you are looking for!

Sources: James Rettig, "The *Jewel in the Crown*: The *Oxford English Dictionary*," in *Distinguished Classics of Reference Publishing*, ed. James Rettig (Phoenix: Oryx Press 1992), 180–197; K. M. Elisabeth Murray, *Caught in the Web of Words: James A. H. Murray and the Oxford English Dictionary* (New Haven: Yale University Press, 1977).

---

change over time, and your understanding of a definition may be tainted by your modern perspective (e.g., "nationalism" or "middle class" or "capitalism"). Whether examining the language of a fourteenth-century legal document describing land ownership or trying to discern the nuances of a modern historian's usage of words, understanding the origins of words and their historical development (*etymology*) is critical to your analysis. Knowing when and where a particular phrase or word came into common usage and the evolution of that usage provides an intellectual context for your research. A plethora of dictionaries and etymologies exist. On slang alone, there are volumes for American slang, southern US slang, "underworld" and criminal lingo, and common language used by the army and navy, as well as slang in other languages. The source for the origins and usage of most words in the English language is the monolithic *Oxford English Dictionary* (*OED*). Available in print and online, the *OED* tells you the part of speech of the word, its definition, its origin, and its change in usage over time. Citing and dating the first documented use of the word in a sentence within a published work, the *OED* establishes when and by whom words entered into common usage and, conversely, when they became seldom used.

To find a slang or etymological dictionary, use your library's online catalog and search by the subject "English Language" (or other language). Then limit by words in the subject dictionaries and what you wish to look for, for instance, "slang." This will locate dictionaries like *Soviet Camp Speech*, which details prisoners' language in Soviet detention camps.[9]

Selected Dictionaries, Etymologies, and Word Origins

Oxford English Dictionary. J. A. Simpson and E. S. C. Weiner, eds. 2d ed. New York: Oxford University Press, 1989. Also available online through subscription.

The New Partridge Dictionary of Slang and Unconventional English. Tom Dalzell, Terry Victor, and Eric Partridge. London: Routledge, 2005.

New Dictionary of American Slang. Robert L. Chapman, ed. New York: Harper & Row, 1986. (rev. ed. of *Dictionary of American Slang.* Harold Wentworth and Stuart Berg Flexner, comp., eds. New York: Crowell, 1975.)

Online Etymology Dictionary. http://www.etymonline.com/ (accessed November 15, 2011).

Book Reviews

Understanding others' thoughts on a work, whether published in the 1800s or last week, can help you with your own comprehension and critical assessment of the work's significance. Book reviews provide relatively short critical overviews and a discussion of a book's thesis and analysis. More than a mere summary, a review in a scholarly journal will usually compare the text of the book to related titles in the field, as well as assess the primary evidence in the notes and bibliography of the book. As stated earlier, an important part of the practice of history is discussion of ideas with one's peers. Book reviews are one way of furthering that discourse. As a new scholar, book reviews can help you to develop a critical eye while reading your research materials. You can compensate, a bit, for your lack of depth of knowledge on a topic by reading others' commentaries. Book reviews also help you understand the intellectual climate of a time period. Looking at book reviews of Margaret Mead's *Coming of Age in Samoa* (1928) tells us as much or more about Western civilization's views on adolescence in the late 1920s as it does about indigenous cultures in Samoa.[10] As a general rule, book reviews are not research articles. They do not present findings with evidence. They are merely educated opinions or evaluations. As such they should not be the major source of information for your paper or project. The exception is if you are using the book review as primary source evidence to gauge the reception of a work or idea in its own time.

The easiest way to locate book reviews of a specific title is to use an index. Begin by determining the first publication date of your book. This tells you if you will be able to use an online index or if the book was published before the coverage of most online indexes. If you will be using a print index, knowing the publication date of your book tells you in which volume to begin searching for references to reviews. For print indexes, be sure to check several years as a book review may take some time to show up in an index. In addition to the sources listed below, most periodical indexes listed in chapter 4 will also index book reviews. There will be some overlap in journal coverage between periodical indexes, but in each case, some unique journal titles will result from your search. Most of the sources below will require you to look up the journal that contains the review. In some cases, the full text may be attached to an online index. *H-Net* (http://h-net. org) contains reviews of select history titles online. Nonscholarly sources of book reviews are problematic because the review's purpose is not for discussion among researchers and to set the work within the context of existing literature. Reviewers in Amazon.com and similar sources may have useful comments about the readability and the contents of a book, but reviewers do not have a vested interest in the whole of the research on the topic. Besides, Amazon's purpose is commercial, to sell books.

Selected Sources of Book Review Resources

Book Review Digest. New York: H. W. Wilson, 1905– . *Book Review Digest Plus*. New York: H. W. Wilson, 2002– . Also available online through subscription. http://www.hwwilson.com/Databases/brdig.htm (accessed March 26, 2006). Fee based online.

Book Review Index. Detroit: Gale Research, 1965– . At the writing of this book, H. W. Wilson had been purchased by Ebsco.

Combined Retrospective Index to Book Reviews in Humanities Journals, 1802–1974. Evan I. Farber, ed. Woodbridge, CT: Research Publications, 1983–1984. 10 vols.

*Combined Retrospective Index to Book Reviews in Scholarly Journals, 1886–
1974.* Evan I. Farber, ed. Arlington, VA: Carrollton, 1979–1982. 15 vols.
H-Net Reviews. http://www.h-net.org/reviews/ (accessed January 1, 2006).
History net is the online organization of professional historians. One section of the website contains book reviews.

Directories

Directories simply provide addresses and contact information for associations, historical societies, archives, and libraries that you may need to contact about some aspect of their collections. Also, you may need to find out
further information about programs or grants that these types of institutions
offer. Many organizations now have websites, so you can often find online
information previously available only in printed directories.

Selected Directories

Directory of History Departments, Historical Organizations, and Historians.
Washington, DC: American Historical Association, Institutional Services
Program, 1990– . http://www.historians.org/pubs/directory2/ (accessed
April 23, 2012).
World of Learning. London: Europa Publications 1956– . Included in each
country's listing are addresses and contacts for museums, historical orga-
nizations, and universities.

Using the Internet as a Reference Resource

The Internet is perhaps the best and the worst reference resource available
today. It has the ability to connect you to an established authority in the field
you are studying, as well as to a self-proclaimed authority who knows very
little. There are several websites set up to act as reference sites, containing
the online equivalent of a shelf of printed reference resources. *Bartleby.
com* (http://bartleby.com) contains a plethora of sources such as *Roget's
International Thesaurus* of English (1922), *Bartlett's Familiar Quotations*
(1919), and more. You can search all of these sources simultaneously or
individually for information. The problem with many free services such as
Bartleby is that these online replicas of print sources are often out of date.
Other websites, such as the *Internet Public Library* (http://www.ipl.org),
offer a different approach by attempting to operate as a library, linking to

websites, as well as to volunteer researchers who will answer your questions, just as a librarian would. Some of these services answer questions mechanically, based on how you have asked the question and how others have asked that question, using natural language processing, or allow anyone, expert or uninformed, to suggest likely answers to your query. See the Registry of Answer Boards (http://answerboards.wetpaint.com/page/Registry+of+Answer+Boards). These services can be useful, but remember that your public, school, and college libraries can usually provide better information for free. Your local library and librarian also are attuned to your professors', teachers', and classes' needs in ways these other services are not. Many libraries offer numerous ways to contact a librarian. You could send an e-mail message, engage in an online chat, initiate an Instant Messaging session or make a telephone call, or simply walk into the library. Personalized, professional service can be delivered to you quickly and efficiently in a variety of ways, but you must first make your needs known.

Case Study—Using Reference Resources to Understand Herodotus

You will use several types of reference resources to find out about people and places mentioned in a passage of Herodotus' *Histories*.

Herodotus, *Histories*, Book V.49.1–51.3

49. . . . It was in the reign of Cleomenes that Aristagoras the despot of Miletus came to Sparta; and when he had audience of the King (so the Lacedaemonians say) he brought with him a bronze tablet on which the map of all the earth was engraved, and all the sea and all the rivers. Having been admitted to converse with Cleomenes, Aristagoras spoke thus to him: "Wonder not, Cleomenes, that I have been so zealous to come hither for such is our present state that the sons of Ionians should be slaves and not free men is a shame and grief to ourselves. . . . Now, therefore, we beseech you by the gods of Hellas, save your Ionian kinsmen from slavery . . . I show you; . . . therein . . . lies that Susa where lives the great king, and there are the store houses of wealth and; take that city, and you need not fear to challenge Zeus for riches. . . ." 50. . . . Cleomenes asked Aristagoras how many days' journey it was from the Ionian Sea to the king. Till now, Aristagoras had been cunning and fooled the Spartans right well; but there he made a false step; for if he desired to bring the Spartans way into Asia he

should never have told the truth. . . . (From *Herodotus: With an English Translation by A. D. Godley*. London: William Heinemann, 1921)

What can you learn from this passage using reference resources?

- *Herodotus*. Greek historian who lived c. 484 to sometime after 424 B.C.E. Considered the "father of history," he published his *Histories* about Greece's defeat of the Persian king Xerxes around 445 B.C.E. From Edwin Yamauchi, "Herodotus," *Encyclopedia of Historians and Historical Writing* (Chicago: Fitzroy Dearborn, 1999).

- *Aristagoras, tyrant of Miletus*. Deputy tyrant of Miletus c. 505–496 B.C.E., who initiated the Ionian Revolt against the Persians. From "Aristagoras," in *Oxford Classical Dictionary*, 3d rev. ed. (London: Oxford University Press, 2003).

- *Miletus*. Modern-day Turkey, coastal city of Asia Minor. Largest city in league of 12 Ionian cities. Destroyed by Persians in 494 B.C.E. Rebuilt and allied with Athens in the Peloponnesian War. In 499 B.C.E. the Ionian Revolt was started here by one of the cities ex-tyrants, Aristagoras. For a long, detailed archaeological history, see G. Kleiner, "Miletos," in *Princeton Encyclopedia of Classical Sites*, ed. Richard Sitewell (Princeton, NJ: Princeton University Press, 1976) and Percy Neville Ure, "Miletus," *Oxford Classical Dictionary*, 3d rev. ed. (London: Oxford University Press, 2003).

- *Cleomenes*. King of Sparta, reigned c. 520–490 B.C.E. Vigorous in his interference in foreign affairs, especially concerning Athens. Refused to support the Ionian Revolt. From Paul Anthony Cartledge, "Cleomenes, (1)I," in *Oxford Classical Dictionary*, 3d rev. ed. (London: Oxford University Press, 2003).

- *Susa where lives the great king*. City in Italy. In this case, you would want to use the bibliography attached to the article in the *Oxford Classical Dictionary* and look up the book *The Royal City of Susa*, R. Tallon, ed. (1992). From "Susa," in *Oxford Classical Dictionary*, 3d rev. ed. (London: Oxford University Press, 2003).

If you wanted to set the context for the entire account, you might wish to read the following articles:

Shalom Perlman. "Interstate Relations." In *Civilization of the Ancient Mediterranean*. Michael Grant and Rachel Kitzinger, eds. New York: Scribner's, 1988.

J. K. Anderson. "Wars and Military Science: Greece." In *Civilization of the Ancient Mediterranean*. Michael Grant and Rachel Kitzinger, eds. New York: Scribner's, 1988.

Also unique to classical and many literary texts are commentaries, line-by-line, or passage-by-passage discussions of the text. In this case, you may want to consult the following:

W. W. How and J. Wells. *A Commentary on Herodotus: With Introduction and Appendices*. London: Oxford, 1967.

NOTES

1. Norman J. G. Pounds, "Steelmaking," in *Dictionary of the Middle Ages* (New York: Scribner's, 1982).

2. "Table F3: Passenger Traffic on Railways," in *International Historical Statistics: Europe, 1750–2000*, 5th ed., ed. B. R. Mitchell (New York: Palgrave Macmillan, 2003).

3. Thomas S. Noonan, "Kizil-Koba Culture," in *The Modern Encyclopedia of Russian and Soviet History*, ed. Joseph L. Wieczynski (Gulf Breeze, FL: Academic International Press, 1976), now titled *The Modern Encyclopedia of Russian and Soviet and Eurasian History*; Ronald Storey, "The Aristocracy of Inherited Wealth," in *Encyclopedia of American Social History*, ed. Mary Kupiec Cayton, Elliott J. Gorn, and Peter W. Williams (New York: Scribner's, 1993); Richard C. Martin, ed., *Encyclopedia of Islam and the Muslim World* (New York: Macmillan Reference USA, 2003); Barbara A. Tenenbaum, ed., *Encyclopedia of Latin American History and Culture* (New York: Scribner's/Macmillan Library Reference USA, 1996); Neil Schlager, ed., *St. James Encyclopedia of Labor History Worldwide: Major Events in Labor History and Their Impact* (Detroit: St. James Press/Thomson Gale, 2004); Joseph R. Strayer, ed., *Dictionary of the Middle Ages* (New York: Scribner's, 1982).

4. *ACLS Humanities E-Book Collection.* http://www.humanitiesebook.com http://www.humanitiesebook.org/ (accessed April 23, 2012).

5. Mary Beth Norton, ed., *The American Historical Association's Guide to Historical Literature*, 3d ed. (New York: Oxford University Press, 1995).

6. Tony H. Chang, *China during the Cultural Revolution, 1966–1976: A Selected Bibliography of English Language Works* (Westport, CT: Greenwood, 1999).

7. Emily Ballew Neff, "Copley, John Singleton," *American National Biography* (New York: Oxford University Press, 2000). http://www.anb.org/articles/ 17/17-00180.html (accessed January 1, 2006).

8. Jane Turner, ed., *Grove Dictionary of Art. From Renaissance to Impressionism: Styles and Movements in Western Art 1400–1900* (New York: St. Martin's Press, 2000). Also available online, *Grove Art Online*, http://www.groveart.com (accessed January 1, 2006).

9. Meyer Galler, *Soviet Camp Speech* (Jerusalem: Magnes Press, The Hebrew University, 1994).

10. Margaret Mead, *Coming of Age in Samoa: A Psychological Study of Primitive Youth for Western Civilization* (New York: W. Morrow & Company, 1928).

Finding Monographs and Using Catalogs

WHAT YOU WILL LEARN IN THIS CHAPTER

- how to define and identify a book or monograph
- how to use subject headings and understand how they differ from keywords
- how to select your search terms and enter them in an online catalog
- how to use an online catalog and the contents of its records effectively

---

What Is a Book? The Changing Nature of Monographs

A book is a book is a book, right? The traditional form of the book, a narrative with an introduction, a body or discussion, and a conclusion, is still the major, standard means of scholarly, and even nonscholarly, written communication. This linear layout of text allows the author to lead the reader through the evidence, arriving together at one or several conclusions. However, this format has not always predominated. Originally, written texts were papyrus rolls that were rolled and unrolled and read aloud to groups. Little attempt was made to draw the text to a conclusion. Instead, the purpose of the document was to record the facts and the story so the narrative could be publicly debated and discussed. Around the fourth century C.E., the codex became the form we now recognize as a book. With pages to turn, the layout and purpose of the printed text changed radically as a result. With the establishment of universities around the twelfth century C.E., monographs (or books) evolved to contain interior organization, such as chapters and subheadings, identifiable named authors (instead of the unnamed "eyewitness" or no attribution at all), documentation or footnotes, and an essay structure that included a conclusion. Further, this structure encouraged the book to become more tightly focused on a single subject, allowing the author to lead an individual reader through an argument.

With the advent of the Internet, in the era that has been called the "late age of print," these assumptions, as well as the linearity of the book text, have been challenged by alternative methods. A website seldom leads visitors to a single conclusion. Rather, much like the early papyrus rolls, such a site must satisfy a number of different types of users. With its use of hypertext, a website allows every visitor to experience the site in a unique way, drawing his or her own conclusions, and no longer coming to a single end.[1] This phenomenon will be further described in chapter 11 on presenting your research.

Historians and publishers are experimenting with new ways of delivering scholarship digitally. A substantial number of monographs are now being replicated in electronic form, and a few are being issued only in electronic form. Such subscription projects as *Ebrary* (http://www.ebrary.com/corp/) and the *ACLS Humanities E-Book Project* (http://www.humanities ebook.org/) provide, through a subscription, online access to databases of monographs selected by participating publishers. In each case, you are able to search through subject headings to retrieve monographs, just as with a library catalog. The added value of each of these services is that you can also search for keywords throughout the *full text* of all of the works contained in each of the databases. The texts in the *ACLS Humanities E-Book Project* are all historical in some manner, whereas *Ebrary* contains a finite number of e-books from all disciplines, including history. Although these projects are expanding, you as a researcher will still primarily be dealing with traditional printed monographs found through a library catalog.

When Are Books the Right Choice for Information?

In this chapter, we look at books, or monographs, as secondary works, those materials that provide analysis or interpretation of primary sources and other secondary works. You will need both books and journal articles to know the field of research for your topic, as well as to enter into the discussion with other historians. They will help you discover what research has not been done and how your unique topic fits into this larger body of research. To omit important works from experts in the field would be a serious flaw in your research. However both forms, book and journal, serve a particular role. Monographs and journal articles will be the core second-ary sources for your research. While many types of books are published, the standard type of secondary book in history is the scholarly nonfiction monograph. Intended for an academic audience, it is an extensive, in-depth discussion of a topic by an individual, or perhaps coauthors. The scholarly monograph is distinguished from other types of books, such as a collection of essays by many scholars around a single topic, a collection of essays by one scholar on many topics, or a *Festschrift* (a collection of essays in honor of a scholar). Because of their length, monographs are able to thor-oughly examine large topics intensively, make extended arguments, and raise many questions around a diversity of issues. By comparison, a journal article is usually limited in page length and, thus, often narrower in scope, distilling the major points of an argument. In fact, journal articles are an excellent source for organizing and focusing a paper topic. Chapter 4 will discuss the uses of journal articles further. In monographs, the secondary works cited as documentation in the bibliography or the notes tend to be at least several years old, even when the book has just been published. Journal bibliographies tend to be more up-to-date, in part because journals publish articles more frequently and because journal article topics tend to be more cutting-edge. Scientists tend to publish their groundbreaking research in professional journals, since the information is deemed time-sensitive and can be disseminated much more quickly in journals than in monographs. Sometimes historians publish parts of their research in journal articles before writing a larger analysis in the form of a book. For instance, historian Mary Kupiec Cayton wrote an article in *The American Historical Review* in 1987 entitled "The Making of an American Prophet: Emerson, His Audiences and the Rise of the Culture of Industry in Nineteenth Century America."[2] Two years later, she published a book, *Emerson's Emergence: Self and Society and the Transformation of New England, 1800–1845*, which in part consid-ers not only the role Emerson's public lectures had on his reception but also his audiences' influence on his message.[3]

Using the building blocks of primary resources, a book will take a broad topic that spans a number of years and examine its impact in-depth. For instance, the book *Tempered in the Revolutionary Furnace: China's Youth in the Rustication Movement,* by historian Yihong Pan, examines the expe-riences of a few dozen of the 17 million urban, educated, middle-school Chinese students sent to the countryside to experience rural life and boost agricultural production between 1953 and 1980.[4] Using oral histories and other primary sources, coupled with secondary works including other his-torians' interpretations of the period, Pan provides new insights into the

---

Box 3.1 Defining and Refining Your Topic Using Monographs

As you do your research, you will be constantly refining and defining your topic. Because monographs usually cover such a breadth of subject, you will use them to begin to see the directions your topic can take. Remember, you cannot fully examine every aspect of a topic in the pages allotted by your teacher or professor or the website space you will design. To help focus your topic and your thoughts, reflect on how the book was classified in the *Library of Congress Subject Headings (LCSH)*. LCSH was designed to classify knowledge in connection to other ideas and may help you to understand the context of your topic in a broader scheme of knowledge. Also look at tables of contents in some of the books that best fit your topic to see how the material is subdivided. Further, look at the bibliographies at the end of what you think are key chapters and select some of those sources to read. Called "snowballing" or "pillaging," you are looking into the same writings, or discourse, that other historians have examined to research your topic. This is an excellent way to begin to build a list of resources, to test the viability of your broad topic, and to find out what has been published on a subject. However, do not limit your research to sources you find in bibliographies. This could limit your research by recycling and duplicating the same ideas, preventing you from discovering new theories. Be sure that you also look for monographs and journal articles through catalogs and periodical indexes.

---

reasons many of these students as adults led protests in 1978 and 1979 that forced the Chinese government to abandon this program. Compared to an article, the topic of the book is fairly broad, covering a number of years and incidents. Yet, in its 284 pages, it is able to explore the topic of the rustication movement comprehensively, in a way that a journal article could not.

How to Use a Book Artfully

While it is often best to read a book cover-to-cover to examine the author's argument from inception to conclusion, it may be that the information or analysis you need is contained in a portion of the text. In order to determine this, always use the book's "navigational" tools to the fullest. Look carefully at the table of contents. In it, you will find information that will help you identify the parts of the book that are most relevant to your research. Many online catalogs now include a book's table of contents in the catalog records, so in some cases you can browse the contents without even having the book in your hands. The index at the back of the book is also an important navigational tool. A good index can pinpoint the information you seek. Even if only one chapter of the book pertains to your research, it is still wise to read the introduction and conclusion of the book as well as the section in which you are interested. This will help you to understand the fuller context of the material you select and the author's overall argument.

Electronic books are presented much like a printed book. Many actually look like their print counterparts, either in a page image or as a website, with webpage navigation. Sometimes their content is divided by pages, looking like an exact image or with page breaks indicating where pages occur in the original printed text. Sometimes e-books present themselves as a long series of linked pages with no relationship to the physical layout of the printed text. This is problematic when you try to cite information and are unable to cite a page or any location in the text. E-books and collections of e-books usually allow for keyword internal full text searching of a single title or of the complete collection of e-books. While this is particularly useful for difficult to find topics (for instance the Gnadenhütten massacre, the killing of a group of Christian Indians in the US Revolutionary War) cross searching across a large selection of books can produce overwhelming numbers of results for more common ideas (American slavery, for example). Generally printing or downloading the whole book, portions, or even individual pages are prohibited. E-books can make it difficult to consult endnotes. When reading a print book you can place a bookmark or your finger in the endnotes section, which is difficult with a book on the screen. Some e-books have hyperlinked notes within the text, which partially solves this issue.

Many e-books are available through commercial publishers and for a subscription cost, paid by your libraries. One important e-book collection for historians is the *ACLS Humanities E-Book Project* (http://www. humanitiesebook.org/). The project contains over 3,000 secondary work monographs, with new titles added each year. Titles are selected by a board of learned societies, university presses, and the University of Michigan, for their importance to the humanities, availability for electronic conversion, and fit with the existing e-book collection. While over 3,000 monographs may seem large, it is still a small collection compared to a library, so it may not contain anything on your topic. This collection allows you to search across all of the titles. Google books may also be a useful source for e-books. A mix of public domain (copyright free and free to use) and copyrighted titles (you can only read portions of, not the complete text), Google Books' original purpose was to provide full text searching of contents of books, but only allow the user to see a snippet of text where their particular criteria occurred if the book was still under copyright.[5] Conflicts arose over copyright and author's permissions, which led to a famous court case that limited Google's ability to outright make publically available some titles.[6] As a result, Google Books is an interesting but eclectic collection of texts. You will find references in Google Books that you would be unable to find any other way, but you will still have to seek the original full text either on your library's shelves or from one of the subscription e-book collections mentioned above.

Most books are still issued in print format, and the older books that you will use are most likely also in print format. However, with the lack of sufficient space in libraries and users expecting electronic access at home, e-books are the trend of the future. Whether you are looking for electronic books or print books, you need a catalog, usually a library's catalog.

Finding Monographs and Using Catalogs

A catalog, in its most basic definition, is a description or listing of a collection of materials. A library catalog simply provides a description and location of that library's holdings and other materials to which the library has access, including book titles (both electronic and print), journal titles (but not their contents, e.g., not the individual article titles), video titles, children's book titles, government documents, special materials (like manuscript collections) and even CD-ROMs, electronic monographs, full-text journals, and sometimes websites. (Some libraries do omit certain types of material from their online catalog, such as US government documents.) The online catalog may also contain materials that are full text, online, which can be delivered to your desktop and are not physically located on the shelves of, or even owned by, your library. If you are unsure about the contents of your library's online catalog, ask your librarian.

Online catalogs provide a number of ways to access a library's collection. Understanding how the catalog operates will reduce your research time, as well as help you discover some amazing information.

Navigating a Library Portal/Finding the Catalog

The front page of most library websites are portals, gateways to the content, services, and information about the library and its activities. These introductory pages are often crowded and confusing, making it hard to find what you need. Yet, if you learn to navigate this front page, you will usually be led to a wealth of quality research materials. However, identifying where the catalog is and what is being indexed in the online catalog can be tricky. Figure 3.1 is a sample of a typical homepage. The big centered search box provides basic search options in different sources (books, databases to find articles, etc.). In this case you would click on the books and more tab and enter your search. Some libraries may also have a tab labeled catalog or may simply provide a link to the catalog/online catalog in a list. Libraries strive to speak to researchers of all levels in terminology that connects the finding of information to the researchers' ideas. Sometimes it is hard as a researcher to figure out if you are where you need to be.

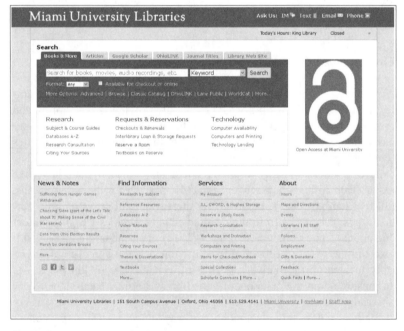

Figure 3.1. An example of a library portal/home page. Access to the libraries' catalog, other research databases, and information about services and staff are accessible from front page links.

Figure 3.2. Indiana University Libraries main research page with one box discovery service searching. Click on the OneSearch box. *Used by permission of Indiana University Libraries.*

Some libraries have begun using what is called a "discovery layer." A discovery layer, sometimes called federated searching, integrates different types of sources and databases, for instance, the online catalog with other selected periodical databases.[7] Your search results would include books in your library, as well as journal articles from indexes like *Historical Abstracts* and *Academic Search Complete/Premiere*. (Read more about periodical indexes in chapter 4.) You will need to look through your results carefully to know what kind of resource you have (book, journal article, or something else). This style of searching is convenient, a sort of "one stop shopping, general store" approach, producing more results quickly. However, you must be sure you understand what indexes this discovery layer is searching through. It might be incompatible with other databases or may leave out a database that is important to your field of research, causing you to miss important journal articles. Often the searching in the discovery layer/federated searching is not as precise because

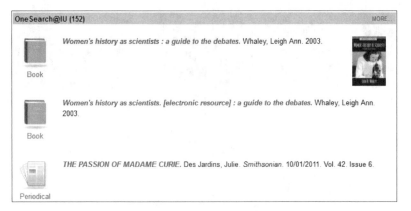

Figure 3.3. Results from Indiana University Libraries discovery layer OneSearch. *Used by permission of Indiana University Libraries.*

subjects are not standardized across databases. For instance, the library's online catalog will use the *Library of Congress Subject Headings*, but *Historical Abstracts* has a different set of standardized subject words. For simple beginning research you will find enough resources through a discovery layer service. For more advanced levels of research, you may wish to talk to your librarian about alternatives and target specific sources or databases.

Whether you have access to a discovery layer service or still use your library's online catalog, skillful use of that search engine will provide you with quality resources for your paper or project. Inability to make that search engine or catalog give you results that match your topic can add to your research time and frustration. The discussion below will address using an online catalog, but the same strategies can be used in a discovery service.

In any library catalog (online, discovery service, the printed card drawers, or even those catalogs of library collections that are printed in book form), you can search for a book by the subject, author, or title. For author, you must usually search by the last name first. For titles of monographs, you must search for the beginning of the title, dropping the initial article but using all of the articles within the title. For instance, the book *Women of the Pleasure Quarters: The Secret History of the Geisha*, by historian Lesley Downer, would be searched by entering "women of the pleasure quarters" in the title field.[8] You need not be concerned with capitalization of words.

Strategic Searching: Keyword vs. Subject Searching

When you begin your research, your search strategy will take the form of either a keyword or a subject search.

- *Keyword.* A keyword search makes an *exact* match of the word that you type in the search box. The computer will be searching through some combination of the titles, notes, table of contents, and subject fields of the catalog record. For example, if you search for the keywords "children and history," the results *might not* include a book entitled *A History of Childhood in the Middle Ages* because you asked the catalog to look for the word "children," not "childhood." You would only find that book listed in your results if the word "children" was listed somewhere in the online record, maybe in the subject headings field.
- *Subject.* A subject search performs a search through an approved, controlled list of words and phrases. Most college and university library catalogs use the *Library of Congress Subject Headings* as a source for approved subject headings. Using a standard word or set of words, a subject heading helps collect synonymous words and ideas under one term or phrase. Using the same example, a search for the word "child" would not find monographs using the word "teenagers." However, you could select the subject headings "Adolescence–United States–History" or "Teenagers–United States–History" or "Children–United States–History" and focus your topic, as well as eliminate those monographs that would technically meet your criteria but not be on your topic. In this case, you need to select the word or phrase that the *Library of Congress Subject Headings* list uses, which is not always precisely the wording you would naturally use.

Guessing a subject heading can be difficult, so unless you are confident of a subject heading, it is best to begin with a keyword search. The subjects that have been assigned to that particular book are listed in the catalog record for the monograph and hyperlinked at the bottom of the screen of the catalog record. These are linked to other records with the same subject heading in the catalog. The catalog will perform a search on this subject heading and generate a list of those items assigned the same subject heading. The smart research strategy is to look at several relevant monographs in your results list and search on the subject headings that are attached to these records. Begin to manipulate these subject headings. Many times these subject headings will suggest additional terms and concepts. Often, they will pinpoint a smaller, highly relevant number of monographs and other materials. Using these subject headings will save you time in your research and will produce more efficient, precise results.

Keyword Searching

When doing a keyword search, it is best to begin by performing a little word association. In the example above, you would need to think of both the words "children" and "childhood." You might even come up with other related words, such as "youth" or "adolescent" or "adolescence." You must remember that the computer and the catalog are not doing the thinking for you. It is your job to think of associative or synonymous words. In fact, it is possible that the first words that come to mind are not the words that best reflect your topic. Language is political, and point of view is critical. For many years, the subject heading used for the Vietnam War was "Vietnamese Conflict 1961–1975." "Vietnam War" was not a subject heading because, technically, the United States never declared war on Vietnam. So you would have done a keyword search on "vietnam war" to find books or monographs with those keywords in the title and then discovered the correct subject heading. While the *Library of Congress Subject Headings* have caught up with current nomenclature, using "Vietnam War, 1961–1975," added subject headings related to the conflict include "Cambodian-Vietnamese-Conflict 1977–1991" and "Sino-Vietnamese Conflict 1979." A more current example is the Bosnian war in the early 1990s. The subject heading for that conflict is "Yugoslav War 1991–1995—Bosnia and Hercegovina."[9] As suggested above, it is always best to use the subject headings in the catalog records of the monographs you have identified to find more monographs and other materials in the catalog.

To compensate for this problem of exact word matching in keyword searching, you can use two techniques: truncation and Boolean searching. The use of truncation, sometimes called "wild cards," allows you to search for many forms of a word in one step. In our example of children and childhood, you could enter the search with an asterisk (*) (sometimes $ or ! is used) after the root word, in this case *"child*."* Using *"child*"* will give you the results "child," "children," "childhood," "childlike," and "children's." However, it will not give you results that contain the words "teenager" or "youth." To expand your search to include those terms, you would want to use Boolean searching and use "or" between words that are synonymous. For instance:

child* or youth or teenage*

Then combine this idea with history using a Boolean "and" to combine concepts:

(child* or youth or teenage*) and history

This particular search is too broad, unless you are in a smaller library, so you would want to limit it further by adding a geographic specification, for instance, "United States." Chapter 4 on journals will discuss Boolean searching in more depth as it is especially useful in searching periodical databases.

Subject Searching

Sometimes, you may know the exact subject heading and will want to begin with a subject search. If you are looking for biographies or histories of a place, the subject headings of these works are automatically the person or place name. For example, to find biographies on Mahatma Gandhi, you would look under his last name, "Gandhi," as a subject. The subjects on Gandhi will then be subdivided by categories such as "Bibliography," "Correspondence," "Philosophy," and "Views on life." Individuals who have pseudonyms are found under both their commonly known names, for instance "Twain, Mark," as well as their real names, "Clemens, Samuel Langhorne." It is always best to check both names. Likewise, buildings and historic sites will be found under their names. Cities, provinces, states, countries, and other political divisions will have subject headings under their names. For instance, the subject heading for Berlin is "Berlin (Germany)." Usually, political divisions are followed by their larger political unit (e.g., cities by province or state) and then have other subject subdivisions attached after that (e.g., "Sydney (N.S.W.)," for New South Wales in Australia, or "Kuala Lumpur (Malaysia)"). However, many times the subject headings are complex: the subheadings that directly follow the main heading in the string do not always include the word "history" even though that is what the results will cover. Additionally, when "history" is a subheading, it is not always the first subheading in the string. Some examples are shown below:

British–Travel–Germany–History–20th century
Interfaith marriage–Germany–Berlin–History–20th century
Architecture–England–London–History
Households–England–History–To 1500

Box 3.2 *Library of Congress Subject Headings* **and Controlled Vocabulary vs. Tags and "the cloud"**

The *Library of Congress Subject Headings* are a voluminous set of books (some libraries have these online) containing agreed-upon words and phrases used in most university catalogs that describe library materials. Designed to classify and arrange the materials in the Library of Congress in 1898, these subject headings merely attempted to classify knowledge into standardized words and phrases so that catalog librarians would always use the same word or words to describe materials instead of choosing synonymous words and phrases. For example, the terms "doctor," "physician," and "surgeon" can be synonymous, yet "doctor" can also mean "professor." While other countries use the Library of Congress system, other classification schemes are also in use. This standardizing of subject headings is called "controlled vocabulary." You will encounter similar systems in many periodical indexes. Increasingly additional methods are being used to classify and collect resources on the same topic. Tagging allows users to customize the content of resources by assigning personal descriptive words or phrases. The websites, Amazon and Flickr are examples of this "third order" of organization. Library of Congress subject headings are hierarchical compared to tagging, which is usually chaotic and very broad. You may find that some of the databases you use, as well as the online catalog, may allow you to do your own tagging and searching through those tags.

Sources: Lois Mai Chan, *Still Robust at 100: A Century of Library of Congress Subject Headings. LC Information Bulletin*, August 1998, http://www.loc.gov/loc/lcib/9808/lcsh-100.html (accessed September 8, 2011) and David Weinberger, *Everything is Miscellaneous: The Power of The New Digital Disorder* (New York: Times Books/Henry Holt & Co., 2007).

In the example above, if you had entered "England–History–Architecture" in the subject field in your catalog, you would not get any search results because the order of the words matters in subject headings. One way around this problem is to do a simple subject search and then to limit the results by selecting words in the subject "history." This allows the word "history" to appear in any order in the string of the subject subheadings. The subject headings above are regular ones found in the *Library of Congress Subject*

Headings list. However, there are "form subject headings" that can be commonly applied to many subjects. Limiting by these can be useful in narrowing your topic. You can use words for types of reference resources, such as encyclopedias, statistics, etc., as subheadings to find those kinds of sources. Limiting by other common words in the subject, or subject subheadings, is also productive, for example, "Africa, West–Civilization" or "Palestine–Antiquities." A selected list is shown below.

Social life and customs	*Politics and government*	*Antiquities*
Civilization	*Bibliography*	*Philosophy*
Pictorial Works	*Description and Travel*	*Dictionaries*

Alternative Searching: Faceted Catalogs and Limiting

Many online catalogs now have the ability to use facets to limit catalog searches. You would perform your search in any of the manners above. Once you get a set or list of results, the catalog provides a list of words or phrases called facets off to the left or right side of your results, which allows you to limit your search. These words or phrases are usually based on common subject headings attached to the records of your results. If you click on these facets, you will begin to narrow your search. Using facets is an excellent way of taking a topic that is too broad and shaping it into a manageable topic. For instance, you could search for the keywords, civil war women and limit by the facet/subject "social conditions" and "sex role" and find books like: Nina Silber, *Daughters of the Union: Northern Women Fight the Civil War* (Cambridge, MA: Harvard University Press, 2005) and LeeAnn Whites and Alecia P. Long, *Occupied Women: Gender, Military Occupation, and the American Civil War* (Baton Rouge: Louisiana State University Press, 2009). Any and all of these searching methods (keyword, subject, and faceted) will produce useful results. One method may prove more useful for your research topic. Be prepared to mix methods.

How to Read an Online Catalog Record

Even though online catalogs have different appearances, the essential information in your library's online catalog record is the same as that contained in every other online catalog record worldwide. The book has a bibliographic citation, that is, the author, title, publisher, and place and date of publication. In addition to these, the record will indicate the number of pages, as well as any illustrations (illus. or ill.) or maps. Sometimes the table of contents is included. At the end of the record are the Library of Congress subject headings assigned to this particular book. Also on the screen somewhere are indications of the location of the book, the call number, perhaps the floor number or library (if your campus has multiple libraries) where the book can be found, as well as information on whether the book is on the shelf or checked out. The call number will begin with either a letter or a number. Most academic libraries use the Library of Congress call numbering system, an alphanumeric system (a combination of letters and numbers) that organizes materials into broad, related categories. History is often classed under "D" (world history), "E" (US history), and "F" (Latin American, local US, and Canadian history). However, because of the interdisciplinary nature of history, you will find history monographs with call numbers throughout the Library of Congress Classification System. For example, John W. Chaffee, *Branches of Heaven: A History of the Imperial Clan of Sung China* (Cambridge, MA: Harvard University Press, 1999), has the call number DS751.3.C35 1999 for Chinese history, but Richard L. Davis, *Court and Family in Sung China, 960–1279: Bureaucratic Success and Kinship Fortunes for the Shih of Ming–Cho* (Durham, NC: Duke University Press, 1986) has the call number HN740.Z9 E434 1986 for the subjects of social history and conditions and social problems, social reform. Browsing on the shelf by call number is usually fruitful in finding other sources, but remember that books can be classified in different places. Many libraries also have storage facilities, so not all the books may be on the shelf together in one location. The full Library of Congress Classification System can be seen at http://www.loc.gov/catdir/cpso/lcco/. See figure 3.4 for an example of a local catalog record.

Finding Monographs and Using Catalogs Outside of Your School

While you should begin your research at your college or university, you may find that you have selected a topic in which your library's collection is not very strong. You may need to look at other libraries' collections and request materials through interlibrary loan. Interlibrary loan is a service offered by most libraries that allows monographs and other types of materials to be borrowed between libraries, as well as providing photocopies of journal articles

Figure 3.4. An example of a record from a local library's online catalog. Along the left side of the screen, the record fields are clearly labeled. When you search for a keyword, typically, you are searching through the words in the author, title, imprint, series, note, subject, and added author fields. When you search for a subject, you are searching only in the subject field. Notice also that the subjects are hyperlinked allowing you to directly search those subjects. *Record courtesy Miami University (Ohio) Libraries.*

from other libraries' collections. This process may involve fees, takes time, and can have borrowing restrictions, so be sure to consult your librarian. The greatest challenge is identifying those monographs and sources that you need and that your library does not own. Many libraries subscribe to a database called *WorldCat* that is used by libraries worldwide to share cataloging. (A free, less robust version of WorldCat is available at: http://www. worldcat.org.) In essence, when you use this database you are searching the holdings of thousands of libraries simultaneously. However, resist thinking of *WorldCat* as a database that contains *every* book *ever* written, in *every* library. It does not. But it is a huge database that can help you find resources that you could never find otherwise.

Because *WorldCat* is an online catalog, it functions in much the same way as your library's online catalog. It contains monographs, titles of journals (not their contents), motion pictures and videos, sound recordings, electronic resources, manuscripts, and even selected Internet sites that libraries have deemed quality resources for inclusion in their catalogs. You can search by author, title, keyword, and subject. You can limit by type of publication (serials, sound recordings, monographs, even Internet resources), date, language, and format (large print, microform). Some of the terminology is different (author phrase and subject genre phrase, etc.), but you are basically doing the same kind of searching as in your home library's online catalog. You should begin with an advanced search option. Of the three choices of search level you are given in *WorldCat* (basic, advanced, and expert), the advanced level gives you the most guidance and will help you to know exactly where in *WorldCat* (author, title, subject, or other limits) you want to search. In the tabbed navigation bar toward the top of the *WorldCat* screen, select Advanced Search, if that is not your library's opening search screen.

In the search portion of the screen, you will find a series of boxes in which you will enter your search words. Next to these boxes are drop-down boxes from which you will select where you want *WorldCat* to look for your search terms. Because librarians also use this database, it will have some unusual choices in these drop-down boxes. For instance, under the general category of Subject, you will have the choice of Subject Phrase, Named Person Phrase, and Genre/Form Phrase, to name a few. Under the general category of Title, you will have the choice of Title Phrase, Series Title, and Series Title Phrase. Although the differences are significant to librarians, do not worry about them as a beginning researcher. When searching for a title, author, subject, and keyword, use the general category (such as Author) and you will be searching all the variations listed in the drop-down box. Remember, though, the distinction between keyword and subject still applies in *WorldCat*, as in any database you will search. If you wish to limit your search, you can check the boxes that appear below the main search box and limit your search by date, by serial (journal, magazine), etc. You can choose to rank your results by relevance or by date (currency). The default is relevance, meaning that items judged as more appropriate for your topic by the database are ranked highest. Sometimes that means the items have more of the keywords in the record or in the subject field instead of the title field (fig. 3.5).

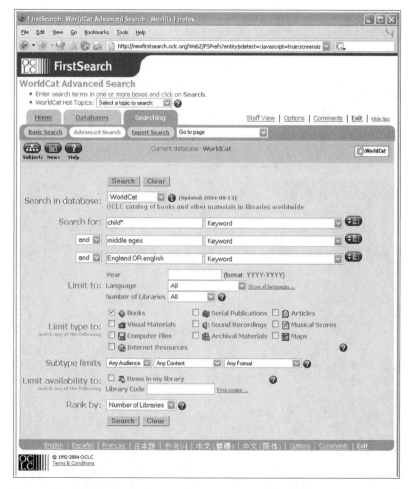

Figure 3.5. The advanced search page in *WorldCat*. Screen shot taken from OCLC's FirstSearch® service. *Used by permission of OCLC. FirstSearch® and WorldCat are registered trademarks of OCLC Online Computer Library Center, Inc.*

Your results in *WorldCat* will be grouped by type of resource, with monographs, serials, archival materials, maps, and so on, all collected separately toward the top of the screen in tabs. An individual record also has the same functionality as your local online catalog, with the subject headings hyperlinked. The results will tell you what libraries own your item. Keep in mind that, unless it is a manuscript, your library probably will be able to request a copy from another library through interlibrary loan (fig. 3.6).

If you know that a particular library is strong in a particular subject area, you may want to search that library's online catalog directly. For instance, if you live in Ohio but are doing a project on the history of the Pacific Northwest, you may want to use the University of Washington's catalog to locate materials because it is a research library and its collection of Northwest regional history would be more substantial than that in most Midwest libraries. Most universities allow outside users to search their catalogs. One of the lists of catalogs below will enable you to link to and search other libraries' catalogs.

Figure 3.6. Results list in *WorldCat*. The tabs divide your results by material type so you can further narrow your search. Screen shot taken from OCLC's FirstSearch® service. *Used by permission of OCLC. FirstSearch® and WorldCat are registered trademarks of OCLC Online Computer Library Center, Inc.*

SEARCH TIPS

1. Connect to your library's online catalog.
2. Begin with a keyword search.
3. Find a title of a good source which reflects your topic.
4. Look at the subject headings linked to the record.
5. Use those subject headings to connect directly to that heading in the catalog.
6. Check *WorldCat* or another library's catalog.

Sources for Catalogs

- Your library's catalog
- *WorldCat.* FirstSearch. http://www.oclc.org/firstsearch/content/worldcat/ (accessed July 28, 2011). Large online catalog of libraries, primarily in the United States but also in other countries around the world. WorldCat.org (http://www.worldcat.org) is a free public version, with fewer features.
- *European Library.* http://search.theeuropeanlibrary.org (accessed September 8, 2011). Simultaneously search the catalogs of the national libraries of Europe.
- Use a web browser to search for another library, university, and/or country.

Where Else Can I Find Monographs?

The online catalogs above are your best source for finding monographs. There are, however, a few other ways to find monographs. As discussed above, you can use an online collection of e-books that will lead you to printed monographs. Libraries generally index most of their electronic books in their online catalog, but you may find searching through an entire database of full text electronic books useful for your research. You can also purchase your personal copy of an e-book for the Amazon Kindle or Barnes and Noble Nook. You may sometimes lend it to a friend, but generally libraries are not able to lend out this kind of e-book in the way they have been allowed to lend out printed books (although technology continues to change). For another source of references to books, you might think of

---

Box 3.3 Book Reviews and Discourse

Book reviews are a useful tool for focusing your thoughts, as well as discovering what others think about the quality of other historians' work. This form of discourse, in which the writers of the reviews are critiquing the author's research and argument, will help you not only to understand what the author intended with his or her work but also to look at the execution of the book's argument and its research flaws. A book review will compare one particular work to other important works on a similar topic, not only leading you to other resources but also helping you to judge their quality. Chapter 5 will talk more about book reviews and evaluation.

---

searching the major online booksellers for research monographs, expecting them to behave like a catalog and a library. Although many scholars are big fans of Amazon.com and BarnesandNoble.com, these are not library catalogs. Their subject control is spotty. Their keyword searching is not fine-tuned, often leaving you with a plethora of results you did not want and without the results you need. The ranking of results is based on an odd algorithm that has more to do with sales and popularity than with your search criteria or appropriateness to your subject. After all, their purpose is to sell books. Also, you have no idea what is in the website, what is missing from the website, and why. They have an interest in telling you what is in print and out of print, but they cannot match the collection of a long-established library. Finally, the companies all have excellent customer service, but they do not have trained librarians who are connected with your professors and courses, have knowledge of the discipline of history, or know exactly what you need.

Case Study Finding and Using Monographs: The Spread of Islam in Western Africa

Your topic is the spread of Islam in western Africa, including the nations of Mali and Ghana. In this part of the world, Islam spread through the work of missionaries and traders, rather than through conquest.

1. Begin by dividing your topic into concepts.

CONCEPT I	CONCEPT II	CONCEPT II
Islam	*West Africa*	*Missionaries*
		Traders

2. List associative or synonymous words.

CONCEPT I	CONCEPT II	CONCEPT II
Islam	*West Africa*	*Missionaries*
Islamic	*West African*	*Traders*
Muslim	*Mali*	
	Ghana	

3. Decide which words will best reflect your topic and do a keyword search. Use truncation (*).

islam* and (mali or ghana)

and limit by words in the subject "history."

4. Select a relevant source in your results list: Nehemia Levtzion, *Islam in West Africa: Religion, Society, and Politics to 1800* (Aldershot, UK: Variorum, 1994).

5. Look at the subject headings assigned to the book and use some to search for more monographs and materials on your subject. "Islam–Africa, West–History".

6. You may wish to combine the terms "missionaries" and "trade" in some way with either or both "West Africa" and the two country names to gain a broader insight on the influences of these two activities.

7. If you need more information, do the same or similar searches in *WorldCat* or another library's catalog.

NOTES

1. Jay David Bolter, *Writing Space: Computers, Hypertext, and the Remediation of Print*, 2d online ed. (Mahwah, NJ: Lawrence Erlbaum Associates, 2001), 77–120.

2. Mary Kupiec Cayton, "The Making of an American Prophet: Emerson, His Audiences and the Rise of the Culture of Industry in Nineteenth Century America," *American Historical Review* 92 (June 1987): 597–620.

3. Mary Kupiec Cayton, *Emerson's Emergence: Self and Society in the Transformation of New England, 1800–1845* (Chapel Hill: University of North Carolina Press, 1989).

4. Yihong Pan, *Tempered in the Revolutionary Furnace: China's Youth in the Rustication Movement* (Lanham, MD: Lexington Books, 2002).

5. Other collections of e-books include: *Ebrary* (http://www.ebrary.com/corp/), *Questia* (http://www.questia.com/), *Google Books* (http://books.google.com/), Project Gutenberg (http://www.gutenberg.org/). *Google Books* and Project *Gutenberg* are public domain, free access books. *Project Muse* and *JSTOR*, currently provide access to digital journal collections, but will shortly start to include secondary source e-books. See also the following list of open access book providers: http://oad.simmons.edu/oadwiki/Publishers_of_OA_books.

6. Robert Darnton, "Six Reasons Google Books Failed," *New York Review of Books*. March 28, 2011. http://www.nybooks.com/blogs/nyrblog/2011/mar/28/six-reasons-google-books-failed/ (accessed September 8, 2011).

7. Major providers of discovery layer tools include: Ebsco Discovery Service, WorldCat Local, Summon, and Primo Central. Your library may or may not identify the provider of the discovery search interface, but many of them will look familiar as they already use a similar interface to provide access to databases you are familiar with.

8. Lesley Downer, *Women of the Pleasure Quarters: The Secret History of the Geisha* (New York: Broadway Books, 2001).

9. In catalogs, librarians will alter subject headings as historical usage changes. For example, over the years the subject heading for African Americans has changed from "Negroes" to "Afro-Americans" to the current "African Americans."

Finding Journals, Magazines, and Newspapers: Using Indexes

4

WHAT YOU WILL LEARN IN THIS CHAPTER
- the differences between journals and magazines and when to use each
- the differences between general and subject-specific periodical indexes
- how to select an appropriate periodical index
- how to search in a periodical index

This chapter will teach you, first, to define and distinguish journals from magazines and newspapers and, second, how to find, use, and construct a search in a specialized periodical index. Locating appropriate and on-topic secondary source journal articles can be difficult because so many exist and because their indexing is not as easily accessible as a book. Not listed in online catalogs, individual journal articles must be discovered through selecting one or more of the appropriate specialized indexes for your field of study.

How to Read a Journal Article

Journals are an essential component of your secondary sources and of the historical discourse and scholarly exchange of ideas. Often, they provide a very focused examination of some aspect of your topic and supply a specific, detailed bibliography that will point you to other valuable secondary works and primary sources. Not just an essential part of secondary source research, journal articles can offer an excellent model for the structure of your paper. Look at the introduction and conclusion and then examine how the subsequent paragraphs line up the discussion and evidence to support the ideas presented in the beginning. By the end of the article, did the author achieve her or his purpose? Because of their length, journal articles must be well organized, keep their argument focused, and have the proper mix of evidence, both primary and secondary sources, directly related to the topic. For instance, in the article "Is Smoking Permissible in Islamic Law? Answers from Arabic Manuscripts in the Beinecke Collection," Felicitas Opwis uses three seventeenth- and eighteenth-century Arabic primary source legal texts supported by scholarly secondary works to examine tobacco use in secular society and the conflicts between secular and religious authorities. Likewise, Scott Levi in his article "The Indian Merchant Diaspora in Early Modern Central Asia and Iran" uses selected contemporary published travel accounts from the sixteenth to the twentieth centuries to examine the roles Indian agents had on the foreign economies of central Asia, Iran, the Caucasus, and much of Russia where they lived and worked.[1] In both of these cases, the topics are specific and the primary source evidence is limited and focused. The primary and secondary evidence is interwoven and directly related. The bibliographies from journal articles such as these can lead you to primary and secondary sources that you may wish to use in your research. You might want to provide a different interpretation, but the bibliography will help you discover sources that you may not have known about.

What Are Periodicals (or Journals, Magazines, Newspapers)?

You will want to make sure you can distinguish a journal article from other types of periodical articles. Periodicals, another important type of secondary work, are materials that are issued "periodically," that is, more than once, usually at regular intervals—for example, quarterly or monthly. This category includes journals, magazines, newspapers, and annual reviews. Unlike full-length books, periodicals include short articles that focus on narrower, more concise subjects. Because they are published frequently, periodicals generally contain up-to-date, timely research. Each type of periodical has a very specific intent:

- *Journals.* The audience for journals includes academics, specialists, and researchers in the field on which the journal focuses. Often, this is a narrow audience. Some examples are *Oral History Review, Early American Review*, and *Nineteenth Century Feminisms.* Journals provide one way for researchers to communicate with one another. The language in these articles can be quite specialized and sometimes less accessible to general readers. The frequency of publication is usually quarterly or less. Articles generally contain many footnotes and a bibliography of sources.

- *Magazines.* Magazines are read by the general public and reflect the culture, ideas, and politics of the day. The language used is more accessible to all levels of readers. These publications usually contain images and either report or provide summary information on research or topical issues. They usually contain little or no documentation, such as footnotes, bibliographies, or complicated tables of statistical evidence. Magazines are usually published more frequently than journals: monthly, weekly, or twice-monthly. Magazines are considered primary sources because they report on events and reflect public attitudes and opinions. See chapter 6 for more information on magazines as primary sources.

- *Newspapers.* Newspapers are generally published daily with the intent of reporting the happenings of the city, town, and nation in which they are issued. They view the world's news from their particular location or perspective, or publish stories from a worldwide wire service or other newspapers to document news from other places. Frequently, newspapers do in-depth reporting on issues relevant to their particular area. Newspapers are usually more suited for primary source research. However, some major newspapers will provide background information for historical events and places that may prove useful to your research. They contain little documentation, such as footnotes, bibliographies, or complicated statistical evidence. Increasingly newspapers are accessible online and updated frequently as news breaks. While online publishing provides up-to-date information and allows errors to be easily corrected, archival stories are harder to find.

- *Annual Reviews.* Published once a year, annual reviews attempt to survey the evolution of scholarship within a discipline during a particular year. Annual reviews are more prevalent in the sciences and the harder social sciences, such as psychology and education, than in the humanities and history.

For the purposes of this chapter, most of our discussion will revolve around journals and magazines, the resources that index them, and the ways they can be used for historical research.

Journals vs. Magazines

Journals are the medium that scholars use most often to communicate new research findings, ideas, and conclusions. By contrast, magazine articles are written by journalists trained in research and reporting techniques and who are not typically specialists in any one specific discipline. These journalists gather their information by interviewing professional researchers and practitioners and by researching and reading some of the same scholarly journal articles that you might use for your own research. For example, if a journalist were writing an article on Martin's Hundred, a plantation located outside of Jamestown, Virginia, and chartered sometime around 1618, he or she could consult journal articles and books written about the settlement, as well as interview the archaeologists who excavated the site. The journalist would not actually be doing the archaeological digging and interpreting of the artifacts found. The archaeologist might publish his or her findings in a journal. Upon completion, the journalist's article, which is a synthesis and explanation of the investigation, goes to an editor, who makes corrections and adjustments and decides the final shape the article will take. This editor also has the power to decide whether or not to publish the finished article. While the journalists and editors at history-oriented magazines like *Smithsonian* and *National Geographic*, as well as more general magazines such as *Time* or *Newsweek*, are educated and informed, their purpose is to speak to a broad, general audience interested in history and other subjects, as opposed to a specialized, high-level audience. This does not mean that these magazines are inaccurate. It just means that their content is often too general to be used as the basis of your secondary historical research.

The physical appearance of magazines is also distinctive. Glossy photographs adorn the cover, as well as the interior. Such magazines contain paid advertisements, helping them remain affordable to a wide readership. Their subjects are broad and their headlines sometimes even sensationalized. For instance, an article about mummies in a glossy magazine called *Archaeology* was titled "The Well Dressed Dead," while a related article in a journal called *European Neurology* was titled "Myotonic Dystrophy in Ancient Egypt."[2]

Journal articles have a very different purpose and, consequently, different identifying qualities. The publishing process is structured so that scholars review, or referee, other scholars' work. Scholars submit articles to a journal on a specialized, focused topic. The articles are then sent to several other experts in the field to read and judge the accuracy of the scholarship. These readers, or referees, suggest changes or point out flaws in the authors' reasoning or arguments. The editor of the journal then decides whether to send the article back to the author for revision or to reject the article for publication. A journal article is judged by its scholarly merit as opposed to its ability to appeal to a mass audience. For an example of the review process, see the March 1997 issue of the *Journal of American History*, where the journal printed all of the reviewers' comments with the original journal article.[3]

Journal articles, like scholarly monographs, have notes, either at the bottom of each page or at the end of the article. Detailed charts, diagrams, and tables of statistics are sometimes included in this documentation. This material, along with other cited primary sources, serves as the foundation of the author's research and findings and supports the author's analysis and interpretation. The material is presented in such a way that other scholars can integrate those sources into their own research. In this way, historical research can be cumulative. The chart below outlines the differences between journals and magazines.

JOURNALS	MAGAZINES
Signed article by author. Author is usually scholar in the field who is an expert.	*Articles often unsigned. Articles often written by journalists or nonspecialists in the field about which they are writing.*
Language is technical and aimed at a specialized audience, usually those who also study in the field. Uses the jargon of the discipline.	*Language is simpler and aimed at a general audience. Anyone who is interested could read and understand the article.*
Documentation in the form of notes, footnotes, and bibliography.	*Has no documentation, but often sources are mentioned in the article.*
Complicated charts and graphs. These might not be present in many historical journal articles.	*Glossy photographs and simple charts or graphs.*
Articles have been through a scholarly referee process, selected by a journal editor, and approved by specialists in the field.	*An editor has approved articles.*

In December 2003, the traditional format of the journal was subjected to an experiment in the *American Historical Review*. The journal published an article solely in electronic format that sought to rearrange the traditional journal article from its usual linear format to a more hypertextual layout. This journal article, "The Differences Slavery Made: A Close Analysis of Two American Communities," challenged that linear format by operating much like a web page that allowed the readers to jump between introduction, summary of argument, points of analysis, and methods. [4] The introductory "page" (fig. 4.1) was similar to a journal article but enhanced by

Figure 4.1. Front navigation page of "The Differences Slavery Made: A Close Analysis of Two American Communities," an electronic scholarly article published in the *American Historical Review. Used by permission of the* American Historical Review, *William G. Thomas III, and Edward Ayers.*

hyperlinks to tables, maps, and footnotes. The methods section provided a description of the technical aspects of the data collection and production of the maps. In a separate tool bar section, readers could select evidence, historiography (bibliography), and tools. These three sections are essentially bibliographies of the primary and secondary sources used in the article with links to the actual sources and links back to the text in the analysis. This article could be read in the traditional manner or broken into bits and reassembled, in whatever manner readers desired to build their own understanding of the argument. Although complex, it was the beginning of electronic scholarship. New software also changes the way scholars participate in the review process and in the way they exchange scholarly ideas. The website, Writing History in the Digital Age, a born-digital, open-review volume edited by Jack Dougherty and Kristen Nawrotzki (http://writinghistory. trincoll.edu) and an Association of American University presses' report, "Sustaining Scholarly Publishing" (http://mediacommons.futureofthebook. org/mcpress/sustaining) connect readers' comments to the applicable paragraphs and pages of the text. While both of these are not strictly journal articles (a set of edited essays and an organizational report), they represent the newer possibilities of "peer review."

The identifying features of journals and magazines are easier to see when you can actually look at the hard copy of these types of secondary sources. A significant number of articles are in a digital format, making it harder to discern just what type of source they are. Some journals and journal-like articles are born digital and have a very different look and feel. Look for the same identifying features. All research articles should be documented and all authors' credentials identified.

Journals usually include letters to the editor, as well as book reviews, two features in which scholars continue their discussion and historical debate. Letters to the editor comment on previously published articles and the quality of their historical interpretation, while book reviews, written by other researchers who are working in the field, evaluate the scholarly contributions of published books. Neither of these forms of historical debate are considered research articles as they present no research evidence. They can be valuable to you to understand other historians' arguments, but consult your professor about using them as sources in your paper.

Commentary Periodicals

A third type of periodical exists, which is relevant to historical research and falls between the categories of journal and magazine. This periodical is often considered a journal even though it has the characteristics of a magazine. Sometimes called "commentary magazines," these publications contain political and social commentary that offer insightful analyses of events and issues. For example, you can read an article written in *The Nation* on March 15, 1919, by playwright, critic, and actor Robert Benchley entitled "The Making of a Red," a parody on the hostility toward supposed communists in the entertainment community. The 1919 article is a primary source. In the January 21, 2002, issue, the same magazine published an article by Benjamin Barber, political philosopher, author, and former advisor to President Clinton, entitled "Beyond Jihad vs. McWorld: On Terrorism and the New Democratic Realism." The article, as with Barber's book of a similar title, takes a capitalistic market focus while contrasting liberals' international interdependence approach with conservatives' war response to terrorism. Usually, the articles contained in these publications are opinion pieces or personal accounts based on learned analysis of primary and secondary source material. Often written by well-known and respected political commentators and intellectuals, these are definitely not the kind of glossy, mainstream articles that journalists write for general magazines. Because they reflect the conservative, liberal, and moderate political and social opinions of the time in which they were written, these commentary articles can also be primary sources and can be used in your own research to document certain areas of thinking and debate. Many of these magazines have been published since the early part of the twentieth century and provide a useful intellectual history of Western philosophical thought.[5] Yet, because they are opinion-based and usually contain few footnotes, charts, or other scholarly documentation, they may not be considered scholarly journal articles by your professor. Even so, these articles can be excellent sources for you as you conduct your research. You can use them to help clarify and formulate your own opinion, as well as to understand other points of view and other approaches to your research topic. Some examples of commentary magazines/journals follow.

TITLE	DATE BEGAN	POLITICAL POINT OF VIEW
Nation	*1865*	*Liberal*
New Republic	*1914*	*Liberal*
Progressive	*1929*	*Liberal*
American Spectator	*1932*	*Conservative*
National Review	*1955*	*Conservative*

The Role of Newspapers in Secondary Historical Research

Newspapers tend to be most useful as primary sources, reporting events and other primary source data. Chapter 6 contains information on using newspapers as primary sources. However, newspapers can occasionally be used as secondary works when they publish stories on historical sites, anniversaries of historical events, or new archaeological discoveries that provide background information. In these cases, the newspaper is functioning more like a magazine than a journal, lacking documentation and complicated charts and graphs. Older newspapers are most often used as primary sources, providing evidence about people and events in particular eras. Before using a newspaper article as a secondary source, check with your professor.

How to Find Articles: Designing a Search and Using an Index

The best method for finding journal articles is to use a periodical index. If you have mastered your college or university's online catalog, learning to use a print or online index is just an expansion of that knowledge. Most major indexes to journals and magazines, as well as the journals you seek, are not available for free via the Internet. (An exception is the *Directory of Open Access Journals*, which provides free full-text access to scholarly journals, see http://www.doaj.org. Often, none of these journals are included in a periodical index or through Google Scholar.) However, many journals, subscription or free, can be accessed, usually online, through your library's catalog. Because of the interdisciplinary nature of history, a wide variety of potentially relevant periodical indexes are available. In the section below, you will learn how to find the right index for your topic.

Before using a periodical index, it is best to make sure your topic is well-defined and organized and that you understand the relationship of the components or concepts of your topic. As you know, journal articles are often more specific than books, so the terminology that you use to search for those articles must be more precise than the words you used in your online catalog search. Divide your topic into its essential ideas or concepts and play word associations with those ideas. For instance, if your topic is "the participation of women in the scientific revolution of the sixteenth through eighteenth centuries in Europe," you would think of the following search terms:

CONCEPT I	CONCEPT II	CONCEPT III	CONCEPT IV
Women	Science	Sixteenth century	Europe
		Seventeenth century	
		Eighteenth century	

Remember that the way *you* may think of your topic is not the way *others* may describe it. You will want to think of synonyms and other words that are close in meaning and reflect your topic. You will want to list similar concepts together, even if you do not use all of these words in your search. For instance, in this example, you may think of the following:

CONCEPT I	CONCEPT II	CONCEPT III	CONCEPT IV
Women	Science	Sixteenth century	Europe
Gender	Math	Seventeenth century	France
Female	Mathematics	Eighteenth century	England
Botany	Chemistry	Early modern	Great Britain
	Physicians	Enlightenment	Germany
	Surgeons		Italy
	Medicine		
	Physics/		
	Physicist		

Once you have made your list, think about the association of concepts, one to another. Must the list of journal articles you are seeking include *all* of the concepts you have listed or just a couple? You are beginning to use Boolean logic when you think this way, creating sets and linking them with the Boolean operators, either "and" or "or" (see fig. 4.2).

The Venn diagram in figure 4.2 would be written as a search statement in a database, as follows (capitals do not matter):

women and (scientist* or botan* or chem* or surgeon* or physician*) and (europ* or england or english or france or french)

Use parentheses to group your concepts and synonyms, or sets, together. This tells the database how to search for your topic, considering first the

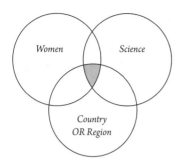

Figure 4.2. Boolean diagram that represents your concepts divided into sets.

words in the parentheses and then connecting the concepts as a whole. You would enter this search statement as a keyword search in a periodical index or database. Remember, the * (sometimes $ or ! in some databases) is truncation or a wild card, as you learned in chapter 3. When doing a keyword search, you must account for spelling variations and forms of your words. So, "botan*" will find "botany" as well as "botanist," "botanical," "botanically," and so on. Your search statement has asked for some form of the word "botany" (or "surgeon," "physician," "england," "europe" or "european") to appear in the database record. The article listings that result must have one of the words in their title, abstract, or subject headings/descriptors corresponding to each of the sections of your search statement that you have separated by an "and." Results of this search will include articles such as the following:

Weber, A. S. "Women's Early Modern Medical Almanacs in Historical Context." *English Literary Renaissance* 33 (Oct 2003): 358–402.

Jacob, Margaret C., and Dorothee Sturkenboom. "A Women's Scientific Society in the West: The Late Eighteenth-Century Assimilation of Science." *Isis* 94(2) (2003): 217–252.

Findlen, Paula. "Becoming a Scientist: Gender and Knowledge in Eighteenth-Century Italy." *Science in Context* 16 (2003): 59–87.

Tosi, Lucia. "Marie Meurdrac: Paracelsian Chemist and Feminist." *Ambix* 48 (July 2001): 69–82.

Klairmont-Lingo, Alison. "Women Healers and the Medical Marketplaces of 16th-Century Lyon." *Dynamis* 19 (1999): 79–94.

Evenden, Doreen. "Gender Differences in the Licensing and Practice of Female and Male Surgeons in Early Modern England." *Medical History* 42 (April 1998): 194–216.

The better your search statement, the more useful your resulting list of journal articles will be. Throughout the course of your research you will refine and even repeat the same search in the same and in different databases. The more you learn about your topic, the more you will recognize relevant articles that previously seemed irrelevant.

SEARCH TIPS

1. Divide your topic into concepts.
2. List synonyms and associated terms.
3. Indicate relationships of terms using the Boolean operators "and" or "or."
4. Use parentheses to make synonymous associations in your search statement.

Using an Online Database: *Historical Abstracts* and *America: History and Life*

Search statements can be used in a variety of online periodical databases. You can use general periodical indexes, such as *Academic Search Complete/Premier*, *Reader's Guide to Periodical Literature*, or *Infotrac*, and/or specialized, discipline-centered indexes such as *Historical Abstracts* or *America: History and Life*. (An Internet search engine generally will not index individual journal articles, the exception being *Google Scholar*. *Google Scholar* has many limitations, which are discussed later in this chapter.) General indexes, such as *Academic Search Complete/Premier*, try to cover major journal articles in a wide variety of disciplines, including history. Often, these general indexes include magazines as well. Because of this "one size fits all" approach, the subject headings lack professional terminology that an index designed for practitioners in the field would have. Using a specialized index will not only save you time but also directly connect you to the appropriate historical literature, eliminating the guesswork as to the quality and acceptability of the article and publication. *Google Scholar*, a search engine designed by the company Google, attempts to provide bibliographic access to academic research journals. Part of the problem with *Google Scholar* is that the coverage is limited to the connections the search engine's bots can make with publishers and others that supply full-text articles, preprint articles, and conference publications. This conglomeration of resources is only a small portion of what is available and may miss key resources for your topic just because *Google* was unable to access a journal's or publisher's website. Search results are returned, arranged on a sort of cited-reference search, what others have cited in their works, as well as the usual *Google* ranking algorithm. *Google Scholar* is not able to provide the subject control or the limiting capabilities that a subject-specialized index can. This often results in huge numbers of results. Often the results are a mixed bag. In a 2011 comparison of the quality of results between *Historical Abstracts* and *Google Scholar*, Hal P. Kirkwood and Monica Kirkwood found that *Google Scholar* more often presented older results and listed books rather than journal articles higher in the results.[6] Ironically little duplication was found between the *Google Scholar* and *Historical Abstracts* results. A significant number of *Google Scholar* results were off topic. *Google Scholar* is a suitable resource if you need just a couple of items and your search strategy is not too complex or too general. With some exceptions the article results of *Google Scholar* are not freely available on the Internet and *Google Scholar* does not completely link to full text. You must rely on your library to pay for online journal subscriptions.

For more precise and quicker results, use a subject-specialized index designed for history journals that uses the language of historians, such as *America: History and Life* or *Historical Abstracts*. These indexes cover "modern" history, roughly 1450 to the present, but also include articles with background information prior to the fifteenth century. *America: History and Life* mainly indexes US and Canadian history, while *Historical Abstracts* covers the rest of the world. Both are multilingual but with a heavy preponderance of English-language articles that have been issued in both electronic/online, as well as paper formats. The focus of this discussion is on the electronic version. However, the print versions are also very useful if that is what your library has. Do not ignore these indexes at your library just because they are not electronic! Print or electronic, they are the best way to connect to the scholarly, historical journal literature.

Like most indexes and catalogs, these indexes have both keyword and subject access. The subject access in this index is not as useful as in many other indexes because subject assignment can be imprecise and somewhat irregular. As a novice searcher, it is best to use the keyword search and your newfound Boolean searching skills. Both of these indexes have extra features that will help you refine your search even more.

Entering a Keyword Search in *Historical Abstracts*

Enter your search in the keyword boxes, using * for truncation as necessary (fig. 4.3). A keyword search statement for the concept of mothers and family in World War II era Germany could look like the following:

(nazi* or german*) and (mother* or famil*)

Your search is asking for articles that include some form of the word "nazi" (including "nazis," "nazism," etc.) and "mother" or "family" (including "mother," "mothers," "motherhood," "family," and "families") in the title, subject, or abstract fields. Your search, however, is also asking for the more general concept of "german" (as well as "germans" or

Figure 4.3. Main search screen for *Historical Abstracts*, one of the major online databases for history. Enter your search in the Keyword box. A unique feature to this database, as well as its companion database, *America: History and Life*, is the ability to restrict the time period the articles cover. In the example above, we have limited by the decades of the 1930s and 1940s. ©2012 Ebsco. Reprinted by permission, all rights reserved.

"germany") and some concept of "family" or "mother." Remember that in Boolean logic, your search results must only match one word from *each* set. Articles may have this broader view of family history in Germany without specifically including some form of the word "Nazi" and thus not directly covering the period of the 1930s and 1940s. In this case, you may want to restrict your search by the time period the articles cover (e.g., the 1930s and 1940s), specify that they be written in English (unless you read German), and perhaps further limit the type of publication to journal articles. Remember, if this does not produce the desired results, you must approach the search from a different viewpoint. Always have at least one other way to think about your topic. A librarian and your professor will help you with this.

When using *Historical Abstracts* or *America: History and Life*, it is important to know about these databases' unique feature that allows you to further limit your general search by historical period. As discussed above, your search may yield articles outside of your desired time period. Using only the search words "german*" and "women*" could provide you with articles on the eighteenth and nineteenth centuries, when what you need is information about the 1930s and 1940s. This is when the special date-limiting feature in *Historical Abstracts* can be useful. You can limit your results by era/decades or centuries by entering 1930 to 1939 or 1900 to 1999 (or even by exact date, although that is usually too restrictive). In this example, you would select the decades 1930s and 1940s. Selecting the entire twentieth century would be too broad as you would retrieve results that would examine German family life before the rise of the Nazis, as well as in East Germany during the Cold War.

The newest interface in Ebsco for *Historical Abstracts* and *America: History and Life* has a feature called SmartText Searching. This method of searching allows you to input long phrases or sentences in a search box and the database will try to interpret your natural language into something searchable. Be sure to click on SmartText Searching under the Search Modes section on the main page. Such a strategy is fine if you are having trouble defining your topic or just need a couple of articles, but not recommended for a more developed major research paper topic.

What You Will Get: Looking at Your Results

The result of your search will be a list of citations, customized to your search criteria. In the case of *Historical Abstracts*, the results are ranked with the most relevant citations at the top of the list, regardless of publication date. Each record consists of the basic information needed for you to locate the article, as well as an abstract, or summary, telling you what the article covers, a list of the descriptors/subject headings assigned to that article, the time period covered by that article, and the primary sources used to write the article (fig. 4.4). To find the actual article, look for either a full text link in the record (usually a .pdf document or an html link) or a link to a "find it" button. In many cases your article will be attached. However, just because the full text is not included in either of these databases, does not mean your library does not have it. We are used to finding (and consuming) journal articles in much the same way

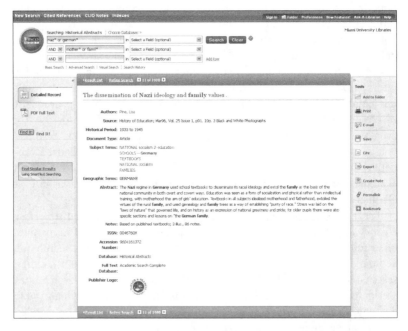

Figure 4.4. One of the results from your search. Provided is the title, author, and page numbers of the article as well as the name, date, and volume of the journal. An abstract or summary of the article is also provided. The abstract might provide you with other terms and names individuals to search for. Notice the documentation note at the bottom. That tells you that the references consist of primary sources and what those primary sources are. ©2012 Ebsco. Reprinted by permission, all rights reserved.

as we purchase music, on a song by song or article by article basis. That is sort of what you are doing in a journal index that links to the full text of the article. You have skipped the whole journal volume with all of a single years' issues bound together (i.e., the album or CD) and zeroed in on the exact article (or song). This is easy if that link to the article is attached to the bibliographic information in the index, but can make it harder to find if it is not. If your library does not automatically link to some sort of method of finding your article, you will need to look up the journal title (not the article title) in your library's online catalog to see if your library subscribes to it in paper, electronically, or not at all. You will then have to drill down from the journal title, to the issue, and then the article. This is the same process if the article is online or in print.

Part of being a good researcher is recognizing good results from your search. Good results fit your topic, are not too general, and are not too many in number to make it impossible to read them all within the time constraints of your research. If your search results include an extremely long list of citations, it probably means that your search terms were too broad. You may be willing to sort through hundreds of bibliographic citations to find those that reflect your needs, but it is better to refine your search using the special capabilities of these databases. As a general rule, between 25 and 50 citations is a good-sized list. Anything over 100–150 exceeds a manageable, browsable list.[7] With any larger yield, add additional search terms or limits to restrict your search statement or rethink your search terms entirely. In the case of *Historical Abstracts* or *America: History and Life*, if you have too many citations, you can restrict your historical time period even further, add additional keywords to your search, or limit your results by the facets or subjects suggested on the left of the screen. Listed under the "subject" link these facets represent the subjects/keywords assigned by the database's indexers. Theoretically if this subject is attached to the record, the article focuses significantly on the idea. Facets are useful to limit your search and to help you discover ideas and aspects of your topic you may not have thought of. If you have too few results, you need either to expand your search by adding other search terms and linking them with "or" or to rethink your choice of terms and keywords. Perhaps there are better, more common, or more descriptive words that reflect your topic. Going back to your word lists when you divided your topic into concepts may help you think of other words to use. If you have tried to expand your search several ways, using new terms each time, it is possible that you have a unique topic on which little has been written. If you suspect this to be the case, you may wish to check with your professor or a librarian.

By its nature, history crosses many disciplines and many other disciplines publish articles on their own history. Searching in other related indexes may be useful. In historical research, or in any research, ignorance and poor search techniques are no excuse for not discovering the works of other scholars who have written on your topic. Look at Selecting Other Indexes, below, to find periodical indexes other than *Historical Abstracts* and *America: History and Life*.

SEARCH TIPS

1. Use the keyword search.
2. Use truncation and Boolean search techniques.
3. Limit your search by time period.
4. Expand or limit your search to produce an acceptable number of results.
5. Use other special sections of the index as appropriate (author or title index or browse by author, title, or subject).

Selecting Other Indexes

Because history is such an interdisciplinary subject, you will often find periodical indexes aimed at other disciplines very useful for certain topics. Ancient historians use *L'Année Philologique* because *Historical Abstracts* and *America: History and Life* do not encompass the time period they study. If your topic looks at some aspect of medical history, in addition to the two main historical indexes discussed above, you would benefit by searching medical indexes like *Medline* (the free general public version is called *PubMed*: http://www.pubmed.gov) or *PsychInfo*. A selected list of the subject-specialized indexes for other disciplines can be found at the end of this chapter. However, you can also look in your institution's online catalog to find out what is available, in print and possibly online. Generally, these indexes are listed in the catalog using very broad subject headings. In the medical example above, the subject heading to use is "Medicine–Periodicals–Indexes." If your topic is in social history, you might want to do a search in your online catalog under "Sociology–Periodicals–Indexes." You would find the subject-specific specialized index, *Social Sciences*

Box 4.1 *JSTOR, Project Muse,* **and Periodical Indexes**

JSTOR and *Project Muse* began as two collections of humanities journals (*JSTOR* does have some social sciences journals). Their original intent was to provide digital archival access (JSTOR = Journal Storage) to the core academic journals in the humanities, social sciences, and selected sciences. With about 1,482 and 490 journal titles, respectively, they contain significantly fewer journal titles than those indexed in *America: History and Life* (about 1,700 titles) and *Historical Abstracts* (over 2,300). *America: History and Life* and *Historical Abstracts* have controlled vocabulary (descriptors or subject headings) while *JSTOR* and *Project Muse* do not.

When researchers conduct a search in *JSTOR* and *Project Muse*, often they use a keyword search, which searches through the entire article text or can be limited to title, and so on. *Project Muse* does use Library of Congress Subject Headings, but searchers can only browse through a list. *JSTOR* provides no subject access. *JSTOR* currently has a "moving wall" that excludes access to the current three to five years of volumes. Project Muse has no such restriction. Both of these databases will be adding selected academic books, and in the case of *JSTOR* some current journal issues. Because these services concentrate more on their full-text contents, they are not good indexes, providing limited options to create an advanced, complex search strategy. *JSTOR* and *Project Muse* are excellent resources for journal articles but should not be confused with periodical indexes like *America: History and Life* and *Historical Abstracts*, which have a greater depth and breadth of journal titles and the capabilities of complex searching.

Index. The subheading "Bibliography" is also sometimes used, for example, "Education–Bibliography–Periodicals."

E-Journals and Electronic Collections of Journals

While using a periodical index is perhaps the most efficient way to locate the best history journal articles, e-journals and collections of e-journals offer a possible second alternative when searching for scholarly articles. Digital collections such as *JSTOR*, the *History Cooperative* (partnering with *JSTOR*), and *Project Muse* provide full text of many journal articles and allow for searching through the full text of an article. These collections, while useful, should not be confused with a periodical index. While many scholars think of them as an index, they have no subject access, only keyword searching. So, if authors used the word "negroes" in their 1911 research and "Afro-Americans" in their 1977 research and "African Americans" in their 1990 research and you use the keyword search "blacks," you would likely miss significant scholarship. If your search words are too general, you will literally get thousands of results because you are searching through every word of the text of the articles. In the case of *JSTOR*, many articles from the most recent two to five years are not included. Called the "moving wall," this means if you use *JSTOR* as an index and restrict your research to its contents, you will be excluding current scholarship. However, in the case of the *History Cooperative*, you can search only through recent issues of history journals. The purpose of *JSTOR*, *History Cooperative*, *Project Muse*, and other collections of full-text journals is to provide the full text of a selected list of journals based on a contractual agreement with the journal publishers. Sometimes this means the publisher will not allow the current issue(s) to be supplied or will not provide digitized versions of older issues.[8] While the reasons for this are numerous, a periodical index simply provides a timely reference to the article's existence in a journal because none of these contractual or copyright issues affects the indexing of articles. But when you have a focused concept or unique term, searching these large full-text repositories can be beneficial. Also, access to a single journal title will allow you to browse quickly and efficiently through the table of contents for its issues. Browsing the table of contents of a very focused journal, for instance, *History in Africa* or *Renaissance Quarterly*, will allow you to catch topics related to your research that you may not have come across with your choice of keywords or subjects in your index searches. (Remember too that you can browse the table of contents of a print journal just as you can that of an online journal.) Your search strategy should integrate the search capabilities of both periodical indexes and full-text journal repositories. Both provide useful research articles.

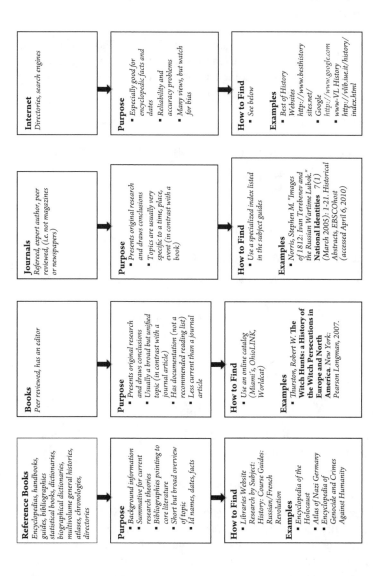

Reference Books
Encyclopedias, handbooks, guides, bibliographies statistical books, dictionaries, biographical dictionaries, multivolume general histories, atlases, chronologies, directories

Purpose
- *Background information*
- *Summative for current research theories*
- *Bibliographies pointing to core literature*
- *Short but broad overview of topic*
- *Id names, dates, facts*

How to Find
- *Libraries Website Research by Subject: History: Course Guides: Russian/French Revolution*

Examples
- *Encyclopedia of the Holocaust*
- *Atlas of Nazi Germany*
- *Encyclopedia of Genocide and Crimes Against Humanity*

Books
Peer reviewed, has an editor

Purpose
- *Presents original research and draws conclusions*
- *Usually a broad but unified topic (in contrast with a journal article)*
- *Has documentation (not a recommended reading list)*
- *Less current than a journal article*

How to Find
- *Use an online catalog (Miami's, OhioLINK, Worldcat)*

Examples
- *Thurston, Robert W.* **The Witch Hunts: a History of the Witch Persecutions in Europe and North America.** *New York: Pearson Longman, 2007.*

Journals
Refereed, expert author, peer reviewed, (i.e. not magazines or newspapers)

Purpose
- *Presents original research and draws conclusions*
- *Topics are usually very specific to a time, place, event (in contrast with a book)*

How to Find
- *Use a specialized index listed in the subject guides*

Examples
- *Norris, Stephen M. "Images of 1812: Ivan Terebenev and the Russian Wartime Lubok."* **National Identities** *7(1) (March 2005): 1-21. Historical Abstracts, EBSCOhost (accessed April 6, 2010)*

Internet
Directories, search engines

Purpose
- *Especially good for encyclopedic facts and dates*
- *Reliability and accuracy problems*
- *Many views, but watch for bias*

How to Find
- *See below*

Examples
- *Best of History Websites http://www.besthistory sites.net/*
- *Google http://www.google.com*
- *www-VL History http://vlib.iue.it/history/index.html*

Figure 4.5. Summary of Secondary Source Literature.

Case Study Searching for Periodical Articles:
Canton Trade System

Explore the following topic: the Canton Trade System (1760–1843), a series of trade regulations used by the Chinese to give domestic traders, known as *cohong*, an advantage over trading tea and textiles with such foreign companies as the British East India Company.

1. Divide your topic into concepts.

CONCEPT I	CONCEPT II	CONCEPT III	CONCEPT IV
China	*Trade*	*Europe*	*1760–1843*
		British East India Company	

2. Think of other related words.

CONCEPT I	CONCEPT II	CONCEPT III	CONCEPT IV
China	*Trade regulation*	*Europe*	*1760–1843*
Cohong		*European*	
		British East India Company	
		Britain	
		British	
		Portugal	
		Portuguese	

3. Select *Historical Abstracts* and perform a keyword search. Enter your search as follows:

(china or chinese) and trade

Remember $ or * or ! is truncation and will give you any number of characters after the root word. In this case, "chin*" is too short of a word and you will get too many results that would match your request but not be related to the word "China." After you receive your results, you will want to limit them by decades and probably by English, unless you read Chinese.

4. Aim for a list of not more than 70 results. A bibliography of 25–50 articles is ideal.

5. Depending on the quantity and quality of your results, you can add some of the words in your list above. For instance, at the time of the writing of this book, "Canton Trade System" yielded no results, but the phrase may be used by an author in the future. The word "Europe" was not used because articles would usually be written about a specific country, in this case probably Britain or Portugal. You could add those words if your results list is too large.

Selected Historical Indexes

These indexes apply to history and either cover time periods not covered by *America: History and Life* or *Historical Abstracts* or are created for a very specific time period of history.

Bibliography of British and Irish History. 1901– . http://www.history.ac.uk/ projects/bbih/info (accessed November 16, 2011). Subject matter covers the Roman period of the British Isles published from 1900 to the present (some limited materials before 1901). Journal articles, books, and other publications, including *Annual Bibliography of British and Irish History. Writings on British History.* Requires a subscription.

L'Année Philologique; Bibliographie Critique et Analytique de L'Antiquité Gréco-Latine. Paris: Société d'édition "Les Belles Lettres." 1924– . Former title: *Dix Années de Bibliographie Classique . . .* 1914–1924. Also available online through subscription. http://www.annee-philologique.com/aph/ (by subscription) and on CD-ROM titled *The DCB: Database of Classical Bibliography.* Atlanta: Scholars Press, 1995– (1974–1989). Index for classical history, literature, art, religion, folklore, early Christian texts, papyrology, and science. Access by subject, classical author, or text. Published in 1995, the CD-ROM covers publications from 1974 through 1989.

Diotima. http://www.stoa.org/diotima/ (accessed November 16, 2011). Index covering issues about women and gender in the ancient world.

TOCS-IN (Tables of Contents of Interest to Classicists), 1992– . http:// www.chass.utoronto.ca/amphoras/tocs.html (accessed November 16, 2011). Searchable list of table of contents of journals in classical studies.

ITER: Gateway to the Middle Ages and the Renaissance, 1784– . http:// www.itergateway.org/ (accessed November 16, 2011). Citations to books, journal articles, and essays concerning the Middle Ages and Renaissance studies.

Feminae: Medieval Women and Gender Index. http://www.haverford.edu/
library/reference/mschaus/mfi/mfi.html (accessed November 16, 2011).
Index to journal articles, book reviews, and essays in books concerning
gender issues but focusing on women and the Middle Ages. Excludes
single-author monographs. Coverage is since about 1990 but not for all
titles in the database.

*Viva: A Bibliography of Women's History in Historical and Women's
History Journals*. http://www2.iisg.nl/viva/ (accessed November 16,
2011). Multilingual bibliography from history and women's studies
journals, as well as selected articles from *Africabib*. Covers 1975 to the
present.

Annual Bulletin of Historical Literature. London: Historical Association.
1911– . Also available online through subscription. http://onlinelibrary.
wiley.com/journal/10.1111/(ISSN)1467–8314 (accessed November 16,
2011). Annual bibliography, classified by historical subject and era, providing access to recent scholarship.

International Medieval Bibliography. Leeds, UK: University of Leeds,
1967– . Also on CD-ROM and available online by subscription. http://
www.leeds.ac.uk/ims/imb/ (accessed November 16, 2011). Covers all
aspects of medieval life (450–1500) and culture, including literature,
politics, history, religion, and philosophy. Lists articles, *festschriften*,
conference proceedings, monographs, and collected essays.

*Isis: Current Bibliography of the History of Science and Its Cultural
Influences*. Chicago: University of Chicago Press, 1913– . Index to history of science journals. Since 1975, *Isis* is included in the electronic
database *History of Science, Technology, and Medicine*.

*C.R.I.S.: The Combined Retrospective Index to Journals in History, 1838–
1974*. Washington, DC: Carrollton, 1977–1978. 11 vols. Index to journals of interest to historians. Index is an enhanced keyword title list; that
is, words in the title, with extra significant words added, are listed in a
column.

IBZ: Internationale Bibliographie der Zeitschriftenliteratur. Munich: K. G.
Saur, 1896– . Also available online through subscription. Covers general
academic journals in all fields but focuses on the social sciences and
humanities. Especially good for European-language journals.

Selected Periodical Indexes of Use to Historians

ABZU. http://www.etana.org/ (accessed November 16, 2011). Index to
books, journal articles, conference proceedings, book reviews, and

websites on the Middle East. Some are full text and some are condensations of the texts.

Africa Bibliography. Manchester: Manchester University Press, 1984– . Indexes articles, books, and essays. Arrangement is by country or region.

Africabib.org. 1974– . http://www.africabib.org (accessed November 16, 2011). A compilation of a series of databases: *Bibliography of Africana Periodical Literature Database; African Women's Database; Women Travelers, Explorers and Missionaries to Africa 1763–2004: A Comprehensive English Language Bibliography.* Indexes books, journals, and conference proceedings. Access is by broad subject heading, keyword, or author/title. You must select and search each database separately.

ABSEES: American Bibliography of Slavic and East European Studies. Urbana-Champaign, IL: American Association for the Advancement of Slavic Studies, 1956– . Annual. http://www.library.illinois.edu/absees/ (accessed November 16, 2011). Annual comprehensive listing of journal articles, books, book chapters, book reviews, dissertations, online resources, and selected government publications produced in the United States and Canada. Has full-record keyword searching. Also available online by subscription.

Alternative Press Index, 1969 – . Index to radical magazines and newspapers worldwide. Also available online by subscription. http://www.ebscohost.com/academic/alternative-press-index (accessed November 16, 2011).

Annual Egyptological Bibliography. Leiden: E. J. Brill, 1947– , and some years available online. http://oeb.griffith.ox.ac.uk/ 1992– (accessed November 16, 2011). In print and online. You must search in each individual year and then by very broad subjects unless you wish to pay for a subscription. Some libraries may subscribe.

Applied Science and Technology Index 1913. http://www.ebscohost.com/academic/applied-science-technology-abstracts/ (accessed November 16, 2011). Applied sciences, such as inventions, mechanical technology, industrialization, and so on. Index to journal articles. Online by subscription.

Art Abstracts. Bronx, NY: H. W. Wilson, 1929– . Also available online through subscription. http://www.ebscohost.com/academic/art-abstracts (accessed November 16, 2011). Journal articles, yearbooks, and museum publications. Useful for art histories, painting, and sculpture. Online by subscription.

Arts and Humanities Citation Index. Philadelphia: Thompson ISI, 1977–. Also available online through subscription. http://thomsonreuters.com/products_services/science/science_products/a-z/arts_humanities_citation_index/ (accessed November 16, 2011). All humanities, including history. Part of the *Web of Science.* Unique system that will also index footnotes. You can find a source that you like and trace what other articles have cited it. Online by subscription.

ATLA Religion Database. Chicago: American Theological Library Association, 1960–. Also available online through subscription. http://www.atla.com/products/catalog/Pages/rdb-db.aspx (accessed November 20, 2011). Indexes journal articles, book reviews, and essays in religion and theology from the American Theological Society. Online is the union of two print indexes, *Religion Index One* and *Religion Index Two.*

BHI: British Humanities Index. London: Library Association, 1962–. Also available online through subscription. http://www.csa.com/factsheets/bhi-set-c.php (accessed November 20, 2011). General humanities index with international coverage.

Bibliography of Asian Studies. 1969–. Also available online through subscription, http://www.asian-studies.org/bassub.htm (accessed April 25, 2012). Multilingual, nearly comprehensive index to all aspects of Asian studies. Includes books, reference works, conference and symposia proceedings, and journals.

Black Studies/Kaiser Index to Black Resources. Also available online through subscription. Bibliography and index of journals, magazines, newspapers, newsletters, pamphlets, reference books, and reports on black life outside of Africa and published 1948–1986. Created by the Schomburg Center for Research in Black Culture of the New York Public Library. Check with your library to see if they have a subscription.

EconLit/Economics Literature/Journal of Economic Abstracts. Evanston, IL: American Economic Association. 1963–. Also available online through subscription. http://www.aeaweb.org/econlit/ 1969– (accessed November 20, 2011). Business and economics focus. Good for journals and papers on economic history.

Film Literature Index. Albany, NY: Filmdex, 1963–. Also available online through subscription. http://webapp1.dlib.indiana.edu/fli/index.jsp (accessed November 20, 2011). Popular and scholarly film and television periodicals.

Gender Studies Database. Combines *Women's Studies International* and *Men's Index.* 1972–. Also available online through subscription. http://www.ebscohost.com/academic/gender-studies-database.

Geobase 1980– . Available by subscription online. Includes journals, books, monographs, reports, and theses in human and physical geography. Historical geography is a field of study that would include information for historical research.

History of Science, Technology, and Medicine. Research Libraries Group, 1975– . http://www.oclc.org/support/documentation/firstsearch/databases/dbdetails/details/HistSciTechMed.htm (accessed November 20, 2011). Database that includes journal articles, conference proceedings, books, book reviews, and dissertations on the history of science and technology and allied historical fields. Electronic equivalent of *Isis Current Bibliography of the History of Science, Current Bibliography in the History of Technology, Wellcome Bibliography of the History of Medicine,* and *Bibliografia Italiana di Storia della Scienza.*

Index to Black Periodicals/G. K. Hall Index to Black Periodicals. Boston: G. K. Hall & Co, 1950– . Indexes the black magazine and journal press. This index has had various titles, so you may need assistance finding all of them in your library.

Lexis-Nexis. Dates vary by publication. http://www.lexis-nexis.com (accessed November 20, 2011). Full-text collection of newspapers and magazines. Many titles reach back into the 1970s. This is probably more useful as a primary source.

LGTB Life with Full Text. LGBT journals, magazines, and regional newspapers, and some full text books. Available online through subscription. http://www.ebscohost.com/academic/lgbt-life-with-full-text (accessed November 20, 2011).

Medline/Index Medicus/PubMed. Washington, DC: National Library of Medicine, 1953– /1879– . http://www.ncbi.nlm.nih.gov/entrez/query.fcgi. (accessed November 20, 2011). Index to medical journals that would include the history of medicine. Online as PubMed.

Middle East Abstracts and Index. Pittsburgh: Northumberland Press, 1978– . Also available online by subscription. http://referencecorp.com/books.html (accessed November 20, 2011). Index that addresses all aspects of Middle Eastern life. Indexes journal articles, editorials, government documents, press releases, annual reports, speeches, news conferences, books, theses, and dissertations.

MLA International Bibliography. New York: Modern Language Association of America, 1956– . Also available online through subscription. http://www.mla.org/bibliography (accessed November 20, 2011). Literary criticism journals. Literature and history are often tied together.

Music Index. Detroit: Information Coordinators 1949– . Also available online through subscription. http://www.ebscohost.com/public/music-index (accessed November 20, 2011). Critiques of music, composers, and culture in journals.

OCLC Public Affairs Information Service (PAIS). 1913– . Also available online through subscription. http://www.csa.com/factsheets/pais-set-c.php (accessed November 20, 2011). Foreign affairs, political history. Index to journals, policy papers, and government, international, and organizational documents.

Philosopher's Index. Bowling Green, OH: Philosophy Documentation Center, Bowling Green State University, 1940– . Also available online through subscription. http://www.philinfo.org (accessed November 20, 2011). Index to journals, articles, books, and essays that would include ancient intellectual history.

Psychological Abstracts/PsychInfo/Psych Abstracts. Washington, DC: American Psychological Association, 1927– . Also available online through subscription. http://www.apa.org/ (accessed November 20, 2011). Journals, books, and book chapters on the development of psychology.

RAMBI. Index to articles on Jewish Studies. Free, online. http://jnul.huji.ac.il/rambi/ (accessed November 20, 2011).

Women's Studies International. Baltimore: NISC, 1972– . Available online through subscription. http://www.ebscohost.com/academic/womens-studies-international (accessed November 20, 2011). Broad range of women's issues, including history.

NOTES

1. Felicitas Opwis, "Is Smoking Permissible in Islamic Law? Answers from Arabic Manuscripts in the Beinecke Collection," *Yale University Library Gazette* (2001 Suppl): 178–184; Scott Levi, "The Indian Merchant Diaspora in Early Modern Central Asia and Iran," *Iranian Studies* 32 (Fall 1999): 483–512.

2. "The Well Dressed Dead," *Archaeology* 57 (May/June 2004): 16; Giacomo Cattaino and Laura Vicario, "Myotonic Dystrophy in Ancient Egypt," *European Neurology* 41 (1999): 59–64.

3. Some flaws are quite evident in the Organization of American Historians' brave experiment. The article itself was not a typical journal article. The nature of the

article led some of the reviewers to guess the writer's identity, destroying the usual anonymity of the author during the review process. If you want to follow the debate, you can also see the article Adam Shatz, "Strange Fruit," *Lingua Franca* (August 1997): 18–20. Still, the exercise is useful to understand how the review process works.

4. William G. Thomas III and Edward Ayers, "The Differences Slavery Made: A Close Analysis of Two American Communities," *American Historical Review* (December 2003). http://www.vcdh.virginia.edu/AHR/ (accessed January 1, 2006).

5. For a less historical list, see Arts and Sciences Library, University at Buffalo (SUNY), *Commentary and Opinion Journals.* http://ublib.buffalo.edu/libraries/asl/guides/jour_comment_opinion.html (accessed January 1, 2006).

6. Hal P. Kirkwood Jr. and Monica C. Kirkwood, "Historical Research," Online 35(4) (2011): 28–32. http://www.infotoday.com/online/jul11/index.shtml (accessed November 20, 2011).

7. Some historians will browse large numbers of search results before deciding on a topic in order to survey the breadth of research activity on a topic. But this is surveying the topic at a preliminary stage of your research process, when you are not really into the core of your focused research topic. If you are not careful, you can be distracted by too many citations.

8. At the time of this writing *JSTOR* and *Project Muse* have begun to offer some current issues of periodicals, as well as scholarly history and humanities e-books.

5

Evaluating Your Sources

WHAT YOU WILL LEARN IN THIS CHAPTER

- how to decide if the resources you have found are reliable and of good quality

---

Evaluation occurs every day and in all parts of our lives. We evaluate what others wear, the movies we watch, which car to purchase, and the accuracy and relevancy of news stories we hear. We like awards shows, reality talent competitions, and best and worst lists. Evaluation is essential both to selecting appropriate sources from the vaguely relevant lists of sources generated from your research queries, as well as evaluating the arguments and evidence presented in those sources. Most of this chapter will discuss how to evaluate the quality of the academic sources you find for your research.[1] On another level, you must use your evaluation skills to closely evaluate the arguments presented in those sources. While some of those techniques are similar, the evaluation of an argument is much more extensive than the evaluation of the quality of sources.

Why Evaluate Your Sources?

Using reliable sources as a foundation for your research is necessary to achieve effective results and produce the best possible research paper or project. It is also essential if you want your work to be taken seriously by your professors and teachers, as well as other historians and researchers. In the previous chapters, you learned how to find secondary sources for your research. This chapter explores how to distinguish quality research from substandard research, a crucial task for a researcher. This can be difficult when you are not an expert in the field and have not spent your life studying a particular geographic area or period of history. However, to be a critical researcher, you must reflect upon the accuracy, value, and authority of your sources.

This chapter provides the basic criteria and some solid research techniques to help you evaluate secondary works. Other chapters will offer more detailed criteria and guidelines for evaluating specific resources: primary resources and Internet resources in chapters 6 and 7, maps in chapter 8, images in chapter 9 and statistics in chapter 10. While basic evaluation strategies can be applied to all types of resources, techniques used for evaluation of primary sources and Internet resources differ a bit from those used for secondary works. For primary sources you must have some knowledge of the time in which they were created and for Internet resources you must have an understanding of website navigation and function.

Basic Evaluation Criteria

The list below summarizes a number of commonly used evaluation criteria and is not exclusive to history. Asking these questions will help you assess the value of the secondary research you have found.

- *Author authority.* Who is the author, and what is his or her affiliation? Most journal articles and many books have biographical information on the author at the bottom of the first page or at the back of the book. Is the author from a reputable institution or organization? Does that institution or organization reflect a political viewpoint through which the author's research might be filtered? Is the author a practicing historian in the topic of history about which he or she is writing? For instance, is this person a historian with a strong economic background in writing on the military-industrial complex and the Vietnam War, or is he or she a chemist by day with an interest in Vietnam-era economics? Perhaps he or she is not a scholar at all. Look at the publisher or website affiliation. In other words, consider why you should trust this scholar's authority. You can also look for other sources of biographical information on this individual by using some of the biographical sources listed in chapter 2. Sometimes the name of a press/publisher can give you a clue to the work's authority and academic value. Most presses that have the word "university" in the name are reliable and scholarly. Many other major commercial presses also produce reliable texts, for instance, Free Press, Scribner's, and Gale. A selected and incomplete list of reputable publishers can be found at http://lib.colostate.edu/howto/publr-com. html and at the Association of American University Presses (http:// www.aaupnet.org/aaup-members/membership-list). However, there are publishers called vanity or subsidy presses, which essentially print works at the request of the author. A legitimate publisher provides editorial services, uses discrimination when deciding what to publish, conducts peer reviews, and provides marketing assistance. Vanity presses have almost none of these quality controls, sometimes resulting in many poorly researched works. However, vanity presses are useful for authors publishing local histories, which have limited appeal and economic viability. If you are not sure if a publisher is a vanity press, look for an online website that describes the publisher's editorial policy.

- *Audience and purpose.* Understanding the audience for which the author wrote the text is important. Is it for other scholars or practitioners who will understand the same professional concepts and terminology? Even if you do not yet fully understand what those terms mean, can you understand the context of such words and phrases as "neocolonialism" or "nihilism"? Can you tell by the language of the book or journal article that the target is a more general audience? If so, is the content scholarly enough to be useful for your research? Checking the footnotes and documentation can help you make this determination. (See the section below on footnotes and documentation, for a better understanding of what you can learn from these citations.) Remember, the best way to understand an author's purpose is to read the introduction of a book or journal article, where the argument is usually spelled out quite clearly.

- *Accuracy and completeness.* Since you have already planned the search strategy you will employ as you consult your institution's online catalog, as well as one or two periodical indexes, you already have an idea about the scope of your topic. Use this knowledge to think about issues that should logically be addressed by the works you are employing as sources. Has the author covered all of the necessary topics, even if he or she disagrees with other scholars? If important issues or themes are excluded, this may affect your research and signal problems with your sources. Then, as you read the text, consider if the author supplies the evidence and discusses the topics she or he promises. If not, this could be a red flag that the work is not of the best quality. Compare content across all sources. If one of your sources does not consider many of the same issues, authors, and pieces of evidence that your other sources do, this may be a clue that it is not reliable. That does not mean an author must agree with all of your other sources, but all of the authors should enter into the same debate. To further understand a book's audience, you can also look for book reviews to see what other scholars thought about the texts you are using. A book review can be useful in a number of ways. It generally contrasts the views and findings of a number of texts on similar topics. This comparison is particularly useful for you because not only does it identify key concepts across a number of works, but it will also highlight the differences in interpretation. Use book reviews to identify other works and key concepts. Book reviews, however, are not research as they present no original data and present the educated opinion of the reviewer. Thus, they are generally not considered peer-reviewed research articles. See chapter 2 for sources on finding book reviews and biographical information.

- *Footnotes and documentation.* Look at the footnotes and documentation. If little documentation is presented in the form of references to primary sources, charts, or graphs, you should look at the source with a very critical eye. An important component of presenting research is to identify findings, include proof for those findings, and document where you have found them so that others may replicate and judge your results. As with scientific fields in which other scientists replicate experiments to see that they get the same results, if you look at another historian's work and cannot replicate the research process based on the documentation, that may signal problems with her or his research process. A footnote or an endnote should contain all of the information necessary to find the "data" or item it refers to in the text. You should be able to go back and look up the referenced journal article, for instance, and see on a particular page what your original source was quoting or referencing. If the footnote references a primary source, that source should be clearly identified, so even if you cannot go to the archive and look at the source, you understand what it is and when it was produced.

How to Read and Evaluate a Book/Monograph or Journal

Actively thinking about the text you are reading will help you to understand and evaluate the usefulness and quality of a book. Books that are full-length narratives (i.e., an idea fleshed out in a number of interconnected chapters and generally written by one or two authors) are constructed in a way that allows the reader to follow an argument throughout all the chapters. Always read the introduction, in the case of a book, or the initial first or second paragraphs of an article. This is where the author lays out the plan for the research that follows. Why is the author's thesis or argument significant? What criteria can you use to judge the significance of that argument? Has the author considered the right questions applicable to the topic?[2] Just like the introduction to your paper, book and article sections highlight the research question and relate the issues that follow to that research question. Subsequent chapters of the book or sections of the article then connect the data/primary source evidence and other scholars' findings. Look at the data presented. As you read, try to connect the evidence back to the question and topics posed in the introduction. Look at the topic sentences of the paragraphs and think about how they relate to the introduction to that chapter. Read the concluding book chapter or article conclusion carefully. These chapters or paragraphs usually draw all of the information presented together and suggest a larger, meaningful significance for the research. If you can be mindful of the author's argument throughout the work, you will absorb the details and be able to discern problems or spot potential differences in the quality of research. Remember to compare your author's findings with other authors' findings, and also look for book reviews and biographical information about the author.

Perspective and Bias: Historians and Interpretation

We believe in a fair society that reports news and research in a factual and objective manner. Yet, varying perspectives and biases are part of life and part of research. When you formulate your research query, you do so with your twenty-first-century sense of curiosity and knowledge. All good historians have a perspective that influences their choice of research topics and the manner in which they plan their investigation and compile their primary sources. Sometimes this perspective can cause quite different analyses to emerge. An example of this phenomenon can be seen in the work of two scholars of Nazi Germany, Christopher Browning and Daniel Goldhagen. Based on a Hamburg police battalion's participation in the killing or deportation of Polish Jews in 1941 and 1942, Browning wrote a book entitled *Ordinary Men: Reserve Police Battalion 101 and the Final Solution in Poland*.[3] Based on the same set of primary sources, Goldhagen wrote a book entitled *Hitler's Willing Executioners: Ordinary Germans and the Holocaust*.[4] Just by looking at the two titles, it becomes evident that the two historians have a very different interpretation of similar evidence. Neither scholar disputes the facts about the atrocities committed. Browning believes the motives of the German soldiers were rooted in allegiance to their country and their fellow soldiers. In a time of war, they would follow their orders. Goldhagen believes that not just the soldiers but most Germans were "eliminationist anti-Semites." While the debate became quite heated and was more complicated than can be discussed here, it is evident that these two scholars framed their research questions differently and that their investigations were influenced by their own perspectives. Goldhagen not only is of Jewish background but also had family members victimized in the Holocaust. Browning came of age in the 1960s during the Vietnam and Watergate eras, when the motives of the US government engaged in war were questioned. Neither book is based on sloppy research, but both authors have perspectives colored by their pasts. You, as a historian and researcher, must realize that research is never just compiling factual information but requires interpretation and that you need to be critical about how others' perspectives shape their interpretations.

Scholarship or Propaganda?

As you conduct your secondary source research, you must carefully evaluate information to distinguish sources that have been created with the *intent* to deceive or to sway opinion. *Propaganda* is defined as "the spreading of ideas, information, or rumor for the purpose of helping or injuring an institution, a cause, or a person."[5] Propaganda uses half-truths or takes facts out of context so that those who read or view it will draw erroneous or over-simplified conclusions. Propaganda is not always evil, although it is often thought to be so; but it must be recognized for what it is. Below is a table that contrasts scholarship and propaganda.[6] Remember that propaganda would be considered a primary source as it reflects attitudes and opinions at a given period of time. Be sure the sources you find for your secondary sources (and the research you produce) fit in the scholarship column.

SCHOLARSHIP	PROPAGANDA
Describes the limits of data	Excessive claims of certainty (we have the way, the view)
Presents accurate description of alternative views	Personal attacks/ridicule
Presents data that do not favor preferred views, as well as data that support these	Emotional appeals
Settles disputes by use of generally accepted criteria for evaluating data	Distortions of data unfavorable to preferred views
Looks for counterexamples	Suppresses contradictory views
Uses language in agreed-upon ways	Suppresses contradictory facts
Updates information	Appeals to popular prejudices
Admits own ignorance	Relies on suggestion (e.g., negative innuendo)
Attempts to discuss general laws/principles	Devalues thought/critical appraisal
Finds own field/area of investigation difficult and full of holes	Transforms words to suit aims
Relies on critical thinking skills	Magnifies or minimizes problems
	Presents information/views out of context

Case Study—Evaluating Sources: Holocaust Historians

As discussed in this chapter, Christopher Browning and Daniel Goldhagen interpreted primary source evidence quite differently in their two books about a German battalion in World War II. The following will help you put into perspective how you as a scholar might evaluate such information:

Shatz, Adam. "Browning's Version: A Mild-Mannered Historian's Quest to Understand the Perpetrators of the Holocaust." *Lingua Franca* 7 (Feb 1997): 48–57.

Shandley, Robert R., ed. *Unwilling Germans?: The Goldhagen Debate*, with essays translated by Jeremiah Riemer. Minneapolis: University of Minnesota Press, 1998.

Using the questions posed in this chapter, ask yourself:

1. How did each scholar's background affect his perspective? How did this background guide the framing of the questions asked of the primary source data and the conclusions drawn?

2. Were the audiences and purposes of each book the same? By reading the *Lingua Franca* article, do you think one of the scholars might have had a more general audience in mind? Was the purpose of each of the books to speak to a different segment of a scholarly audience? Do you think other scholars' perspectives influenced their analyses of this debate and, thus, the reception of these two scholars' research?

3. Did either author include or ignore evidence included by the other? This may be discussed by other scholars in their examinations of the books. It may be useful to browse the original texts and look at the bibliographies and footnotes. You may also want to read book reviews.

NOTES

1. Andrea A. Lunsford and John J. Ruszkiewicz, *Everything's an Argument.* (Boston, MA: Bedford/St. Martins, 2010), 286–287.

2. Ibid., 288–290.

3. Christopher R. Browning, *Ordinary Men: Reserve Police Battalion 101 and the Final Solution in Poland* (New York: HarperCollins, 1992).

4. Daniel Jonah Goldhagen, *Hitler's Willing Executioners: Ordinary Germans and the Holocaust* (New York: Alfred A. Knopf, 1996).

5. "Propaganda," *Merriam-Webster Collegiate Dictionary.* http://www.m-w.com/dictionary/propaganda (accessed September 26, 2011).

6. Sonia Bodi, "Scholarship or Propaganda: How Can Librarians Help Undergraduates Tell the Difference?" *Journal of Academic Librarianship* 21 (January 1995): 21–25. Adapted with permission.

6 The Thrill of Discovery: Primary Sources

WHAT YOU WILL LEARN IN THIS CHAPTER
- how to differentiate many types of primary sources
- how to search for primary sources
- how to locate and use archives
- how to evaluate primary sources

Primary sources, or primary evidence, are the foundation of historical research. Whether it is a collection of personal letters of one of the first African American surgeons, plaster casts of the remains of former residents at Pompeii that captures them in their moment of death, or an archive of vintage radio broadcasts, primary sources are what excite and compel historians to pursue their craft and are the material from which historians formulate questions. Identifying and appropriately using primary sources often present the greatest challenges to novice and skilled researchers alike. To be an effective researcher, you must be able to identify the variety of primary sources and understand the relationship among them. Integration of government documents, photographs, and oral histories, if these are available, can help you to form a more balanced analysis and assessment of a past event or situation.

This chapter first defines and then provides categories of primary sources to help you imagine the types that exist for your research. As each category of primary source is explored, search tips to find primary sources as well as major collections, both in print and online, will be included. Primary sources can be found in manuscript, print, and online forms. Chapter 7 will explore the Internet, which can be quite valuable for primary sources (although it can be used for research in a variety of ways well beyond primary research). In the conclusion of this chapter, a list of criteria to evaluate your primary sources is provided. Just as with secondary sources, you must evaluate the quality and accuracy of your primary sources. Much of the time, you will have to try to think like someone in another century to understand the perspective and intent of individuals who existed in different environments and possessed different knowledge from you. Doing so will allow you to develop search and evaluation strategies to help you find, utilize, integrate, and evaluate primary sources in your research. Chapters 8, 9, and 10 consider other forms of primary sources such as maps, nonprint sources (images, artifacts, art, etc.), and statistics in greater depth.

Definitions

Distinguishing a primary source from a secondary source is essential. Regarding primary sources, historians have two basic rules. First, you cannot make anything up. Second, you cannot ignore inconvenient evidence.[1]

- *Primary sources* are items that are directly associated with their producer or user and the time period in which they were created. Examples include diaries, newspaper articles, government documents, clothing, photographs, oral interviews, and news broadcasts. A primary source reflects the authority and perspective of someone who directly experienced what they are describing.

- *Secondary works* are analyses and interpretations based on primary sources and other sources, which can include other secondary works such as books and journal articles, and tertiary sources, such as encyclopedia articles. A secondary source usually reflects the authority and perspective of a professional historian who did not experience what they are describing but who is trained to analyze primary sources and contextualize them within a bigger picture.

These definitions can become confused, however, when a secondary text becomes a primary source because the analysis it presents is actually an example of the intellectual and cultural thought of the time in which it was written. For instance, Denis Diderot's *Encyclopédie, ou, Dictionnaire raisonné des sciences, des arts et des métiers* was an attempt by the philosophers and intellectuals of the eighteenth century to compile the known information about the world into a set of volumes. In the eighteenth century, Diderot's *Encyclopédie* was useful as a secondary work, a text that compiled and interpreted the world's knowledge. Many scientific advances and changes in cultural attitudes have occurred in the intervening centuries, transforming this encyclopedia from a secondary work of the eighteenth century into a primary source in the twenty-first century. The volumes tell us what eighteenth-century intellectuals knew and how they perceived their world.

Nature and Categories of Primary Sources

When looking for primary sources, it is necessary to think about the variety and types of sources available. There are many ways primary sources can be categorized. Thinking of them in the following categories will help you search for them:

- *Public records.* Governments are and have always been in the business of keeping a myriad of records in order to define their populations, create policies and procedures, and otherwise maintain civil order. Generally, these records were never intended to be published, are unique copies, and were for the internal operation of a government. Census records, court records, certain types of statistics, wills, local administrative records, and tax records are all examples of public records. Sometimes church records may count as public records as the Catholic Church was a governing body during certain eras and in certain regions. See chapter 10 for more about statistics and census records.

- *Official records.* To operate, governments have laws and guidelines, the documentation of which becomes a valuable official record that provides a wealth of information. Often, these records are published and more than one copy exists. These records are intended to make citizens aware of the rules and regulations, as well as the actions of their civil government. Sometimes the differences between public and official records are slight. Examples of official records include laws, civil codes, legislative hearings, and treaties.

- *Personal documents.* Individuals have always generated amazing amounts of documentation that can teach us a great deal about their lives and societies. Diaries, letters, e-mail correspondence, oral histories, financial records, and household accounts are all incredibly rich research sources. With the advent of e-mail, personal correspondence on paper has declined, along with some of these other types of primary sources historians have been used to examining.

Instead, researchers will need to incorporate artifacts and other material to discover the daily lives and thoughts of ordinary people.

- *Artifacts/relics.* Individuals leave behind "stuff," including material possessions and general debris, such as refuse. Analyzing what items humans produced, used, consumed, and discarded provides insight into the lives of the vast majority of humankind, few of whom leave any written or other personal records to be studied. Examples include furniture, paintings, tools, machines, clothing, textiles, firearms, cooking tools, farm implements, music, and art. See chapter 9 for more about art as a primary source.

- *Business and other organizations' documents.* Corporations and other organizations, such as unions, civic clubs, charities, and churches, produce materials that document their activities, as well as the roles and identities of their workers, members, constituents, and clients. Shipping manifests, inventories, financial records, meeting minutes, and production schedules can provide insight into a business, its goods, and its influence, for example, on the local economy, society, and labor pool.

- *Images.* Photographs, posters, paintings, engravings, icons, and videos are valuable records of events but also serve as chronicles of changes in the texture of individuals' lives. Families grow and change. Cities and buildings damaged by war and decay fall apart and are rebuilt. Images provide glimpses not only of dress and decoration but also of values. How was a middle-class home decorated in Victorian England? What did Red Square look like in revolutionary Russia? How did illuminated Bibles reflect medieval culture? How did propaganda films reflect Nazi ideology? Chapter 9 explores visual and audio media as primary sources.

- *Architecture, city plans, and maps.* A city's map, neighborhoods, and mix of architectural styles indicate how individuals rich and poor relate as a society. Maps indicate how traffic flowed and how land was used. Rural land uses, environmental history, and landscape archaeology all tell us how individuals relate to the land and the importance of land in their society. Documents that provide this kind of information include photographs, city plans, blueprints, house drawings and house plans, as well as maps. Actual buildings also provide information about their past. See chapter 8 for more about maps and this chapter for more about architecture.

- *Media and other public communication.* News and its path of communication have certainly changed over time, but its significance as a primary source has not. With the rise of commercial and industrial societies, individuals as well as governments and commercial interests needed to effectively find and disseminate information. What they have left behind is vast amounts of fertile material for study, including newspapers, magazines, learned societies' publications, television news broadcasts, broadsides, and radio broadcasts. See chapter 9 for audio and video resources.

- *Literary texts.* The text of a novel, essay, poem, play, short story, music, or religious work is a primary source. Written in a specific time and place, these works reflect the culture and thought of an era and location, even if the work is critical of the status quo or set in another time. Historians sometimes analyze popular novels and works of music alongside other primary source material in their research. See chapter 9 for more about music.

Planning Your Project with Primary Sources

Now that you have a sense of the variety of primary sources, a bit of planning before you begin your search is wise. You will need to be attentive to what materials are available locally and those that may require interlibrary loan, assistance from an archive at a distance, or even a trip to that archive. You should locate and request these materials or at least correspond with the archivist early in your research, even if it turns out that you will not use those sources. When querying an archive, do not ask for everything on, for example, the Battle of Gettysburg; instead, ask a more specific question, such as, does the archive have information on a specific person from the town or battle? Be prepared for a bit of a wait and for a possible trip. Most repositories and archives do not have the staff or the finances to describe collections in detail, to search through many boxes for specific material at the request of an individual researcher, or to photocopy large amounts of material to send to you. If your project must be finished within a semester or less and you are unable to travel to the archives, you must quickly determine how central certain pieces of primary evidence are to your research. If you cannot access the needed sources in the time you have, you will need to quickly discuss this with your professor or teacher. Acquiring primary materials can take time, and you do not want to be caught short in your effort to obtain and analyze important sources. Missing key evidence weakens your argument.

Locating Primary Sources

Considering these categories and examples of primary sources helps you to imagine the kinds of primary evidence that might exist to support your research question. Sometimes your research question arises from your curiosity about a primary source. You will need to locate additional primary sources that will effectively support your thesis. As you read secondary works and discover primary sources, you will refine your research questions, causing you to search for more supportive evidence in the form of additional primary and secondary sources. As a beginning researcher, you may have difficulty selecting a topic and keeping yourself focused as you begin to discover so many related resources. Asking the following questions will help you think about what kind of evidence to look for and how to link your evidence directly to your research question.

SEARCH TIPS

1. What types of primary materials might have been produced? Remember to think about both printed materials, such as documents, as well as physical representations of culture, such as artwork and architecture.
2. Who would have produced these primary sources?
3. Who would have used and/or critiqued these primary sources?
4. When would these primary sources have been produced?
5. Would these primary sources have been published, unpublished, or represented in another form (e.g., an audiotape of an interview)?
6. What would historians of that period have used to do their research?
7. Why does this source still exist? Why was it important enough for someone to preserve?

Fixing the "authorship" in a specific place and time, as well as identifying the types of resources you hope to find, will help you to figure out where to look for sources. Published sources (magazines, books, etc.) are the easiest to find because they have been cataloged and multiple copies were produced (and likely saved). Locating artifacts, personal documents, and audio and video images is often more challenging as these are one-of-a-kind materials and often uncataloged in libraries and archives.

In searching for primary sources, you must think like the people who lived in the place and time you are studying. This means that you must consider their language, terminology, and way of life. Important differences between British and American English will affect the way you must search in current and historical catalogs and indexes. While Americans refer to "Queen Anne's War," the British call this same military action the "War of the Spanish Succession." Information about African Americans is often indexed under the archaic term "negro," bars are found under "saloons," housekeeping is found under "domestic economy," and "mental hygiene" is used to explore mental illness. Medicine and illnesses always present a challenge. "Hysteria" was a common diagnosis given to women in the past, but it actually refers to a very nonspecific ailment, making it much more difficult to locate primary source documents.

Before you begin your search, take a quick look at a subject encyclopedia, like those discussed in chapter 2, to get an overview of a topic. This will give you a number of terms, definitions, and associations that will make your search for primary sources as effective as possible. Additionally, reading a journal article or two or at least the introduction of a book on your topic will help to refocus your twenty-first-century mind.

Much of the primary source material you find will be in the traditional printed format, either in a published book or in manuscript form. Some manuscripts, however, have been filmed, reproducing many pages on microfiche (a 4 by 6 inch piece of film) or microfilm (a roll of 35 mm film). Some primary source material is also available in digital form via the Internet, but since the digitizing process is time-consuming and expensive, a large portion of this material is still available only in print, microfilm, or microfiche. See chapter 7 for a more complete discussion of how to locate, access, and interpret online primary source materials.

Dividing primary sources into published and unpublished sources will help you develop your search strategy (fig. 6.1). Published sources will be the easiest to locate through your library. These were mass-produced, so, at least at one time, more than one copy existed. You will probably be able to locate a copy to borrow through interlibrary loan or find a microfilmed copy of your printed primary source. Unpublished sources are typically one-of-a-kind items and often held in a single location, such as a museum or archive, although some may have been microfilmed or digitized and made available on the Internet. Documents, diaries, business records, parish records, an individual's papers, and photographs are all examples of unpublished primary sources. Before visiting a museum or archive, you should contact the curator or archivist to find out about the collection. Sometimes copies can

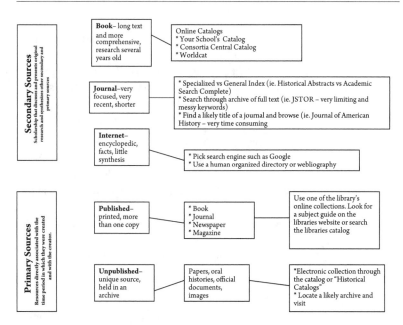

Figure 6.1. Categorizing Primary and Secondary Sources

be made of the items you want. More often, archives receive high volumes of requests, so if you do not know fairly clearly what you are looking for and what collection it might be in, they will be unable to assist you. They will not search through boxes of manuscripts looking for your evidence. Here are some general characteristics of the types of institutions and organizations that hold primary sources:[2]

- *Archives*. Archives hold official documents of official bodies. Federal and state/provincial archives hold materials relating to the activities of the country or other civil unit. For example, the National Archives holds an original copy of the US Declaration of Independence.

- *Local historical societies*. Historical societies hold documents of local interest, individual and family papers, local council minutes, local company records, and church and parish records, if not held by the church. For example, the Wisconsin Historical Society has a number of databases for local history topics (http://www.wisconsinhistory.org/ genealogy/).

- *Museums.* Museums contain artifacts, relics, and sometimes supporting documentation, such as the papers of the archaeologists or perhaps the painters whose works they collect. The Louvre (http://www.louvre.fr/minisite) and the British Museum (http://www.britishmuseum.org/) have sections on their website with samples from their collections. You can also visit in person and see more of their collections, as well as talk with one of their curators about items not publically displayed.

- *Universities.* As institutions of higher learning, universities can have a combination of all of the above and function as all of the above. Special collections may exist at different institutions. For example, the University of Sussex holds some papers of the British novelist and critic Virginia Woolf.

- *Libraries.* Libraries tend to hold published primary source material, such as old books, but can have unpublished materials. Usually, they have a special library within the library or on campus for these materials.

Knowing the nature of an institution helps you determine which ones are likely to hold the types of sources you are looking for. However, lines can blur between these types of institutions, especially in small towns. The local university or public library may be the repository for all of the local history, as well as the current and primary source printed materials. Local historical societies may have archival materials, and archives may have information about the city in which they are located, as well as papers of individuals who have lived in the town. Sometimes an institution may hold the primary source material simply because it has the ability and space to preserve it, even though the institution does not appear a likely source for the item. Contact more than one organization when looking for primary sources for your research.

Digitization and Electronic Access to Primary Sources

The sections that follow in this chapter discuss primary sources in a very traditional way, considering that a significant number of digitized primary sources began in a physical, nondigital format. Online/electronic sources have either been digitized from their original format or born digital, for example, a company's collection of emails or the Library of Congress's *Twitter* archive. Increasingly many of the traditional formats of primary sources, for example, memos are now born digital, never existing in paper form. Over time historians will adapt research strategies and topics to reflect the switch in formats and the availability of primary sources. At the moment paper, digital copy, and born digital data exist, presenting preservation challenges to libraries and archives worldwide.

Access to these digital collections can challenge some of the methods described in the rest of this chapter. Individual items of collection may be discovered in isolation from the rest of the contents of a collection, perhaps through a search engine like *Google*. Much can be learned by looking through a sequence of primary source documents in a folder, or for any source in some sort of context. For instance *Youtube* clips are often taken out of their original context. Traditionally a researcher would have found the item in a collection, in an archive (e.g., a video clip in the context of the whole video), and used that context to evaluate the item. Many of us use keyword searching whether through a search engine, on a website, or in an online catalog. Such searching through the text of a single item can produce, "a field of electronic haystacks," total information overload. Certainly you may find information that you would have had to read for months to find, but also you may spend a long time searching through irrelevant results. For example, if you are searching through a collection of e-mails, sometimes participants in the conversation use reply over and over and the conversation strays from the original subject line. Yet, when you search for a specific word, that irrelevant source will be included in your results. It is impossible to electronically assign a subject on an item by item, page by page basis for these types of primary sources. So, if you are looking for evidence of race class or gender in a collection of papers of a labor union, those words probably would not have been used, after all, the purpose was to support the information the union need to operate, not what researchers might use the collection for later.[3]

Published Sources for Mass Consumption

Of all of the types of primary sources for which you will search, printed and published primary sources are the easiest to locate and to obtain. The invention of moveable type by Johannes Gutenberg in 1455 made the printed word more affordable and thus more easily disseminated. Since Gutenberg's invention, society has not stopped printing information and news for mass consumption. Prior to Gutenberg, book production was laborious as each individual copy was handwritten or block-printed and considered as much a piece of artwork as a container of knowledge. Post-Gutenberg, books were valued more for their content and owned by a larger number of literate individuals. With improved printing and transportation, journals and newspapers became the primary means of public communication for centuries. Newspapers not only provided political news but also fostered debate, announced what goods were entering various cities and ports, and reported births and deaths. Journals allowed scientific societies and specialized audiences to exchange new discoveries and debate ideas. Magazines channeled some of those ideas to the masses, reported fashion and news, serialized novels, published other fiction and poetry, and provided all manner of entertainment and general knowledge to their readers. When looking for published primary sources to use in your research, it is important to remember that each of these types of sources will require different approaches and search strategies.

Books as Primary Sources

The major tool for finding primary source books or monographs is your library's online catalog. Remember, a book is considered a primary source only if the author was involved in a particular event, lived during or close to the time period you are studying, or expressed the intellectual ideas of a particular era. For example, Nicholas Culpeper's book *A Directory for Midwives; or, A Guide for Women . . .*[4] contained sections on the formation of the child in the womb, cures for diseases, miscarriages, and "suckling" directions. This edition, "newly correct from many gross errors," gives us an idea about the depth and limits of the reproductive knowledge of the seventeenth century, but it is clearly outdated for a modern-day obstetrician or a basic sex education class.

Locating published primary source books is quite similar to finding secondary source books. Because you will be looking for older materials, you will want to use broader subject headings and keyword searches in the catalog. The more you work with an online catalog, the easier it will become to use. Despite libraries' and archives' best efforts, many institutions have uncataloged materials. Checking with your librarian or archivist may reveal valuable collections that will not turn up in your library's catalog. The following search tips need not be executed in order, but individual tips can be helpful, depending on the information you know about your topic. You will want to try several of these techniques in more than one library's catalog or *WorldCat* at various points in your research.

SEARCH TIPS

1. *Search by keyword.* Use the keyword search in your library's online catalog. Think as broadly as you can and use Boolean operators to link similar concepts together. For instance, "obstetric*" or "midwi*" (for "midwifes" or "midwives"). Often, online catalogs, as well as databases, have a method to limit or narrow your search by the date of publication. Look for the limit button/method, enter the date or dates that define your time period of interest, and let the computer do the search for you!

2. *Search by corporate author.* Try to figure out the identity of the author of your primary source. *Corporate author* means not an individual but a group of some type, perhaps a government, an organization, or a company. This can be difficult to determine at times. Such official bodies produce documents in the organization's name even if individuals associated with the official body write them. If you are looking for documents by the African National Congress, for example, enter that phrase as an author. Sometimes guessing the official name of an organization is tricky. Most online catalogs will help you, for instance, giving you a referral from "Nazi Party" to the "Nationalsozialistische Deutsche Arbeiter-Partei."

3. *Search by keyword and limit your search by words in the subject headings.* Remember, a keyword search is for the exact word or words in the book title, subject headings, and sometimes the content notes of the catalog record. After you have done a broad keyword search, limit your search by using one of the following terms in the subject headings: "Diaries," "Personal Narratives," "Sources," "Documents," "Statistics," "Antiquities," or "Correspondence." For example, a keyword search with "women and medieval and japan" with a limit of "correspondence" would find *Letters of the Nun Eshinni: Images of Pure Land Buddhism in Medieval Japan.*[5]

4. *Search by very broad subject.* Often, primary source materials are assigned very general subject headings, have titles that might seem strange to twenty-first-century researchers, and will not be readily found by some of the methods described. You can do a broad search, such as "Women–United States," and use the catalog's limiting ability to narrow the search

> to those entries that also have "Periodicals" in the subject. For example, doing a subject search for "Women's Rights" and limiting the search to "Periodicals" could turn up Amelia Bloomer's (a nineteenth-century women's rights and temperance reformer) magazine *The Lily: A Lady's Journal Devoted to Temperance and Literature* (1849–1856).

Your local library will be limited in its primary resources. Even major research libraries will be limited in some areas of their collection. Understandably, no library can collect the breadth of material available. However, you can discover what other libraries hold, as well as a way to borrow those materials. The database *WorldCat*, discussed in chapter 3, is an excellent source for locating published primary source material at other institutions. Remember, *WorldCat* is not comprehensive, even for the libraries included; still, it is an invaluable tool to find published primary sources that will be useful for your research.

Your search techniques for primary sources in *WorldCat* will not differ much from those discussed in chapter 3 on finding books as secondary sources, and you will follow the same patterns described above for your local catalog. One of *WorldCat's* most helpful features is its ability to categorize your search results into types of materials, for example, books, manuscripts, audiovisuals, periodicals, and Internet sites.

Several other means of more comprehensive book indexing exist and can be quite useful. Bibliographic book catalogs, or bibliographies, contain references dating back to the late fifteenth century. Most of these bibliographies use the traditional catalog format of author, title, and subject. They are more generally available in print, although some libraries have access to online versions that allow for additional, more thorough searching. In all cases the online versions have improved upon the print versions, updating and correcting the contents and providing unique full text access. A selection of these follows.

Catalogs and Bibliographies for Books

English Short Title Catalog (ESTC) (1475–1800). http://estc.bl.uk (accessed December 14, 2011). This catalog provides a bibliographic description of works printed in any language in England or its dependencies or printed in English anywhere in the world. The print version is often referred to as "Pollard and Redgrave" or "Wing," but is also known as *Short-Title Catalogue of Books Printed in England, Scotland, & Ireland and of English Books Printed Abroad, 1475–1640.* 2d rev. and enl. ed. A. W. Pollard and G. R. Redgrave, comps. (London: Bibliographical Society, 1976–1991); and *Short-Title Catalogue of Books Printed in England, Scotland, Ireland, Wales, and British, America, and of English Books Printed in Other Countries, 1641–1700.* 2d ed. rev. and enl. Donald Wing, comp. (New York: Index Committee of the Modern Language Association of America, 1972–). The catalog also refers to a set of microfilm that contains the complete text of the book referred to in this index. Many libraries will loan the microfilm.

Early English Books (EEBO) (1475–1700). http://eebo.chadwyck.com/home (accessed December 14, 2011). Covering a smaller time period than the ESTC, the EEBO provides access to the full-text electronic edition of the books listed in its pages.

American Bibliography: A Chronological Dictionary of All Books, Pamphlets and Periodical Publications Printed in the United States of America from the Genesis of Printing in 1639 Down to and Including the Year 1800 (Chicago: Privately Printed for the Author by Blakely Press, 1903–1959). This bibliography (called "Evans") is also available online through subscription as "Early American Imprints." http://www.newsbank.com/readex/ (accessed December 14, 2011).

Bibliotheca Americana: A Dictionary of Books Relating to America, from Its Discovery to the Present Time, 29 vols. (New York: Sabin, 1868–1936) (called Sabin).

Hathi Trust. http://www.hathitrust.org/ (accessed December 14, 2011). Huge, downloadable collection of digitized books by major US (primarily) academic libraries. Some full-text sources are publically available and some will only refer you to the title of a book.

Google Books. http://books.google.com/advanced_book_search (accessed December 14, 2011). Mix of current and historical books. If a book is not in the public domain, you will only see a selection. Coverage is not systematic as with some of the sources above.

Internet Archive. http://www.archive.org/details/texts (accessed December 14, 2011). Aggregates other digital book projects. Books must be in the public domain.

SEARCH TIPS

1. Search for primary source books in your home catalog. (Use the general search tips for books as primary sources.)
2. Search for books in *WorldCat*.

3. Use bibliographies and footnotes of other secondary sources on your subject to find other primary source books.

Magazines and Journals as Primary Sources

Magazines, journals, and newspapers were the primary means by which social, cultural, political, and intellectual information traveled prior to the advent of radio and television. Magazines and journals grew in prominence and frequency in Western society starting in the eighteenth century and acted as a medium for political debate, as well as entertainment. Magazines serialized novels, printed poetry, reported gossip, discussed local news, debated politics, and called upon individuals to rally around political movements. They can also tell you what knowledge was available to common people, for example, what was commonly known about diseases and their causes and treatments, as well as about nations and peoples around the world. Journals contributed to the transfer of scientific and philosophical ideas among researchers. Journals were and indeed continue to be published by learned societies and groups as a means of exchanging knowledge among intellectuals and practitioners. Journals also allow these societies to communicate their beliefs and scientific findings to their members and initiate professional debate. Through journals you can understand, among other things, the development of psychoanalysis, the discovery and evolution of germ theories, and treatments, both valid and invalid, of diseases. Magazines and journals are fruitful sources of primary material and usually easily obtainable.

Two searching techniques can be used for locating magazines and journals. Since older publications often are not indexed or are self-indexed (providing an annual index in the last issue of the year or the first issue of the next year within the publication), you must first know of a magazine's or journal's existence to be able to find its index. You can use a catalog, such as your library's online catalog or *WorldCat*, to look for a journal title by subject. For instance, if your research topic is "abolitionism," you could search under the subject heading "Antislavery Movements" and limit the results by using the subject subheading of "Periodicals" or using material type "Serials." You will likely have to learn about the existence of magazines and journals in this manner and then read them issue by issue for relevant material. Many times, no index to individual articles within the periodical will exist. Then, you must be a smart researcher and know a bit about your topic from your secondary sources. Often, you can pin down a period of activity that relates to your topic in order to limit the number of issues you would need to read.

For more popular magazines and journals that were published during or after the nineteenth century in the United States and Great Britain, good bibliographic and subject indexing does exist. Listed below are the major indexes or collections, which many libraries will have, either in paper or online. Always remember that these indexes were created at the specific time these periodicals were published and, as a result, use the terminology of that time. Some of the online periodical indexes have attempted to rectify this archaic, and sometimes offensive, language with more modern terminology.

Indexes for Magazines and Journals as Primary Sources

This list details the basic sources available in most libraries. A more extensive list of less common indexes appears at the end of this chapter. Many major magazines have their own archives (e.g., *The Economist* (http://www.tlemea. com/economist/home.asp), *Time* (http://www.time.com/time/archive), and *Life* (through *Google Books*)). Check with your library to see if you have access. These are not true "indexes" because they just provide access by keyword in the text of the article and not through assigned subject headings.

Poole's Index to Periodical Literature, rev. ed. William Frederick Poole. Gloucester, MA: P. Smith, 1963 (1802–1907) (commonly called Poole's Index). Also available through online subscription, *19th Century Masterfile*™ *Poole's Index* is a bare-bones index to nineteenth-century periodical literature of the United States and Britain. As both of these countries had empires and colonial holdings, the information, however biased, does cover other world regions. *Poole's* in print can be difficult to read but is worth the perseverance because of its breadth. Reading the instructions at the beginning of volume 1 will help you navigate and decipher this complicated reference work. Some libraries subscribe to the enhanced online version of *Poole's*, which is called *19th Century Masterfile*. The online version is only slightly easier to use than the print version but includes some other smaller indexes to magazines of the same era, which are not included in *Poole's* in print. *19th Century Masterfile* also includes other primary indexes, such as selected years of the *New York Times*, the *Times* (London), some coverage of the *British Parliamentary Papers* and *US Congressional Publications*.

Readers' Guide to Periodical Literature. Minneapolis: H. W. Wilson, 1890– . Online title *Readers' Guide Retrospective* (1890–1982) EBSCO. *Reader's Guide to Periodical Literature* has been a staple for libraries and researchers since before 1900. Indexing both popular and scholarly journals, the print and online versions provide bibliographic citations to the articles. The online version compensates for differences in historical terminology, so searching under "polio" also retrieves articles on "infantile paralysis," the 1930s term.

The Waterloo Directory of English Newspapers and Periodicals, 1800–1900. Waterloo, Ont.: North Waterloo Academic Press, 1997. While a directory, this source would lead to titles that could be browsed for articles.

The Wellesley Index to Victorian Periodicals, 1824–1900; Tables of Contents and Identification of Contributors, with Bibliographies of Their Articles and Stories. [Toronto]: University of Toronto Press, 1966. http://wellesley.chadwyck.com/home.do (accessed December 14, 2011). Major nineteenth-century British periodicals, with listing of table of contents, issue by issue. In print and online by subscription and also part of *British Periodicals* and *19 Century* (also by subscription).

Major Historical Collections of Magazines and Journals

American Periodical Series (APS). UMI/Proquest. Available microfilm. Divided into three periods (1740–1800, 1800–1850, and 1850–1900), the APS is a microfilm and digital collection of over 1,100 magazines (and technically not an index). An online version has selected some of the periodicals and digitized their contents (see http://www.proquest.com/products/pt-product-APSOnline.shtml).

Harpweek. http://app.harpweek.com/ (accessed December 14, 2011). By subscription. Full text of *Harpers Weekly*, an important magazine that reflects nineteenth-century American culture.

British Periodicals (accessed December 14, 2011). By subscription. Nineteenth- and twentieth-century periodicals.

Gallica: La Presse Quotidienne. http://gallica.bnf.fr/html/editorial/presse-revues (accessed December 14, 2011). Primarily nineteenth-century French journals.

SEARCH TIPS

    1. Use one of the general indexes (*Poole's* or *Readers' Guide to Periodical Literature*) to do a subject search through many

journals or magazines. (See a longer bibliography of indexes at the end of the chapter.)

2. Use *WorldCat* or your local catalog to find titles of journals and magazines on your specific topic by doing a keyword or subject search and then limiting your results by using the subject word "Periodicals."

Newspapers as Primary Sources

Newspapers have a different purpose from magazines and journals and provide different types of primary source evidence. They tie communities together, report events, and provide political commentary. They allow individuals within communities to share information, sell products, and announce births, deaths, and other life events. In the past, they often reported the arrival of commercial goods in ports and cities or the activities of the royal courts. Newspapers did not and still do not always report the facts of a particular event, but they are nonetheless an excellent primary source for discovering public opinion and the issues and activities that surround particular events. The two longest published and farthest-reaching newspapers in the world are the *New York Times* and the *Times* (London). However, almost every town throughout the world, whether large or small, has at least one newspaper. You can use one of the directories listed below to locate the title and date of origin of a newspaper for a particular city, town, county, or country. Sometimes a local library or historical society will have an in-house index to the newspapers in the area it serves. At times, those indexes will include other local historical publications (magazines, journals, and other published histories).

SEARCH TIPS

1. Look for your topic in one of the major newspaper indexes listed in the following section.
2. Look for the title of a newspaper in a particular city or country by using one of the directories or bibliographies listed below.
3. Look at the bibliography of your secondary works.
4. Use *WorldCat,* the guide to the US Newspaper Program participants (http://www.neh.gov/us-newspaper-program), or your catalog to look up newspapers by city.

Indexes for Newspapers

New York Times Index. New York: Bowker and New York Times Company, 1851– . As the United States grew as a world economic power with New York City at its center, the *New York Times* reported the significant national and international events that shaped the world. Most libraries will have the print index referenced above. Several companies offer indexes and full-text access. *Paratext (19th Century Masterfile)* and *ProQuest (New York Times Historical)* offer different dates and forms of the *New York Times* either as an index or as full text.

Times Index /Palmer's Index to the Times. Sheperton, UK: Palmer/London: Times Publishing Co., 1785– . The *Times* grew from a small "sheet" designed to "register the times" to the official newspaper of the capital city and its nation's government. The United Kingdom was a major world power from the seventeenth to the mid-twentieth centuries. Consequently, the *Times* reported stories that were of concern to all of its colonies and territories, including the story of a new nation in the New World, now better known as the United States of America. The print index changed titles a number of times and is sometimes also called *Palmer's Index to the Times*, as well as *Official Index to the Times*. *Chadwyck-Healy* and *Paratext* also provide some online indexing and some full-text access to the *Times*.

Proquest Historical Newspapers. Subscription to the online versions of the *New York Times, Wall Street Journal, Boston Globe, Atlanta Constitution, Hartford Courant, Christian Science Monitor, Los Angeles Times, Chicago Tribune,* and *Washington Post.* For details, see http://www.proquest.com/en-US/catalogs/databases/detail/pq-hist-news.shtml (accessed December 14, 2011).

America's Historical Newspapers/ Early American Newspapers. http://www.newsbank.com/readex/?content=96 (accessed December 14, 2011). Subscription required. Many smaller newspapers, 1690–1922.

British Library Online Newspaper Archive. http://www.bl.uk/welcome/newspapers.html (accessed December 14, 2011). Access to nineteenth- and twentieth-century British newspapers, some titles, some full text.

Google News Archive. http://news.google.com/ (accessed December 14, 2011). Now closed, but still useful. Aggregator for many newspapers that have been digitized by Google and other projects. Has many gaps. Do your search and limit by the date at the left.

ICON: International Coalition on Newspapers. http://icon.crl.edu/digitization.htm (accessed December 14, 2011). List of digitization projects, worldwide.

List of Online Newspaper Archives. Wikipedia. http://en.wikipedia.org/wiki/Wikipedia:List_of_online_newspaper_archives (accessed December 14, 2011). Country by country listing. Dates of coverage vary.

Klaus Graf's List of Newspapers. http://www.delicious.com/Klausgraf/digi_zeitungen (accessed December 14, 2011). Especially good for German newspapers.

How to Read a Bibliographic Entry in a Printed Newspaper Index

Reading an entry in a newspaper index can be complicated. While the information varies from index to index, the entry usually contains the date (month and day only, the year is listed on the outside of the volume), the page number and section (a number, a letter, and/or a Roman numeral), and column number (sometimes a number, sometimes a letter, counting over from the left side of the page). Sometimes the entries are listed by the headline; more often the entry is a paraphrased summary of the scope of the article. Usually, the articles are listed under a subject heading in chronological order. Broad subject headings will encompass common types of information, for instance, "Motion Picture Reviews," "Book Reviews," "Shipping News," "Murders," "Deaths," and so on. In most cases, you will not find information listed under a title of the book or movie or the name of the ship. In the case of the *New York Times Index*, a reference is printed only once, so you may be referred to another subject in the same volume. For instance, in figure 6.2 the subject heading "Hindenburg (Airship)" suggests another subject heading, "Aeronautics–Commercial Service–Ocean." While coverage of the story began on May 7 (1937), looking down the list of descriptions of articles, you find major coverage with "witnesses describe fire." This is a summary of a series of articles on May 8, 1937, on pages 2–4 in the front section of the paper, as well as another major article published on May 8 on page 18, located in column 1, listed as "(18:1)."

Bibliographies to Locate Historical Newspaper Titles

These indexes will help you locate the titles of newspapers, the dates they were published, and if and when they ceased publication, changed title, or were absorbed by a competitor.

Historical Newspapers and Indexes on the Internet—USA. http://www.researchguides.net/newspapers.htm (accessed December 31, 2011). Links to digitized collections of local newspapers.

1024 THE NEW YORK TIMES INDEX *Year 1937*

HINDENBURG, Paul von Beneckendorff und von (1847-1934)
Por, Ja 31, IV, 5:1
Book, Hindenburg the Wooden Titan, banned, F 4, 7:2
Por, Ap 4, IV, 2:3
1927 war guilt s assailed by Gen Ludendorff in book, Ag 23, 4:3

HINDENBURG (Airship)
See also Aeronautics—Commercial Service—Ocean
Destroyed by fire and explosions while landing at Lakehurst, N J; 33 reptd killed or missing; notables aboard; Capts Pruss, comdr, and E Lehmann, former comdr, injured; comment; German reaction; illus, My 7, 1:3-8; rept on mail carried; return passenger list; survivors and missing; ship's history; disaster 1st on passenger line, My 7, pp 18-21; U S Commerce Dept and German investigating comms apptd; experts discuss causes of fire; repts of sabotage denied; death list at 33, including Lehmann; F T Birchall on German reaction, My 8, 1:5-8; witnesses describe fire; illus; repts on survivors' condition; list of casualties; comments; ship insured; originally built for helium; films of disaster released; some of mail salvaged; Eckener to aid inquiry; repts threatening lrs, My 8, pp 2-4; ed, My 8, 18:1; disaster occurred on day before 22d anniversary of Lusitania sinking, My 8, 21:3; U S Navy appts investigating bd; death list at 35; Prof O Stern on hydrogen combustion as cause, My 9, 1:6-8; German survivors return by ss, My 9, 4:3;

Figure 6.2. Excerpt from the printed version of the 1937 *New York Times Index* providing references to the Hindenburg airship disaster. ©*1937 by the New York Times Co. Reprinted with permission.*

Historical Newspapers Online (Penn State Guide). http://gethelp.library. upenn.edu/guides/hist/onlinenewspapers.html (accessed December 31, 2011). Links to digitized collections of local newspapers.
Newspaper Indexes: A Location and Subject Guide. 3 vols. Anita Cheed Milner. Metuchen, NJ: Scarecrow Press, 1977–1983. Guide to locations

of indexes, both published and unpublished, of newspapers held in the United States (but not necessarily limited to American newspapers).

United States Newspaper Program: National Union List. Dublin, OH: OCLC, also available http://www.neh.gov/us-newspaper-program (accessed April 27, 2012). Complicated but comprehensive list of newspapers held in United States and its territories. Subject, title, geographic, and audience index. The website provides links to each of the states, some of which may have online indexes or bibliographies to their newspapers.

Center for Research Libraries (CRL) Newspapers. http://www.crl.edu/collections/topics/news (accessed December 14, 2011). Index to the titles of CRL's extensive newspaper collection. Searchable by title, place (city and country), language, years held. You may use the index but will be unable to get the papers from CRL unless you are a member.

Willings Press Guide. London: Willings Service. 1928 Annual. Directory of newspapers in Great Britain and worldwide.

British Newspaper Library Catalogue. http://explore.bl.uk (accessed December 14, 2011). Listing of UK newspapers since 1801. Use the drop down menu on the left to select newspapers.

Newspapers in Microform: Foreign Countries: 1948–1983. Washington, DC: Library of Congress, 1983. Gives worldwide holdings of foreign newspapers available in microfilm or microfiche.

Gale Directory of Publications and Broadcast Media. Detroit: Gale. 1869– . Annual. [title varies] Provides addresses and dates of inception of current newspapers, by city. Many papers have been around a long time, and this directory is mostly useful for those papers that have been continuously published since the nineteenth century.

Sources of News

Chronicling America. http://chroniclingamerica.loc.gov/ (accessed December 31, 2011). Search and view newspaper pages from 1880 to 1922 and find information about American newspapers published between 1690 and the present.

New York Times Historical. ProQuest. By subscription. Full-text image and indexing of the *New York Times*. Databases for other major newspapers also exist (e.g., the *Chicago Tribune*, the *Washington Post*, the *Los Angeles Times*)

Times Digital Archive. Chadwyck Healy. By subscription. Full-text image and indexing of the *Times* (London).

Google News Archive. http://news.google.com/ (accessed December 31, 2011). Searches a number of sources, including historical newspaper archives digitized by Google. No longer being updated and dates of inclusion are erratic for many of the papers.

Americas Historical Newspapers. Full text of more than 1,000 US newspapers published between 1690 and 1922, including titles from all 50 states. By subscription.

Television News Archive (Vanderbilt University). http://tvnews.vanderbilt.edu/ (accessed December 14, 2011). Since 1968, Vanderbilt has been recording network news (ABC, CBS, NBC, some CNN) and making the newscasts available to researchers. Use its "TV News" search to find news programs. Copyright restrictions will not permit you to use these clips on a website. Check to see if your library has a subscription.

LexisNexis Academic: News. http://www.lexisnexis.com (accessed December 14, 2011). Subscription service. In the "News" section, a transcripts database provides transcripts for news outlets such as the major networks, public radio, and television, as well as *Burrelle's Transcript Service* and some foreign news services. Dates of coverage vary by source in the database but are concentrated in the last 30 years.

Benn's Media Directory. Tonbridge, UK: Benn Business Information Services. 1846– . Annual. [title varies] Directory of television and cable stations worldwide. Provides contact information for paper/media outlets.

World News Connection. http://wnc.fedworld.gov/ (accessed December 14, 2011). *World News Connection*, a fee-based service, provides translations of newspaper articles, conference proceedings, television and radio broadcasts, periodicals, and some technical reports from other countries. It is the continuation of the Foreign Broadcast Information Service (FBIS) begun in 1941. The older translations, titled "Daily Report," were issued to US government depository libraries in various forms (print, microfilm).[4] While *World News Connection* is issued today as a depository item in CD-ROM format, access is restricted due to copyright rules. If you think this would be a useful resource, check with your librarian. Readex has a more extensive collection (http://www.readex.com/readex/product.cfm?product=246), but your library must subscribe.

Unpublished Sources and Manuscripts

It might be said that manuscripts and other unpublished sources are the most exciting finds for the historian. Looking at a document in the handwriting of

Box 6.1 How to Use an Archive or Special Collections

If you find you need to visit a library, archive, or special collections in person, use some of the following tips to make your visit productive. Prior to your visit:

1. *Do your research!* Read several secondary source texts and encyclopedia articles. You should be versed enough in the topic to broadly understand the nuances of it and have identified the potential useful sources the archive holds. You may not know exactly what you are looking for, but do not go in and say, "I'm doing a paper on the US Civil War, what do you have?" To go in unprepared may cause both you and the archivist to miss relevant sources. Ignorance of your topic is also disrespectful of the archivist's time and knowledge. The archivist is not your personal research assistant but a conduit to the sources you need. Archives are notoriously understaffed and cannot devote all of their time to you.

2. *Look at the archives website and do a search through WorldCat.* On the archives website look for a section of finding aids, collection descriptions, and an online catalog. Many archives will have finding aids that describe the collection and list the categories and sometimes folders contained in the collection. Be sure that the collection you need to see has not already been digitized. If it has and you want to see the originals, you will need to make a case to the archivist why the digital copies are not sufficient.

3. *Correspond with the archivist.* Give him or her as much detail, succinctly, as you can about your project and what collections interest you. Tell the archivist who you are and what your interest is, for example, "I am a student at Xavier University in Cincinnati in Dr. Alexandra Korros's Cincinnati History class. I am working on a research paper on..." In this example, this lets the archivist know that you are not a company looking for materials, perhaps for commercial use or a genealogist working on family history. The archivist can better plan for your visit. Make sure to ask about reading room hours and other restrictions. Some archives are closed on certain days. Some collections have restrictions for their use or may be in offsite storage, which will take a couple of days for delivery. Inquire about photocopying, some materials may be too fragile, or taking digital pictures, there may be restrictions.

During your visit:

1. *Bring pencils and paper.* Most archives will not permit ink pens because they fear damage to the materials. You will also probably have to leave your personal belongings in a locker outside the reading room. Make sure you have your materials to do your research. Running back and forth wastes time.

2. *Be organized about your research.* You may only be allowed one folder or box at a time. Start with the important materials and work logically through the collection so you know what you have seen and need to look at, perhaps the next day or in the future. You will find your work fascinating and can easily get lost in the collection and run out of time.

3. *Record basic details about the item you find information from.* This includes the collection's name, the folder, the name of the participants (e.g., correspondents) and basic details about the item. Also note if there are any copyright or use restrictions. Most archives do not own the copyright and if you use a facsimile or a copy in your research you will need permission from the copyright holder. (This mainly applies to thesis and dissertations and not to an unpublished research paper for class. Thesis and dissertations are considered publications, just as any other work.) If you are quoting and paraphrasing (not copying a complete chart), you can simply cite your source.

4. *Talk with the archivist about your topic* (but do not monopolize their time). They usually possess in-depth knowledge about the collection you are using, as well as other collections in the archives. They may be able to offer a perspective that you had not thought of.

After your visit:

1. *Send a note or email to the archivist, thanking him or her for their time and assistance.* Not only is this the polite thing to do, but also if you find that you need further information about the collection after you return home, it establishes good relations. Make sure you credit the archive in your footnotes.

someone who lived hundreds of years ago is exciting. Imagine that you were researching Jane Addams, founder of Hull House, the Chicago settlement house established in 1889 as a social agency for immigrant women and children and the working poor. Addams worked tirelessly for daycare, established after-school activities for girls, and taught English classes. Finding a letter in Addams's own handwriting in which she lobbied both the Illinois state government and the federal government for aid for these women and children connects you to her thoughts and to the issues of the day. Diaries, correspondence, household and business account books, surveys, court and parish records, and land books are all unique primary sources that can illuminate historical periods.

There are several ways to begin looking for locations of manuscripts. Always start with what you know. If you are searching for the papers of an individual, look at some of the standard biographical sources listed in chapter 2 on reference materials. Many biographies and biographical dictionaries will list where an individual's papers are held and if those papers have been published. Use what you know about the person's life, look at websites, and correspond with libraries and historical societies in the region in which the person lived to see if those institutions hold any papers relevant to the individual's life. If not, they will probably be able to give you some leads. If you are looking for manuscripts that relate to an event, a similar strategy applies. Look for the papers of famous individuals involved. Correspond with the libraries and archives in the area. In addition, check *WorldCat*. If you are doing a general search for manuscripts on a topic, you may want to try the indexes listed below. One quick note about manuscripts and other primary source material on the Internet: increasingly, archives are putting *portions* of their collections on the Internet for researchers, and although the quality of these sites continues to improve, you must be sure that these sites are legitimate and accurate. Chapters 7 and 9 provide more details.

Well-organized manuscript collections are categorized in folders and boxes with a finding aid to help the library staff and researchers navigate their way through the collection. The term "finding aid" refers to various unpublished indexes that archivists and librarians create to more easily access documents in manuscript collections. Sometimes finding aids are simply a chronological listing of the boxes with a general description of the material contained in them. In other cases, a list might identify every item in the collection, down to the fishing lure enclosed in someone's letter. Unfortunately, there will be many instances when no finding aid exists.

Some archives and repositories have put their finding aids online. Called EADs (encoded archival description finding aids), they describe and list the contents of the archival collection. One very useful example is the Library of Congress's EAD page (http://findingaids.loc.gov/). It is unlikely that your local historical society or archive will have EADs, however. If you are trying to determine whether an archive has material that will be useful in your research, more often than not you will have to write to the archivist with a specific request.

Catalogs, Bibliographies, Directories, and Indexes for Manuscripts

Subject Collections: A Guide to Special Book Collections and Subject Emphases as Reported by University, College, Public, and Special Libraries and Museums in the United States and Canada. 7th ed. New York: Bowker, 1993. Subject, author, and title bibliography of major manuscript collections held in libraries and archives across the United States.

National Union Catalog of Manuscript Collections Collective Catalog of Manuscripts and Related Textual Material Held in Archives in the United States (NUCMC). Washington, DC: Library of Congress, 1959–1993 (in print and through *WorldCat* thereafter). Begun in 1959 as a print index and later placed online, first through an RLG database (1985) and then *WorldCat* (1993), NUCMUC contains a wealth of references to manuscripts throughout any time in history. Prior to 1986, you must use the printed catalog. For a more detailed discussion, see http://www.loc.gov/coll/nucmc/.

Women's History Sources. Andrea Hinding, ed. New York: R. R. Bowker, 1979. Index to women's manuscripts in US repositories.

ArchiveGrid. http://archivegrid.org/ (accessed December 16, 2011). From *WorldCat.* Libraries, museums, and archives contribute collection descriptions.

Archives Finder. http://archives.chadwyck.com/ (accessed December 16, 2011). Requires subscription. Current directory of over 5,480 repositories and over 132,300 collections of primary source material across the United States. Sponsored by Chadwyck-Healy, a large publisher of primary source microfilm and microfiche.

Guide to Federal Records in the National Archives of the United States. Robert B. Matchette, et al., comps. Washington, DC: National Archives and Records Administration, 1995. http://www.archives.gov/research/

guide-fed-records/index.html (accessed April 28, 2012). Discusses what is available in each record group at the archives. Some examples of what the federal archives saves and provides access to are records and documents from the Indian Claims Commission, War Production Board, Civil War Pension, Rural Electrification Service, Forest Service, and other administrative offices of government.

National Archives and Records Administration. http://www.archives.gov/ (accessed December 16, 2011). The National Archives is the major documentary preservation agency of the United States. Included in this site are indexes to their collections, as well as actual digitized collections. Enter the "Research Room" and browse. Use *ARC* (http://www.archives.gov/research/arc/) to do some searching.

The European Library. http://search.theeuropeanlibrary.org/portal/en/index.html (accessed December 16, 2011). Unified catalog of major European national libraries. Includes their digital collections as well.

WorldCat. Online, available through subscription and free. Some differences in access. http://www.worldcat.org/. Many archives and libraries catalog their collections in *WorldCat.*

Historical Manuscripts Commission. http://www.nationalarchives.gov.uk/archon/ (accessed December 16, 2011). Online reference for British manuscripts. It provides access to locations of collections and archives. See also *Archives HUB.*

Archives HUB. http://archiveshub.ac.uk/ (accessed December 16, 2011). Online index that connects UK universities' archives into one catalog.

Other national libraries and archives of note (there are many other sites like these, see the Directories to Archive Repositories section below to find others):

- *National Library of France.* http://www.archivesdefrance.culture.gouv.fr/ (accessed December 16, 2011).

- *Bibliothèque Nationale de France.* http://www.bnf.fr/ (accessed December 16, 2011).

- *Biblioteca Nazionale Centrale "Vittorio Emanuele II."* http://www.bncrm.librari.beniculturali.it/ (accessed December 16, 2011).

- *Russian Federation National Library.* http://www.nlr.ru/eng/ (accessed December 16, 2011).

- *National Library of China.* http://www.nlc.gov.cn/ (accessed December 16, 2011).

Directories to Archive Repositories

When you need to locate a library, archive, or historical society, use one or more of the directories below. In general, the books are more comprehensive than the Internet sites.

Directory of History Departments, Historical Organizations and Historians. Washington, DC: American Historical Association, 1975– . Annual. See also http://bibpurl.oclc.org/web/45 or http://www.historians.org/pubs/directory/index.cfm (accessed December 16, 2011). Directory that includes addresses of historical associations in the United States and Canada. Often includes websites and e-mail addresses.

Europa World of Learning. London: Allen and Unwin, 1947– . Annual. Directory of learned societies worldwide, including archives, libraries, and museums.

European Archive. http://www.europarchive.org/ (accessed December 16, 2011). Fairly comprehensive listing of European archives. Includes links to archive home page. Aimed at historians.

Repositories of Primary Sources. http://www.uiweb.uidaho.edu/special-collections/Other.Repositories.html (accessed December 16, 2011). Worldwide listing of archives and historical societies with primary source material. Organization is geographic.

National Libraries of the World. http://en.wikipedia.org/wiki/List_of_national_libraries (accessed December 16, 2011). Country listing of national libraries, which are often the holders of the major manuscripts, government documents, and other unpublished documents from that country. Includes web addresses.

British Archives: A Guide to Archive Resources in the United Kingdom. 4th ed. New York: Palgrave, 2002. Listing by city of archives and special libraries and their holdings.

SEARCH TIPS

1. Look at the bibliography in an entry in a biographical encyclopedia to find the location of an individual's papers.
2. Locate a library or archive in the place where your person lived or an event occurred and correspond with that library. Use one of the directories above to find the contact information.
3. Search *WorldCat* and your local library's catalog. Some manuscripts may have been put into microformat and may be available outside of the archive.

4. Check the Internet. (See chapter 7 for specific search techniques.)

___

Documents from Governments and Other Official Bodies

Finding official publications of governments and other governing bodies can be challenging. Every government operates differently, has changed its operation over time, and has preserved different records depending upon its administrative needs. As mentioned throughout this chapter, having a general understanding of the secondary literature is always useful before searching for the primary sources. Find an encyclopedia article that will explain the structure of the government for the time period that interests you. Know the name of the governmental agency or ministry and in which department it resided or how it fits in the government's structure. Begin by doing a keyword search in your library's catalog and in *WorldCat*, understanding that some libraries do not put government documents in their online catalogs. Check with your librarian to be sure. Once you have determined your department's or agency's official name, search for that name as an author. The United States has many avenues to search for government documents. Several indexes are listed below. For a substantial listing of indexes and sources, use the Sears and Moody book in the Directories/Bibliographies section below.

Finding documents from governments of other nations can be especially tricky if you have a limited knowledge of those nations. Nations with long democratic and parliamentary traditions, such as the United States and many of the European nations, have huge numbers of records, documenting government procedures, laws, and the like. Many developing nations that have had monarchies, dictatorships, and forms of government not open to their citizens have kept fewer documents and have made (and continue to make) fewer government documents available. Many of these nations might have been colonies before independence, so governmental records would be included not only in that colonial power's government documents but also in its language and from its viewpoint. An example is Great Britain's Foreign Office, which administered many of its colonies and thus kept records on such places as India and Canada. Sometimes, oppressive regimes have sealed or hidden records. Finding reliable and accurate Soviet government documentation of Stalin's purges in the Soviet Union, during which more than 20 million people perished, has proven challenging. Only in 1998 did President Boris Yeltsin order secret state documents concerning Stalin declassified. Much material from the Soviet regime remains difficult, if not impossible, to access, even for experienced scholars.

Other government documents are those records produced by quasi-governmental organizations. The United Nations is the prime example of such an organization, as are the European Union and the World Bank. They all have or had a representational organizational structure that creates legislation that is theoretically binding to its members. In addition, there are reports, studies, and statistical publications created and issued for a general public to read. These sources are especially useful for topics in the post-1945 era and as a means of discerning a wider world viewpoint. The same search techniques apply for these organizations as for government documents.

The process of using your online catalog and *WorldCat* is much the same as looking for information in the United States. For public records at the national level, searching can also be difficult. Again, if you know what you are looking for, your library's catalog and *WorldCat* are good starting points. Search by the government or the office of the government as an author, for example, "United States. Congress. House," "Great Britain. Parliament. House of Lords," "League of Nations," or "France. Parlement." If you are not exactly sure of the records you are looking for, you might browse through the guides to public records listed below. Major collections have been issued in large multivolume sets or in microformat. You can determine their availability by looking in *WorldCat*, although in this complicated area, asking a librarian for assistance would be a good idea. Also, the Guide to Official Publications of Foreign Governments (listed below), while intended for contemporary use, will assist in identifying when governments began producing selected publications, such as journals of assembly proceedings and statistical publications.

Indexes and Bibliographies of Government Documents

Many governments and agencies have begun to put historic documents online, full text. Some documents also appear in *Hathi Trust* and *Google Books*. Note that this is a very abridged selection of indexes to US government publications. There are too many to list here.

Monthly Catalog of United States Government Publications. Washington, DC: GPO, 1895– . Provides bibliographic citations to government documents produced by US government agencies (i.e., not Congress, the president, or the judiciary).

CIS U.S. Serial Set Index, 1817–1969. Washington, DC: Congressional Information Service, dates vary. The Serial Set includes selected House and Senate reports and documents, including documents submitted by government agencies to Congress. Indexes are divided into parts, by years. Parts of this index and or the material included in the serial set may be included in other indexes available at your library. Consult your librarian. Also available online by subscription.

British Parliamentary Papers. http://parlipapers.chadwyck.co.uk/marketing/index.jsp (accessed April 17, 2012). Project to make available copies of papers from the eighteenth century (1688–1800) and available free to the UK higher education academic community. Still in progress. See also a selection from Hansard (http://hansard.millbanksystems.com/) and for other efforts, see the directory: http://www.parliament.uk/business/publications/parliamentary-archives/archives-electronic/ (accessed April 27, 2012). There are fee-based products as well.

Great Britain, Parliament, House of Commons. *Journals of the House of Commons.* London: Various Printers, 1503– .

Great Britain, Parliament, House of Lords. *Journals of the House of Lords.* London: Various Printers, 1503– . Journals are the official record of the proceedings of the two legislative bodies of Great Britain. There are numerous indexes to these that have been commercially published, as well as annual indexes to each session. Check with your library to see in what format they own these and who is the publisher.

Great Britain, Parliament. *British Sessional Papers.* London: Various Printers. Bills, reports, and papers presented to Parliament. Check with your library to see in what format they own these and who is the publisher.

LexisNexis Congressional. http://web.lexisnexis.com/congcomp (accessed December 16, 2011). Subscription database, *LexisNexis* includes congressional hearings, public laws, and other congressional publications, dating back to 1789. Includes the US Serial Set.

United Nations. http://www.un.org; *United Nations System of Organizations*, http://www.unsystem.org/ (accessed December 16, 2011). The first site is the official website of the United Nations and has records of the general assembly and some of its commissions. The second site provides an alphabetical list with links to websites of UN agencies that are often hard to find. In both cases, the documents associated with the sites are relatively recent, late twentieth century to the present.

Directories/Bibliographies for Governments/Guides to Government Publications

Using Government Information Sources: Electronic and Print. 3d ed. Jean L. Sears and Marilyn K. Moody. Phoenix: Oryx Press, 2001. Heavily oriented to publications in the United States but also includes a chapter on foreign countries. Discusses current and historical publications. Offers concrete search strategies. Many of the sources listed in this book are now online.

Guide to Official Publications of Foreign Governments. 2d ed. Bethesda, MD: CIS/American Library Association, 1997. Under each country is listed the types of government publications they produce, statistical yearbooks, court decisions, annual budgets, and census materials, for example.

Genealogy and Public Records

Genealogy, the search for family history, has often been dismissed as a legitimate method of historical inquiry by practicing professional historians. Recently historians have incorporated genealogical research techniques in their research. In *Communities of Kinship: Antebellum Families and the Settlement of the Cotton Frontier,* Carolyn Earle Billingsley argues that just as historians consider race, gender, and class in their research, they should also include kinship to understand the structure and function of communities. Using genealogical methodologies, she traces a southern family's migration and settlement patterns, marriages, land purchases, finances, religious affiliations, and political alliances to build a picture of US southern society and culture. Billingsley discovered relationships between the westward migratory patterns of southerners, the family structures that supplied financial capital, political stability, and the rich society of the antebellum South.[6]

The materials of genealogical research are most often public and vital records. The best place to begin is to use the census, if it covers the time period in which you are interested. (See chapter 10 for more about censuses.) Most censuses have two parts, the population schedules and statistical reports. The population schedules gather raw data on an individual level. An enumerator goes house to house recording, on a specific day, names and details about the residents and their neighbors. Organized roughly by street address, these census rolls allow you to build a picture of a neighborhood. The information collected on each individual varies by census year, country, and the ability of the enumerator to both follow instructions and to locate individuals. Statistical reports provide the total numbers of the characteristics of the population, for example, women and men, or unemployed.

Other vital records of use include birth, death, marriage, wills (probate), taxation, land transfer, cemetery burials, obituaries (in newspapers), and military service records. Most of these records are kept by the local or federal government and churches and vary in availability by locality and throughout time. Written records were created and maintained when governments and/or state churches (for example, the Roman Catholic Church or the Church of England) felt the need to count individuals, to record property, to tax, and to adjudicate disputes between its inhabitants or when businesses needed to keep track of their transactions. It can be challenging to figure out what the names or titles of the branches of government that administer these records are called in different countries. For example, the Exchequer, the treasury, is the main governmental office in Great Britain that collected taxes.

Locating these records can be difficult. Many are unique, single copies. However, databases like Ancestry.com (http://www.ancestry.com/) and Family Search (https://www.familysearch.org/) have tried to collect, digitize, or film these local records. Ancestry requires a subscription, either by your library or by individuals. Before you begin to look for public records, it will serve you well to look thoroughly at the primary sources listed in your secondary works' notes. This will give you a clue as to the terminology and the types of sources for which you will be looking. Follow up on those footnotes in your library and by looking in *WorldCat* to see if some of these primary sources may be available in microformat or in some other format besides the original document in the archive.

SEARCH TIPS

1. Search your catalog, *WorldCat*, or other online catalogs using the name of the office or the department of government as an author.
2. Use the footnotes in your secondary sources to lead you to government departments or agencies.
3. Use one of the guides below to locate the records that exist for your country of interest.

Guides for Genealogy and Public Records

The WPA Historical Records Survey. A Guide to the Unpublished Inventories, Indexes, and Transcripts. Loretta A. Hefner, comp. Chicago: Society of American Archivists, 1980. From 1935 to 1942, the Works Project Administration (WPA) took a state-by-state inventory of all available public records. This guide updates those records' locations and other supplemental inventory projects since the ending of the WPA's survey.

Vitalrecords.com. http://www.vitalrec.com/links1.html (accessed December 12, 2011). Aimed at genealogists, this source provides links to many state and local pages, which include directions for requesting information, as well as summaries of holdings of each state or locality.

Cyndi's List. http://www.cyndislist.com/ (accessed December 12, 2011). Comprehensive, worldwide list of genealogical sources in print and online. Will provide links to other countries' resources, including locations of local records.

Basics of Genealogy Reference: A Librarian's Guide. Jack Simpson. Westport, CT: Libraries Unlimited, 2008. Good starting place.

Sources and Methods for Family and Community Historians: A Handbook. Michael Drake, Ruth Finnegan, and Jacqueline Eustace. Cambridge: Cambridge University Press in association with the Open University, 1997. British focus. Good for working through the types of sources that are unique to Britain.

Geography and Genealogy: Locating Personal Pasts. Dallen J. Timothy and Jeanne Kay Guelke. Aldershot, England: Ashgate, 2008. Good at contextualizing types of sources for research.

Your Guide to the Federal Census for Genealogists, Researchers, and Family Historians. Kathleen W. Hinckley. Cincinnati, OH: Betterway Books, 2002. Basic guide to using the US census.

Genealogy, Geography, and Maps: Using Atlases and Gazetteers to Find Your Family. Althea Douglas. Toronto: Ontario Genealogical Society, 2006.

Forensic Genealogy. Colleen Fitzpatrick. Fountain Valley, CA: Rice Book Press, 2005. Incorporates database searching with evaluation of sources (i.e., how to date a photograph).

Maps and Plans for the Local Historian. David Smith. London: B. T. Batsford, Ltd., 1998. Explains types of maps and how to extract and use information from them.

Maps for Historians. Paul Hindle. Chichester, West Sussex, England: Bookcraft Ltd., 1998. Explains types of maps and how to extract and use information from them.

Business Records

All corporations keep records. What is publicly available beyond what is mandated by law is at the discretion of the corporation. Contemporary business archives are a relatively new development in archival preservation and are maintained primarily for the use of the corporation. If a company is still in existence, you will need to make direct contact to inquire about the availability of its records. Be explicit about what you want and how you will use the information. Companies are often more forthcoming with information when they understand that your request is for a student paper and not for a competitor's marketing report or an exposé of the company. If the company is no longer in existence, you will need to check with the local historical society or public library to see if the records are in their collections. Sometimes, however, company records do not exist. In this case, look for supporting documentation such as labor union publications, newspaper articles, and advertisements to fill some of the gaps.

SEARCH TIPS

1. Use one of the directories below to determine if the corporation is still in existence and has a library.
2. Search in *WorldCat* for the corporation as an author.
3. Contact the local historical society or public library.
4. Look for supporting primary source information such as labor union materials and newspaper and magazine articles.

Directories and Resources

The directories below do not specifically list individual collections within business archives. However, they will lead you to the depositories and libraries of corporations that hold those records. You will have to contact the organizations, libraries, or corporations directly with your research query.

Directory of Corporate Archives in the United States and Canada. Society of American Archivists http://www.archivists.org/saagroups/bas/directory/corporat.asp (accessed December 13, 2011). Contains description of the collections, gives contact information, and indicates if the archive is open to the public.

American Library Directory. New York: R. R. Bowker. 1912– . Annual. [title varies] Directory that provides contact information by state and county for libraries of all types including public, academic, and corporate.

World Guide to Special Libraries. 7th ed. Willemina van der Meer and Helmut Opitz, eds. Munich: K. G. Sauer, 2007. Directory to locate libraries that would have archival or corporate materials in countries other than the United States.

Directory of History Departments, Historical Organizations and Historians. Washington, DC: American Historical Association, 1975– . Annual. See also http://www.historians.org/pubs/directory2 (accessed December 13, 2011). Searchable directory that includes addresses of historical associations in the United States and Canada. Often includes websites and e-mail addresses. Defunct companies' archives may be deposited at a local historical society.

Proquest Historical Annual Reports. Fee based. http://www.proquest.com/en-US/catalogs/databases/detail/pq_hist_annual_repts.shtml (accessed December 13, 2011). Corporate annual reports since 1884.

Oral History

Oral history is a somewhat recent addition to the historian's repertoire of primary sources. Hearing the voices or reading the words of individuals who experienced the common and uncommon events of history enlivens the historical narrative. For example, the words of Japanese Americans who lived in internment camps provide a fuller picture of the American home front during World War II. Oral histories can be found both as audio files (various methods of audio recording such as cassette tapes, reel-to-reel tapes, or streaming audio on the Internet) and as transcripts (typed testimony of the interviewee). Remember that you can gather and create your own primary source material by collecting your own oral histories. Countless books offer instruction on the technique. Your professor can offer assistance on the technique of collecting oral testimony as well. Two guides that are useful are Valerie Raleigh Yow, *Recording Oral History: A Guide for the Humanities and Social Sciences*, and Donald A. Ritchie, *Doing Oral History: A Practical Guide.*[7] When using oral history, be aware of the problems of fallible memory and the inadvertent influence that the interviewer may have on the interviewee.

Indexing of oral testimonies has been spotty at best until the advent of the Internet and streaming audio, which allows sounds to be broadcast to your desktop. In the past, large oral history projects, such as the Works Project Administration's (WPA) 1930s interviews with former American slaves, have been the most accessible to researchers, mainly through printed transcripts. Now, however, a much wider range of oral history material is available. Begin by using your online catalog and *WorldCat*. Do a very broad keyword search. For instance, if your topic is the "WPA slave narratives," described above, begin by doing a keyword search with the words "slaves" or "slavery" (or as you learned earlier in this book, truncate the word and search under "slave*"). Then limit (remember, all databases have the ability to narrow a search by adding extra criteria) by using the subject words "personal narratives." Another strategy would be to do a search using both the phrase "oral history" and the name of your topic in its broadest terms. For example, you can do a keyword search for "african american" (with truncation) and "oral history."

Many local historical societies and special interest groups collect oral histories of their members, and the Internet has become a useful resource for making these local oral history projects available. Doing an Internet search using the name of your topic and the phrase "oral history" can be fruitful. Carefully check the legitimacy of a web-based source. Look for the producer and that individual's purpose. For more on evaluating Internet sites, see chapter 7.

SEARCH TIPS

1. Use the words "personal narratives" or "oral history" when searching in your catalog or in *WorldCat*.
2. Use the guides in the following section to locate large oral history repositories and printed resources.
3. Search the Internet (see chapter 7 on Internet searching).

Guides to Oral History Repositories

Oral History Collections and Centers Online. http://www.h-net.org/~oralhist/centers.html (accessed December 13, 2011). Maintained by *H-Net*. Some of the centers may have transcripts or streaming audio recordings of oral histories online.

Oral History Association's List of Centers and Collections. http://www.oral-history.org/wiki/index.php/Main_Page (accessed December 13, 2011). List with links to centers. Some of the centers may have transcripts or streaming audio recordings of oral histories online.

Australia's Oral Histories. http://www.nla.gov.au/ohdir/about.html (accessed December 13, 2011). Large, searchable database of Australian oral histories.

Directory of Oral History Collections. Allen Smith. Phoenix. Oryx Press, 1988. General listing by library of collections probably still on cassette tape. Because of the date of the publication, contact the libraries to verify the existence of the materials and their condition before visiting.

The Oral History Collection of Columbia University. Elizabeth B. Mason and Louis M. Starr, eds. New York: Oral History Research Office, 1979. http://library.columbia.edu/indiv/ccoh.html (accessed December 13, 2011). Columbia is one of the pioneers in oral history and has amassed a large collection of interviews of famous or significant individuals. Some of the transcripts of written interviews are available on microform. Columbia also provides a set of links to other online oral history programs.

UCLA Oral History Program. http://oralhistory.library.ucla.edu/ (accessed December 13, 2011). Large collection of oral histories. Similar in scope to Columbia above but a more recent program.

Oral History Index: An International Directory of Oral History Interviews. Westport, CT: Meckler, 1990. Index to holdings worldwide. Again, because of the date, you would need to contact the libraries before a visit.

Oral History Collections. Alan M. Meckler and Ruth McMullin, eds. New York: Bowker, 1975. Name and subject index to US and foreign oral history centers. Because of the date, check with the archive to see if the collection and the archive still exist.

Material Culture: Buildings, Artifacts, and Objects

While textual primary sources are probably the easiest to find and more commonly used by researchers, nontextual sources, objects, artifacts, or buildings (architecture) provide a unique window on the lives of common people, who often left no written record. Objects or artifacts tell stories about the past. Sometimes they are passed down in families with a story about some ancestor's use, creation, or discovery of the artifact. Laurel Ulrich in *The Age of Homespun: Objects and Stories in the Creation of an American Myth* discusses an Indian basket given to a white woman living in a Colonial Rhode Island fort. The basket, a homemade gift from a grateful Indian mother represents an idealized view of white/Native American relations. The details of the story and its participants cannot be completely confirmed as factual (while parts can be proved inaccurate or improbable), but through the object we have a sense of colonial American life.[8] The object acts as a conduit of information. Consumption and consumer patterns, the hallmarks of material culture, tell us about the social status, values, and aspirations of common people.[9]

Historical studies using artifacts can be either "object centered" or "object driven". Object centered focuses on the details of the object and responses to the object, whereas object driven connects the object to the everyday lives of people.[10] Giorgio Riello, in "Things That Shape History" suggests thinking about how you might use artifacts, objects, and buildings in your research in the following ways.[11]

- *History from Things.* Use the object as one piece of evidence, such as a butter mold, to interpret the past. Look at the object's use, if you know, and why it was discarded or how it might have been recycled.

- *History of Things.* Use the object, along with other objects to explain the relationship of people and society to that object.

- *History and Things.* Remove the object from its contexts and study it as an object. Museums often do this when they display an object, for example, a pewter teapot, separate from the setting in which it would have been used. The object is discussed in terms of it being an unusual, common, average, etc. example of teapots.

Searching for objects, artifacts, and buildings may be in some cases easier than most primary sources. Often you or someone in your family possesses the object or lives in the house. You can also go to a museum, art exhibit, or just walk down a neighborhood or city street and look at the buildings. Buildings and architecture reveal the everyday lives of their inhabitants. When using a physical building, look at the outside setting. What is the relationship of the structure to the neighborhood and to the other structures around it? What was the building used for? Is it still serving that function today? How has technology changed the use of the building, as well as its structure? Internally how does the space reflect the lives of the inhabitants? Look at the layout and the ornamentation. Once you have "read" the building, look for other sources to help you evaluate its significance. Look for public records and information about the people who lived or worked in the building. If you need to work from printed materials (books, photographs, etc.) instead of witnessing the actual structure, try some of the strategies below.

SEARCH TIPS

1. In a keyword search, in your library's catalog, be as specific as you can, craftsmen houses, Rookwood pottery, and so on. Look for the words il. or illus. in the description of the item.

2. Use one of these general subject headings: *"Architecture, Domestic"*; *"Architecture, American, sometimes Architecture, United States"*; *"Clothing and Dress"*; *"Interior Decoration"*; *"Costume"*; *"Teapots"* (or the object you want to look at).

History before 1400: Ancient and Medieval Cultures and Those with Substantial Oral and Material Culture Traditions

Many factors make finding accessible primary resources prior to the fifteenth century challenging. The documentation of some cultures' histories relies more heavily on material culture, such as pottery, or oral stories that have been passed down through generations of storytellers. The ancient and medieval European worlds used terms like "rolls," "royal skins," "day-books," "formularies," and "charters," which are more reflective of their physical form and function (skins were written on skins, rolls are lists) than indicative of content. So, as a researcher in these eras and cultures, you must know something about the type of primary source and its form.

The availability of written sources prior to the twelfth century varies according to place and culture. Much of what has been handed down to present-day scholars exists as copies of originals. If the original still does exist, few researchers are ever allowed to view it. Copies are seldom exactly true to the original document and could have been altered inadvertently because of copying or dictating errors or purposely by scribes who objected to their content. Undoubtedly, you will be working with facsimiles and reprints. Even modern printers make mistakes, and authoritative editions make textual changes to account for language and translation conflicts. In addition, these sources are often translated from their original language, usually Latin, Greek, Hebrew, or older versions of English, French, or other vernacular languages. Translation is a skill practiced by a scholar who knows the language and understands the culture of the speakers and writers of the language. Part of translation is also conveying the meaning of the words, as well as the literal equivalent of the text. It is important to use a reliable edition of the text for your research.

What has survived to be studied also depends upon the medium on which it was recorded. At certain times, paper did not exist or was expensive, so documents were written on clay, papyrus, leather, and other less durable materials. Some cultures' records survived because climatic conditions were conducive to their preservation. For instance, sand and a dry Middle Eastern climate preserved many Egyptian papyrus records. In other cases, cultures purposely destroyed records and documents during war and conquest. During and immediately after the French Revolution, many medieval French documents were destroyed because of their association with the monarchy. Sometimes information is preserved by accident, such as when clay potsherds used as "scrap" were thrown into a fire and accidentally fired and hardened.

The sheer increase in quantity of production and survival of documents, as well as artifacts, speaks to the prosperity and literacy of a population. Certainly, if more documents are produced and survive, there must have been more people to read and save them at some point. A shift from oral memory to documentary evidence indicates that documents and literacy became more common.[12]

For various reasons, some cultures have stronger oral traditions than written ones. This does not mean that these societies were not literate but that they functioned governmentally and socially more efficiently with a spoken record of their past and of their laws than with a written record. Just as classical cultures had the *Iliad* and medieval cultures had traveling bards, African cultures have griots who pass local history and folklore down through the generations. Linguistically, you can follow cultural influences to see how words and phrases have evolved.

Material culture, the buildings, tools, and artifacts left behind by humans, can be especially useful in learning about cultures that leave scant written records. Archaeologists dig up former sites where people lived and try to re-create past communities and the lives of those who lived in them. For instance, historians use archaeological reports of Mayan and Incan ruins to understand the customs and the social and political structures of these ancient societies often by excavating refuse pits, graves, and sites of towns and cities. Environmentally, you can study how crops, plants, and animals migrate and spread and how trade and conquest by other nations bring new foods and diseases into a culture.

As students of ancient and medieval cultures, you must rely on a multitude of types of primary sources and, in many cases, become a "jack of all trades" when it comes to analysis and interpretation.

Ancient History

When looking for primary resources for ancient civilizations, thinking about the types of information that a civilization would produce will be helpful. For instance, ancient Egypt, Greece, Rome, and many of the civilizations of the Near East were highly bureaucratic and recorded laws, day-to-day governmental activities (in the forms "royal skins" of Persian kings or daybooks of Roman officials), finances of the operation of the kingdom, finances of the income and personal property of the ruler (land surveys, deeds, and tax records), and private business contracts.[13] While these types of primary source records are not that different from those discussed throughout this chapter, locating such records, many of which no longer exist in their original form, presents a special research challenge.

Thinking of your ancient history sources in the following groups will help you search for the appropriate source for your project.[14] Literary works, such as histories, epic poems, plays, speeches, and some private letters of individuals, have survived by various means but, again, rarely in their original manuscript form. You will be working with authoritative translations by eminent scholars of important ancient texts by Homer, Herodotus, and Thucydides, for example, and such texts as the Christian Bible or the Torah.

Unique to ancient history, especially studies of Greece and Rome, is *epigraphy*, words inscribed on stone or metal. These inscribed objects could be displayed publicly, heralding the outcome of a great battle or the memory of an individual; hidden in a tomb for only its occupant to see; or placed on coins. Not meant to be preserved, clay tablets and potsherds were used as early "scribbling pads" and accidentally heated in the fire and preserved. Ancient Greece and Rome even had graffiti. Epigraphs are found in a multiplicity of languages throughout the Mediterranean, even as far east as Romania and as far south as the Persian Gulf.[15] *Numismatics*, or the study of coins, is also important to ancient Greek and Roman historians. Looking at the circulation of coins provides clues to commerce and how people traveled. Debasement of the metal indicates the political health of the empire. Themes and inscriptions (names and images) on the coins can be interpreted alongside other primary sources. Another specialized area of study for ancient historians is *papyrology*, the study of ancient documents written on papyrus. However, papyrology by its nature is restrictive because only certain cultures in Middle and Upper Egypt and parts of the Near East had the climate to preserve the material. These documents can be both public and private accounting records, as well as letters. Archaeological evidence is also another key component to primary evidence in ancient societies, especially Greece and Rome. Studying the artifacts that individuals left behind tells us about their lives. Archaeological reports discuss the size and location of towns, as well as the decoration of clay pots, wall murals and mosaics, structures of houses, garbage heaps, and layouts of cities.

SEARCH TIPS

1. Think about the types of sources that might be useful for you to study, look up that term as a subject in your library's online catalog (e.g., "Numismatics" or "Inscriptions"), and then look at the subdivisions by country or region. You can also look by subject, "Coins, Roman" or "Inscriptions, Latin" (or whatever language you are looking for).
2. In your library's online catalog, search for the culture or country as a subject and limit by words in subject "Sources" or "Antiquities." For example, "Roman Law" as a subject and then limit by words in subject "Sources." Remember, there may be intervening words between these two subject words, for instance, "Roman Law–History–Sources."
3. Another subject term to use is "Excavations, Archaeology" and limit to the country or region by words in the subject.

Selected Ancient History Primary Sources

Ancient History Sourcebook. http://www.fordham.edu/halsall/ancient/asbook.html (accessed December 13, 2011).

Loeb Classical Library. Translated texts of classical authors. See the publisher's website for the complete list of titles. http://www.hup.harvard.edu/collection.php?cpk=1031 (accessed April 27, 2012).Your library will probably have most of these. If not, you should be able to order them through interlibrary loan.

Individual authors (e.g., Herodotus, Livy).

Orientis Graeci Inscriptiones Selectae: Supplementum Sylloges Inscriptionum graecarum. Wilhelmus Dittenberger, ed. Hildesheim: G. Olms, 1960.

Inscriptiones Graecae ad res Romanas Pertinentes. R. Cagnat, ed. Paris: E. Leroux, 1906–1927.

Inscriptiones Latinae Selectae. Hermannus Dessau, ed. Berolini: Apud Weidmannos, 1954–1955.

Corpus Inscriptionum Latinarum. Berolini: Apud G. Reimerum, 1869–1963.

Bibliotheca Scriptorum Graecorum et Romanorum Teubneriana. Leipzig: Teubneri, 1866– .

Perseus Digital Library. http://www.perseus.tufts.edu/ (accessed December 13, 2011).

Motif—Index of Folk Literature: A Classification of Narrative Elements in Folktales, Ballads, Myths, Fables, Mediaeval Romances, Exempla, Fabliaux, Jest-books, and Local Legends. Rev. and enl. ed. Stith Thompson. Bloomington: Indiana University Press, 1955–58. Also available online by subscription.

For more suggestions, see *Sources for Ancient History.* Michael Crawford, ed. Cambridge: Cambridge University Press, 1983.

Medieval European History

Medieval history has its own language and specialties, which makes the search for primary sources different compared to some of the other topics described in this chapter. The greatest number and variety of sources are available from the twelfth century forward. Prior to that, there are significant numbers of sources available, but coverage is geographically and chronologically scattered.[16] Historian R. C. van Caenegem divides medieval sources into two types, narrative and nonnarrative. Narrative sources include annals, chronicles, histories, tracts, letters, biographies, and genealogies. Because medieval European society saw God associated with all aspects of life, common sources of history are ecclesiastical histories that attempted to explain how the Christian God affected historical events. Chronicles, ecclesiastical in origin, compiled facts and commemorated events. Annals were yearbooks of happenings. Genealogies, often part of chronicles, trace the histories of papacies, bishoprics, abbeys, kingdoms, princedoms, and their leaders. Biographical works chronicle the lives of saints and secular leaders. Letters were a form of public conversation, used as teaching tools or pieces of propaganda. Examples of nonnarrative sources are charters, laws and legislation, writs and mandates, chancery registers and rolls, formularies, land surveys, rolls of persons, and account books, all materials that documented property or regulated behavior. Charters are deeds or proof of ownership of land or goods. Court records are both from secular cities and ecclesiastical courts. Writs and mandates are documents that the rulers, local authorities or papal authorities used to inform the public of regulations, orders, or facts. Chancery registers or rolls list (sometimes abstract or include the complete text of) charters or documents that were dispatched abroad. Sometimes these documents were grouped by concern or subject. Formularies were frequently used form letters and documents. Surveys of local lands, as well as of counties and crown holdings, were put into registers so that local lords, municipalities, and the king knew what was owed to them by their tenants, as well as what they owned and where the crown's money came from (tolls, taxes, fishing rights, etc.). One of the most famous of these surveys is the Domesday Book, a one-year (1086) snapshot, county-by-county survey of England, recording by household names each estate and its value, yield in taxes, and production. Records for individuals exist also in rolls registers of deaths, births, funerals, and marriages, although not until late in the medieval period and frequently not in a continuous chronology so that you can study a significant time period. Some examples of records of individuals include parish registers, registers of freedmen, and rolls of deaths in religious communities. Lords of manors kept records that traced taxes, tithes, land transactions and deeds, crime and civil complaints, and the births, deaths, and marriages of their tenants.

Just as for ancient societies, literature is very important to the interpretation of medieval society. Few books were widely available yet. Individuals and libraries attached to churches and the newly founded universities had both learned works such as summas (something like a collection of someone's works), as well as copies of the pagan (Greek and Roman) classics. Liturgical books, such as holy scriptures, missals, prayer books, and books of hours, were also popular and prized. Many of our modern ideas about fiction/literature and fact/history were developed from the Renaissance to the Enlightenment. The medieval mind had no expectation or concept of such distinctions, so chronicles and historical narratives are not factual history as you might expect. They contain "fictional" elements that enhance the story or narrative. Their formats vary from verse and ballads to prose.[17]

Many of these sources have been published or printed in modern texts and collections. Remember that even though these documents are printed, they were intended both to be read by the educated portion of the population and heard and recited by memory by the less literate. Britain was one of the best, most meticulously documented medieval societies, but similar sources exist for continental Europe. Many of these texts have been reprinted in a series by learned societies. Your key to finding these sources is to use many of the kinds of books (rolls, registers) in the above paragraph or one of the finding aids listed in the bibliography below or available online. To search for rolls, registers, annals, charters, writs, and mandates as keywords in your library's catalog or online could be useful. Language could be a barrier since until about the twelfth century most documents were written in Latin. After that, the vernacular or spoken languages gained in popularity, but they will be an older form of the modern language you are used to. Many times, translations into English or into a modern form of the original language are provided.

SEARCH TIPS

1. In a keyword search, in your library's catalog, use one of the terms that describes what you are looking for ("writ," "charter," etc.) and combine it with place, ruler, topic, or office (e.g., the name of a court).
2. You may wish to limit your results by publication date or to limit the time the content covers.
3. You can also use the word "sources" in the subject heading to indicate primary sources.

Bibliographic Guides to the Study of Medieval History

Medieval Studies: A Bibliographic Guide. Everett Uberto Crosby, Charles Julian Bishko, and Robert L. Kellogg. New York: Garland, 1983. Contains a list of primary sources and major secondary works. The categories are quite extensive (e.g., "National Laws," "Art," and "Folklore") and cover more geographic areas and cultures than just Europe.

Guide to the Sources of Medieval History. R. C. van Caenegem. Amsterdam: Elsevier/North-Holland, 1978. Content includes sections on the sources of medieval history, as well as listing libraries and archives.

From Memory to Written Record: England 1066–1307. M. T. Clanchy, 2d ed. Oxford: Blackwell, 1993. Highlights the explosion of documents in British history. Wealth of references to the types and titles of sources.

The Labyrinth. http://labyrinth.georgetown.edu/ (accessed December 11, 2011). Digitized selection of primary documents with reference materials.

Medieval History Sourcebook. http://www.fordham.edu/halsall/sbook. asp (accessed December 11, 2011). Digitized selection of primary documents.

What Every Medievalist Should Know. James Marchand. http://www.the-orb.net/wemsk/wemskmenu.html (accessed December 11, 2011). Guide to research. Contained in *ORB: The Online Reference Book for Medieval Studies.*

Rosenthal, Joel Thomas. *Understanding Medieval Primary Sources: Using Historical Sources to Discover Medieval Europe*. Abingdon, Oxon: Routledge, 2012.

Using Bibliographies to Locate Primary Sources

In some cases, you may find a comprehensive bibliography on your country or time period that highlights the major primary resources relevant to your research. While this bibliography will not list every resource available, published or unpublished, it will usually suggest the principal groups and the records they produced. Such bibliographies will provide a survey of documents produced by the governing bodies, common literary texts, famous personal accounts, diaries and correspondence, statistical collections, and records of statesmen. A list of seminal bibliographies follows, including some websites. Many of the multivolume histories listed in chapter 2 will also have extensive bibliographies that will lead you to seminal primary sources. Looking through these lists may lead you to other resources. However, the topics of the bibliographies are too broad and may not be the place to begin your research if your topic is not well defined. You may find too many sources that will be too focused for your topic.

Bibliographies Containing References to Primary Sources

The American Historical Association's Guide to Historical Literature. 3d ed. 2 vols. Mary Beth Norton, ed. New York: Oxford University Press, 1995.

Sources for Ancient History. Michael Crawford, ed. New York: Cambridge University Press, 1983.

Latin America: A Guide to the Historical Literature. Charles C. Griffin, ed. Austin: University of Texas Press, 1971.

Africa, Asia, and South America since 1800: A Bibliographical Guide. A. J. H. Latham, comp. Manchester: Manchester University Press, 1995.

Chinese History: A Manual. Rev. and enl. ed. Endymion Wilkinson. Cambridge, MA: Harvard University Asia Center for the Harvard-Yenching Institute, 2000.

Medieval Studies: A Bibliographic Guide. Everett Uberto Crosby, Charles Julian Bishko, and Robert L. Kellogg. New York: Garland, 1983. Contains a list of primary sources and major secondary works. The categories are quite extensive (e.g., "National Laws," "Art," and "Folklore") and cover more geographic areas and cultures than just Europe.

Guide to the Sources of Medieval History. R. C. van Caenegem. Amsterdam: Elsevier/North-Holland, 1978. Content includes sections on sources for medieval history, as well as libraries and archives.

From Memory to Written Record: England 1066–1307. M. T. Clanchy, 2d ed. Oxford, UK: Blackwell, 1993. Highlights the explosion of documents in British history. Wealth of references to the types and titles of sources.

A Bibliography of British History, 1914–1989. Keith Robbins, comp. and ed. Oxford: Clarendon, 1996.

A Bibliography of English History to 1485. E. B. Graves, comp. Oxford: Clarendon, 1975.

Bibliography of British History: Tudor Period, 1485–1603. Conyers Read, comp. 2d ed. Totowa, NJ: Rowman and Littlefield, 1978.

Bibliography of British History: Stuart History, 1603–1714. G. D. Davies and M. F. Keeler, comps. 2d ed. Oxford: Clarendon, 1970.

Bibliography of British History: The Eighteenth Century, 1714–1789. S. Pargellis and D. J. Medley, comps. Oxford: Clarendon, 1951.

Bibliography of British History, 1789–1851. L. M. Brown and I. R. Christie, comps. Oxford: Clarendon, 1977.

Bibliography of British History, 1851–1914. H. J. Hanham, comp. Oxford: Clarendon, 1976.

WWW–Virtual Library History Index. http://vlib.iue.it/history/index.html (accessed December 11, 2011). Massive directory of sites focused on history and covering all eras and countries imaginable. Look for the sections on archival materials under each country or time period.

Stanford University Library Guides. http://library.stanford.edu/depts/hasrg/index.html (accessed December 11, 2011). Many of these guides have an extensive list of primary sources.

Yale University Library Subject Guides. http://guides.library.yale.edu/ (accessed December 11, 2011). Many of these guides have an extensive list of primary sources.

Evaluation

Once you have located your primary sources, you must examine their interrelatedness. Much like a detective or a crime scene investigator, you must read and review your evidence carefully, looking for obvious omissions, as well as clues the past has left you. The following questions will be helpful in determining the usefulness of a source:[18]

1. Who produced this source? Clearly identify the author and find out as much as you can about that individual in the secondary literature and biography and encyclopedia resources.

2. What was the purpose of the primary source? Is it still used for its intended purpose or has it changed over time?

3. Who was the intended audience? Who would have used the object or lived or worked in the building.

4. Is something or someone missing? Did the author intend to omit something or someone on purpose? Why? Do the facts seem incomplete or too complete? Are the conclusions too logical or illogical? Would the individual creating this primary source really have access to all of this information? Should she or he have been able to include more information? For objects, is some feature missing that might be hidden, for example a fireplace behind a wall.

5. What is the perspective of the author and how might this affect the contents of the source? Architects, artists, and photographers, as well as authors of a document, all have a perspective that is evident in their work.

6. How does the document reflect the time in which it was written? What other sources or materials might support or refute this evidence? Compare different primary sources from the same period. What voices are missing? Does it reflect a particular gender, racial, ethnic, regional, religious, or political perspective?

7. Is something implicit that would be clear to the original audience but might be hidden from the modern researcher? Is there a set of values, assumptions, or biases that the audience would have had that the modern researcher does not?

8. What other sources or materials might support or refute this evidence? How was the primary source received at the time? If it is a book or a famous building, a review might have been written, or some public comments might have been made.

9. Compare the primary source to other similar sources. If it is a building or object, look at others that had a similar purpose. How is your source similar, different, or unique?

10. Is the document believable? That is, could it have been created in the time in which it appears to have been created?

11. When thinking about buildings and objects, think about the space they occupy and how their space is arranged. Do specific rooms have a specific function (i.e., a sewing room or a nursery)?

Case Study—Finding Primary Sources: Tobacco through the Ages

Now that you have an idea about the variety and types of primary sources available, putting them all together is the challenge. Below is an example that will help you think about primary sources and their role as the foundation for your research.

Tobacco use was, and still is, a controversial economic and social issue in virtually all societies. You can find information about its commercial, social, and medical influence in almost every century throughout the history of its use by Europeans. Some of the potential sources are as follows:

1. *Published sources for mass consumption.* Looking in your catalog, as well as resources such as *Early English Books*, using "tobacco" as a subject and limiting the results by date of publication will produce all sorts of discussions on tobacco's influence. Prior to 1800, you might find a book by Giles Everard entitled *Panacea; or, The Universal Medicine: Being a Discovery of the Wonderfull Vertues of Tobacco Taken in a Pipe, with its Operation and Use Both in Physick and Chirurgery* (London: Printed for S. Miller, 1659). After 1800, when smoking was often regarded as a vice, you would find a book entitled *Smoke Not: An Essay, by Miss E.S.C., to whom a prize has been awarded by a committee of the British Anti-Tobacco Society* (Richmond: Macfarlane & Fergusson, 1861). Using *Poole's Index* or *Readers' Guide to Periodical Literature* (or their online counterparts, if available at your institution) or a newspaper index, such as the *New York Times Index* or the *Times (London) Index*, and looking up "tobacco" would also be revealing. You could read "The Dangers and Delights of Tobacco," in *St. Pauls: A Monthly Magazine* in 1868–69, or an editorial from the *New York Times* in 1866 discussing Baron Bramwell's suggestion that tobacco was necessary for English children.

2. *Manuscripts.* Using one of the manuscript indexes above or *WorldCat*, and doing a keyword search, and looking at the results in the archival materials section, you would find materials like the John B. Hutson papers (1933–1957). Hutson was the assistant to the secretary-general of the United Nations and undersecretary of agriculture. These papers include scrapbooks, speeches, articles, and letters centering on Hutson's involvement in the tobacco industry.

3. *Government documents.* Using your local catalog or some of the bibliographic sources above, such as the *Monthly Catalog*, you might find a report, "Smoking and Health; Report of the Advisory Committee to the

Surgeon General of the Public Health Service," by the US surgeon general's Advisory Committee on Smoking and Health, issued in 1964.

4. *Public records.* Public records for tobacco can be extremely varied, depending on the time and geographic location. You could look for local revenues of taxes placed on tobacco. You could find market prices for tobacco. Health records of populations and aggregate statistics might be available but not for individual smokers. In each of these instances, the records would be located at a local historical society, library, or the city or state's department of health. Use the guides listed previously to locate the contact information for these institutions and ask them if such information exits. Doing a keyword search on *WorldCat* for "tobacco" and your state or locale might also prove fruitful.

5. *Business records.* Using some of the directories listed, you could look for the archives of Philip Morris/Altria Group or another of the major tobacco companies still in existence. Because of recent controversies, your access to the archives would probably be restricted.

6. *Oral testimony.* Searching one of the directories provided above or looking in *WorldCat* (searching for keywords "tobacco" and "oral history"), you would find a reference to the Southern Folklife Collection at the University of North Carolina at Chapel Hill and a manuscript collection entitled "Collection 1941–1946; 1987," which is a series of interviews with Anglo-American musicians who grew up on tobacco farms or were involved in the tobacco business.

7. *Media and advertising.* Search the sources provided in the media section in chapter 9 to see what might be available. Do not forget that some advertisements might be in print sources. Check with your librarian. See chapter 7 on using the Internet.

FOR FURTHER READING

Alexander, Christopher. *The Timeless Way of Building.* New York: Oxford University Press, 1979.

Alexander, Christopher, Sara Ishikawa, and Murray Silverstein. *A Pattern Language: Towns, Buildings, Construction.* New York: Oxford University Press, 1977.

Teachers: Using Primary Sources (Library of Congress) http://www.loc.gov/teachers/usingprimarysources/ (accessed April 27, 2012).

Barber, Sarah, and C. M. Peniston-Bird, eds. *History beyond the Text: A Student's Guide to Approaching Alternative Sources*. Abingdon, Oxon: Routledge, 2009.

Brundage, Anthony. *Going to the Sources: A Guide to Historical Research and Writing*. 4th ed. Wheeling, IL: Harlan Davidson, 2008.

D'Aniello, Charles A., ed. *Teaching Bibliographic Skills in History: A Sourcebook for Historians and Librarians*. Westport, CT: Greenwood Press, 1993.

Dobson, Miriam, and Benjamin Ziemann, eds. *Reading Primary Sources: The Interpretation of Texts from Nineteenth- and Twentieth-Century History*. London: Routledge, 2009.

Fisher, Steven, ed. *Archival Information: How to Find It, How to Use It*. Westport, CT: Greenwood Press, 2004.

Harvey, Karen, ed. *History and Material Culture: A Student's Guide to Approaching Alternative Sources*. London: Routledge, 2009.

Howe, Barbara J. *Houses and Homes: Exploring Their History*. Nashville, TN: American Association for State and Local History, 1987.

Kyvig, David E., and Myron A. Marty. *Nearby History: Exploring the Past around You*. Lanham, MD: Rowman & Littlefield Publishers, 2010.

Lusker, Marilyn. *Research Projects for College Students: What to Write Across the Curriculum*. New York: Greenwood Press, 1988.

Rosenthal, Joel Thomas, ed. *Understanding Medieval Primary Sources: Using Historical Sources to Discover Medieval Europe*. Abingdon, Oxon: Routledge, 2012.

Using Primary Sources on the Web. http://www.ala.org/rusa/sections/history/resources/pubs/usingprimarysources (accessed December 11, 2011).

Yale University Guide to Primary Sources. http://www.yale.edu/collections_collaborative/primarysources/ (accessed December 11, 2011).

Bibliography of Advanced Indexes to Published Primary Sources

Below are titles of specialized journal indexes that span much of the twentieth century and, in some cases, also cover portions of the nineteenth. The main title is the current or latest title. Listed underneath are the previous titles.

Alternative Press Index 1969– . Index to the radical press of the 1970s. Find out what antiwar, labor, and women's publications were discussing.

L'Année philologique; bibliographie critique et analytique de l'antiquité gréco-latine, 1924– . Multilingual index to articles concerning classical culture. Good for ancient history.

Art Index, 1929– . Index to articles about art, including art history, folk art, sculpture, architecture, painting, and anything art-related.

Biological Abstracts, 1926– . History of biology and scientific development.

- *Abstracts of Bacteriology,* 1917–1921.
- *Botanical Abstracts,* 1918–1926.

Biological and Agricultural Index, 1964– . Agricultural/farming developments.

- *Agricultural Index,* 1916–1964.

Chemical Abstracts/Chem Abstracts, 1907– . History of chemistry and related industries.

- *Review of American Chemical Research,* 1905–1906.

Combined Retrospective Index to Book Reviews in Scholarly Journals, 1886–1974. Index to book reviews.

Education Index, 1929– . History of education and educational theory.

Essay and General Literature Index, 1900– . Indexes essays in books.

Index Islamicus, 1906– . Index to the study of the Islamic world.

Index Medicus, 1879– . Index to articles on all aspects of medicine. (Online version, *Medline* 1966– and *Old Medline* 1953–1965.)

Industrial Arts Index, 1912–1957. Index to publications in the trades, business, technical sciences, and so on. Later split into the two titles below.

- *Applied Science and Technology Index,* 1958– .
- *Business Periodicals Index,* 1958– .

International Index to Periodicals, 1901–1965. Index to scholarly journal articles. Parallel index to *Readers' Guide to Periodical Literature,* which indexes popular articles. Split into the indexes below.

- *Social Sciences and Humanities Index,* 1965–1974.
- *Humanities Index,* 1974– .
- *Social Sciences Index,* 1974– .

PAIS International/Public Affairs Information Service, 1990– . Index to articles in public administration and the operation of governments.

- *Bulletin of the Public Affairs Information Service Bulletin,* 1915–1986.
- *PAIS Bulletin,* 1986–1990.

Psychological Abstracts, 1927– . History of the study of psychology.

NOTES

1. Definitions from a discussion with Dr. Andrew Cayton, December 14, 2011.

2. Howell and Prevenier have a nice discussion about the evolution of archives from private collections to this current organizational division. Martha Howell and Walter Prevenier, *From Reliable Sources: An Introduction to Historical Methods* (Ithaca, NY: Cornell University Press, 2001), 34–42.

3. Edward Hampshire and Valerie Johnson. "The Digital World and the Future of Historical Research." *Twentieth Century British History* 20(3) (2009): 396–414. The phrase "a field of electronic haystacks" appears on page 410.

4. Nicholas Culpeper, *A Directory for Midwives; or, A Guide for Women, in their Conception. Bearing; and Suckling their Children* . . . (London: printed, and are to be sold by most booksellers in London and Westminster, 1693).

5. James C. Dobbins, *Letters of the Nun Eshinni: Images of Pure Land Buddhism in Medieval Japan* (Honolulu: University of Hawaii Press, 2004).

6. Carolyn Earle Billingsley, *Communities of Kinship: Antebellum Families and the Settlement of the Cotton Frontier.* (Athens: University of Georgia Press, 2004), 1–39, 147–153.

7. Valerie Raleigh Yow, *Recording Oral History: A Guide for the Humanities and Social Sciences*, 2d ed. (Walnut Creek, CA: AltaMira Press, 2005); Donald A. Ritchie, *Doing Oral History: A Practical Guide*, 2d ed. (Oxford: Oxford University Press, 2003). See also Nancy MacKay, *Curating Oral Histories: From Interview to Archive* (Walnut Creek, CA: Left Coast Press, 2007).

8. Laurel Ulrich, *The Age of Homespun: Objects and Stories in the Creation of an American Myth* (New York: Knopf, 2001), 42–45.

9. Karen Harvey, "Introduction," in *History and Material Culture: A Student's Guide to Approaching Alternative Sources*, ed. Karen Harvey (London: Routledge, 2009), 5, 9.

10. Ibid., 2.

11. Giorgio Riello, "Things That Shape History: Material Culture and Historical Narratives," in *History and Material Culture: A Student's Guide to Approaching Alternative Sources*, ed. Karen Harvey (London: Routledge, 2009), 24–26.

12. M. T. Clanchy, *From Memory to Written Record: England 1066–1307* (Oxford: Blackwell, 1993).

13. Ernst Posner, *Archives in the Ancient World.* (Cambridge, MA: Harvard University Press, 1972), 3–4.

14. Michael Crawford, ed., *Sources for Ancient History* (Cambridge: Cambridge University Press, 1983).

15. Emilio Gabba, "Literature," in *Sources for Ancient History*, ed. Michael Crawford (Cambridge: Cambridge University Press, 1983), 1–80.

16. R. C. Van Caenegem, with the collaboration of F. L. Ganshof, *Guide to the Sources of Medieval History* (Amsterdam: Elsevier/North-Holland, 1978), 15.

17. Lister M. Matheson, "Vernacular Chronicles and Narrative Sources of History in Medieval England," in *Understanding Medieval Primary Sources: Using Historical Sources to Discover Medieval Europe*, ed. Joel Thomas Rosenthal (Abingdon, Oxon: Routledge, 2012), 25–26.

18. Some of these questions came from Marilyn Luzker, "The Undergraduate Researcher and Primary Sources," in *Research Projects for College Students: What to Write across the Curriculum* (New York: Greenwood Press, 1988),

43. An in-depth discussion of evaluating primary sources can be found in Howell and Prevenier, *From Reliable Sources*, 62–68. For material culture, see David E. Kyvig and Myron A. Marty, *Nearby History: Exploring the Past around You* (Lanham, MD: Rowman & Littlefield Publishers, 2010), 177–192; Barbara J. Howe, *Houses and Homes: Exploring Their History* (Nashville, TN: American Association for State and Local History, 1987); and Giorgio Riello, "Things That Shape History: Material Culture and Historical Narratives," in *History and Material Culture: A Student's Guide to Approaching Alternative Sources*, ed. Karen Harvey (London: Routledge, 2009), 24–26. For evaluating primary sources on the Internet, see *Using Primary Sources on the Internet* (Instruction and Research Services Committee of the Reference and User Service Association, History Section, American Library Association), http://www.ala.org/rusa/sections/history/resources/pubs/usingprimarysources (accessed December 10, 2011).

7

History and the Internet

WHAT YOU WILL LEARN IN THIS CHAPTER

- when the Internet is appropriate for history research
- how to perform efficient searches using a search directory, search engine, or meta-search engine
- how to evaluate your search results
- how historians use the Internet to communicate

The Internet and Research

The Internet and its contents influence if not alter, the traditional methods of historical research. Resources, especially primary sources, are quickly available without the item being physically present at the location of the researcher. However, some novice researchers treat it as a virtual library, equivalent to the collection of monographs, journals, and primary sources discussed in the previous chapters. A website can integrate a collection of primary sources, documents, images, and maps, for instance, that a single researcher or organization has collected, as well as connect these sources with interpretive materials such as explanatory essays or reference-like texts such as encyclopedias and glossaries. A powerful tool, the Internet can allow greater communication between teacher and learner, regardless of the purpose of the website. For instance, a website on the Song Dynasty in China (http://afe.easia.columbia.edu/song/) examines the economic and social history of twelfth-century China as seen through a scroll painting. The site contains images with explanatory text and a bibliography of further readings. Yet, while sites such as this are amazing research tools, the Internet does not have the organization (precise, controlled subject headings) of an online catalog or index, nor does it employ the peer review process that many publishers of journals and monographs use to assure quality publications. Scholars and nonscholars alike take advantage of the freedom of the Internet, creating websites of varying quality. Because of this you can waste a lot of time searching for websites and finding nothing of value. As a researcher, you must learn to efficiently search for and evaluate websites, just as you do all the other sources you gather. When used appropriately and in conjunction with monographs and journals, information from websites can enhance your research. Understanding what the Internet is and how it functions will allow you to use it appropriately.

Thinking about the types of common Internet sites will help you decide which are most valuable for certain aspects of historical research. Websites fall into the following categories, and many are combinations of these categories (an example of a historical site in each category is listed in parentheses):

- collections of primary sources (*Avalon Project*, http://avalon.law.yale.edu/subject_menus/major.asp)

- papers and projects (*History Matters: Student Projects on the Web*, http://historymatters.gmu.edu/browse/studhist/)

- webliographies (*Latin American Network of Information Center*, http://lanic.utexas.edu/)

- collections of an organization's documents, policies, and activities (*The American Historical Association*, http://www.historians.org/)

- blogs or personal reflections on topics (History News Network's list of blogs, http://hnn.us/departments/86.html)

- connections to listservs for scholarly discussions (*H-Net Humanities and Social Sciences Online*, http://www.h-net.org/)

- reference or encyclopedia sites (*Ecole Initiative: Creating a Hypertext Encyclopedia of Early Church History*, http://www2.evansville.edu/ecoleweb/), an exhibit of artifacts and interpretations on a subject (*Turning the Pages* [British Library] http://www.bl.uk/onlinegallery/ttp/ttpbooks.html) and current scholarly research and analysis (*History Cooperative's Online Proceedings* [for a fee], http://historycooperative.press.uiuc.edu/proceedings/)

When Is the Internet Appropriate for Historical Research?

Again, if used correctly and critically, the Internet can be a valuable source for your historical research. Knowing when it is useful and when books and journal articles are more appropriate is the key to being a good and accurate historian. Historian Carl Smith in his oft-quoted, groundbreaking article "Can You Do Serious History on the Web?" answers in the affirmative.[1] He defines serious history "to mean original work that is responsibly based on primary sources, is intelligently informed by relevant scholarship, and makes a clear argument or group of arguments." If a website meets these criteria, it contains serious history. So what kinds of serious history can be found on the web?

- *Primary sources.* Many historical societies, museums, and archives are beginning to digitize *parts* of their collections and place them online. Sometimes universities, other research agencies, or individual faculty members create a collection of out-of-copyright or primary materials on a subject. For example, *The Labyrinth* (http://labyrinth.georgetown.edu/) categorizes both primary and secondary materials about medieval life and culture. The Internet is especially useful for modern historical primary source material such as video clips and oral interviews. Websites such as *History and Politics Out Loud* (http://www.hpol.org/) at Northwestern University contain audio versions of political speeches and include transcripts online. Other primary source materials are the Cambodian Genocide Program (http://www.yale.edu/cgp/) and the Paris Siege and Commune (http://www.library.northwestern.edu/spec/siege/). Youtube (http://www.youtube.com/) is also a good source of classic historical videos.

- *Bibliographies/webliographies.* Collections of references to secondary source materials, such as journal articles, books, and some websites, are widely available. Individuals, organizations, or research institutes interested in a particular subject often will compile lists of key references, allowing you to build on someone else's research. If you are lucky, such resources will include an internal search engine or some sort of topical arrangement to facilitate your search. If you are very lucky, you may find some links to full-text articles that have no copyright restrictions. For an example, see *Africabib* (http://www.africabib.org), a site that, among other components, contains three major searchable bibliographic databases: *Bibliography of Africana*

Periodical Literature Database, African Women's Bibliographic Database, and *Women Travelers, Explorers, and Missionaries to Africa 1763–2003.* It is compiled by Davis Bullwinkle, director of the Institute for Economic Advancement Research Library at the University of Arkansas-Little Rock.

- *Organizations' and governments' documents.* Many organizations have begun to link their current and historical documents to an online page. Numerous projects are creating collections of digitized historical documents. For example, *Eurodocs* (http://eurodocs.lib.byu.edu/), while not a site by a government, organizes full-text historic European countries' and territories' documents by country. The *United Nations* (http://www.un.org) makes a large portion of its official documents from the last 10 years available through its website. For example, you can find International Court of Justice proceedings against Yugoslavia for genocide in Bosnia, Herzegovina, and Croatia, as well as Economic and Social Council programs on health. Seldom will you find documents older than the late 1980s/1990s (although collections continue to grow retrospectively) placed online by an organization or government, although some notable exceptions exist. The African National Congress has a growing collection of documents (http://www.anc.org.za/). *American Memory* (http://memory.loc.gov/ammem/) has an online collection of the proceedings of the US Congress from 1774 through 1875.[2]

- *Specialized reference sources.* The Internet's use of hyperlinks makes it an ideal vehicle for reference sources, such as definitions and longer articles of explanation on topics that can be too specialized to be published in book form or that can be enhanced by multimedia. For an example, see the *Encyclopedia of Cleveland History* (http://ech.cwru.edu/). In this encyclopedia, you will find images and historical information about Cleveland, Ohio. Remember to be careful of out-of-date resources. The edition of *Roget's Thesaurus* that Bartleby.com supplied was published in 1922.

- *Cutting-edge secondary source research.* Historians usually engage one another to work out theories they have devised based on their research, and some of this discussion takes place on forums on the Internet. At the *Roy Rosenzweig Center for History and New Media* (http://chnm.gmu.edu/), selected essays are posted by the authors to promote discussion among historians about doing digital history. The site also contains a number of primary source collections as well. In the same way, some of the chatter on the *H-Net* (http://www.h-net.org/) series of listserv groups cites cutting-edge research. What the Internet will not provide, generally, is access to published, refereed journal articles or books. While there are exceptions, usually access to such materials requires a paid subscription by your library. An exception is *Google Scholar* (http://scholar.google.com/), a separate section of the search engine *Google*, which does provide links to some full-text academic journals (see chapter 4 for a discussion). There are also some academic journals that do publish freely online and will not be indexed in a periodical index. As discussed above, the search engines will not search in a fee-restricted database or in an online journal. For a list of online history journals, some free, some subscription, see http://aac.sub. uni-goettingen.de/en/journals/history/ and http://www.doaj.org. Many universities are creating scholarly commons or institutional repositories that collect and make freely available via the web, the published and unpublished works of their scholars. This is done with the permission of both the scholars and the publications in which the works appeared (for an example, see University of Nebraska's DigitalCommons, http:// digitalcommons.unl.edu/disciplines.html). An Internet search may turn up these sources.

- *Communication.* Many scholars belong to a listserv, and some read blogs or create their own blogs. With a listserv, you subscribe to a list on which you can ask, view, and reply to questions about topics around a central theme, for instance, early modern history. Blogs are public, personal diaries in which anyone can participate. Finally, *RSS (Really Simple Syndication)* allows you to receive notifications, much like a personal newsletter, of new postings in selected blogs. More about blogs and listservs below.

- *Syllabi.* Sometimes online course syllabi can be useful in research. Professors create specialized guides for their students to use in a course. Be very careful to evaluate your source. Make sure that the person writing the document has some authority and is not a student completing an assignment. Be careful using websites by other students. Some will be of excellent quality, while others may be poorly constructed and researched. It is difficult to judge quality if you do not yet know much about the subject you are studying. Be cautious about using syllabi and the documents linked to them as sources. See the online American History survey *History Matters*

Box 7.1 How to Read a URL

Your browser "reads" a URL (uniform resource locator) or the address of a website, which is the location of the computer where the web page you want resides. Knowing how to read a URL is essential to understanding where you are on the Internet. See figure 7.1 for an example of a URL.

http://www.dohistory.org

Server or host computer of an organization or institution where the information is kept.

Domain name, in this case an organization. This gives you an idea as to the type of information provided. Other common domains are: .edu for education, .com for commercial and .gov for government.

http://www.dohistory.org/on_your_own/toolkit/writing.html

Folder Names

Document Name

Figure 7.1. The parts of a URL (uniform resource locator). By stripping each of the file names, separated by a forward slash (/), you can discover the origin or hosting computer.

Using the diary of Martha Ballard, an eighteenth-century midwife, this website illustrates how the past can be pieced together using fragments of evidence. The first URL takes you to the main website, an organization called "dohistory" that provides materials to study Martha Ballard's diary. The second URL above leads you to a guide on deciphering eighteenth-century handwriting. By reading the URL itself, you will see the name, or host, of the website you are visiting, the kind of site (domain) it is (.com, .edu, .org, etc.), and which particular part of the file you are looking for. You can actually use your knowledge about a URL's structure to evaluate a website. Even though you know nothing about the content of the website, by peeling off the file names back to www.dohistory.org, you know that an organization, in this case the Center for History and the New Media Film Study Center at Harvard University cited at the bottom of the page, has made this website available on the Internet. That should prompt you to ask questions about the purpose and intent of the organization and the influence that might have on the content of the site.

(http://historymatters.gmu.edu/) and *World History Matters* (http://chnm.gmu.edu/worldhistorysources/) for examples of an online course and the integration of multimedia into the basic American civilization course. Also see the section of *History Matters* (http://historymatters.gmu.edu/) titled "Syllabus Central," which provides links to other syllabi that may have web pages with explanatory material useful for your research. MERLOT (http://history.merlot.org/) has a section of learning materials that include class activities and simulations.

Using the Internet: The Basics

To access the World Wide Web and all of those wonderful sites mentioned, you will use a piece of software called a browser. *Foxfire*, *Internet Explorer*, *Chrome*, and *Safari* are just a few. If you have problems reading a website, it could be that the webmaster did a poor job in creating the site and it can only be read by the particular browser for which that site was created. Be careful not to confuse browsers with a database or with the search engines, or the search directories, discussed below.

How Do I Access Websites on the Internet?

Most of us have a favorite search engine that we use, such as *Google*, and we simply type some words in its search box and hope for the best. You can waste a great deal of time "surfing" on the Internet, looking for useable information, finding very little, and getting lost on interesting but unrelated websites. Before you become mired in your Internet search, you need to be sure that the time you spend will be worth the effort when you find results. Performing efficient searches in the right places, just as you learned in using online catalogs and indexes, will improve your time-investment-to-results ratio. Using effective search strategies in search directories, search engines, and meta-search engines will produce useful results from quality websites. Each of these three Internet tools has different uses for specific kinds of research.

Search Directories

A search directory is a very large but limited collection of links categorized by knowledgeable people (often librarians or researchers). Purposely selective and not comprehensive, the collection of links implies quality and reliability simply by any one link's inclusion. Search directories are useful when you have a very broad subject that you are unable to focus into a research topic. Because they are organized by subject categories, you can do a keyword search *within* the directory, discover a subject category, and browse through that category, still within the directory. You have already practiced this same technique in an online catalog by doing a keyword search and then searching by the subject headings attached to the catalog record. But you still must use your evaluation skills. Not all websites, even though they have been selected for a directory, will necessarily be of good quality or meet *your* research standards. Follow the evaluation guidelines later in this chapter and think about your research needs as you search for online sources.

SEARCH TIPS

1. Choose a search directory.
2. Using the search box, do a keyword search within the directory.
3. When the results appear, use the subject headings/subject categories attached to one of the results to browse for other similar websites in the directory.

General Search Directories

Internet Public Library. http://www.ipl.org (accessed September 6, 2011). Very selective but extensive list of hundreds of thousands of quality sites. Not all are history-related, but this is a good place to start looking.

BUBL Link. http://bubl.ac.uk/ (accessed September 6, 2011). A directory, similar to the *Internet Public Library* but somewhat smaller in scope, with thousands of highly selected sources. However, because of its British origin, it contains many more British and European sources that may not be listed in some of these other directories. While the site is no longer being updated, the recommended resources will remain useful for several years.

MERLOT (Multimedia Educational Resource for Learning and Online Teaching). http://www.merlot.org (accessed September 6, 2011). Provides ratings and descriptions of websites that are more academic in nature and usually designed to supplement teaching. Includes links to assignments created by professors and teachers.

Voice of the Shuttle. http://vos.ucsb.edu/ (accessed September 6, 2011). Scholarly directory established in 1994 at the University of California, Santa Barbara. Long lists to search through but useful.

Open Directory. http://dmoz.org (accessed September 6, 2011). Billed as the "most comprehensive human-edited directory of the Web," *Open Directory* has the usual categories. It also has a number of links to directories in other languages.

INFOMINE. http://infomine.ucr.edu (accessed September 6, 2011). Directory created by librarians from a number of university libraries for students and faculty using the Internet for research. The search interface is a bit different from most, looking much like an online catalog with options to search in author, title, subject, description, and full text.

The Internet Scout Report. http://scout.wisc.edu/ (accessed September 6, 2011). A searchable, weekly newsletter of recommended Internet sites. Lengthy reviews. Not a directory in the true sense of the word but a good place to begin looking.

Yahoo. http://www.yahoo.com (accessed September 6, 2011). The original directory. It is vast, though not approaching the size of a search engine. When it comes to scholarship, there are good finds as well as lots of junk in *Yahoo.* This directory is not as selective as the previously listed ones, but its organization is good. Use your evaluation skills carefully.

General History Search Directories, Webliographies, and Print Bibliographies

WWW-VL History Central Catalog. http://vlib.iue.it/history/index.html (accessed September 6, 2011). Part of the *World Wide Web Virtual Library*, a massive directory of sites focused on history and covering all eras and countries imaginable. There is no search feature included, so you must browse through the categories. Some marginal sites are included in this site's attempt to be comprehensive. Still, a gem.

Best of History Websites. http://www.besthistorysites.net/ (accessed September 6, 2011). Selective collection of sites for students and teachers of all levels and all areas of history.

Library of Anglo-American Culture and History. http://aac.sub.uni-goettingen.de/en/history/guide (accessed September 6, 2011). Very comprehensive. German site but multilingual with scholarly websites. European focus.

Stanford University Library Guides. http://library.stanford.edu/depts/hasrg/index.html (accessed September 6, 2011).

Box 7.2 Google

Habitually, many of us go straight to the search engine Google to perform our searches. In fact "google" has become a part of speech, for example, to google, googling, googled, and so on. According to Siva Vaidhyanathan, author of *The Googlization of Everything: (And Why We Should Worry)*, "Google is on the verge of being indistinguishable from the web itself" (3). The Google search engine has revolutionized not only the way we find information, but how we expect to acquire that information—fast, free, and highly relevant. The technologies that Google has invented and uses, as well as the company's practices can shape public conversation, as well as your personal views. Because Google collects and organizes information/websites, it has no editorial responsibility to seek and highly rank authoritative sources. News outlets, such as newspapers, wire services, and television news are expected to vet their stories and judge the credibility of the information they have gathered (33–35). Google's ranking is based upon criteria that includes popularity of a link, your past search strategies in google and the sites you have looked at, where you are located (Google knows where you are searching from and makes assessments as to what US residents want compared to their European counterparts), and how many other pages link to a particular page (140). Google often seems to defer to Wikipedia, whose articles often end up on the first page if not in the first five results (63). Google's ranking has the potential to give false importance to information because of a website's ranking within the results. To be fair, Google's desire is to make information past and present, printed and digital, easily and accurately accessible to a wide audience. Google Books and Google Scholar, despite their failings (see chapters 3 and 4 of this book) are a step toward creating a digital library that allows us to do research in different ways. Many other search engines do have similar practices to Google. Because of this, you must use more than one search engine and creatively evaluate not only the accuracy of the information presented but also what information may be left out.

Source: Siva Vaidhyanathan, *The Googlization of Everything: (And Why We Should Worry)* (Berkeley: University of California Press, 2011).

Yale University Library Subject Guides. http://guides.library.yale.edu/ (accessed September 6, 2011).

Trinkle, Dennis A., and Scott A. Merriman, eds. *The History Highway: A 21st Century Guide to Internet Resources.* 4d ed. Armonk, NY: M. E. Sharpe, 2006. Huge print bibliography of websites organized by country and general subject. However, because a printed book can be dated and websites disappear, some links might be out of date.

Search Engines

Search directories, while incredibly useful for a topic that is not well developed, cover only a small portion of the available Internet resources. Search engines attempt to index a larger portion of the Internet. Scouring the Internet for websites and remembering their locations, a *bot* or *spider* (essentially a piece of software) crawls into servers, the machines that house web pages, looks at the links and words on the top page(s), and stores and catalogs the locations of those web pages and links, returning regularly (every month or so) to update its information.[3] This means that if a page disappears before the spider or bot returns to make updates, you will find a *dead link*, a nonworking connection to the web page that previously existed. Unlike print documents of the past, little of the Internet historical record is being preserved. One attempt is the *Internet Archive or Wayback Machine*, http://www.archive.org/.)[4]

When you perform a search, the search engine posts the results, matching the keywords and web pages with uniform resource locators (URLs) related to your search request. In this process, there is no human intervention. The search, as well as the posted and ranked results, is the result of a mechanical process. Traditionally, search engines searched only through HTML (or web) pages.[5] Now, many search engines also compile locations of .pdf documents (.pdf), excel files (.xls), adobe postscript (.ps), Microsoft *Word* files (.doc), *PowerPoint* files (.ppt), and rich text files (.rtf). While more sophisticated search engines and processes continue to be developed, some contents on the web may not be able to be discovered by a bot or spider. The invisible or deep web material, not searchable by a bot or spider is discussed below.

Because of its immense inventory of websites and lack of subject control, a search engine requires a good search strategy. Your Boolean logic skills (see chapter 4) will be useful in constructing a productive search in a search engine. When you enter your keyword search in the search box, most search engines assume you want all of the words to appear in the web page, but not as a phrase. This is the Boolean concept of "and." (Always check the "search tips" section that each search engine provides for the peculiarities of that search engine.) For instance, a search for "Dust Bowl California" could get you a website advertising a maid service located in California, if they claim to dust your ceramic bowls carefully! A more precise search would be *"Dust Bowl" California*. The quotation marks indicate you want to do a phrase search for the words "dust bowl" and that the word "California" should be included. One result would be *Dust Bowl Refugees in California* (http://www.sfmuseum.org/hist8/ok.html), a website maintained by the Museum of the City of San Francisco. Google has a limited advanced search. Look to the bottom of the screen of results. Select "Advanced Search". You can limit by language, domain type, last update, reading level, and other criteria. Don't forget on the left side of the basic search screen you can also limit by such criteria as images, maps, and so on. Most search engines also allow you to restrict your searches to a particular domain. Restricting your search to .edu (site: .edu) is sometimes useful, if you think academic websites will provide more authoritative information (as opposed to .com or .org). Sometimes an .org website will give you an organization's unique view, for instance, that of the Institute for Historical Review (http://www.ihr.org/), which denies the Holocaust.[6] (An .org is not necessarily nonprofit as originally intended in the domain extension monikers. It is given for any organization and often for any group that does not fit into any of the other domain categories.) Each search engine has features in its advanced search that are unique to that search engine. Again, look at the help files of the search engine and decide which tips will be useful for your particular research project. *Google* advanced search techniques can be found at: http://www.google.com/support/websearch/?hl=en. Other search engines have similar support pages.

An algorithm, which varies by search engine, ranks your results. *Google*, for instance, has a sophisticated ranking system that combines the number of times a page is linked on other web pages, as well as the number of occurrences of your query words and their location in the web page. (For the technical explanation, see the *Google* help pages.) So, if a web page is linked often to other websites, it will be ranked higher in *Google's* results list. Web designers have tried to influence rankings by having a large number of websites link a phrase, usually a derogatory phrase, to a website. This practice, called *"Google* bombing," has recently been used to link George W. Bush's biography to the phrase "miserable failure." *Google* has fixed this particular instance of google bombing, but the practice persists.[7] Regardless of your view of these individuals and issues, this is a way to manipulate *Google* search results. Other search engines have their own ranking techniques. In some cases, a search engine charges fees to website producers to have their website appear higher in a results list.

Each search engine listed below (and the numerous others that you may encounter) has different devices and techniques for searching and creating the database. Remember to read their search help files to determine their unique features. Because each search engine's spider or bot collects and indexes sites differently, use more than one search engine. The same search strategy in different search engines will yield different results.

SEARCH TIPS

1. Use Boolean search techniques such as "+" (for "and") and "term." (put your phrase in quotation marks). Check the "help" section for your search engine to see how to indicate Boolean connectors, such as "and". Many search engines assume that you want all of the words included in your search.
2. Use the advanced search features and limit by domain, such as .edu, .gov, or .org.
3. Be as concrete and specific with your search terms as you can. General searches often produce voluminous results that are even more vague than your search and will waste your time.
4. Use more than one search engine.

General Search Engines

This list below is a selected list, see footnote 8 for a comparison of search engines.[8]

Google. http://www.google.com (accessed September 6, 2011).
Teoma. http://www.teoma.com (accessed September 6, 2011). Teoma is now indexing meta-sites, those large sites with many links and complicated subject organizations.
Yippy. http://yippy.com/ (accessed June 1, 2012).
Bing. http://www.bing.com (accessed September 6, 2011).
The Search Engine List, http://www.thesearchenginelist.com/ (accessed April 29, 2012). A nice comprehensive list of choices by type of search engine and function.

Search Engines for History

No *true* search engines exist specifically for history. Others will cite search engines for historical resources, but technically they are really collections of websites and/or directories with a search engine that searches within that directory.

Meta-Search Engines

The concept of meta-search engines can be a bit daunting and frankly engages in overkill when it comes to academic Internet research. Meta-search engines search many search engines and directories simultaneously. If your topic is not well defined or unique, these aggregators create an overwhelming amount of redundant information and are therefore not recommended for your academic research.

Selected General Meta-Search Engines

Webcrawler. http://www.webcrawler.com/ (accessed September 6, 2011).
Dogpile. http://www.dogpile.com/ (accessed September 6, 2011).
Metacrawler. http://www.metacrawler.com/ (accessed September 6, 2011).

SEARCH TIPS
Use the same research techniques with meta-search engines as with search engines.

What Am I Missing? The Deep Web or Invisible Web

Because of the technology that search engines use to crawl the web, there are places and types of information that they may not be able to find. Referred to as the "deep web" or "invisible web," this portion of the Internet is inaccessible by most of the common search engines. While a search engine may find the existence of a project or a website, it is unable to search within a database. An obvious example is the website eBay, which offers personally owned items for sale. If someone wishes to sell his or her ancestor's Civil War surgical instruments, searching for "surgical instruments 'civil war'" generally does not find the eBay auction listing. A more scholarly example is the *Cambodian Genocide Program* at Yale University (http://www.yale.edu/cgp/), which is a site that contains three databases: a bibliographic section, a biographic database, and a photographic database. These databases

Box 7.3 Databases verses Search Engines

Databases and search engines have some distinct differences, although they may not be clear to student researchers. In fact, the distinctions may be blurring as the information keeps changing.

Databases	General-Purpose Search Engines
Collects material: Utilizes submission processes based on peer review, editorial boards, and other review processes	**Collects material:** Uses a Web crawler or by submission
Indexing: Information and data are stored in a uniform way utilizing "fields." Fields allow for the retrieval of specific pieces of information.	**Indexing:** Retrieval is facilitated across several formats
Retrieval of Information: Finds results by matching information listed in fields. All fields are searchable	**Retrieval of Information:** Find results by searching for keywords found in text. (Relevancy determined by algorithm or similar such criteria.)
Scope: Databases are organized with a special purpose or subject in mind or are intended for a specific audience or membership. All entries in the database relate to its subject, purpose, or some kind of specialization.	**Scope:** General-purpose search engines provide across-the-board coverage.
Authority: A submission process is in place to ensure authority	**Authority:** Search engine does not evaluate information or Web sites.
Updating: Every day new information can be added to a database easily.	**Updating:** New Websites and Web content created every day. Search engines are always crawling for new content and revisit Web sites on a regular basis, although frequency varies from one search engine to another.

Cost: Free or fee-based access may depend upon membership in a professional association	Cost: Free access.
Examples: America: History and Life (fee-based); Historical Abstracts (fee-based); Africabib (free)	**Examples:** Google; Yahoo

Table adapted from Jane Devine and Francine Egger-Sider, *Going Beyond Google: The Invisible Web in Learning and Teaching* (New York: Neal-Schuman Publishers, Inc., 2009), 11. Used with permission.

attempt to provide access to Pol Pot's security police archives, which document a portion of the 1.7 million Cambodians who were killed in the genocide between the years 1975 and 1979. *Google* will list the URLs for the databases themselves, but it will not be able to search within their contents, for instance, to find an individual's name. Another example of a hidden database to which common search engines might not go is Northwestern University's collection of photographs on the Siege and Commune of Paris, 1870–1871. Doing a search for "siege Paris" would find the web page. However, if you were looking for a photograph of the Chateau de Meudon, contained in the database, searching for "chateau meudon" might not find the photographs contained in this site. To search within a database, you must fill out a search query form with your desired search terms. Searching through fields unique to that database, the internal search engine dynamically generates a list of results; a webpage specifically tailored to your query. These results exist only for the one time you use them. Once you close your browser window, those results no longer exist as a single site. The url is considered dynamic, not static or stable, as normal websites or even the journal articles in JSTOR. A dynamically generated or temporary url will have symbols like "?" or cgi in it. For instance searching in the website/collection of primary resources that make up *American Memory* for civil war hospitals yields 1,293 results with a url of http://memory.loc. gov/cgi-bin/query. This url cannot be entered into a browser to produce the same results at a later date. (You may find some of the referenced sources in this book have dynamically generated urls. To find the source, you may have to do an Internet search for its title instead of typing in the url.) Many times dynamically generated urls are very long. As technology changes, the ability to search within these kinds of databases may also change.[9]

A database such as *DOAJ: Directory of Open Access Journals* (http://doaj.org) contains full-text articles of open-access journals, academic journals that are subscription-free. A search engine is unable to search in the contents of these journals. You will have to know about the *DOAJ* site and use its internal search engine. Likewise, fee-based periodical databases, such as *Historical Abstracts* or *America: History and Life*, or a collection of online scholarly full-text journals, such as *Project Muse*, will not allow search engines to index their sites. This is one reason you will not find journal articles from subscription-based journals *freely* available on the Internet. Not only can the bots and spiders not get to the journals' servers but also the particular journals control what is published and how and to whom it is delivered. Remember, usually if you want refereed journal articles, you must go to a periodical index, such as *Historical Abstracts* or *America: History and Life*. Not all information is free. Other web portals/ invisible web search engines try to search through important websites for a specialized subject. For instance, Science.gov (http://www.science.gov/) indexes resources from 50 science-related databases and about 2,100 federal agency websites. Science Research.com (http://scienceresearch.com/scienceresearch/search.html) intermixes journal articles (but does not provide full text of those articles) and other public science databases.[10] Parallel portals/invisible web search engines do not exist for history, as of this writing.

Other types of information not accessed by some search engines include files that are images (.jpg, .gif), audio files (.wav, .mp3, .ra, .au, .aiff,), and movies (.mov, .mpg). Some search engines have special sections that allow searching for these types of files. Below are websites that compile other websites generally inaccessible by many search engines. For a graphic representation of the invisible web, see: http://www.juanico.co.il/main%20frame%20-%20english/issues/information%20systems.htm.

General Sites for Searching the deep or invisible web

Complete Planet. http://www.completeplanet.com/ (accessed March 26, 2006). Searchable access to databases contained in its site.

Deep Peep. http://www.deeppeep.org/ (accessed November 3, 2011). Less academic. Allows you to search in forms.

Incywincy. http://www.incywincy.com/ (accessed November 3, 2011). Provides access to other sites with search engines and your search words.

Special Search Techniques: Finding Primary Sources on the Internet

The Internet has made primary sources available to many more scholars and others who would previously have been unable to view and use them. A wide range of primary source material exists on the Internet. These sources range from simple scanned images or a collection of oral histories from a local historical society (e.g., *Shema, Arizona Jewish Historical Society*, http://www.asu.edu/lib/archives/shema/shema.htm) to an elaborate museum exhibit (e.g., *Colonial Williamsburg*, http://www.history.org/history) or a collection of an individual's papers (e.g., *Thomas Jefferson's Papers*, http://memory.loc.gov/ammem/collections/jefferson_papers/). The Internet can also provide a group's documents (e.g., *European Union*, http://europa.eu/documentation/official-docs/index_en.htm) or a selection of primary sources from a given time period (e.g., *Civil Rights in Mississippi Digital Archive*, http://digilib.usm.edu/crmda.php; *The American Museum Congo Expedition, 1919–1915*, http://diglib1.amnh.org/) or region/country (e.g., *American Memory*, http://memory.loc.gov/ammem/amhome.html; *Gallica* [France], http://gallica.bnf.fr/). All of these sites are invaluable to a researcher. There are, however, some issues to consider with primary sources found on the Internet. Unlike a collection in an archive but similar to a printed collection, when you view a collection online, you have no idea what might be omitted by those who have created and compiled it. Digitizing an online collection is costly both in human time and in computer (server) space, so collections are necessarily selective and items may be left out. When working with a box of individual manuscripts, you select the important documents for your research and ignore other documents. You can look at all of the original markings on the documents. However, the well-meaning individuals doing the scanning may clean up a scanned image for readability and destroy the historical integrity of the original, including some peripheral marks, which may offer clues to its significance. High-quality collections should offer the original scanned image along with an electronically enhanced image. Collections may include guides that explain that what is online is only a selection from a larger collection and give more information about the whole collection.

Searching for Primary Sources

Searching for primary sources on the Internet can be just as challenging as searching for primary sources in print. The Internet has no assigned subject headings. First, browse one of the academic search directories listed above to find a specialized website that might include primary sources among its contents. Next, use several of the search engines to find a website that contains your primary source material. As already noted, search engines gather information from the web differently, so your results may differ from search engine to search engine. When searching in a search engine, use the most specific and concrete terms you can. For instance, do not enter broad search words that are really concepts, such as "imperialism." Rather, you should search for something like "(britain or british or england) and (india or empire)." Alternatively, you could do an image search or search for files that have an extension of .jpg or .gif. If you are looking for the Treaty of Greenville, a treaty between the United States and the Northwest Indian Confederation that ceded portions of territory in areas that are now known as Ohio and Indiana to the United States, then type in the title of that treaty. If you are looking for a specific form of primary source, an oral history for instance, incorporate that term into your search. The Internet will often use more common language, unlike an online catalog, as previously discussed, which uses controlled vocabulary, or standard subject terms. You may be able to guess at the searching terminology on the Internet, but unlike in the online catalog and other indexes, there is no guarantee others are using the same words.

SEARCH TIPS
1. Use specific and concrete search terms.
2. Use the advanced search features to search for images or to exclude words.
3. Type in specific titles of documents and speeches.

Historians Communicating: Using *H-Net* for Information

Other very important Internet tools for the historian are listservs or discussion lists and blogs. Until now, the casual but public conversations of professionals went largely unrecorded. *H-Net* (http://www.h-net.org/) contains a series of discussion lists where specialists query, respond to, and debate issues in the humanities. For example, on the *H-Slavery* list in March 2005, a scholar had a question concerning a ca. 1800 account of the West African slave trade that discussed the fuller tribe, referred to white slavers as "Baccaranas," and called slave ships "monstrous birds." The scholar wanted to know what others on the list knew about these references. Respondents suggested that "Fulani" were called "Foulah" and located on the Upper Guinea Coast. Another suggested that "Baccaranas" was really a reference to buccaneers. Another suggested that this term could have ties to an African or European language, citing possibilities from Portuguese, Spanish, and local languages, an example being "barracoon," a term for a slave pen to hold persons at the coast until sold onto a ship.[11] This virtual discussion opened up numerous avenues for further research and drew upon a number of different experts. Undoubtedly a discussion list for whatever area of history you are researching exists. Representing both the cutting edge of research and topics that continue to be of central concern to scholars, these lists will often include information that is impossible to find elsewhere. All of the lists at *H-Net* are searchable, so if you want to see what has been discussed on your topic, you can select a list and search within it. If you are serious about becoming a historian, you should join a list in your area of interest and follow its discussions. This is where you will make professional contacts, as well as see trends in the discipline. If you are struggling with an advanced history project and have already talked with your professor and your local librarian, you may wish to post, or perhaps ask your professor or teacher to post, a query to the appropriate list. Most of the participants on these lists would expect you to ask an advanced question after having done some research on your own.

Blogs continue to influence historical and political ideas and discourse. A blog, the word formed by the union of the words "web" and "log," is, in the words of historian Ralph Luker, "a commonplace journal maintained on the Internet, where it is accessible to other readers. . . . Blogs take a variety of forms from daily personal journals to occasional essays."[12] This form of communication offers a new avenue, other than the forms above, for historians to engage in historical discussion. For example, Sharon Howard, a British academic, on her website *Early Modern Resources* (http://earlymodernweb.org/), runs the *Early Modern Notes Weblog* (http://emn.sharonhoward.org/). Her weblog discusses such topics as eighteenth-century reactionaries, sources for research funding, and early modern "blood sports"/ball games. Blogs and listservs (e-mails distributed among a list of individuals to create an online discussion around a focused topic) are informal means of historical discussion. The website *History News Network* maintains a list of historical blogs called *Cliopatria* (http://hnn.us/blogs/2.html).[13] The history lab at the Institute of Historical Research (University of London) has created the History Blogging Project (http://www.historybloggingproject.org/) to help academic historians in the blogging process "as a method of public engagement for post-graduate historians." Modern blogs have evolved and become more like a website that integrates historical analysis, discourse, research, and resources, as opposed to simply a means to express its author's opinions. Be cautious and identify those blogs that seek academic discussion and contributions from those that are really more personal opinion on issues. See chapter 11 for a discussion on using blogs as a presentation method for your research.

Evaluation of Websites

No matter where your information originates on the web, you must be careful about its quality. The process of evaluating websites is not entirely different from the process of evaluating print secondary sources discussed in chapter 5. You must still consider the author's/creator's credentials and the accuracy of the information. In addition, you must consider the readability of the site and its currency, as well as certain navigation issues. Below is a basic checklist that will help you evaluate Internet material. There are numerous variations on these criteria. Your library may even have a set they recommend.

General Websites

Listed below are generally accepted criteria that are based on two excellent guides developed by Esther Grassian, a retired librarian from University of California Los Angeles.[14]

- *Authority*. Who produced the website and what do they know? Is this someone who has studied in the field? Is this person or organization the logical one to be creating a website about this topic? Look for a biography of the author and that author's credentials on the site. Check the domain (.edu, .com) that the website comes from. Is the website trying to sell you something? Is there a conflict of interest?
  - Example: *Institute For Historical Review* (IHR). http://www.ihr.org. An organization that argues with the documentation of the Holocaust, among other issues. Many historians question the authority of the authors of the articles published by the IHR and its publications and website. Authors often lack advanced historical credentials like a Ph.D. or practice in a related field or are journalists or not practitioners of history at all. Many historians also argue that the

primary sources used by the IHR to make claims, such as that the gas chambers never existed in the concentration camps or that there was no Nazi-organized attempt to exterminate the European Jews, are weak and used in a biased manner.

- *Audience.* For whom was the site created? If it was for Mrs. Smith's fourth-grade social studies class, the information may be too basic. If it was created for a general audience, it may not be academic enough to use in a scholarly research paper. This is the equivalent of using the *World Book Encyclopedia* for your research, a fine encyclopedia when you are in grade school but unacceptable for college-level research.

- *Accuracy and content.* Does the information appear accurate based on your research? Make comparisons with other web pages, journal articles, and books. Watch for inaccuracies with dates and other material. How is this website unique compared to other websites and print resources you have examined or read? In comparing other sources, can you detect controversy by looking at differences in the facts and analyses presented? Do you detect bias? Has the website been created by a person or an organization that has a viewpoint that might bias data? Is the collection and arrangement of the information sloppy? Look for inaccuracies if documents have been transcribed or retyped.

  • Example: Compare *Martin Luther King Jr.—A True Historical Examination* (http://martinlutherking.org) to *The King Center* (http://www.thekingcenter.org). The first site is created and maintained by someone who is sympathetic to the white supremacist movement. Not providing any individual author information but sponsored by Stormfront, a "white pride" organization, the site not only focuses on the controversial issues of Martin Luther King's life, such as plagiarism in his writings, but also includes tangential issues such as rap lyrics, Kwanzaa, and Jews and the civil rights movement. Heavily showcased is a book by David Duke, who is closely affiliated with the Ku Klux Klan. In contrast, *The King Center*, the recognized authority site, seeks to present and preserve King's papers and scholarly writings and to publicize programs about his legacy.

  • Example: History of Robots in the Victorian Era (http://bigredhair.com/robots/). Although the url is a dead giveaway (but useful sites can have unconventional urls), this site looks rather credible until you realize that the state of technology in the Victorian era would prohibit the creation of these robots.

- *Currency.* When was the website last revised? Old information can be false, inaccurate, and, in some cases, harmful. Websites unrevised for over two years probably are not very useful for scholarly research. While historical information does not have a "shelf life," abandoned websites will not be checked for inaccuracies nor add new findings and current debates.
- *Navigability and structure.* Do the links work well, or are most of them dead? Is the site logically organized? If you cannot find your resources, does it matter what the site contains? Websites lend themselves to the integration of "chunks" or distinct paragraphs of text coupled with illustrative photographs, documents, and links to other websites. This method of conveying information is a different process from a printed book or journal article. Does the website use the web/hypertext format well?

Rely on your own gut instinct as well. If the website appears too good to be true and you cannot find an authoritative author or producer, then it probably is not as good as it seems. Another way to help you decide the quality of a website is to evaluate the web pages that list it as a link. In the *Google* or *AltaVista* search box, you can type "link:" in the search box and then copy the address of the web page in which you are interested. The results will have links to that particular page. Remember that a popular page does not always mean quality; it could be the universal example of a bad page.

Evaluating Sites Concerned with Primary Sources

The Public History Resource Center offers additional criteria for websites that include primary sources.[15]

- *Quality of scans of documents and images.* Has the integrity of the original image been preserved? Are there mechanisms such as enlarging to enhance the image for better examination? Has the document been transcribed to assist you in reading the handwriting?
- *Searchability.* Is the text of the documents searchable? Is there also a subject search? As historical concepts are hard to find through a keyword search, a directory or subject listing for a website is useful.
- *Bibliography or webliography.* Is a list of materials for further research, both print and web-based, included?

▪ *Interpretive or descriptive materials.* Are there added materials that help you understand the collection? Since you cannot see the original "box" of materials, how will you get a sense of the whole collection? Is the interpretation by someone who is an authority?

The Internet can be a valuable resource for your historical research. However, just as with any other research tool, you must know how to use it critically and effectively, as the *Institute for Historical Review* and the *martinlutherking.org* sites illustrate.

Case Study—Using the Internet: Japanese Americans and Internment Camps

You have selected your general topic of Japanese Americans and their incarceration in camps in the United States during World War II. While you develop a thesis statement with your professor, you can begin searching on the web.

1. Use a search *directory* to begin your search. Often, you will find the best information without having to search through pages of irrelevant results from a search engine. For instance, if you go to *WWW-VL: History* and search by decade 1940–1949, you will find a section entitled, *Major Events—Japanese American Incarceration* with a listing of about 16 websites. For example:

▪ *Suffering under a Great Injustice: Ansel Adams's Photographs of Japanese American Internment at Manzanar.* http://memory.loc.gov/ammem/aamhtml/aamhome.html.

▪ *Camp Harmony Exhibit.* http://www.lib.washington.edu/exhibits/harmony/Exhibit/

2. Use one or two of the search engines listed to find other resources to add to your list above. Using *Google*, you could, in this case, use the basic search and type in the keyword box "japanese american internment camps." As you know search engines search through many thousands more sites than a search directory organizes, you would want to be more specific, perhaps the name of a camp or a location, with your search criteria as you have no subject categories to browse once your search is complete.

Historically, American soldiers were also "interned" as prisoners in Japan, so your results may reflect a completely different topic if you are not careful. Some possible useful results follow:

- *Japanese American Relocation Digital Archives*. http://jarda.cdlib.org/.
- *Children of the Camps*. http://www.pbs.org/childofcamp/.

If you felt you wanted more images, you could do *Google* search and click on the images link on the left. You could also look through Flickr (http://www.flickr.com/).

3. Make sure you evaluate your sources. Use the criteria above.

FOR FURTHER READING

American Social History Project, Center for Media and Learning and the Center for History and New Media. *History Matters*, http://historymatters.gmu.edu/ (accessed January 10, 2006).
  Online history textbook for American history. Has many links to projects, readings, and assignments, as well as other websites.
Center for History and the New Media. *World History Matters*, http://chnm.gmu.edu/worldhistorysources/ (accessed April 28, 2012).
  Online history textbook for world history. Has many links to projects, readings, and assignments, as well as other websites.
Center for Teaching History with Technology, http://thwt.org/ (accessed April 28, 2012).
  List of sites that include teaching techniques for K–12.
Craver, Kathleen W. *Using Internet Primary Sources to Teach Critical Thinking Skills in History*. Westport, CT: Greenwood Press, 1999.
  Assignments with study questions for upper-division secondary school students and college-level students.
Drobnicki, John A., and Richard Asaro. "Historical Fabrications on the Internet: Recognition, Evaluation, and Use in Bibliographic Instruction." *In Evolution in Reference and Information Services: The Impact of the Internet*. ed. Di Su. Binghamton, NY: Hayworth Press, 2001.
Trinkle, Dennis A., and Scott A. Merriman, eds. *The American Highway: A Guide to Internet Resources on U.S., Canadian, and Latin American Resources*. Armonk, NY: M. E. Sharpe, 2007.
  Print bibliography of websites focused on world history. Some duplication in the "general" section with the *History Highway* below.

Trinkle, Dennis A., and Scott A. Merriman, eds. *The History Highway: A 21st Century Guide to Internet Resources*. 4d ed. Armonk, NY: M. E. Sharpe, 2006. Huge print bibliography of websites organized by country and general subject. However, because a printed book can be dated and websites disappear, some links might be out of date.

Trinkle, Dennis A., ed. *Writing, Teaching and Researching History in the Electronic Age: Historians and Computers*. Armonk, NY: M. E. Sharpe, 1998. Series of essays that include using computers in the classrooms to teach history, as well as examples of nontraditional history projects.

Vaidhyanathan, Siva. *The Googlization of Everything: (and Why We Should Worry)*. Berkeley: University of California Press, 2011.

NOTES

1. Carl Smith, "Can You do Serious History on the Web?" *AHA Perspectives* (February 1998), http://www.historians.org/perspectives/issues/1998/9802/9802COM.CFM and http://chnm.gmu.edu/resources/essays/serioushistory.php (accessed September 6, 2011).

2. Library of Congress, *A Century of Lawmaking for a New Nation: U.S. Congressional Documents and Debates, 1774–1875*, http://memory.loc.gov/ammem/amlaw/lawhome.html (accessed September 6, 2011).

3. Ran Hock, "A New Era of Search Engines: Not Just Web Pages Anymore," *Online* 26 (September/October 2002): 20–27; Jane Devine and Francine Egger-Sider, *Going Beyond Google: The Invisible Web in Learning and Teaching* (New York: Neal-Schuman Publishers, Inc., 2009), 5–6, 12.

4. For some of the initiatives, see *Web Archiving Bibliography*, from the Austrian Online Archive, http://www.ifs.tuwien.ac.at/~aola/links/WebArchiving.html (accessed September 6, 2011).

5. HTML is the scripting language used to create the traditional web page.

6. *Institute for Historical Review*, http://www.ihr.org/ (accessed September 6, 2011). Not to be confused with the very reputable British *Institute of Historical Research*, http://history.ac.uk (accessed September 6, 2011).

7. "Google Bomb," *Wikipedia*, http://en.wikipedia.org/wiki/Google_bomb, and "Google Bomb," *Links and Law: Information about Legal Aspects of Search Engines, Linking, and Framing*, http://www.linksandlaw.com/technicalback-ground-google-bombing.htm (both accessed December 30, 2011).

8. For an interesting comparison of search engines, see Greg Notess's web page, http://searchengineshowdown.com/. See also http://searchenginewatch.com (both accessed September 6, 2011).

9. Charles Deering McCormick Library of Special Collections, Northwestern University Library. *The Siege and Commune of Paris, 1870–1871*, http://www.library.northwestern.edu/spec/siege/ (accessed December 30, 2011). A more in-depth discussion of the invisible web can be found in Devine and Egger-Sider. See also *Beyond Google: The Invisible Web: Invisible Web-ography*, http://library.laguardia.edu/invisibleweb/webography (accessed November 3, 2011).

10. Devine and Egger-Sider, *Going Beyond Google*, 104–105.

11. Eric Gardner, "Fuller Tribe, Baccaranas and Monstrous Birds," *H-Slavery*, March 23, 2005, http://www.h-net.org/~slavery/; Rachel G. Malcolm-Woods, "Fuller Tribe, Baccaranas and Monstrous Birds," *H-Slavery*, March 23, 2005, http://www.h-net.org/~slavery/; Christopher Lowe, "Fuller Tribe, Baccaranas and Monstrous Birds," *H-Slavery*, March 23, 2005, http://www.h-net.org/~slavery/; Jacqueline Knoerr, "Fuller Tribe, Baccaranas and Monstrous Birds," *H-Slavery*, March 23, 2005, http://www.h-net.org/~slavery/ (all accessed September 6, 2011).

12. Ralph E. Luker, "Were There Blog Enough and Time," *Perspectives* (May 2005), http://www.historians.org/perspectives/issues/2005/0505/0505tec1.cfm (accessed November 3, 2011).

13. Ibid.

14. Esther Grassian, *Thinking Critically and World Wide Web Resources*, http://www.library.ucla.edu/libraries/college/11605_12337.cfm (accessed November 3, 2011) and *Thinking Critically about Discipline-Based World Wide Web Resources*, http://www.library.ucla.edu/libraries/college/help/critical/discipline.htm (accessed January 5, 2006); see also *Evaluating Web Pages: Techniques to Apply and Questions to Ask* (U.C. Berkeley Library), http://www.lib.berkeley.edu/TeachingLib/Guides/Internet/Evaluate.html (accessed November 3, 2011). For an alternative approach, see Marc Meola, "Chucking the Checklist: A Contextual Approach to Teaching Undergraduates Web-Site Evaluation," *portal: Libraries and the Academy* 4 (July 2003): 331–344. See also Esther Grassian's website at https://sites.google.com/site/teachinfolit/ (accessed November 3, 2011). Esther Grassian, retired librarian, still maintains a website for information literacy with many of her former websites. See: https://sites.google.com/site/teachinfolit/.

15. Debra DeRuyver, Jennifer Evans, James Melzer, and Emma Wilmer, *Evaluating Web Sites* (Public History Resource Center Rating System, April 30, 2000), http://www.publichistory.org/evaluation/index2.html (accessed November 3, 2011).

Maps: From Simple to Geographic Information Systems

8

WHAT YOU WILL LEARN IN THIS CHAPTER

- the historical uses of maps
- how to understand the components of modern maps
- how to read and evaluate a map
- how to find maps and atlases for your research
- how Geographic Information Systems work and how to plan a small historical map

---

Maps as Representations of Our World

Our lives are filled with geographical references, conveying a sense of place and space. It is hard to imagine life without the visual representation and accuracy of the maps we use to navigate city streets, mark land plot ownership, and watch weather patterns. Historically, maps were not always so representational of a spot on the globe. Prior to ca. 1450 and the Age of Discovery, large area and world maps tended to express worldview philosophies, indicative of the religious and spiritual beliefs or concerns of the mapmakers and their nations. Local maps of villages and cities did often reflect actual on-the-ground features but were not drawn with accurate measurements or "to scale." Driven by exploration and trade, *cartographers*, or drawers of maps, were compelled to create more accurate navigational maps.[1] Not until after World War II did the maps and atlases commonly used to express sociocultural trends begin to appear in textbooks and in many newspapers and magazines. Contemporary maps and atlases, such as Collins' *Atlas of Twentieth Century History*, contain maps on desertification, sea pollution, and incidences of acquired immunodeficiency syndrome (AIDS) worldwide.[2] Maps and atlases also compare and illustrate data such as gross domestic product, life expectancy, and water quality. More recently, technology has enabled individuals other than cartographers to create maps and to incorporate data that allow for in-depth study of geographic patterns. Studying history through the use of visual material, including maps, can dramatically change certain long-held historical beliefs. For instance, the maps associated with the *Salem Witch Trials Documentary Archive* (http://etext.lib.virginia.edu/ salem/witchcraft/) reveal that the concentration of accusations of witches was greater in Andover than in Salem, Massachusetts. This new way of compiling and examining data geographically has changed the traditional focus of witchcraft from Salem to Andover.[3]

This chapter presents a short history of the evolution of maps and atlases and discusses common types and uses of maps throughout history to help you to knowledgeably incorporate this primary source into your research. Then, the components of a map, "reading" and evaluating a map, and finding maps are covered. Finally, you may decide you want to make your own, using Geographic Information Systems (GIS) or other mapping software. Some tips on using this software and organizing a map will be offered.

A Short History of Maps and Cartography

Geographers define a map as a "graphic representation, drawn to scale and usually on a flat surface, of features—for example, geographical, geological, or geopolitical—of an area of the Earth or of any other celestial body."[4] Yet, Chinese philosophy saw the world in concentric rings drawn around a globe. Babylonians drew the world as flat plains connected by stairs. Neither of these maps of the world was based on observation of the physical environment of the earth or the sky.[5] The Age of Discovery, fueled by trade and colonization, made world and large regional navigational maps necessary. These maps contained greater detail, included physical features, and encompassed larger areas and regions. In early maps, the hallmarks that are valued in modern maps, such as scale and legend, were seldom present. Maps come in all shapes and sizes and have been drawn on clay tablets, parchment, and animal skin, as well as paper.

In 1595, the first publication using the term "atlas" in the title originated with a collection of European maps from the cartographer Gerhardus Mercator (1512–1594) (aka Gerhard de Kremer).[6] Several types of historical atlases exist. In fact, the term "atlas" covers the more traditional collection of maps, as well as something that looks and reads much more like a book or encyclopedia in that it contains more explanatory and analytical text than a map. Other atlases assemble a collection of color-coded maps that display information including the changes of territory over time, the spread of a particular disease, or the measure of economic stability in a certain period. Some provide a significant amount of textual explanation, while others are simply maps. Technically, an atlas could also take the form of a website, one example being *Images of Early Maps on the Web*.[7] In this chapter, "map" will refer to the many forms in which maps are created, including atlases.

Maps for Navigation and Commercial Use

Much of what has been discussed above refers to maps as commercial or navigational primary sources. Each of these necessary functions changed the map from a more philosophical expression to a more practical object. As navigational and commercial tools, maps highlighted the best trade routes for goods (the Silk Road, for example, the caravan trade route that connected Mediterranean Europe and the Middle East and China [Asia]); charted the sea coasts of North and South America for explorers as early as the 1500s; and provided road highway routes for vacationers in the post–World War II US vacation boom.

Maps as Political Tools

Maps can be used as political tools to purposely or inadvertently indicate control over a particular territory, country, or peoples. English monarch Elizabeth I commissioned Christopher Saxton to perform a topographic survey of England and Wales, resulting in a large, decorative, printed atlas entitled *Atlas of England and Wales* (1579). The atlas unified England in a book of maps just as Elizabeth ruled a unified England. It was a symbol of her controlling power.[8] Artwork on the map identifies Elizabeth as the patron of geography and astronomy.[9] However, it was not until later, in the nineteenth century, that the genre of nationalistic atlases produced other maps. Beginning in the 1920s and 1930s, colonies of European nations gained their freedom, and some began producing atlases as one method of declaring independence.[10] Prior to independence, in the seventeenth to the nineteenth centuries, many peoples on the continents of Africa and Asia were colonized by the United States and western European nations, creating disputed claims over territory. Mapmakers of neutral nations were often faced with trying to decide whom to label as colonial rulers or occupiers.[11] In other cases, disagreement between two nations caused different names to be given to the same land features. The name for the body of water between Japan and Korea has been in dispute for many centuries, with Korean maps labeling it the "East Sea" and Japanese maps the "Sea of Japan." Historically, cartographers have also labeled it the "Sea of Korea" or the "Oriental Sea." Nations may also have political agendas that lead them to exclude or even distort certain aspects of their countries.

In a twentieth-century example of unintentional cultural dominance, geographer Robert Rundstrom reports on a health project using GIS (Geographic Information System) to map Zuni Indians' residences in their small towns and villages (*pueblos*) to enhance health-care delivery. These residences have no house numbers, nor do the pueblos have street names. The data collectors ended up using mostly English names to identify locations, with a few Zuni words if they could be rendered into English and were "not too humorous."[12] This is an example of assimilation by map, even if the intentions of the mapmakers were to improve the delivery of health care to the Zuni.

Maps as Propaganda

Maps can also be used to create a skewed opinion or present a desired version of reality. In the 1920s and 1930s, many English-language textbooks used Ellsworth Huntington's (1876–1947) map of "The Distribution of Civilization," which was blatantly imperialistic and racist and differentiated the "civilized" nations from the "backward" nations. In 1939 and 1940, Nazi cartographers portrayed Germany as surrounded by hostile neighbors, to gain sympathy and sway support from a still neutral American public.[13] In the twentieth century, *The Nuclear War Atlas* attempted to illustrate the horrors of the effects of a nuclear war by showing the numbers of anticipated deaths and in what areas those deaths would occur. In none of these cases are the data on these maps so much "wrong" as they are so subjective that even when scientifically based, as in the *Nuclear War Atlas*, they have a specific message to convey that sometimes obscures other facts.[14] Understanding purpose is especially important in understanding how maps can be used in your research. Chapter 5 provides tips on how to identify and evaluate propaganda.

Maps Marking Territory

Maps have also been used to indicate personal and public territory. Roman landowners, as well as medieval landlords, paid mapmakers to draw the extent of their estates. Hardly the epitome of modern mapmaking replete with precision or scale, such a map symbolized the landowner's reach of authority, as well as served the purpose of a record for collecting taxes owed by those living and farming on these lands on behalf of the landowner.[15] These maps not only marked who lived where but also indicated crop yields, size of livestock herds, and forests for hunting. To register land ownership for taxation purposes and redistribution, governments, churches, and other official bodies used this kind of mapping, called *cadastral*. For example, in ancient Egypt, the Nile River flooded annually and land ownership boundaries had to be reestablished. In post–World War II Europe, such maps were used to redistribute land confiscated by the Nazis.[16]

Maps in War

Poorly made maps have wrought havoc in military maneuvers. In *How to Lie with Maps*, Mark Monmonier provides excellent examples of the problems of poor maps. During the U.S. Civil War, part of General George B. McClellan's inability to reach Richmond, Virginia, and take control of the Confederate capitol in 1862 was due to inaccurate topographic maps that did not indicate obstacles, such as hills, which hindered Union troop movements. In the 1983 invasion of Grenada, US troops relied on outdated and inaccurate British topographic and tourist maps, which led to both the bombing of a mental hospital, not indicated on the map, and an air strike that killed US troops because the field commanders and the bombers had different maps and grids.[17] As a ploy to protect their country from enemies during the Cold War, Soviet cartographers intentionally moved, distorted, or omitted cities and natural features, such as rivers or coastlines, on maps.[18]

Components of Modern Maps

Understanding the basic parts of a modern map, one that pays great attention to physical detail and accuracy, will help you to evaluate the evidence it provides. Maps have certain features, some of which are generally common to all well-designed maps. Legend, scale, and direction are essential

Land Use

Cultivated

Woodland

Pasture

Fallow

Settlement

Figure 8.1. Example of a map legend which defines the symbols on a map.

to understanding the markings and their spatial relationships on a map. The other features addressed below are commonly, but not universally, found on maps.

- *Legend.* The legend defines the features and symbols of the map. It tells you what the colors and symbols mean and may include measurements. It is often located near one of the corners of the map (see fig. 8.1).

- *Scale.* The scale describes the relationship between the paper map space and the actual physical space on the earth. This is reflected in two ways, by a bar which allows for physical measurement, with a ruler, and by a ratio scale such as 1:100,000, where 1 centimeter on the map reflects 1 kilometer on the face of the earth. Maps are sometimes referred to as "large-scale" or "small-scale." Large-scale maps show greater detail because they cover a smaller area. But, for example, Native American maps do not have scale. Digital delivery of maps makes scale problematic. Scale is often useless on the Internet because the size of computer screens, as well as type size vary and thus prevent measurement with a ruler. Imprecise drawing of scale is one reason that using historical maps with modern maps in GIS is difficult (see fig. 8.2).

1 inch equals 67 miles

0   30   60   120   180   240

Miles

Figure 8.2. Example of scale with verbal scale. The scale, the ruler-like line, graphically defines the relationship (area) on the paper to the real, physical world. Above the line is a verbal scale which describes this relationship in words.

- *Coordinates.* Every place on earth has a location that crosses latitude and longitude. Obviously, city streets and cross streets lie in the same latitudinal and longitudinal plane; thus, a city street map would not have this feature, nor do many older maps.

- *Direction.* Compass points, or at least a direction marker indicating north, should appear on the map.

- *Elevation.* Wavy lines, called *isolines*, denote how high or low land is as well as landforms above and below sea level. These are prevalent on topographical maps.

Of these features, the legend is the most crucial to your research and to understanding the map. The legend tells you, for instance, that gray arrows on a US Civil War map might mark the movement of Confederate troops at the Battle of Gettysburg. Looking next for some directional marker, you would see if they moved north or south across the field of battle. A legend might also tell you that a skull-and-crossbones icon on a map illustrates the spread of the plague in fourteenth-century Europe.

Finding Maps

Categories of Historical Maps

Thinking historically about maps and their formats, types, and perspectives will help you integrate them into your research. Some specific types of maps and their uses include:[19]

1. *Itinerary maps.* In the Middle Ages merchants and pilgrims used strip maps that marked a single route with the hostels, areas of dangers, and impeding geographic features that travelers would encounter. Modern types of itinerary maps would include highway maps and *Google* maps that identify roads, interstate stops, restaurants, gas stations, and other landmarks.

2. *Birds-eye views/Town views/Aerial Maps.* Cartographers created the perspective of looking down on a city or area, enabling users to see street interconnectivity and locations of places of interest. Early maps in this format were not to scale, but still indicated locations and helped individuals navigate through a city. In World War I and the succeeding decades, cartographers and governments used aerial photography to produce images of a battlefield, a house, or an area for prospective development. In recent years, digital satellite maps, such as *Google Maps* and *Google Earth*, previously only available to defense agencies, can be used by the general public to

zoom in from space to a specific address and show images of buildings and streets.

3. *Ordinance and Plat Maps.* These types of maps tend to be more accurate, as they are drawn to scale and are the result of an official survey. Generally, they indicate boundaries of land, land ownership, and land use (for instance, agricultural or manufacturing). Often local or national governments commission their creation. Historic county atlases often provide similar information. While ward maps are slightly different, they too mark territory for census and other local government activities. Generally, ordinance is a British term and plat is an American term for maps that demarcate land boundaries.

4. *Fire Insurance Maps.* These types of maps were created to look at urban areas to assess fire liability and potential. Maps indicate individual buildings, the purpose of those buildings, and the type of construction. For instance, where dwellings or commercial buildings were located, what they were used for, and if their construction was brick, frame, and so on. In the United States a major producer was Sanborn; in the United Kingdom, Charles E. Goad.

Map Resources

Many general and very specific collections of historical atlases and maps are available both in print and on the Internet. Below are examples of atlases and maps available in print and on selected websites. All have copyright restrictions. (See chapter 9 for a discussion on copyright.) For maps, there is a copyright-free solution with a series called *Maps on File* and *Historical Maps on File*, which provides outline maps onto which you can draw your own features. The result is fairly low-tech but will provide you with a custom map, without having to learn geographic information software like ArcGIS. Another copyright-free solution is, of course, creating your own maps from scratch.

To find other maps, use the following search tips in your library's catalog or in *Worldcat*.

SEARCH TIPS

1. Do a broad subject search on a country, continent, or region.
2. Limit the results by words in the subject maps or words in the title atlas.

Selected Historical Atlases

Atlas of American History. 2d rev. ed. New York: Scribner, 1984. Black-and-white maps arranged chronologically. Indexed. Supplements the *Dictionary of American History*.

Times History of the World. 5th ed. Geoffrey Barraclough, ed. London: Times, 1999. The *Times* atlas is a standard, high-quality world atlas with a European view of world history.

Atlas of World History. Jeremy Black, ed. New York: Dorling Kindersley, 2000. Richly illustrated atlas of world history.

Historical Atlas. 9th ed. rev. William R. Shepherd. New York: Barnes & Noble, 1980. Standard historical atlas that covers 1450 B.C.E. to 1980. Includes color maps and index.

Atlas of Islam, 1800–2000. Andreas Birken. Leiden: Brill, 2010. New and up to date.

Routledge Atlas of Russian History. 3d ed. Martin Gilbert. New York: Routledge, 2002. Black-and-white line-drawing maps with boxes to explain significance of maps and their markings. This is an example of a number of historical atlases Routledge has published. Search in a catalog for *Routledge Atlas* by title to see a fuller listing.

David Rumsey Map Collection. http://www.davidrumsey.com (accessed December 30, 2011). Vast collection of historical maps from private collector, David Rumsey. With the use of GIS, some maps are three-dimensional.

Map Collections: American Memory. http://memory.loc.gov/ammem/gmdhtml/gmdhome.html (accessed December 30, 2011). From the Library of Congress' collections. A wide variety of maps, mostly concentrated on the United States, but includes some from other countries.

Maps for Students. http://www.unc.edu/awmc/mapsforstudents.html (accessed December 30, 2011). Maps of the ancient world.

Historical Maps on File. New York: Facts on File, 1984– . Updated periodically. Maps of events and places of historical significance. Designed to be photocopied and altered.

Outline Maps. Houghton Mifflin Online. http://www.eduplace.com/ss/maps/ (accessed December 30, 2011). For educational purposes (.pdf files).

Examples of Sites with Interactive or Online Historical Maps

Africa Maps. http://library.stanford.edu/depts/ssrg/africa/map.html (accessed December 30, 2011). Listing of maps, in various formats.

Afriterra. http://www.afriterra.org/ (accessed December 30, 2011). Nonprofit organization to preserve rare African maps. Small but growing online collection.

Alabama Historical Map Archive. http://alabamamaps.ua.edu/historicalmaps/ (accessed December 30, 2011). Digital images of maps from a number of Alabama institutions, although coverage is worldwide.

Blaeu Atlas. http://www.library.ucla.edu/yrl/reference/maps/blaeu/ (accessed January 1, 2006). Seventeenth-century atlas of Europe.

China Historical GIS. http://www.fas.harvard.edu/~chgis/ (accessed December 30, 2011). Historic maps and sketches of Chinese land throughout history.

Cyndi's List of Maps. http://www.cyndislist.com/maps.htm (accessed December 30, 2011). Part of a genealogical list, good for local maps.

Electronic Cultural Atlas Initiative. http://www.ecai.org/ (accessed December 30, 2011). Links to online atlas projects. Worldwide in coverage, all time periods.

Euratlas. http://www.euratlas.com (accessed December 30, 2011). Swiss company specializing in reflection European history in modern renderings.

Great Britain Historical GIS Project. http://www.port.ac.uk/research/gbhgis/ (accessed December 30, 2011). Collection of digital information about Great Britain, useful for creating electronic maps.

Hargrett Rare Map Library. http://www.libs.uga.edu/hargrett/maps/index.html (accessed December 30, 2011). Primarily US historical maps.

Historic Cities. http://historic-cities.huji.ac.il/ (accessed December 30, 2011). Maps of cities of the world throughout history, as well as future renderings taken from books, documents, and other similar sources.

Historic Maps in K–12 Classrooms. http://publications.newberry.org/k12maps/ (accessed December 30, 2011). American history maps for teaching from the Newberry Library.

Historical Atlas of the Twentieth Century. http://users.erols.com/mwhite28/20centry.htm (accessed December 30, 2011).

Historical Text Archive: Maps. http://historicaltextarchive.com/links.php?op5viewslink&sid50&cid510 (accessed December 30, 2011). Links to other collections.

Mapping History. http://mappinghistory.uoregon.edu/ (accessed December 30, 2011). Interactive maps to highlight issues in American, Latin American, African, and European history.

Maps of Scotland. http://maps.nls.uk/ (accessed December 30, 2011). Covers 1560–1929.

Perry Castañeda Map Collection. http://www.lib.utexas.edu/maps/map_sites/hist_sites.html (accessed December 30, 2011). From the University of Texas at Austin's collection of maps. Historical section organized by continent, country, or region.

Salem Witch Trials Historical Maps. http://jefferson.village.virginia.edu/salem/maps.html (accessed December 30, 2011).

Sanborn Fire Insurance Maps. Teaneck, NJ: Chadwyck-Healy/ProQuest, http://sanborn.umi.com/ (accessed December 30, 2011). Maps of US cities and towns with buildings and their uses marked. Used by fire insurance companies. The *ProQuest* database is fee-based. Check with your library to see if you have access. Some individual states have been providing free online access to selected maps of cities in their own states. For example, Utah, http://www.lib.utah.edu/digital/sanborn/browse.html, and Virginia, http://fisher.lib.virginia.edu/collections/maps/sanborn/. In addition, many libraries have print and microfilm copies.

Historical GIS Network. http://www.hgis.org.uk/resources.htm (accessed December 30, 2011). Links to other collections of interactive maps.

National Historical Geographic Information System (NHGIS). https://www.nhgis.org/ (accessed December 30, 2011). Mostly US census data.

Gazetteers

Another geographical tool useful for locating places on a map are *gazetteers*, or dictionaries of places. Places include cities, states, administrative divisions, and natural features. Gazetteers provide facts about a place (such as population) and include coordinates (such as longitude and latitude) to locate that place on a map. They are especially useful for those places that have disappeared or are difficult to locate because they are so small.

Selected Gazetteers

Columbia Gazetteer of the World. Saul B. Cohen, ed. New York: Columbia University Press, 1998. Provides population, exact location, and very brief description of cities, states, countries, areas, territories, and so on.

Place-Name Changes 1900–1991. Adrian Room. Metuchen, NJ: Scarecrow Press, 1993. Name changes in all countries, especially post–World War II and the post-Soviet era. Refers to new name of place.

Getty Thesaurus of Geographic Names. http://www.getty.edu/research/tools/vocabularies/tgn/index.html (accessed December 30, 2011). Place-names related to history, archaeology, and art.

How to Read a Map

Reading between the latitude and longitude, or between the lines as it were, when interpreting a map is a bit more complex. Remember, by their nature maps are a distortion of reality or a representation of the perception of reality. They represent a three-dimensional object, the earth, on a flat surface. Often, what is at the center of a map is what the cartographer has chosen as the focus of attention. This will give you a clue as to the purpose of a particular map. It is just as important to identify what has been left off of a map as it is to analyze what has been included.[20] For example, Martin Gilbert, in his map "The Intifada, February 1992" from *The Atlas of the Arab–Israeli Conflict*, includes a box of information with statistics indicating that Palestinians were killed by Israeli and Palestinian troops.[21] However, Gilbert makes no mention of the Israeli-backed occupation of Lebanon, even though he makes mention of the border. He also includes the West Bank as a part of Israel, when Palestinians consider this area independent territory. Gilbert is not intentionally trying to deceive, and his atlases are excellent and instructive; but like any other author, he has a perspective from which he is presenting his information.[22]

Questions to Ask When Reading a Map

While some modern-day cartographers and others who create atlases may have unintentional biases, mapmakers in the past have had both overt and covert agendas in their creation of maps and atlases. Be sure to "read" and evaluate your map. Ask these questions[23]

1. What is at the center of the map? The culture of the mapmaker tends to be at the center of the map. This is evident in maps of the Indians of North America as well as in twelfth-century Islamic maps.

2. What is in the margins? More than just artwork, decoration in the margins of maps can be signs of a monarch's power (what he or she has dominion over), examples of the local flora or fauna, or symbols of the local religion or mythology. More modern maps might include points of interest that no longer exist.

3. Who was the map made for and why? Every map has a purpose and an audience. This would explain why certain features are included on a map and some are excluded.

4. What is missing from the map? Not only does this help you to date the map, but it hints at the quality of the map as well as the possibility

that the cartographer is intentionally trying to deceive his or her audience. What is absent from a map can create just as interesting a study as what is on it.

5. What is the perspective of the mapmaker/cartographer? Understanding this perspective is just as crucial as understanding the perspective of the author of a text. Aside from cultural influences, the cartographer also has a purpose for creating the map and perspective from which he or she analyzes the contents.

6. Was the map part of a collection of single-sheet series maps, a printed atlas, or another printed work, such as a book or magazine? In the latter two cases, might it have been meant as a visual companion to a verbal description, which could affect what is included on the map? In the former case, a single legend may exist on one of the sheets that may fit together to form a larger map.

7. How was it made? By professional survey? What is the quality of the drawing and engraving or printing? This is particularly crucial if your map was created before the advent of modern mapmaking tools and common survey practices.

Planning Your Own Map: Simple to Complex

You may decide that you have collected some interesting and unique facts and data and that you want to illustrate your results by designing your own map. With the development of desktop GIS software, you can create a fairly simple map in a short amount of time. However, before beginning a project, you need to understand that GIS is not simply the computerization of colored pencil drawings on an outline map. Instead, it is a new way of visually and analytically thinking about your historical research. Although simple maps can be created with the software, you need to think about whether or not GIS is the proper tool for your needs because it can be challenging to use.

Simply put, GIS allows you to take layers of data that have a spatial relationship and stack them together on a map. The following is a more complex definition from geographer Anne Kelly Knowles:

[GIS] digitally links locations and their attributes so that they can be displayed in maps and analyzed, whether by their geographical characteristics such as location, proximity, density, and dispersal, or by their attributes, such as social, economic, and physical characteristics.[24]

In their article "Using GIS for Spatial and Temporal Analyses in Print Culture Studies,"[25] library historians Bertrum H. MacDonald and Fiona A. Black graphically show how the layers of variables of book culture can be compiled and explained geographically in a city. In this case, they consider the variables of book production and locations of bookstores and libraries with migration patterns, demographic information, and transportation routes. These data on a map would show the relationship of the availability of text (bookstores, libraries, and publishers) to readers (migration, transportation, and demographics such as population) (fig. 8.3).

By layering data, much in the same way one might layer transparencies of maps, although in much greater complexity, GIS allows the discovery of new spatial relationships. If you change the arrangement of your data, it is possible to arrive at different conclusions, as in the case of the Salem witch trials discussed earlier in the chapter. Through animation, GIS also has more complex features that will allow you to reflect change over time.

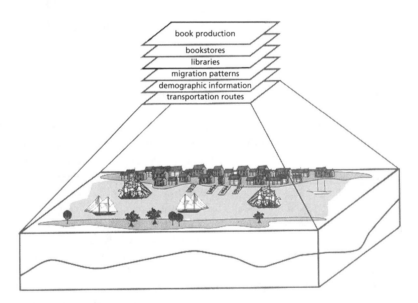

Figure 8.3. A graphic representation of the way GIS layers data or variables. MacDonald and Black's suggested ways in which GIS could be applied to understand a fuller picture of literacy rates and the availability of the printed word (through libraries and booksellers). Bertrum H. MacDonald and Fiona A. Black, "Using GIS for Spatial and Temporal Analyses in Print Culture Studies," *Social Science History* 24 (Fall 2000): 510. ©*Elsevier and reprinted with permission Elsevier, MacDonald and Black.*

You should consult your professor or librarian if you wish to reflect this kind of complex geographic relationship of ideas.

In preparation for creating your own map, first consider a few issues. Planning out what you want your map to include and what features it will illuminate is the most important step. Much like planning a website or preparing to do a bibliographic database search, you must decide on your major topics and components. What are you trying to compare and correlate? Can your ideas be reflected in data (a statistical table), or are they more conceptual (more bookstores mean a more literate population, as in the example above)? Why are these ideas reflected better visually, on a map, rather than in a chart, bar graph, or textual description? Will you need more than one map to reflect your data? Cramming too much information onto one map will dilute your analysis because no one will be able to see your correlations.

To set up the contents of your map, think in terms of themes and attributes (sometimes called "features"). For example, if you are trying to map troop movements during a battle, a theme could be something as simple as roads with attributes such as name, width, length, type (gravel or dirt), location (east, west), control (French or British), number of troops transported, and so forth. When you combine your data for roads, trenches, and field movements for a specific geographic area, you have a database. You may also want to think in layers. In the past, complex maps were created by laying a series of transparencies over a basic outline map. This is one way to reflect change over time. The most common piece of software used for creating maps, ArcGIS, has the ability to create tables and layers, as well as to link these to maps. Thinking through the relationship of your data and the components of the map prior to beginning your map project will help you produce a meaningful map.

You might think that overlaying a historical map onto a modern map to demonstrate change over time would suit your purposes. Beware: superimposing a historical map onto a present-day map is sometimes impossible. Prior to aerial photography, map scales were imprecise.[26] For instance, placing an eighteenth-century map of London on a modern map of London to illustrate change will probably not work because the scales would not match, due to the earlier cartographer's imprecise measurements. If you do decide to use an older map, it is recommended that you scan the map at a higher resolution.[27] Then you can perform a process known as *georectifying*, which assigns real-world coordinates to the historical map. In addition, if you decide to build a map using historical data that is preformatted for a GIS project, websites are available that will provide that computerized data for you to insert in your map program. In both of these examples, you are getting into complicated mapping exercises and should probably seek assistance from your library, professor, or someone in your geography department. The provider of the ArcGIS software also has a tutorial page (http://www. gis.com/). If you find that ArcGIS is too complex, several other, simpler alternatives exist to create a basic map using historic data. NYPL (New York Public Library) Map Warper is a tool to georectify NYPL's collection of historic maps onto modern maps. Watch the tutorial to learn to use the system. You are limited to the collections of the NYPL.[28]

FOR FURTHER READING

History of Maps and Cartography

Andrews, John Harwood. *Maps in Those Days: Cartographic Methods before 1850.* Dublin: Four Courts Press, 2009. Nice survey of map history.

Barber, Peter, and Tom Harper. *Magnificent Maps: Power, Propaganda and Art.* London: British Library, 2010. Reproductions of historic maps with discussions on how they were used.

Black, Jeremy. *Maps and History: Constructing Images of the Past.* New Haven, CT: Yale University Press, 1997. Thorough history of the development and use of maps but not focusing on the science of cartography. More of a social history of maps.

Black, Jeremy. *Maps and Politics.* Chicago: University of Chicago Press, 1997. Similar to *Maps and History*, this volume takes a more contemporary focus and examines the uses of maps in twentieth-century world politics.

Clark, John Owen Edward. *100 Maps: The Science, Art and Politics of Cartography throughout History.* New York: Sterling Pub, 2005. Examples of historic maps and how they have changed/been used over time.

Goffart, Walter A. *Historical Atlases: The First Three Hundred Years 1570–1870.* Chicago: University of Chicago Press, 2003. Interesting history of the development of atlases and their cultural, as well as practical, value.

Harris, Nathaniel. *Mapping the World: Maps and Their History.* San Diego: Thunder Bay Press, 2002. Individual histories of significant maps, 2300 B.C.E. to 2001 C.E.

Knowles, Anne Kelly, ed. *Past Time, Past Place: GIS for History.* Redlands, CA: ESRI Press, 2002. Excellent introduction to the use of GIS in history. Includes case studies of actual online projects with lots of illustrations.

Monmonier, Mark S. *Bushmanders & Bullwinkles: How Politicians Manipulate Electronic Maps and Census Data to Win Elections.* Chicago: University of

Chicago Press, 2001. Discussion of how politicians gerrymander maps to create political districts and how such mapping with GIS speaks to the notions of community, identity, and the construction of the American political body.

Monmonier, Mark S. *How to Lie with Maps*. 2d ed. Chicago: University of Chicago Press, 1996. Excellent discussion of how maps have been purposely or inadvertently used to mislead and misconstrue information. Chapters include "Maps for Political Propaganda," "Maps that Advertise," and "Blunders that Mislead."

Rumsey, David, and Edith M. Punt. *Cartographica Extraordinaire: The Historical Map Transformed*. Redlands, CA: ESRI Press, 2004. North and South America's change from wilderness to civilization.

Short, John Rennie. *The World through Maps: A History of Cartography*. Buffalo, NY: Firefly Books, 2003. Broad, heavily illustrated history of mapmaking.

Thrower, Norman Joseph William. *Maps & Civilization: Cartography in Culture and Society*. Chicago: University of Chicago Press, 2007. How maps have shaped and reflected society.

Maps and General Geography Texts

Campbell, John. *Map Use and Analysis*. 4th ed. Boston: McGraw-Hill, 2001. Excellent, in-depth primer on map terminology and construction.

Dorling, Daniel, and David Fairbairn. *Mapping: Ways of Representing the World*. London: Longman, 1997. Textbook that integrates the history of maps with the newer trends in mapmaking.

Tufte, Edward R. *The Visual Display of Quantitative Information*. 2d ed. Cheshire, CT: Graphics Press, 2001. Discussion of graphs, including maps and their evolution in the display of data.

Wood, Denis, Ward L. Kaiser, and Bob Abramms. *Seeing through Maps: Many Ways to See the World*. Amherst, MA: ODT Inc., 2006. Simpler discussion of maps, including how to read a map.

Geographic Information Systems

Software

ArcGIS. http://www.esri.com/software/arcgis (accessed November 12, 2011). Website for the producer of the leading GIS software. Site contains tutorials and guides for using the software.

Guides and Resources

Davis, David E. *GIS for Everyone: Exploring Your Neighborhood and Your World with a Geographic Information System*. 3d ed. Redlands, CA: ESRI Press, 2003. Simple introduction to GIS for beginners. Includes free software.

ESRI Website. http://www.esri.com (accessed November 12, 2011). The full range of GIS software provided by ESRI.

GIS.com: Your Guide to GIS. http://www.gis.com (accessed November 12, 2011). Beginner's guide to GIS including training modules. Provided by ESRI.

Gregory, Ian, and Paul S. Ell. *Historical GIS: Technologies, Methodologies, and Scholarship.* Cambridge: Cambridge University Press, 2007. Step-by-step guide to planning a history project using GIS techniques, including software package.

Krygier, John, and Denis Wood. *Making Maps: A Visual Guide to Map Design for GIS.* New York: Guilford Press, 2011. Step-by-step guide.

NOTES

1. Daniel Dorling and David Fairbairn, *Mapping: Ways of Representing the World* (London: Longman, 1997), 6–7.

2. Jeremy Black, *Maps and History: Constructing Images of the Past* (New Haven: Yale University Press, 1997), 204, 240.

3. Benjamin Ray and University of Virginia, *Salem Witch Trials: Documentary Archive and Transcription Project: Regional Accusations Map*, http://jefferson. village.virginia.edu/salem/maps/ (accessed November 12, 2011).

4. "Map," *Encyclopædia Britannica*, http://www.britannica.com/search?query= map (accessed April 28, 2012). For an interesting discussion concerning the definition of the word "map" since 1649 to the present, see J. H. Andrews, "What Was a Map? Lexicographers Reply," *Cartographica* 33 (Winter 1996): 1–11.

5. Dorling and Fairbairn, *Mapping*, 9.

6. Ibid., 52.

7. *Images of Early Maps on the Web: WWW-VL: History*, http://www.maphistory. info/webimages.html (accessed November 12, 2011).

8. Mark Monmonier, *How to Lie with Maps*, 2d ed. (Chicago: University of Chicago Press, 1996), 88–89.

9. Mark Monmonier, "The Rise of the National Atlas," *Cartographica* 31 (Spring 1994): 2.

10. For a history of the national atlas, see Monmonier, "The Rise of the National Atlas," 1–15. See also Monique Pelletier, "Cartography and Power in France during the Seventeenth and Eighteenth Centuries," *Cartographica* 35 (Autumn/ Winter 1998): 41–53.

11. Monmonier, *How to Lie with Maps*, 90.

12. Robert A. Rundstrom, "The Role of Ethics, Mapping, and the Meaning of Place in Relations between Indians and Whites in the United States," *Cartographica* 30 (Spring 1993): 21–28.

13. Dorling and Fairbairn, *Mapping*, 138–139; for more on Huntington, see David N. Livingstone, *The Geographical Tradition: Episodes in the History of a Contested Enterprise* (Oxford: Blackwell, 1992), especially the chapter "A 'Sternly Practical' Pursuit: Geography, Race and Empire."

14. Dorling and Fairbairn, *Mapping*, 154; William Bunge, *Nuclear War Atlas* (New York: Blackwell, 1988).

15. Dorling and Fairbairn, *Mapping* , 82–83.

16. Ibid., 84–85.

17. Monmonier, *How to Lie with Maps*, 45–47.

18. Ibid., 117–118.

19. William Cronon, Brien Barrett, and Genya Erling, "Learning to Do Historical Research: Sources Maps: Visualizing Place, Space, and Time," Learning to do Historical Environmental Historical Research: A Primer For Historical Research for Historians and Others, http://www.williamcronon.net/researching/maps.htm (accessed October 30, 2011); Jean Manco, "Historic Maps," Researching Historic Buildings in the British Isles, http://www.buildinghistory.org/maps.shtml, and "How to Research Historical Aerial Photographs," *Google Earth Library*, http://www.gelib.com/research-historical-aerials.htm (accessed October 30, 2011). Both are excellent basic sources for using and contextualizing historic maps.

20. Dennis Wood, Ward L. Kaiser, and Bob Abramms, *Seeing Through Maps: Many Ways to See the World* (Amherst, MA: ODT, 2006), 4–5.

21. Martin Gilbert, "The Intifada, February 1992," in *Atlas of the Arab–Israeli Conflict*, 6th ed. (London: Oxford University Press, 1993).

22. Black, *Maps*, 217, fig. 46. Black suggests that Gilbert's Zionist beliefs caused him to represent certain controversial issues in a certain way, "but mention of the Lebanon–Israeli border was made without reference to the Israeli-backed occupation of part of southern Lebanon, the use of Judea and Samaria was questionable and the West Bank was presented as part of Israel." The map is identical in the 7th edition, *The Routledge Atlas of the Arab–Israeli Conflict* (New York: Routledge, 2002).

23. For a fuller explanation of some of these points, see J. B. Harley, "The Evaluation of Early Maps: Towards a Methodology," *Imago Mundi* 22 (1968): 62–74; J. B. Hartley, "Deconstructing the Map," in *Human Geography: An Essential Anthology*, ed. John Agnew, David N. Livingstone, and Alisdair Rogers (Oxford: Blackwell, 1996), 422–443.

24. Anne Kelly Knowles, *Past Time, Past Place: GIS for History* (Redlands, CA: ESRI Press, 2002), xiv.

25. Bertrum H. MacDonald and Fiona A. Black, "Using GIS for Spatial and Temporal Analyses in Print Culture Studies," *Social Science History* 24 (Fall 2000): 505–536.

26. David Rumsey and Meredith Williams, "Historical Maps in GIS," in Knowles, *Past Time, Past Place*, 4–5.

27. Ibid., 5.

28. Other systems that have yet to be used with historical data exist and might also be useful. Open Street Map (http://www.openstreetmap.com) is an editable map of the world. Google Fusion Tables (http://www.google.com/fusion tables/Home) allows the visual publication of data on a modern map. You can enter locations and data and publish it as points on a map. You can also create your own, simple map using Google My Maps (http://maps.google.com/ click on "my places." Directions at http://maps.google.com/support and then select Map Your World and custom maps). Google Earth (http://www.google.com/earth/index.html) also has possibilities, although it can also be very complex. For an example of plotting historical buildings and their changes using Google Earth see the Miami Google Earth Project (http://www.miami.muohio.edu/bicentennial/reflectonthepast/google_earth.cfm), Miami University in Ohio (accessed October 30, 2011).

Beyond the Written Word: Finding, Evaluating, and Using Images, Motion Pictures, and Audio

9

WHAT YOU WILL LEARN IN THIS CHAPTER

- how to use and interpret different types of media (visual media, motion pictures, and audio)
- how to search online catalogs, special media collections, and the Internet to find historic media
- how to incorporate media into your paper or website

The Role of Media in Historical Research: Media as Historical Evidence

The previous chapter focused on maps as a primary source and their development from print to a multidimensional, Geographic Information Systems project. Another set of primary sources that deserves more in-depth analysis is visual media and audio resources. Different from the written word as primary evidence, these categories of media require different and additional searching and evaluation techniques from those already discussed. A quick overview of the purpose of each type of image and its evolution will assist you in using visual media as primary source evidence in your research. Audio materials are different in certain ways from visual media and will be discussed separately.

Images throughout History

Images have been reflective of humankind's culture since the first cave drawing in prehistoric times.[1] Whether symbolic of the hunt or of a noble's position in life or documentary proof of war crimes, they offer a wide variety of visual evidence through different mediums of expression. Images often reflect the social norms and public opinion of the time in which they were taken or created as a reaction to those norms. Images, both moving and still, as well as other types of multimedia highlight political rhetoric, chart economic trends, provide glimpses of daily life and its material trappings, and show the imagination and intellectual ideas of a society.[2] Seeing President Teddy Roosevelt give a speech or listening to an African American discuss his or her life under slavery can focus and even alter our feelings and assessments of current and historical issues and events.[3] Printed materials such as books, magazines, and newspapers have always incorporated images, ranging from illuminated Bibles to lithographs and, later, photographs in magazines and newspapers. People displayed first painted portraits and then photographs of their loved ones on the mantle in the parlor. Images add a dimension to historical discussion that words or text alone cannot convey. We will divide a quick study of images and their use into the categories of photographs, artwork (primarily paintings but also including sketches and nonphotographic illustrations in printed material), and motion pictures. However, there are a number of other types of images that this chapter will not deal with or will deal with only peripherally, such as murals, graffiti, scientific illustration, advertising art, and political cartoons, which can be treated in a manner similar to artwork or photography.

Photography: Real Life Captured?

A photograph can metaphorically highlight the idyllic family, the delinquency of youth, or the romanticism of war. It may be, though, that no photograph is a true reflection of a time passed. Additionally, photographs have value, for instance, as commercial products to sell newspapers or magazines or as evidence of the worth of an investment. Photographs were used to document the westward US land survey, not only for scientific purposes but also to inform and persuade the US Congress that the money allocated to purchase the territory was well spent. What photographers choose to "record," where they stand to take the shots, and what they decide to include in the shot are all part of their viewpoint, or perspective. Photographers who sought to document social conditions, such as Jacob Riis in the slums of 1870s New York City and Dorothea Lange and Walker Evans during the Great Depression in the United States in the 1930s, had their own visual idea of poverty and sought to have their photographs convey their social views.[4] Riis and also Lange were known to have staged photographs. The purpose of these photographs that portrayed the lives of the poor was to incite societal reform. Lewis Hine, the twentieth-century photographer who documented child labor in the United States accused Riis of practicing "yellow photography," sensationalizing atrocious conditions as a means to reform.[5] This idea of viewpoint is particularly evident in political cartoons and propaganda posters, of course, but it is present in all images. Carefully examining your visual evidence before you incorporate it into your paper or website is important. Below are some more detailed examples of how perspective, public opinion, and the social norms of an era have affected the meaning of photographs and images.

News photography, or photojournalism, is a relatively recent field. Prior to the 1940s, the reporter who was responsible for writing the story also took the photos. Until the end of World War II, news photographs were considered sensational.[6] Recording the atrocities in concentration camps at the close of the war brought new focus to the use of photography as documentary evidence, by both amateurs and professionally trained photographers, giving photojournalism respectability in news reporting.[7]

War photography had always been treated with a different sort of fascination. During the US Civil War, there was a public demand for tragic, patriotic images of the war, leading photographers like Alexander Gardner to stage a photograph at the Battle of Gettysburg for such a dramatic effect. In his book *Gettysburg: A Journey in Time*, historian William A. Frassanito chronicles pictorial evidence of Gardner moving what is probably a Confederate infantryman's body into a sharpshooter's position at Devil's Den for a more picturesque shot. *American Memory*, a virtual library of primary source materials at the Library of Congress, explores this issue of authenticity with this photograph in their online exhibit, "Does the Camera Ever Lie? The Case of the Moved Body."[8]

Photographs can give us a limited and sometimes false image of the social context of an era. For instance, *Life* magazine in the 1950s often presented photographs of the perfect, white, suburban middle-class family but ignored the civil rights issues brewing throughout the United States.[9] Images were selected for inclusion in the magazine both because they reflected the interests of the magazine's readers and because the editors needed to sell magazines by appealing to their audience's political and philosophical viewpoint and image. Certain images may offend an audience and cause a drop in sales. Yet images, photographs, and paintings used in a different way can give an accurate glimpse into everyday life. For instance, the old town of Warsaw, Poland, nearly completely destroyed by bombings in World War II, was reconstructed based on historical prints and paintings. A similar process was used for a restoration project at St. Paul's Cathedral in London.[10] Advertisements in magazines and on radio and television can reflect idealized views of cutting-edge culture, since not everyone may have been able to afford the newest fashions of the day. Remember, advertising may not be entirely reflective of society as a whole, especially since its goal is to influence consumer buying and fashion trends.

Questions to Evaluate Photographs/Still Images

Because of all of these issues, there are many factors when incorporating a photographic/still image in your research. Asking the following questions will help you to understand the image creator's intent, what you need to learn about the society in which the image was captured, and how to integrate the image into your analysis.[11]

1. What is the social and historical context for this image?

2. What might have happened before and after this image was created?

3. What is outside the frame of the image? What has been left out? What should be in the image that is missing?

4. What gender, race, and class issues are reflected here? How has the photographer addressed or not addressed these issues?

5. What relationships or connections do the people have to the objects?

6. How did the photographer set up the photograph? Can you tell that the photographer made choices about the angle, lighting, and focus (foreground, background) that might influence how you perceive—and how the photograph's contemporaries may have perceived—the image's meaning and effect? Be careful not to label or stereotype people or objects as this may lead you to erroneous conclusions.

7. Has technology changed the image's natural state? Today we can use software such as *Photoshop* to alter images. In the past photographers could change and manipulate aperture settings and exposure lengths to create an artistic image. Ansel Adams, a famous photographer of the western United States uses special aperture settings for crisper, more detailed images.

8. In published collections of text, how are the images juxtaposed to the text? Look at the language the captions use. Does this change the way we perceive the image?

9. Does the photograph or image ignore issues and details contemporary to its depiction or present them in a certain way that may lead you to a certain view about the image? The purpose of a photograph may be to record what is in the foreground. Use the background to look for evidence of everyday life, the clothing, advertising signage, and so on.

Analyzing the image in figure 9.1, "Behind the Teller's Window at Oxford National Bank 1916," you can learn about women in the workforce in 1916. In this case, the female teller seems to be treated as an equal, using the same machinery as the men, as well as having the same contact with bank patrons. Perhaps it is significant that the photographer snapped the photograph with the woman at the center of the frame. Was he (assuming the photographer was a man) trying to draw attention to her because he knew her or because her position in the bank was unusual? The image also leads to a discussion about a financial and commercial operation in a small town and its mechanization.

Art as Visual Media: Painting and Drawing

Art historians analyze works of art in a way that is unique to their discipline. Art has many features beyond the content and historical significance, such as physical features (line, color, texture), composition (the organization of

Figure 9.1. "Behind the Teller's Window at Oxford National Bank 1916," Frank Snyder Collection of Photographs, Miami University Libraries. *Used with permission of Miami University Libraries.*

the piece), and style (traits that associate the piece with others like it). While you may also be concerned with these features, you will be looking primarily at the artwork's association to real life and how it reflects the social and intellectual philosophy, as well as the material culture, of the time. How an artist paints a landscape or a portrait conveys a particular understanding and opinion of the political, social, and intellectual climate of the era and place in which both artist and subject lived. Painting and art in general have different themes of interpretation across cultures. Unlike photography, art style differs drastically by culture and time period, making it difficult to provide a synopsis of its historical uses and development. For instance, it is difficult to compare style and cultural meaning and to connect historical development between northern Song painting of the Song Dynasty (960–1279 C.E.) that expressed Neo-Confucian ideals and a nineteenth-century American Impressionist landscape painting.

By its nature, art intends to send its messages through symbolism and allegory. The artist has more control over a creation than a photographer over a photograph, so a separate list of evaluation criteria needs to be applied.

Questions to Evaluate Art

1. What is the context of this image? How was it meant to be displayed? Publicly? In a private home? On a wall? Is it a reproduction? Was it used for a purpose other than the way you see it now?[12] Remember, many buildings were designed to include art and art was often designed to be part of a structure, such as frescos in the villas of Pompeii.[13]

2. What cultural presuppositions do you bring from your time that the contemporary viewer would not have had? (For example, what do you know about science, politics, etc. that the viewer did not and, conversely, what did the viewer know that you do not understand?)[14]

3. Why was the art object created? Was it commissioned? Was it a portrait for a family? By a patron? Was there an expected perception? (For instance, was a painting created to show a pastoral view of the countryside or to make a nobleman look like a "manly man"?)

4. What iconography is used in the scene? Paintings often use objects to symbolize philosophies or ideals, for instance, a skull for the presence of death or scientific instruments for learned men. Roman coins used iconography to honor emperors.[15] Several dictionaries exist that would explain these symbols. How realistic is the scene or piece of artwork? Is the piece of artwork realistic or depictive?[16]

5. What was the artist's philosophy or viewpoint when the piece of artwork was created? This is similar to the photographer setting up the photograph. The artist paints with an overt or covert philosophy in mind. Whether a modern-day Marxist sensitive to class issues or, prior to Marxist philosophy, sympathetic to the oppressed masses, the artist has a viewpoint. Just as history has "schools," art history has "methodologies."[17]

6. What is the artist's message? Look at what is central to the piece of art to discern what the artist wanted to tell you.[18]

7. What was the artist's source for the piece of artwork? Was the artist the eyewitness, creating from the event, looking at the landscape, or posing the individual? Or was the artist working from a newspaper description or from memory?[19]

8. Was the artwork intended as a therapeutic act to assist the creator in dealing with a traumatic event, for instance, sketches from the aftermath of the bombing of Hiroshima by someone in the city?

9. What was the artworks reception? How has the interpretation changed over time? *Pilgrims Going To Church*, painted by George Henry Boughton in 1867, portrays a group of pilgrims walking to church, with part of the group obviously startled by something threatening in the distance. In 1867, the painter suggests the threat is Indians, appropriate to the worries on the western frontier in the late 1860s. By 1893 the painting is discussed in New England Magazine in the context of pilgrims yearning for liberty, with no mention of the Indian threat.[20]

Moving Images: Fact and Fiction: Newsreels, Documentaries, Motion Pictures, and Television Programs

Images can be factual or metaphorical, photojournalism or art—and anything in between. Newsreels and documentaries while centered on real people and events have a perspective and bias of their creator. Feature films and television programs begin as fictional stories (art) even if they are intended to evoke a feeling of time, place, and attitude or appear very realistic. Portrayals of the past in popular entertainment are never "pure" but are filtered through the social and cultural norms of the period in which they were created. Historians would never use popular media as primary evidence about the time portrayed, even though the creators want us to believe they are allowing us, the viewers, to experience authentic history.

The HBO series *Deadwood*, which explores the "wild west" in the town of Deadwood, South Dakota, tells us as much about urban social life in the early twenty-first century as it does about frontier life in the United States in the late 1870s, with its overt emphasis on sex, violence, and foul language.[21] This contemporary view of frontier life can be contrasted with PBS's reality TV show *Frontier House*, which immersed three different modern families in a homestead experience in Montana. *Deadwood* is popular television; *Frontier House* is reality TV, despite its attempts at authenticity. Neither program is the real nineteenth-century American frontier and should not be confused with primary sources. Newsreels, however, did intend to bring reality to the public in the form of moving pictures.

About 10 minutes in length and shown before the featured motion picture, newsreels brought world cultures, world wars, and other noteworthy national events to local audiences. Begun in the late nineteenth century with kinescopes and lasting until about the 1970s in cinemas and movie houses, these short news stories had a voice over by a narrator explaining what the audience was "witnessing" in the video images. Sometimes governments, mostly in Europe and the United States, influenced the presentation of their content, but mostly newsreels were another form of news in an age before television news entered into the home.[22]

Documentaries also present "real" images, but they differ from newsreels in several ways. The newsreel is more immediate and was generally viewed within a time frame relatively close to the event's occurrence. Similar to photojournalism, documentaries attempt to interpret or influence the way we understand a particular event or issue. Multiple types of evidence reconstruct events. Sometimes actors may be used to create the idea that you are eyewitnesses to events that are part of the evidence, for instance, you view one of the Jack the Ripper murders. Documentaries have a built-in perspective as they intend to expose some issue. It may be hard to determine authenticity. The documentary, *Song of Ceylon* (1934) uses travel accounts to show the benefits of British rule, while *Las Hurdes/Land Without Bread* (1933) displays the poverty and ill health of a people in the north central regions of Spain. In the case of *Las Hurdes*, several animals were killed to stage the drama of conditions. Documentaries can be valuable to a historian, but remember to consider their intended audience and the societal ideas of the times. Do not confuse documentaries with news.[23]

Feature films and most television programs are yet another kind of moving image of use to historians. Films are not meant to be a record, representation, or explanation of an event or time in the way documentaries or newsreels are. Even though they depict events and people's involvement in those events, films and television programs are art and begin as fiction.

Roots (1976), an ABC mini-series, addressed the lives of Alex Haley's (the author) African and American ancestors. While the representation of slave life was accurate, some of the characters were fictional and Haley's idealistic portrayal of Africa was inaccurate. *Roots* tells us as much about race relations in 1970s America as it does about eighteenth- and nineteenth-century slavery and the South. When you use films and television programs in your research, you must consider dual meanings of the time (when the work was created, as well as the setting).[24]

Questions to Evaluate Visual Media

Asking the following questions will help you to understand the intent of the film and to integrate this type of primary source into your research.[25]

1. Who is the audience? Films are often commercial and are intended to make some kind of profit, even if it is for the cause of an organization.

2. What is the purpose of the film? Who are the producer(s), director, writer(s), and actor(s)? How have they affected the message of the film?

3. Try to identify the artistic portions of the film and the parts rooted in fact. What might have been changed: interpretation, facts, characters and characterizations that might affect your understanding.

4. Watch how the director and film editor use such film techniques as camera view and movement (wide angle shots, large overview shots, close ups, over the shoulder shots, etc.); use of light and shadows; timing (Is the scene moving fast, slow, or lingering at a spot?); cross-cutting and juxtapositions that create storyline associations.

5. How have transitions been used? Filmmakers can cut back and forth between scenes. Dissolving between scenes usually indicates changes in or passing of time and location. Fading of scenes usually indicates a beginning or ending.

6. How was the film received by critics and audiences? Look for reviews in magazines and newspapers just after the release of the film. Look both in national news sources and local news sources. What is well received in a big city like Chicago may not play well in a smaller town (i.e., "but will it play in Peoria").

Searching for Visual Media

Still images and images of artwork can come from a number of sources. You must remember that copyright for images is always a central issue for a website, an honors or master's thesis, or a Ph.D. dissertation. In these cases, your result will be a published document, even if you have designed a website, and you will need to secure the creator's or publisher's permission to reproduce an image. You can search for and obtain images in several places:

- in a book
- from images you own or have created
- in an archive at your institution or historical society
- on the Internet through specially designed search engines
- on the Internet in special collections of images

Using your local online catalog, you can find printed resources, usually books, with photographs and other images contained in them. Do a search, just as you would for any information on your topic, but look through the catalog record for "il." or "illus." in the notes field. If a book consists mostly of images, the subject subheading "pictorial works" will be applied and, if applicable, a credit line will be given to the photographer or illustrator. You could do a search for your topic and limit your search by words in the subject "pictorial works." Images in published books are definitely copyrighted.

SEARCH TIPS

1. Select keyword search.
2. Find a book or two in the list that is about your subject.
3. Look at the subject headings attached to those books and use the same subject headings to search in the catalog.
4. In the catalog record, look for the abbreviation "il." or "illus." to appear in the notes/description.
5. Or limit your search by words in the subject "pictorial works."

If you have photographs that you have personally taken, you usually can freely incorporate those images into your website or paper. Also, you may have photographs passed down through your family that are now in your possession. All you need to do is scan them and save them in the appropriate format. You must be cautious about using photographs of works of art, though, as most museums have restrictions on taking photographs of items in their collections. In this case, even if you have taken the photograph, you do not have the copyright. You also must obtain permission to use snapshots of individuals. If you conducted an oral history and included a photograph of the individual interviewed, you need permission to use his or her image.

You may also go to a local historical society and use its historical collections. Many have vertical files and other collections of photographs. Sometimes a reproduction fee is involved if you want something more than a photocopy. Some collections may be too fragile to copy. Probably the most frequent and easiest method of finding still images is through search engines and websites of collected images on the Internet. Most of these images can be immediately downloaded and incorporated into your website or paper with little or no adjustment by the available software programs. You can search for historical images in two ways on the Internet, either through a site that organizes images or by using a search engine designed to look for images. Below is a list of *mostly* free sites, meaning that you may search the site without paying a subscription. Each site has its own restrictions about the use of its contents, and some will charge you fees for downloading actual images. Increasingly, many historical societies and organizations are placing photos on the web. Look for information about copyright and use of the images on the website. Just because you have found an image on the Internet, though, does not imply it is copyright-free. For large collections of images, the search tips below are useful. For smaller collections, browsing through categories designed by the website may be more fruitful.

Using a general search engine designed for images, whether or not solely historical, will yield the largest number of results. Look for a button or special section for image searching on the major search engines. The quantity of results may be a problem. A vague and imprecise search will often produce overwhelming numbers of results. To search for an image, you must use specific, concrete search terms. You are in essence looking for the graphic representation of an object, an image. If you are looking for images of African Americans in the military, think of specific instances of their participation in the American military and search terms such as "Tuskegee airmen" or "Buffalo soldiers." While you can search for images of the Cold War or the Iron Curtain, your results will be messy and you might miss better images because you are relying on someone to associate those words with an appropriate image. Instead, you must search for images that represent those concepts, such as the Berlin Wall. Another source for images is *Flickr*, an image-sharing website. Individuals and institutions (like libraries) contribute and share their images. You will find more contemporary images than historical ones, but many libraries have uploaded their images for everyone to find. You must also be careful as not all images in *Flickr* are in the public domain. Look at the symbols attached to the image record to determine how you can use the image.

SEARCH TIPS (WITHIN AN ONLINE COLLECTION)

1. Use one of the collections listed in the section below.
2. Search for an object. Make sure that the subject you search for would be in the collection you have selected. For instance, *American Memory* does have images from around the world, but the British Library is probably a better choice for British images. The *Acunet/AP PhotoArchive* has mostly mid-twentieth-century photos, so you would be unlikely to find many US Civil War photographs in that collection.
3. Be as specific as you can. Check to see if there is a date/time period limit or sort to focus your search.

Collections of Historic Images

Collections Providing Free Images

American Memory. http://memory.loc.gov/ammem/ (accessed December 20, 2011). Collections of photographs and moving pictures mostly concerning the United States. Covers nineteenth to twenty-first centuries.

New York Public Library Digital Collections. http://digitalgallery.nypl.org/nypl-digital/ (accessed December 20, 2011). Thumbnails of photographs from collections and exhibits. See also New York Public Library digital galleries.

Images Canada. http://www.imagescanada.ca/ (accessed December 20, 2011). Images, primarily photographs, from a number of cultural institutions throughout Canada, searchable in one single spot. You may use these images for noncommercial purposes for no fee.

British Library Images Online. https://imagesonline.bl.uk/ (accessed December 20, 2011). Images from the British Library throughout British history. Searching is free. There is a cost for reproduction.

Unesco Photobank. http://photobank.unesco.org/exec/search.htm?lang=en (accessed December 20, 2011). Photos of UNESCO's activities. Search for particular historical landmarks.

Image Base (Fine Arts Museums of San Francisco). http://deyoung.famsf.org/search-collections (accessed December 20, 2011). From the collections of the fine arts museums of San Francisco. Non-commercial use is permitted. Sometimes the zoom will not work, so the images are hard to view.

Old Life Magazine Covers. http://oldlifemagazines.com/ (accessed December 20, 2011). Commercial site that sells old covers. Organization is much easier than the official Life site. http://www.life.com/archive/ gallery.

Americana Museum of Photography. http://www.photographymuseum. com/ (accessed December 20, 2011). Fascinating exhibits at this virtual museum on topics related to American history.

PBS's American Photography. http://www.pbs.org/ktca/americanphotography/ (accessed December 20, 2011). Exhibits of photography.

Harrapa. http://www.harappa.com/ (accessed March 28, 2006). Images of South Asia prior to 1947.

Digital Library for the Decorative Arts and Material Culture. http:// decorativearts.library.wisc.edu/ (accessed December 20, 2011). Documents and images about and of American material culture at the University of Wisconsin–Madison.

Web Gallery of Art. http://www.wga.hu/ (accessed December 20, 2011). Searchable database of European painting and sculpture, twelfth to nineteenth centuries.

Harvard Visual Image Search. http://via.lib.harvard.edu/via/deliver/ advancedsearch?_collection=via (accessed December 20, 2011). Search Harvard's union catalog called VIA of visual resources owned, held, or licensed by Harvard. Catalog is accessible to the general public, but access to some of the images may be restricted.

Pictures Catalogue: National Library of Australia. http://www.nla.gov.au/ what-we-collect/pictures (accessed December 20, 2011). Searchable database of photos of Australian life, including history.

Digital South Asia Library Images. http://dsal.uchicago.edu/images/ (accessed December 20, 2011). Group of four collections of photographs mainly of India from the nineteenth century to the present.

Ad* Access. http://library.duke.edu/digitalcollections/adaccess/ (accessed December 20, 2011). Advertisements in US and Canadian newspapers and magazines from 1911 to 1955.

UK History Photofinder. http://labs.nationalarchives.gov.uk/wordpress/ index.php/2010/03/uk-history-photo-finder/ (accessed December 20, 2011). J. Dixon-Scott's photographs of England and Ireland.

British Library Online Gallery. http://www.bl.uk/onlinegallery/index. html (accessed December 20, 2011). Many of the collections are photographic.

Asian Historical Architecture. http://www.orientalarchitecture.com/index. php (accessed December 20, 2011). Photographic survey of Asia's architectural heritage.

Collections Requiring a Library Subscription or
Commercial Collections Charging Fees (but Allowing Searching)

Acunet/AP Photo Archive. http://www.apimages.com/ (accessed December 20, 2011). A subscription-based product. Contains photographs, current and historical, in the Associated Press' archive. Coverage is worldwide. Includes an audio section. Check the online agreement for reproduction rights.

ARTStor. http://www.artstor.org/ (accessed December 20, 2011). A subscription-based product. Contains images of all types of artwork: paintings, statues, architecture, material culture objects, and more. Coverage is worldwide and of all periods of history.

Time/Life Picture Collection. http://www.thepicturecollection.com/ (accessed December 20, 2011). Selected collection of photos from *Time/Life* photographers. If you wish to use most of these photographs, there will be a fee involved. You must register to use the database, although registration is free.

George Eastman House. http://www.eastmanhouse.org/ (accessed December 20, 2011). Click the Collections Online button. Search by a number of different ways, including photographer, subject, and type or style of photograph. Access is generally by menus. Reproduction Right discusses print and not web use. Contact the Eastman House for details.

GettyImages. http://www.gettyimages.com/ (accessed December 20, 2011). Collection of royalty-free, as well as rights, images, motion pictures, and other types of images. The Creative section contains archival photographs. Most photos, however, are from the twentieth century.

SEARCH TIPS (FOR SEARCH ENGINES)

1. Select one of the specialized search engines listed below and click on the section that searches just for images.
2. If it has an advanced search section, select that.
3. Enter words that describe the *object* you seek. For instance, the name of a place or person or event such as "Mahatma Gandhi," "slaves," or "Buddhist temple." You would not want to enter a concept like "nonviolence" or "civil disobedience." However, "Gandhi" and "protests" will bring up examples of nonviolent civil disobedience.

4. If your search engine allows, you may want to limit your search to certain image formats (.jpg or .tif) or color/greyscale. These terms are explained later in the chapter.

Search Engines and Meta-Search Engines for Images and Indexes to Image Collections

Google.com. http://images.google.com/ (accessed December 20, 2011).

Yahoo.com. http://search.yahoo.com (accessed December 20, 2011).

Picsearch. http://www.picsearch.com/ (accessed December 20, 2011).

Visual Search Lab. http://labs.ideeinc.com/visual# (accessed December 20, 2011). Find visually similar images from the Alamy set of stock photos.

TinEye Reverse Image Search. http://www.tineye.com/ (accessed December 20, 2011). Upload a photograph and find out where it was used before.

Digital Library Federation: Public Access Collections. http://dlf.grainger. uiuc.edu/dlfcollectionsregistry/browse/ (accessed December 20, 2011). Index to over 34 institutions and 600 collections. Not all are truly public-access.

Images on the Internet: Some Cautions

It is likely that the majority of your images will be acquired through searching on the Internet. Many organizations such as historical societies or libraries digitize and mount portions of their collections on the Internet to preserve them and to make them available to a wider audience. However, these images, as well as those you may find in published sources, present some issues that you must consider if you use them on your website or for your project.[26]

- *Images on the Internet can be altered—intentionally and/or accidentally.* To make an image clearer and cleaner, it may be sharpened, cropped, or changed in some way by the piece of software used to scan and mount it on the web. Individuals with the best intentions can wipe away valuable historical evidence. When you add images to your website, be careful not to alter their integrity. Do not edit out tears, watermarks, flaws, blemishes, or marks on the original image. These marks give the image authenticity and are part of the original historical record/artifact. Possibly someone contemporary with the image may have left notes and identifying markings, such as names of individuals or buildings, on the image that your cleaning would erase. Sometimes the image is intentionally altered to create the desired illusion. For instance, the website *The Commissar Vanishes* (http://www.newseum.org/berlinwall/commissar_vanishes/) shows photographs Joseph Stalin and the Soviet government altered to provide a version of Russian society and politics that was not necessarily realistic. There are countless other examples of intentional deception on the web. Use the techniques to evaluate sources listed in chapters 5 (Evaluation) and 7 (Internet) to make sure you have an image that is representative of the evidence you wish to present.

- *Be aware that you are viewing only part of a collection.* Seldom are entire collections digitized because of the time and expense involved. Therefore, you cannot know how the image fits into the whole of the collection. If a photograph of the Taj Mahal was included with a letter to Aunt Sophie detailing niece Clara's Grand Tour of Asia in the 1850s, complete with letters describing Agra, India, and its inhabitants, you may not get the letter to Aunt Sophie in the digital collection, only the image. Thus, the image is isolated from its author's purpose and perspective. Also, you may not see all of the photos of a building that has undergone a number of renovations and, therefore, you might miss a crucial phase of its development.

- *Unknown selection criteria have been applied.* You have no idea why these images have been selected. If the images are part of an exhibit, they may have been selected by someone to exemplify an issue and therefore reflect someone's point of view.

- *The scanning process loses some of the information of the image.* When images are scanned and translated into *pixels*, the series of dots arranged in rows and columns that create the image, they lose some of their visual information. A scanned image is not as sharp and clear as the original; its tone is reduced and its color, changed. Images are often compressed to save space and to speed their transfer over the Internet, which further degrades the information. These factors are true of all digital information, not just images; but it is less of an issue for text-based documents because they are less complex than photographs.

- *Monitors and printers differ in their ability to display and print colors, including greyscale or shades of grey.* No matter how high the quality of scan you provide, the image will only be as good as the equipment used to display it. The image may be crisp and show incredible historic detail on your monitor but look quite ordinary on another viewer's monitor.

- *Some items are intended to be viewed from a distance.* Posters and paintings were meant to be hung on a wall and viewed from a distance and in person. Mounting them on a webpage may destroy their scale and sometimes their impact.

Scanning and Downloading Still Images

If you are going to add images to your website, regardless of their source, you will need a basic understanding of image types, image format, and image resolution. In creating and using digital images, you will encounter or create several types of file formats. Knowing their purposes and when to use them is essential.

Common Image Files

Images will have the following file extensions or formats at the end of the name of the file. Different formats are useful for different types of images.

- *.gif (Graphics Interchange Format).* Useful for line-art drawings and other black-and-white drawings. Even black-and-white photographs have shades of grey and are not reflected well in GIFs.

- *.jpg/.jpeg (Joint Photographic Experts Group).* Used for most photographs and artwork, both color and black and white, which does have shades of grey. JPGs are compressed files (files that are made smaller, thus easier to store), so some information is lost in their creation. All browsers (*Internet Explorer, Firefox, Safari,* etc.) can recognize and display them. Generally, this is the format in which you will want to save your scanned images. JPG is the best format for printing.

- *.png (Portable Network Graphics).* PNG is a patent-free improvement to the GIF format. It is a format that is best used for line drawings. While it is a search limit option in some of the image search engines, not all browsers support it.

- *.tif/.tiff (Tagged Image File Format).* TIFF is an archival image format used for all types of images (color, black and white, and greyscale). Since the file is uncompressed, no information about the image is lost, making the file extremely large. Also, some browsers cannot read the file unless you use a special plug-in as the purpose is to preserve the image. Many libraries use this as the digital image from which they make JPG copies.

Now that you understand the types of images you may encounter or create, you will have to make some choices about downloading or scanning images.

Downloading Images

When you download images from the Internet, many of the choices discussed in the scanning section below will have been predetermined for you. You may not be able to change certain aspects of the image to meet the aesthetic requirements of your website. For instance, enlarging the image will cause a distortion and possibly result in an unclear and unusable image because its original scanned resolution was too low. Download the image you desire to your desktop. *Never* link to an image on someone's webpage as it increases your page's loading time and, if the other webpage disappears or moves, your link is broken. You will then be able to make adjustments to the downloaded image by using such software as *Adobe Photoshop* and place it in your website or paper. Rename the image file and record the bibliographic information such as the website address, title, and author. You will need to attribute your sources of images just as you do your other primary and secondary sources. In a website, it is customary to provide a link to the site of origin for your images. (In a paper, you will need to supply a footnote.) For many sites, this link is their requirement for permission to use the image.

Scanning Images

If you decide to do your own scanning, you need to understand the color and physical construction of digital images.[27] The scanning and image manipulation software you are using will require you to make decisions about the image type, resolution, and format. We have already discussed the formats above (.jpg, .gif, .png, .tif). Understanding the color, resolution, the physical structure, and size are the last components to creating your scanned image.

Dividing images into two broad categories will help you understand how to scan and save them. Think of your image as either a line drawing or photograph-like image. An example of a line drawing is a piece of clip art that is basically black and white with definite lines. Black-and-white cartoons might be another example. Just about every other kind of still image could be considered photograph-like. Even black-and-white images have shades of grey and therefore do have "color." Having some sort of perception of color will help you decide in which category to scan and save your image.

Digital Video and Audio Files

The challenge in using digital video and audio files is delivering them to the desktop. Because of their size, having the entire file on your computer is usually impractical. Most digital video and audio files are streamed, that is, delivered to your desktop in small sections so that you can view or listen to the clip as it is being sent. To see or hear the files, you will need special software to decompress them.

Digital Video: Using Moving Images

Digital video is becoming increasingly easy to find on the Internet Many historical video clips are uploaded by individuals and institutions who either have some association with the event or have the ability to copy existing video. Libraries, museums, and historical societies use *Youtube* as a way to create awareness of their collections and provide an easy way for a large audience to find and view the digital video. The relative ease of creating and or converting digital video makes historic videos available as never before. Be very careful as these digital videos can be readily edited. Sometimes multiple copies of videos of varying lengths are available from unknown sources. Be sure the video you use is complete and accurate. Copyright issues apply to digital video just as to still images or any other work. However, interpreting copyright for digital video is more complex.

Searching on the Web

Finding digital moving images on the web is difficult because, like finding photos, deciding on search terminology is difficult. You will have to be creative about how you perform your keyword searches in the search engines below. You can combine your search term with the word "history" or "historical," but often the descriptions will not include that word. Instead, they might say something like "New York City skyline, 1910." In some cases, you may just have to keep looking through your results until you find something useful. Collections of historical video exist but are usually copyright-protected and require fees to link their movies to your website. Read the terms of use on the websites carefully.

Selected Sites with Historical Video Collections

American Memory Motion Pictures. http://memory.loc.gov/ammem/browse/ListSome.php?format5Motion1Picture (accessed December 21, 2011). Films include early Thomas Edison silent shorts, 1950s advertisements, and reactions to the events of September 11.

Internet Archive Moving Image Archives. http://www.archive.org/details/movies (accessed December 21, 2011). Archive of freely available shorts, clips of movies, advertisements, and so on.

Museum of the Moving Image. http://www.movingimage.us/ (accessed December 21, 2011). Online exhibits on themes such as presidential campaigns, 1952–1994.

Television News Archive (Vanderbilt University). http://tvnews.vanderbilt.edu/ (accessed December 21, 2011). Subscription service that indexes most of the nightly news broadcasts since the late 1960s.

Living Room Candidate. http://www.livingroomcandidate.org/ US presidential campaign commercials, 1952–2008.

Digital Newsreel Archive: Movietone News. http://www.movietone.com/n_index.cfm (accessed December 21, 2011). Movie/television and newsreels. Site has become restrictive and requires registration to view any of the contents.

Newsfilm. http://nfo.ac.uk/ (accessed December 21, 2011). Selected news film and video from ITN and Reuters. Historical and current.

Gaumont Pathé Archives. http://www.gaumontpathearchives.com/ (accessed December 21, 2011). Click on the English version. French newsreels since early in the twentieth century. For full access you must register.

Wochenscahu Archives. http://www.wochenschau-archiv.de/ (accessed December 21, 2011). German newsreels.

Archiv Violuce. http://www.archivioluce.com/archivio/ (accessed December 21, 2011). Italian newsreels.

ITN Archive. http://www.itnsource.com/en/ (accessed April 28, 2012). A wealth of footage that you can browse through if you register, which is free. However, there is a fee to actually use the footage. Includes such organizations as British Pathé, Fox News, Reuters, and ITN for much of the twentieth century.

Film Archives Online. http://www.filmarchivesonline.com/ (accessed December 21, 2011). Another site that you must register to use. Similar to the above.

Colonial Film: Moving Images of the British Empire. http://www. colonialfilm.org.uk (accessed December 20, 2011). 150 films created about the British Colonies. Information about 6,000 films contained in the site.

Travel Film Archive. http://www.travelfilmarchive.com/ (accessed December 21, 2011). Travelogues and educational and industrial films shot between 1900 and 1970.

Critical Past. http://www.criticalpast.com/ (accessed December 21, 2011). Royalty free stock footage. Mostly US government sources, which may also appear in some of the above websites.

Television News of the Civil Rights Era. http://www2.vcdh.virginia.edu/ civilrightstv/ (accessed December 21, 2011). News footage from 1950 to 1970. Some local videos.

World History in Video and American History in Video. http://alexander-street.com/products (accessed April 28, 2012). Requires a subscription. Two sources from Alexander Street press that provide video from documentaries, newsreels, and other sources. Some from PBS, The History Channel, BBC, and Arts and Entertainment Network.

National Archives Public Information, Films. http://www.nationalarchives. gov.uk/films/ (accessed December 21, 2011). British films from the Central Office of Information, 1945–2006.

Europa Film Treasures. http://www.europafilmtreasures.eu/ (accessed December 21, 2011). Network of 30 European film archives.

Audio, Music, and Speech Resources

No longer are scholars denied access to brittle cassette tapes or reel-to-reel tapes (a recording format even older than cassette tapes). Increasingly, speeches, interviews, and musical recordings are available through streaming audio on the Internet. As a researcher, you can now hear famous speeches given by dictators, such as Hitler, or presidents, such as John F. Kennedy, and can experience their charismatic vocal inflections. Likewise, musically you can hear the blues of Lead Belly (Huddie Leabetter, 1888–1949) recorded while he was in prison in the 1930s or famous recordings of pieces of classical music or examples of other cultures' music.

To analyze the content of speeches, the following criteria will be helpful. Many times you will have only the written text and, thus, will be limited to a critical analysis of the words. However, if you are able to obtain a copy that actually allows you to hear the delivery of the speech, be sure to incorporate that into your assessment.

Questions to Ask about Speeches

1. Who is the audience, and who else is the speaker trying to reach? Many times the individuals attending the speech are not the only audience. You may not know this or may have to do additional research.[28]
2. Do other versions of the speech exist? How do all the versions differ?[29]
3. How does the speaker have the authority to speak?[30]
4. How does the speaker's voice reflect the time in which he or she is speaking?[31]
5. How does the style or type of speech affect the delivery, for instance, a sermon has a specific format and style of vocal delivery?
6. What powers of persuasion does the speaker use? If you can listen to the speech, how does the speaker use his or her voice? Listen for voice inflection and tone, as well as for repetitive phrases.

Analyzing music presents a more complicated task, especially if you do not understand the conventions, notations, and terminology of music. Still, music is integral to life and culture and can be a revealing piece of evidence in your research. Music can reflect or define an age, for example, ragtime, popular in the United States from the end of the nineteenth century to about 1918, couples black rhythms with European classical musical influences to evoke an era when American society was changing. Music can inspire nationalism, for example, Wagnerian opera in Nazi Germany, or define classes, for example, middle-class urbanites in 1950s Brazil rejected samba style music, which was based on folk traditions, for the bossa nova style but by the 1960s returned first to idealized traditional music and then to embrace protest songs against the military regime. Music can define social movements, for example, the civil rights movement in the United States, or incite spiritual commitment, for example, revival songs for tent meetings in nineteenth- and twentieth-century America.[32] For your analysis, it will help you to think of music in two categories, that which has been written down and that which is from an oral tradition and may have variations (although much of this music has been written down in order to preserve it). The former is often performed before groups in formal concerts, and the latter is often "common" people's music, such as folk music, jazz, lullabies, or songs performed by troubadours, and sung in casual company, often improvised. In the study of music, three categories of participants are involved: the composer, the performer, and the listener. So, as a researcher, you must consider not only the intent of the composer but also the interpretation of the performer(s) and the reception of the audience. In many cases, this both changes over time and place, in the case of the performer(s) and the listener, and is affected by the time in which the composition was written or created. With folk music, the composer is often undefinable, and many performers have changed the song over time, muddying your interpretation. Yet, each performance of a written piece of music is different as well.

Questions to Ask About Music

Use the following criteria to help you analyze the influence of a piece of music. [33]

1. Is the work organized in some way and according to a recognized musical format (e.g., a sonata)?

2. Is the composition part of a series of compositions?

3. How does the composition relate to other compositions written around the same time? What is unique to this composition? What made this composition an example of its age? What does it say about fashion and convention?

4. How does the composition fit in with the composer's other works?

5. How does contemporary culture affect this composition? Can you see literature, art, and other forms of culture reflected in it?

6. How does the delivery of the composition affect its meaning? Was the piece meant to be performed in a concert hall? Sung in cotton fields? By troubadours in the manors of nobles? As a rally for protest? As part of a religious service?

7. Who would have heard this composition and how? Live, recorded? Was it a best seller in its time? To research the market of a composition, look at such magazines as *Cashbox* and *Billboard*, as well as other popular magazines of the day and histories of music. See chapter 6 on primary sources for general research techniques.

8. What was the composer's purpose in writing the composition? Was there a political purpose? Was the composition sponsored by a patron or by an organization such as a church? Was the composition written for a specific performer or a specific occasion?

9. How did the audience, as well as critics, respond? Look at concert reviews.

10. Are there other editions of the work? Especially with folk music that passes down melodies and lyrics, many variations by region and time period exist.
11. What is the message of the lyrics?
12. What emotions does the composition evoke?
13. If you are able, you may want to examine the meter, rhythm, melodic phrases, repetitions of phrases, and harmonies.

Searching for Audio Materials

A growing number of websites provide audio links to speeches, interviews, and historic recordings, although in some cases the links are to transcripts and sheet music, both of which can be valuable for your research. Many of the same search techniques for images apply for audio materials. If you are searching on the Internet in one of the search engines, use the topic, place, or person for a speech, the music genre, country, and/or words "historic music" or "sheet music" for recordings and "interviews" or "oral histories" for oral interviews. (See chapter 6 for a fuller discussion of oral history.) You may also find that your library has a collection of these types of materials. Use the directions in the search box below to search your library's catalog.

Below is a list of the most common file formats you will find on the Internet. Quality often depends on many factors, both the size of the file and the device over which the sound is played.

- *.aif.* Developed by Apple Computer and will work with most browsers.
- *.au.* Created by Sun Microsystems and compatible with most browsers.
- *.wav.* Developed by Microsoft and one of the most common formats supported by most browsers.
- *.mp3.* With the IPOD's popularity, this format is increasing in its prevalence, even for files of older audio material.

SEARCH TIPS (FOR A SEARCH ENGINE)

1. Use the topic, place, or person for a speech, the music genre, country, and/or words "historic music" or "sheet music" for recordings and "interviews" or "oral histories" for oral interviews.

SEARCH TIPS (FOR AN ONLINE CATALOG)

Note: these tips are independent of each other and not to be done step by step.

1. Do a keyword search and limit the results by words in subject speeches.
2. Do an author search with the name of the speaker. Look through the listing for a subheading "Oratory" or "Speeches, Addresses, etc.," for example, "Cicero, Marcus Tullius– Speeches, Addresses, etc."
3. Take special care in looking for music. Music is classified by the genre of music, (e.g., *jazz*) or by the type of song (e.g., *protest songs*). You will need to select your subject heading and then limit your results by the type of material, a sound recording or audio-visual, depending on how your library's catalog allows you to do such a limit. The same pattern follows for a particular composer. Use the composer's name as an author and do the same limit.

Sources for Speeches and Music

Vital Speeches of the Day. 1935– . A magazine that prints important speeches. Check with your library.

History Channel Speeches. http://www.history.com/speeches/ (accessed April 28, 2012). Collection of excerpts of speeches from famous individuals in all areas of public life. Mostly mid-twentieth century to the present.

History and Politics Out Loud. http://www.hpol.org/ (accessed December 18, 2011). Significant political speeches, primarily from the 1960s and 1970s.

American Rhetoric. http://www.americanrhetoric.com/ (accessed December 18, 2011). Audio and video of selected famous American speeches.

Historical Voices. http://www.historicalvoices.org/ (accessed December 18, 2011). Links to other collections of speeches in the twentieth century.

Online Communication Studies Resources (U. of Iowa). http://www.uiowa. edu/~commstud/resources/speech.html (accessed December 21, 2011). Mostly political speeches.

Presidential Rhetoric. http://www.presidentialrhetoric.com/ (accessed December 21, 2011). Speeches since George Washington (some are not video).

Miller Center Presidential Speech Archive. http://millercenter.org/president/speeches (accessed December 21, 2011). Audio and video.

American Memory. http://memory.loc.gov/ (accessed December 18, 2011). Click on the collections for sound recordings. Many folk music recordings and oral interviews are included in the list. Collections include *Voices from the Slave Days*, http://memory.loc.gov/ammem/collections/voices/ and *National Juke Box*, http://www.loc.gov/jukebox/.

American Rhetoric: Online Speech Bank. http://www.americanrhetoric.com/speechbank.htm (accessed December 21, 2011). A large collection of speeches of all kinds. Some fall into the realm of entertainment.

CSpan. Video. http://www.c-spanvideo.org/videoLibrary/ (accessed December 21, 2011). Records, indexes, and archives all *C-SPAN* programming for historical, educational, research, and archival uses.

Archival Sound Recordings. British Library. http://sounds.bl.uk/ (accessed December 18, 2011). Collection includes historical, as well as many other kinds of sounds.

Historic American Sheet Music 1850–1920. http://library.duke.edu/digitalcollections/hasm/ (accessed December 18, 2011). Large searchable collection from Duke University. Only includes front of the sheet music, not the music itself. Part of the Scriptorium collections.

Virtual Gramophone: Canadian Historical Sound Recordings. http://www.collectionscanada.gc.ca/gramophone/index-e.html (accessed December 18. 2011). Early Canadian music.

Dismuke's Virtual Talking Machine: Vintage Phonograph Recordings, 1900–1939. http://dismuke.org/ (accessed December 18, 2011). Digital files from an individual's collection.

Maine Music Box Collection. http://mainemusicbox.library.umaine.edu/ (accessed December 18, 2011). Collections of sheet music, with some audio, 1845–1997.

Smithsonian Folkways. http://www.folkways.si.edu/index (accessed April 28, 2012). Index to Smithsonian recordings of folk music and other recordings. See *Smithsonian Global Sound* below for online access.

Classical Music Library (Alexander Street Press). http://www.alexanderstreetpress.com/products/ (accessed April 28, 2012). Subscription database that provides access to authoritative versions of classical recordings.

Smithsonian Global Sound (Alexander Street Press). http://www.alexanderstreetpress.com/products/ (accessed December 18, 2011). Subscription database that provides historical tracks of folk, country, African American, world, and ethnic music.

Naxos Music Library. http://www.naxosmusiclibrary.com/ (accessed December 18, 2011). Subscription database of classical, jazz, and world music from major recording labels.

Audio Search Engines and Directories

Fagan Finder. http://www.faganfinder.com/audio/.
Political Speeches (Wakeforest University Guide). http://www.wfu.edu/~louden/Political%20Communication/Class%20Information/SPEECHES.html.

Copyright

Copyright is a sticky and difficult issue. Just as you cannot take someone else's idea and claim it as your own, you cannot take an image and reprint it without the producer's permission. There are some basic rules you can follow. If you find that your situation becomes more complex, you will want to consult your library. If you are using an image in a paper that will be turned in to your professor, simply documenting your source and attributing its authorship (i.e., the photographer and/or the source, such as the book, website, or archive) is sufficient. If you have created a website or written a master's thesis or doctoral dissertation, these are considered forms of publishing and you must obtain permission to use images just as you would for a book. Many sources of images, such as libraries, historical societies, and other websites, will allow you to include their images if you acknowledge them as the source, do not make money from your website or project, and use them for educational purposes as opposed to advertising something like a historic tour business. Look for instructions on the website. Usually, there is a link under the word "copyright." If you do not wish to reproduce the image, all you need to do is refer to it in your analysis and list the site as a source.

Manuscripts, oral histories you have collected, and photographs you have taken also have copyright issues. If you have taken a photograph or collected an oral history as part of your project, discuss the process with your professor. All oral history projects require release or consent forms from the individuals you have interviewed.[34] In the case of unpublished documents, such as letters, created after 1978, the general rule is that the author or the author's estate for the life of the author plus 70 years retains the copyright, unless renewed by the author's estate. Works published before 1923 are in the public domain and are copyright-free. However, you would have to digitize the original source, for instance, a photograph or document, and not download someone else's *copy* from a website. Copyright is complicated. When in doubt, assume that the item is copyrighted. Again, if you have any doubts, seek help at your library. A very detailed chart that clearly explains these rules is provided by Cornell University (http://copyright.cornell.edu/resources/publicdomain.cfm).

FOR FURTHER READING

Baigrie, Brian S., ed. *Picturing Knowledge: Historical and Philosophical Problems Concerning the Use of Art in Science.* Toronto: University of Toronto Press, 1996.

Bellman, Jonathan. *A Short Guide to Writing about Music.* 2nd ed. New York: Pearson Longman, 2007.

Berger, John. *Ways of Seeing.* London: British Broadcasting Corporation and Penguin, 1972.

Brett, Guy. *Through Our Own Eyes: Popular Art and Modern History.* Philadelphia: New Society Publishers, 1987.

Brugioni, Dino A. *Photo Fakery: The History and Techniques of Photographic Deception and Manipulation.* Dulles, VA: Brassey's, 1999.

Burke, Peter. *Eyewitnessing: The Uses of Images as Historical Evidence.* Ithaca, NY: Cornell University Press, 2001.

Cameron, Ardis, ed. *Looking for America: The Visual Production of Nation and People.* Malden, MA: Blackwell, 2005.

Care, Handling and Storage of Photographs. Library of Congress and International Federation of Library Associations and Institutions Core Programme Preservation and Conservation, http://www.loc.gov./preservation/resources/care/photobib.html (accessed December, 21, 2011).

Caring for Your Treasures: Photographs. American Institute for Conservation of Historic and Artistic Works, http://aic.stanford.edu/library/online/brochures/photos.html (click on the left: Caring for your Treasures, then photographs.) (accessed December, 21, 2011).

Dasilva, Fabio, Anthony Blasi, and David Dees. *The Sociology of Music.* Notre Dame, IN: University of Notre Dame Press, 1984.

Fitzpatrick, Colleen. *The Dead Horse Investigation: Forensic Photo Analysis for Everyone.* Fountain Valley, CA: Rice Book Press, 2008.

Fitzpatrick, Colleen. *Forensic Genealogy.* Fountain Valley, CA: Rice Book Press, 2005.

Godfrey, Donald G., ed. *Methods of Historical Analysis in Electronic Media.* Mahwah, NJ: Lawrence Erlbaum Associates, 2006.

Harvey, Karen, ed. *History and Material Culture: A Student's Guide to Approaching Alternative Sources.* London: Routledge, 2009.

Herbert, Trevor. *Music in Words: A Guide to Researching and Writing about Music.* New York : Oxford University Press, 2009.

Hogarth, Paul. *The Artist as Reporter.* New York: Reinhold Publishing, 1967.

Holliday, Peter James. *The Origins of Roman Historical Commemoration in the Visual.* New York: Cambridge University Press, 2002.

Howells, Richard, and Robert W. Matson, eds. *Using Visual Evidence.* Maidenhead, Berkshire: McGraw Hill/Open University Press, 2009.

Langford, Martha. *Suspended Conversations: The Afterlife of Memory in Photographic Albums.* Montreal: McGill-Queen's University Press, 2001.

Levine, Robert M. *Images of History: Nineteenth and Early Twentieth Century Latin American Photographs as Documents.* Durham, NC: Duke University Press, 1989.

Monaco, James. *How to Read a Film: The World of Movies, Media, and Multimedia: Language, History, Theory.* New York: Oxford University Press, 2000.

Nickell, Joe. *Camera Clues: A Handbook for Photographic Investigation.* Lexington: University Press of Kentucky, 2004.

O'Connor, John E., ed. *Image as Artifact: The Historical Analysis of Film and Television.* Malabar, FL: Robert E. Krieger Publishing, 1990.

Ostrow, Stephen E. *Digitizing Historical Pictorial Collections for the Internet.* Washington, DC: Council on Library and Information Resources, 1998.

Staley, David J. *Computers, Visualization, and History: How New Technology Will Transform Our Understanding of the Past.* Armonk, NY: M. E. Sharpe, 2003.

Stokstad, Marilyn. *Art History.* 2d ed. New York: Prentice Hall, 2002.

Trachtenberg, Alan. *Reading American Photographs: Images as History.* New York: Hill and Wang, 1989.

Tucker, Amy. *Visual Literacy: Writing about Art.* Boston: McGraw-Hill, 2002.

Tufte, Edward R. *The Visual Display of Quantitative Information.* 2d ed. Cheshire, CT: Graphics Press, 2001. Unique history of graphs and their use and development as a tool to summarize and create visual information.

UVA Electronic Text Center. *Image Scanning: A Basic Helpsheet.* http://etext.virginia. edu/services/helpsheets/scan/scanimage.html (accessed December 21, 2011).

Webmonkey: The Web Developer's Resource. http://www.webmonkey.com/ (accessed December 21, 2011).

Wingell, Richard J. *Writing about Music: An Introductory Guide.* 4th ed. Upper Saddle River, NJ: Pearson Prentice Hall, 2009.

Zelizer, Barbie. *Remembering to Forget: Holocaust Memory through the Camera's Eye.* Chicago: University of Chicago Press, 1998.

NOTES

1. Louise Schneider Adams, *Methodologies of Art* (New York: HarperCollins/Icon Books, 1996), xv–xvi.

2. Peter Burke, *Eyewitnessing: The Uses of Images as Historical Evidence* (Ithaca, NY: Cornell University Press, 2001), 9–10.

3. Motion Picture, Broadcasting, and Recorded Sound Division, Library of Congress, "Theodore Roosevelt: His Life and Times on Film," *American Memory*, http://memory.loc.gov/ammem/trfhtml/trfhome.html; American Folklife Center, Library of Congress, *Voices from the Days of Slavery: Former Slaves Tell Their Stories*, http://memory.loc.gov/ammem/vfshtml/vfshome.html (both accessed January 1, 2006).

4. James West Davidson and Mark Hamilton Lytle, "Mirror with a Memory," in *After the Fact: The Art of Historical Detection* (New York: Knopf, 1982), 216.

5. David Phillips, "Actuality and Affect in Documentary Photography," in *Using Visual Evidence*, ed. Richard Howells and Robert W. Matson (Maidenhead, Berkshire: McGraw Hill/Open University Press, 2009), 59–68.

6. Barbie Zelizer, *Remembering to Forget: Holocaust Memory through the Camera's Eye* (Chicago: University of Chicago Press, 1998), 12–18.

7. Ibid., 16–48.

8. William A. Frassanito, *Gettysburg: A Journey in Time* (New York: Charles Scribner's and Sons, 1975), 191–192; Library of Congress, "Does the Camera Ever Lie? The Case of the Moved Body," *American Memory*, http://memory.loc.gov/ammem/cwphtml/cwpcam/cwcam3.html (accessed December 19, 2011). (See also the Learning Page on the *American Memory* website.) Other examples of staged photographs during wartime include the raising of the flag at Iwo Jima and the return of MacArthur to the Philippines. See also Drew Gilpin Faust, *This Republic of Suffering: Death and the American Civil War* (New York: Alfred A. Knopf, 2008).

9. Zelizer, *Remembering*, 7; Wendy Kozol, *Life's America: Family and Nation in Postwar Photojournalism* (Philadelphia: Temple University Press, 1994).

10. Burke, *Eyewitnessing*, 85.

11. See Robert M. Levine, *Insights into American History: Photographs as Documents* (Upper Saddle River, NJ: Pearson/Prentice Hall, 2004), 11; Frank Goodyear, *"Scholars in Action: Frank Goodyear Analyzes a Daguerreotype,"* History Matters, http://historymatters.gmu.edu/mse/sia/photo.htm (accessed December 20, 2011); Elspeth H. Brown, "Appendix A: Reading the Visual Record," in *Looking for America*, ed. Ardis Cameron (Oxford: Blackwell Publishing, 2005), 362–370; conversation with Lisa McLaughlin, Miami University Faculty, May 2004; Derek Sayer, "The Photograph: The Still Image," in *History beyond the Text: A Student's Guide to Approaching Alternative Sources*, ed. Sarah Barber and C. M. Peniston-Bird (Abingdon, Oxon: Routledge, 2009), 56–60; Phillips, "Actuality and Affect in Documentary Photography," 61.

12. John Berger, *Ways of Seeing* (London: British Broadcasting Corporation and Penguin Books, 1972), 21, 25–26.

13. Ibid., 19.

14. Ibid., 7–8, 50.

15. Ibid., 90–94. Francis Haskell, *History and Its Images: Art and the Interpretation of the Past* (New Haven: Yale University Press, 1993), 1–25.

16. James Hall, *Illustrated Dictionary of Symbols in Eastern and Western Art* (New York: IconEditions, 1994). Use the subject heading in your library's catalog "Symbolism in Art" and look at the subdivisions by country and by type of reference source, encyclopedias, and dictionaries; Sarah Barber, "Fine Art: The Creative Image," in *History beyond the Text: A Student's Guide to Approaching Alternative Sources*, ed. Sarah Barber and C. M. Peniston-Bird (Abingdon, Oxon: Routledge, 2009), 19–25.

17. Adams, *Methodologies*, 58–78.

18. Mark Roskill and David Carrier, *Truth and Falsehood in Visual Images* (Amherst, MA: University of Amherst Press, 1983), 3.

19. Ibid., 1–28.

20. Barber, "Fine Art: The Creative Image," 15–17; David Morgan, "Painting as Visual Evidence," in *Using Visual Evidence*, ed. Richard Howells and Robert W. Matson (Maidenhead, Berkshire: McGraw Hill/Open University Press, 2009), 16.

21. A nice discussion of this in the context of film and television can be found in John E. O'Connor, ed., *Image as Artifact: The Historical Analysis of Film and Television* (Malabar, FL: Robert E. Krieger Publishing, 1990), 6–7.

22. Luke McKernan, "Newsreels Form and Function," in *Using Visual Evidence*, ed. Richard Howells and Robert W. Matson (Maidenhead, Berkshire: McGraw Hill/Open University Press, 2009), 95–106.

23. Pierre Sorlin, "Documentaries: A Goldmine Historians Should Begin to Exploit," in *Using Visual Evidence*, ed. Richard Howells and Robert W. Matson (Maidenhead, Berkshire: McGraw Hill/Open University Press, 2009), 107–121.

24. John E. O'Connor, "Framework 1: The Moving Image as Representation of History," in *Image As Artifact: The Historical Analysis of Film and Television*, ed. John E. O'Connor (Malabar, FL: R. E. Krieger Pub. Co, 1990), 36.

25. Mary E. Beadle, "Visual Evidence," in *Methods of Historical Analysis in Electronic Media*, ed. Donald G. Godfrey (Mahwah, NJ: Lawrence Erlbaum Associates, 2006), 67–112; Michael Paris, "More Than Just Entertainment: The Feature Film and the Historian," in *Using Visual Evidence*, ed. Richard Howells and Robert W. Matson (Maidenhead, Berkshire: McGraw Hill/Open University Press, 2009), 123–138.

26. Many of these issues are discussed at length in Stephen Ostrow, *Digitizing Historical Pictorial Collections for the Internet* (Washington, DC: Council on Library and Information Resources, 1998).

27. For excellent, succinct instructions, see UVA Electronic Text Center. *Image Scanning: A Basic Helpsheet*, http://etext.lib.virginia.edu/services/helpsheets/scan/scanimage.html and UVA Electronic Text Center, *Text Scanning: A Basic Helpsheet*, http://etext.lib.virginia.edu/services/helpsheets/scan/scantext.html (both accessed December 20, 2011).

28. Carla Peterson, "Scholars in Action, Carla Peterson Analyzes Speeches," *History Matters*, http://historymatters.gmu.edu/mse/sia/peterson.htm (accessed January 1, 2006).

29. Ibid.

30. Ibid.

31. Ibid.

32. Fabio Dasilva, Anthony Blasi, and David Dees, *The Sociology of Music* (Notre Dame, IN: University of Notre Dame Press, 1984), 92–105.

33. The criteria listed here are a combination of those suggested in the following guides: Richard J. Wingell, *Writing about Music: An Introductory Guide*, 3d ed. (Upper Saddle River, NJ: Prentice Hall, 2002); Trevor Herbert, *Music in Words: A Guide to Researching and Writing about Music* (London: Associated Board of the Royal Schools of Music, 2001); Jonathan Bellman, *A Short Guide to Writing about Music* (New York: Longman, 2000); and Dasilva, Blasi, and Dees, *The Sociology of Music*, 150–156.

34. Some universities even require your projects to be approved by a group of people called something like the "Institutional Review Board for the Use of Human Subjects in Research" (IRB). Interpretations as to whether oral histories fall under "human subject" regulations are fuzzy. It is best to check with your university or college.

Statistics: Quantifying History   **10**

WHAT YOU WILL LEARN IN THIS CHAPTER
- How statistics as a discipline developed and how they have been collected over time
- How to think about the categories and kinds of statistics
- How to understand, use, and evaluate historical statistics
- How to find statistics and data sets

A Society of Statistics

Statistics and statistical findings permeate our daily lives. Look at any newspaper, listen to any radio or television news broadcast, read any popular magazine and you are likely to find some reference to a statistic and probably even data presented in graph form. In our society facts are often equated with truth and legitimacy. Quoting a statistic that highlights your topic or thesis gives the cause or the idea being discussed validity. We use statistics to understand how we compare, how we prosper or fail, or the seriousness of a particular problem. For instance, we know the causes of death for defined age groups or how much corn is produced, where, and its value.[1] Whether you are antitax or you want more funding for government services, you can see the increase or decrease in taxes paid over time in constant dollars. Further, through market studies published in 2009, we know that seven out of ten men prefer plain ice cream flavors, while 74% of women look for ice cream with chocolate or candy bits. (And neither seems interested in fruit flavors.)[2]

As a researcher, how you understand, interpret, and use the existing statistics is crucial to your research. Faulty use of data or ignorance of existing data will weaken or even negate your argument. However, finding and using data and statistics are often difficult for historians. Historians take evidence and discuss its broader significance, but the nature of data is precise and particular. The data historians try to use is often not standard, not collected in the same fashion over a period of years, nor regularly gathered. Sometimes historians use data and statistics in ways that the original collector never intended. These factors can make data incomplete, incomparable, or even biased in its content. Yet, the very existence of a piece of data tells us what society was concerned with at a given time, even if the data itself is incomplete.

Finding and using data and statistics are difficult for all historical scholars, whether you are new to history research or a seasoned professional. This chapter will discuss the types of statistical data that are available and how they have evolved over time and by producer and product. It will suggest research strategies to find statistics and provide guidance about how to use and evaluate the data you find. Finally, the chapter will conclude with a look at using large datasets. Throughout the chapter the words "statistics" and "data" will be used interchangeably, with the exception of the final section that discusses datasets. Technically, statistics are associated with numbers, and data, a broader concept, includes statistics, as well as facts, which may or may not be entirely numerical. However, for the purpose of this chapter, no such distinction will be made. Much of this chapter focuses on statistics from the United States and the United Kingdom. It is important to remember that the evolution of the collection of data and statistics differs from country to country, depending on government needs and policies and the social developments within the country. The general methods for finding statistics can be applied to any country or time period. The bibliographies at the end of the chapter attempt to include statistical sources from major countries beyond the United States and United Kingdom. However, many, many more print and online sources exist, not just for those two countries, but for countries around the world.

A Short History of the Evolution of Statistical Collection and Analysis: What Can You Expect to Find?

Understanding what types of statistics are available for a particular time and place will help you to plan your research topic and strategy. While statistics of some kind exist for most periods of history and regions of the world, their existence is inconsistent until about the seventeenth century. Prior to the seventeenth century, statistics were not really conceived in the way we think of statistics today. Mostly they were used to count people and goods for tax and conscription purposes, providing money and soldiers to support the government and wars. The elites (nobles, those in power, the "best" of society) needed to know what their loyal subjects had to give. The elites kept household books that tracked their spending.[3]

In the seventeenth century, governments and businesses began to use statistics in planning. Using birth, death, and marriage records, Sir Edmund Halley calculated life expectancy and created tables for insurance companies.[4] The British Government created the Bills of Mortality to count the numbers of deaths during the years of the plague as a means of anticipating outbreaks of the disease.[5] By the end of the eighteenth century, several major studies had been done using the information gathered by census counts to characterize the social and economic health of the population. In the multivolume *Statistical Account of Scotland* (1791–1799), Sir John Sinclair collected numerical data from church parish records, the traditional keeper of vital statistics, as well as earnings and estimates of material goods to create a social picture of the "average man."[6] Also in 1791, Antoine-Laurent Lavoisier, famous as the father of chemistry, gathered data on the annual consumption of food and wine in urban areas in France, which he coupled with a census of land under cultivation to estimate how much agricultural land was required to sustain a growing urban population.[7] Eighteenth-century individuals began to think about and use statistics in their everyday lives. Thomas Jefferson not only kept detailed estate records, but even informed Abigail Adams in a letter that he had 10 ½ grandchildren and 2 ¾ great-grandchildren. He applied this statistical mindset to calculating state representatives' apportionment to the federal government. Benjamin Franklin calculated the probability of contracting small pox from the controversial inoculation procedure, suggesting that the inoculation was safer than natural infection.[8]

The nineteenth century's collection and use of statistics is similar to what we are familiar with today. Statistical societies, and national and local groups of learned men gathered to discuss and collect statistics and disseminate statistical studies. Governments started collecting data on the moral state of society, including statistics on insanity rates, alcoholism, prostitution, suicide, property damage, criminals, and crime and its types (e.g., bribery, rape, robbery). Using this data, they looked at frequencies and tried to correlate it with other data, for example, how educational characteristics were tied to criminal activity.[9] By the late eighteenth and early nineteenth century, censuses, the counting of the population of a country, were common and regularly conducted across much of Europe and the United States (the first census for the United States was in 1790, for Norway and Denmark, 1795, and Britain, 1805). Common people became interested in statistics and facts in general, resulting in an explosion of publications of collections of statistics in the form of compendiums and almanacs.[10] As the nineteenth century progressed, the social reforming Victorians began using statistics to highlight societal conditions and prompt reform. Charles Dickens and Thomas Carlyle opposed governmental use of statistics as political leaders often used data to justify not assisting the poor. Dickens and Carlyle felt that numbers and averages desensitized the compassion of the general population and could not accurately reflect the despair of the poor. Using these statistics governments would deem small numbers of deaths acceptable when weighed against profits and costs of business.[11]

The late nineteenth century brought a more organized and independent (i.e., nongovernmental) surge of statistics and data collection in the form of social surveys and public opinion polls. Initially these two modes of gathering social information were unscientific and driven by individuals' and organizations' desire to reform some perceived social or economic problem. At the turn of the nineteenth century, Victorian reformers worried over the effects of urbanization on public health, family life, and on the working classes in general.[12] In 1895 in the United States the Hull House Association published a study of the residents of Hull House, a settlement house founded by Jane Addams, to highlight women's public health and security issues. In 1899 W. E. B. Du Bois studied the African American community in Philadelphia.[13] Academically trained as a sociologist, Du Bois was an early adopter of social science methodology, but was not taken seriously probably because of his race. In 1909 in the magazine *Charities and the Commons*, an extensive survey looked at Pittsburgh Steel Workers' families' health, work-related injuries, and the general conditions in which they worked.[14] In 1912, Arthur Bowley attempted to collect a random sample of Reading, England householders to look at urban conditions.[15] In the 1930s interwar Germany began collecting data on labor and living conditions, especially rural areas. In France small groups, called *enquêtes*, collected the data, which was used by government agencies.[16]

The early twentieth century saw the rise of scientific principles and the notion of research design applied to the collection of statistical data. By the 1930s, US corporations began surveying consumer markets and consumers' thoughts about the taste and value of products for advertising purposes. Even then, methodological data gathering was problematic because a limited number of people had telephones, which excluded opinions from less wealthy consumers.[17] The twentieth century also brought nationwide opinion polls and more intensive surveying of a population's interests and consumer preferences, for instance, more scientific election polls to predict winners.

Using Statistics: The Nature of Data, Simple to Complex

Using statistics in your research can be revealing, but it can also be difficult to do in a way that is useful to your argument. Understanding how statistics might be presented by identifying categories or types will help you to interpret them. In *History by Numbers*, Pat Hudson suggests categories useful to historians:

- *Descriptive.* Generally simpler data such as a table that shows simple numbers or tallies. This kind of data can be categorical: using such identifiers as names, occupations, gender (called nominal) or using measures or values such as temperature or price-to-earnings ratios (called numeric).[18]

- *Inferential.* Essentially probability about a population in a time and place, for instance, coupling crime and unemployment. Economic theories use descriptive data to predict trends. For example, in 1950, Cornell University studied 1,500 middle-aged men and women and found that 65% of college-educated women were married, compared to 93% of college-educated men. Unmarried women were, "three times more numerous" among college-educated women as among women of the general population. (The study failed to consider that perhaps college was attractive to women who chose not to marry.)[19]

- *Time series.* Looking at the change of measures over time. A time series can use both descriptive and inferential data, but generally looks over a rather long period of time, decades, and at regular intervals. Time series usually have an index, or a base year from which the other statistics are measured, for instance US dollars 1800 = $1.00, so that all of the monetary measures are in the same value.[20]

- *Sampling.* When the whole of a population is too large to count every individual or every item, researchers select a representative group to reflect the larger group. Examples include studies of households by using probate records or looking at an industry, such as the barrel-making industry by examining the records of companies that manufactured the product. This is easier to do with more modern populations. Most historians find themselves dealing with records that are incomplete or irregularly collected data, and thus it is hard to have a true sample to reflect a larger trend. For instance, if you use church records to look at birth and marriage trends, historically, they tend to exclude populations such Jews and Muslims that did not attend "state" churches.[21]

- *Large-scale studies.* Looking at many statistics about a large group of people over a long time. Often these are large, national studies, such as the change in income in the United States in the past century.[22]

- *Mathematical modeling.* Modeling as a whole is trying to predict what might happen based on a collection of variables, for instance, how sectors of the economy behave if certain variables change, or would have changed in a given time. For instance, could slavery have endured as a viable staple of the southern US economy if it had not been abolished by the Civil War?[23]

Most of your research may not be as complex as the examples above, but it is important to understand how others may have gathered and calculated their data. If you do decide to take on a project that is data or statistic intensive, be sure to read some of the resources listed in the bibliography at the end of this chapter and consult with your professor or teacher. You will want to avoid setting up a study using historical data only to find that the assumptions you make in your data collection turn out to be false, inconclusive, or nonrepresentational.

Categorizing Statistics: How They Are Collected and Organized

The categories above help you think about the ways in which historians use data, but finding basic statistics and data require you to think about how the raw numbers would present themselves. Demographic and vital statistics, economic statistics, social statistics, and public opinion data are all categories of statistics that you may find useful. Using these categories will help you in planning your research strategy, identifying potential collectors and producers, and determining value and deficiencies. In each case, you must consider who counted or collected the data and what their purpose was, always considering that this might change over time.

Demographics/Vital Statistics/Census Data

Demographics are statistics about people, including their age, health, earnings, and educational levels. Generally demographics give us a picture of the human condition. Vital statistics are those statistics that directly reflect living: birth (nativity) and death (mortality). Censuses count people in a particular country, for a particular time, and gather other information, such as occupation, about those individuals. Generally, governments who wish to know how many "subjects" they have and some basic information about their lives collect these demographics. Censuses have been taken ever since formal government began. Rulers and ruling bodies needed to know the loyalties of their nobles or elites, as well as the wealth of their citizenry for taxation and conscription. From the sixteenth to the eighteenth centuries some western European nations made several attempts to count and characterize their populations. In the mid-sixteenth century (1547, 1563, 1603, 1676, 1688), the Church of England tried to measure its "communicants," its members, in the wake of the Reformation.[24] In 1607, France tried to estimate its population.[25] These earlier censuses are rather vague, recording simple information such as the number of male heads of household and the number of household residents by gender, or sometimes they only presented total numbers of individuals. Additionally, from time to time the worth or value of a household and its goods was also recorded.

It was not until late in the seventeenth and eighteenth centuries that what we recognize as a modern census came into being. With numerous colonies around the globe, Britain needed to count and measure her subjects. Between 1623 and 1775, England conducted 124 censuses in its 21 colonies including modern-day Canada, United States, and the Caribbean.[26] Ironically, it was not until 1790 for the United States and 1801 for Great Britain that a *regular*, decennial population census was conducted. In modern times, each of these nations conduct a counting of the general population *regularly*, every 10 years. These early censuses usually counted only heads of households, numbers of household members, and some vague economic statistics, such as value of possessions or income. In the United States after the 1850 census, the census rolls, the documents that list individual names, began to reflect each individual in the household with information that included such details as birth date, number of children, and occupation. Collected by an enumerator (usually male), the quality of the information and the data collected depended on his or her competence. In some countries, at various times, enumerators were paid by the number of people they recorded.[27] Census data collected varies from country to country and even from census to census. After the collection of the raw data, the government spends many years aggregating and packaging the data to publish in census publications, abstracts, and almanacs. In addition to a population census, many nations also have agricultural, manufacturing, and industrial censuses at regular intervals. These censuses count industrial and agricultural products, types of land use, resource production and consumption, industry wages and employment.

Vital records record events of individuals' lives, such as birth, death, and marriage statistics. They can be tricky to find. Early collectors of those statistics were local parish churches. Mostly interested in counting their membership, churches recorded births, marriages, and deaths. Not until some time in the nineteenth century did many municipalities and other governing bodies even have a system, let alone a requirement, for collecting such data.

Economic Statistics

Economic statistics help us to understand the strength and prosperity or depression and decline of a nation, region, or selected population. Such statistics include:

- individual and corporate income
- levels of poverty, average wages/earnings
- value of currency
- financial data (debt, savings, interest rates, inflation rates), revenues, as well as levels of taxation
- production and consumption of goods (such as commodities or consumer goods)
- balance of trade between nations (exports and imports)
- gross domestic product

These types of statistics can be hard to find and use, because you must know something about how the statistic was calculated and what it really means. We hear about corn futures and pork bellies, contracts on the projected price of corn in a given time period and the selling price of a side of pork, respectively. Economists use phrases like leading economic indicators that are hard to understand in the present, let alone translate into the past to find comparable statistics. Yet economic statistics tell us about the lives of common people in ways that other types of primary sources cannot. What is produced and what individuals choose to purchase tells us about the values of a time and a culture. Economic statistics, however, are not always comparable because of how they were collected and how they are expressed; for instance, purchasing power due to inflation changes over time so values of goods must be expressed in constant dollars.

Social Statistics

Social statistics, data about the lives and well-being of individuals and populations, have been important tools of governments and rulers, as well as social reformers.

Statistics and data have been collected and analyzed to reflect the social conditions of the general population for many years. In many ways the Domesday Book, a land survey of England in 1085, could be considered an early form of social survey, although its purpose was to collect information on the worth of resources (such as livestock) and land in England for taxation. Yet, it reveals a bit about the material life of the people surveyed.[28] Social data and the social survey became more sophisticated in the late eighteenth and nineteenth centuries.

In 1791, Sir John Sinclair published *The Statistical Account of Scotland,* an early attempt at gathering social statistics, providing data on economics, health, climate, and agriculture. Into the nineteenth century, reform-minded Victorians collected data reflecting the poverty and general state of the population. Reformers were worried over the rural/agricultural population shift to urban areas and how that transition affected public health, public housing, family life, and employment. Many of these social surveys were driven by moral questions and not the objective social science methodology of modern sociological research.[29] The data collectors were often women reformers, medical practitioners, and journalists who sought to bring a societal problem to the attention of the government and the upper classes. Believing that data and statistics could guide their legislation and governmental policy, federal and local governments created commissions to study social problems, for example, collecting data that allowed for a comparison between crime statistics and levels of education.

By the late nineteenth and early twentieth centuries trained sociologists, using a defined methodology, carried out scientific social surveys. In 1899, W. E. B. Du Bois conducted one of the earlier methodologically driven social surveys concerning African Americans in Philadelphia. The survey examined the community as a whole rather than a single or related set of society problems.[30] Listed at the end of the chapter is a representative list of major British and American social surveys and bibliographies of other social surveys.

Public Opinion and Consumer Preferences

Measuring public opinion has always been a challenge. Creating representative samples that accurately predict outcomes of a political race or consumer purchasing preferences is difficult. Not until the late nineteenth century did pollsters use social science methodologies to accurately predict public opinion. While many nations at one time or another have been interested in public opinion, historically the Americans, British, and French seem to have generated more public opinion data.

Pre-Revolutionary France's salons and eighteenth-century British coffeehouses were central places for opinions to be openly, publicly discussed. To gauge public opinion, monarchs and rulers often monitored these gatherings. British coffeehouse discussions were published in such newspapers and magazines as the *Tatler*, *Spectator*, and *Guardian*. Until the twentieth century most opinion gathering focused on local issues, rather than larger national concerns.[31] Straw polls were another way to predict public sentiment. Straw polls were originally conducted orally to gauge a political candidate's popularity. In the early nineteenth century citizens would conduct their own polls, with local newspapers publishing the results. A Buffalo, New York newspaper published a straw poll about the 1856 Buchanan/Fremont presidential race. While at a local prominent citizen's house, 24 survivors of the War of 1812 pledged 21 for Fremont and 3 for Buchanan.[32]

The twentieth century brought modern techniques for conducting polls, as well as a wider, national focus. The *Literary Digest*, a US magazine, conducted a national straw poll of their readers and correctly predicted Woodrow Wilson's election in 1916. Apparently *Literary Digest* readers reflected national attitudes. However in the 1936 election, the magazine incorrectly predicted Alf Langdon over Franklin Roosevelt for US President. George Gallup, with a doctorate in psychology and founder of the American Institute of Public Opinion in 1933, correctly predicted Roosevelt. *Literary Digest* ceased publication in 1937 and the influence of the modern polling organization began.[33]

With the mass production of consumer goods in the late nineteenth century, consumer opinion became more valuable. Corporations began to conduct market research surveys as early as the 1880s.[34] Because the United States has been a leader in public opinion survey, probably more sources of data exist for the United States than for any other country. As you look for public opinion data, remember that some forms of government and some cultures do not encourage public participation or individual expression. To conduct this kind of research could put individuals at risk. You simply may not be able to find actual data because it was not collected or because no one was interested in that data in the time period you are studying.

Gleaning Statistics from Primary Sources

Thus far we have talked about the characteristics and origins of actual statistics that are collected and published for a purpose. There are other sources that contain statistics within them, but that do not have a primarily statistical purpose. Newspapers are a wealth of information. Many times in the back of the paper in the advertising section or just a general short news section, there will be reports of what goods arrived at the port ("Shipping News"), classified ads advertising goods and services for sale or legal notices that might provide information. Further, newspapers have letters to the editor and editorials. You may find indications of public opinion there and perhaps some reports of other quantifiable activities. Public records available at local and state levels also contain data, for instance, probate courts will have wills that might indicate value of goods or estates or include earnings information. Local municipalities might have public criminal statistics. Imagine who might have produced the statistics and how they might have been recorded or reported. Chapter 6 talks about primary sources in depth.

Finding Statistics

How to Think about the Sources

At this point in your quest for statistics, you know historians have a particularly hard time finding reliable and consistent statistical data in a meaningful way. Plain and simple, the data you want may not exist or may be so difficult to compile that it is essentially inaccessible for a semester or yearlong project. Often existing statistics are not collected uniformly over time and contain gaps in data, which creates problems with comparability. You must also be careful to interpret your data or statistics without bias or assumptions. For instance, using wills as a source of data overrepresents wealthy, white males, and civil and criminal court records underrepresents the vast majority of the population, who never were arrested or charged with a crime.[35] Further, the US census never counted religious affiliation in the census (although several special religious censuses were conducted early in the twentieth century), nor until the more recent census, did it count individuals of mixed race, so reliable statistics for certain time periods and kinds of statistics may be hard to find.[36]

Once you have determined what might be a meaningful measure for your research, think about who would be interested in the results, who would have collected the data and why (and would their bias be reflected in the results), and what terms would another generation use to reflect what you wish to measure. In searching for your data, remember that, like other primary sources discussed in chapter 6, you must look for concrete, countable things and not ideas. You cannot count imperialism, but you can count the number of British citizens in India and the number of people who immigrated and emigrated from England and Britain in a given time period. You cannot count modernized nations, but you can use the number of television sets and computers as suggestive qualities of a developed country.

Search Strategies

Statistics are packaged in a number of ways, the most obvious being in their original format, the unprocessed raw data. Look at the original data collection tools, the census rolls, questionnaires, or tables of tabulations. However, probably the most common way to find statistics is in a compilation, an abstract, or the published results of a study. Many collections of statistics exist in the form of almanacs, yearbooks, and abstracts. These sources compile, organize, and index data on a particular subject (often by a single country, or a broad topic: political statistics, statistics on women, etc.), and often from different sources or raw data. In many ways these compilations can provide both interpretation and an index to sources that you would never know existed as they will cite (in a footnote) the original source of the statistics. Almanacs are an old tradition, having existed since written records were kept, but became popular among the general public in the late eighteenth century. Beginning in 1758, the *Annual Register* listed basic information on countries, politics, and current events and included demographic and economic information and statistics on countries and their subregions. For instance, the

1801 volume lists the average price of wheat 1595–1800 for Britain and investment figures for India in China.[37] While almanacs (and yearbooks as well) contain both text and statistics, abstracts tend to contain tables of data compiled, often, but not exclusively, from governmental and other official sources (fig. 10.1). "No. 138. - Population Gainfully Occupied: Adults and Children By Sex and By States and Territories Census Year 1900,"[38] is a table from the *Statistical Abstract of the United States* that combines data from the Bureau of the Census and Department of Commerce and Labor.

Questions to Think about as You Begin Your Research

In general, asking the following questions will help you work through some of the search tips listed below. By answering these questions, you may find statistics and participants that will help you develop search terms. For example, if many of the New York City police were Irish Immigrants, you may want to look for statistics on Irish immigration and information provided by police unions and organizations, as well as basic statistics on New York City. You may not know the names of these organizations, but you have an idea about the kinds of data you are looking for.[39]

1. What do you want to measure? Think in terms of objects and concrete data, not ideas. When you find your statistics ask yourself what is actually being measured.

2. What is a reliable and valid measure of your question? Again think in concrete terms, not middle-class salaries, but by category of salaries by age, region, gender, and so on and not average earnings or wages, but mean or median.

3. Can you find a representative population? Would the population that you want to count be represented or even be countable, for instance, all African Americans in the US South?

4. Who or what (such as an organization) would be the participants and who would be interested in the findings? Governments might be interested in crime or education statistics. The National Urban League, a civil rights organization founded in 1910 in the United States, publishes an annual yearbook entitled the *State of Black Americans*, which includes data about African Americans social and economic conditions.

No. 138.—POPULATION GAINFULLY OCCUPIED: Adults[1] and Children,[2] by Sex and by States and Territories, Census Year 1900.

[From reports of the Bureau of the Census, Department of Commerce and Labor.]

State or Territory.	Men.	Women.	Children.		Total.
			Boys.	Girls.	
Alabama	482,190	158,345	80,989	41,664	763,188
Arizona	45,226	6,162	1,358	624	53,370
Arkansas	358,195	62,532	49,747	15,321	485,795
California	549,158	85,790	7,187	2,132	644,267
Colorado	187,394	27,369	2,903	597	218,263
Connecticut	290,133	83,898	6,838	4,741	385,610
Delaware	57,243	11,894	2,781	1,078	72,996
District of Columbia	84,415	40,382	1,365	779	126,941
Florida	152,708	33,459	11,281	4,122	201,570
Georgia	568,470	182,037	77,462	36,502	864,471
Idaho	56,772	4,375	1,395	141	62,683
Illinois	1,458,400	275,105	50,994	19,541	1,804,040
Indian Territory	108,544	10,020	12,950	2,196	133,710
Indiana	755,783	111,024	26,454	5,692	898,953
Iowa	657,957	102,037	24,564	4,846	789,404
Kansas	431,865	53,386	20,304	2,185	507,740
Kentucky	593,233	98,181	53,676	7,441	752,531
Louisiana	365,562	109,484	39,620	21,427	536,093
Maine	220,868	49,917	3,979	2,013	276,777
Maryland	342,721	91,097	17,034	7,886	458,738
Massachusetts	862,981	317,558	16,393	11,475	1,208,407
Michigan	752,776	126,517	19,523	7,174	905,990
Minnesota	531,973	90,887	16,973	6,041	645,874
Mississippi	402,860	144,254	63,906	34,103	645,123
Missouri	914,245	145,498	52,621	9,028	1,121,392
Montana	104,061	9,539	929	270	114,799
Nebraska	315,072	44,121	12,282	2,495	373,970
Nevada	17,626	1,969	183	31	19,809
New Hampshire	134,414	39,807	2,547	1,951	178,719
New Jersey	584,780	142,718	18,457	11,804	757,759
New Mexico	56,723	5,766	2,987	544	66,020
New York	2,269,211	635,319	55,218	36,726	2,996,474
North Carolina	478,595	127,740	77,986	32,421	716,742
North Dakota	100,423	13,073	3,125	1,019	117,640
Ohio	1,265,716	233,177	34,165	12,894	1,545,952
Oklahoma	115,129	9,708	7,309	549	132,695
Oregon	148,869	17,916	2,331	521	169,637
Pennsylvania	1,932,857	395,656	84,195	35,881	2,448,589
Rhode Island	134,686	48,203	5,143	3,891	191,923
South Carolina	333,282	142,433	56,363	38,917	570,995
South Dakota	115,636	14,425	5,876	1,219	137,156
Tennessee	547,672	103,553	63,711	12,651	727,587
Texas	819,037	122,425	73,604	17,967	1,033,033
Utah	71,745	10,334	2,095	430	84,604
Vermont	110,011	21,852	2,170	900	134,933
Virginia	492,232	114,438	44,651	11,094	662,415
Washington	201,799	20,203	2,807	578	225,387
West Virginia	272,159	28,680	22,343	2,481	325,663
Wisconsin	595,549	106,474	20,842	9,673	732,538
Wyoming	40,469	2,893	795	111	44,268
Total	22,489,425	4,833,630	1,264,411	485,767	29,073,233

Geographical divisions.[3]

North Atlantic	6,539,941	1,734,928	194,940	109,382	8,579,191
South Atlantic	2,781,825	772,160	311,266	135,280	4,000,531
North Central	7,895,395	1,315,724	287,723	81,807	9,580,649
South Central	3,792,422	818,502	445,512	153,319	5,209,755
Western	1,479,842	192,316	24,970	5,979	1,703,107
Alaska	28,905	3,428	802	200	33,335
Hawaii	83,219	5,955	828	170	90,172
Military and naval	90,179	142	9		90,330

[1] Persons 16 years of age and upward.
[2] Persons 10 to 15 years of age.
[3] For States and Territories included in each division see note 5, p. 43.

▶ **Figure 10.1.** How to Read a Statistical Table. This table, entitled "Population Gainfully Occupied" is from the *Statistical Abstract of the United States for the Year 1910*. The *Statistical Abstract* was an annual compilation of data collected by the US government and other sources the US government uses. Note the table number in the upper left and the page number in the upper right. In some years the index at the back of the volume refers to the table number and sometimes the page number. The title, "Population Gainfully Occupied: Adults and Children, by Sex and By States and Territories, Census Year 1900." Even though this is the 33rd *Statistical Abstract*, the figures reflect the last decennial census. (The government will not have any new statistics to report until the next decennial census in 1910, and it will take some time to compile that data. Do not expect 1910 data in the 1911 *Statistical Abstract*.) The footnotes at the bottom of the page clarify how the government defined Adults (persons over 16) and children (persons aged 10–15). Below the title, the sources of the statistics are listed, in this case Bureau of the Census and the Department of Commerce and Labor. If you want more detailed statistics, you can look in the annual reports of these agencies or other agency documents. In this particular case the numbers listed are actual numbers. In later years, as the United States grew, the numbers are reflected in thousands. That means the figure listed in the table would have three zeros (,000) after it.

Source: "No. 138. Population Gainfully Occupied: Adults and Children by Sex and By States and Territories, Census Year, 1900," *Statistical Abstract of the United States 1910*, 33rd ed. (Washington, DC: Government Printing Office, 1911).

SEARCH TIPS
Collections and Compendiums of Statistics

1. Use one of the general statistical sources, abstracts, or almanacs listed below and look at the sources used to create the table of statistics in which you are interested. That will often lead you to related statistics. To find other statistical collections, search for the subject: "Country—statistics." For example, "India—statistics" finds *Indian Agricultural Statistics* (Delhi [etc.]: Directorate of Economics & Statistics, Ministry of Agriculture & Irrigation [etc.], 1885), as well as *Annual Report of the Mysore Department of Health* (Bangalore: Printed at the Mysore Government Press, 1929) and *Memorandum on the Age Tables and Rates of Mortality of the Indian Census of 1901* (Calcutta: Office of the superintendent, government printing, India, 1905).

2. In your online catalog or *WorldCat*, search by a broad topic either in a keyword or subject search (e.g., "women" or "social conditions") and limit your search by "statistics" in the subject. (If this does not work, then add "statistics" in as a keyword search with your other terms.)

3. In your online catalog or *WorldCat*, use one of the common
   subject subdivisions that reflect what you are searching for
   and then limit your search either by subject, "statistics" (which
   itself is a common subject subdivision) or keyword "statistics."
   Some of the more common and useful subject subdivisions are:
   "social conditions," "economic," "public opinion," "economic
   conditions," "policy," and "politics and government."

4. Many organizations, corporations, and government
   departments issue annual reports that contain data from
   the previous year about issues they are concerned with or
   administer. Identify those likely to be concerned with your
   issue and in your online catalog or *WorldCat*, search by
   author, the organization or person that could have produced
   the statistics. For example, "United States. Department of
   Commerce," "European Commission," "South Africa, Bureau of
   Statistics," or "American Federation of Labor."

Demographic and Census Statistics

Official bodies of the ruling government conduct most censuses. Those
countries that have democratic systems and more stable governments produce censuses on a more regular basis and probably with more reliable content. Always question the motives of a government and the likelihood that
a census would have been conducted. In some cases, there will be none.

1. In an online catalog, use the subject heading "country–
   census"; sometimes "United States–1880 census" and
   even sometimes "United States, Census 10th, 1880," also
   "country–population–statistics."

2. Search for keywords in the author field "census" or author,
   country. Bureau of the Census (e.g., "United States. Bureau of
   the Census," but sometimes the form is "US Census Bureau" or
   "United States. Census Office"). However, not every country
   will have the formal agency title "bureau." For instance, for
   India, the author would be "India. Census Commissioner"
   and for Great Britain, "Great Britain. Census Office" or
   "Great Britain. General Register Office." The key to looking
   for "author" is to look for the name of the agency that
   administered the census *at the time*.

3. In an online catalog, search by subject, "Country or
   State–Statistics, Vital" (Ohio–statistics, vital) or by type of
   statistic, "Mortality–Country–Statistics" (Mortality–Great

Britain–Statistics) or "country–population–statistics" (United States–population–statistics).

4. Organizations also gather statistics, sometimes from these official sources, and sometimes through studies of their own. Think about who else might be interested in demographics and see if they have published a report.

Economic Statistics

1. Be sure, especially for this type of statistic, to look at the abstracts and compendiums listed at the end of this chapter. For basic economic statistics much of the collection, adjusting for time, and standardization, has been done for the basic categories.
2. Decide what kind of broad economic statistic you want and search for that as a subject. For example: "Prices–Great Britain–History," "Money–France–History," "Economic history– Statistics," "England–Economic conditions–century," Follow the pattern. The difficulty is in figuring out the category of economic term.

Social Statistics and Social Surveys

1. In an online catalog, use the subject term "social surveys."
2. In an online catalog, search for a particular place, such as Liverpool (England) and limit by the words in the subject, "social conditions." Then limit by publication date.

Public Opinion and Consumer Preferences

1. In an online catalog, do a broad keyword search with your topic and limit by the phrase "public opinion."
2. Many polls are published in newspapers. Browse through a local newspaper or through a major newspaper such as the New York Times or Washington Post during the period you are studying. Also check the letters to the editor section.
3. Use the subject "Public Opinion Polls" in an online catalog. Usually the subject is divided by country, so limit by the name of a country.
4. Look for publications by the major polling agencies and organizations. (Harris Polls, Russell Sage Foundation, Gallup, Crossley, Pew Research).

Evaluating Statistics: Common Problems with Data Collection and Results

Remember that data over time has not always been collected in the same way, nor have questions been uniformly asked. Critically thinking about the statistics you have is important so that you do not overstate the significance of what you are trying to analyze and discuss. Misusing statistics can result in your argument falling apart. Begin with some benchmark numbers, like the total population of a country or locality, the total number by gender, age, or in general the total number of a broad category, such as deaths, regardless of type. Find other data with which to contextualize your statistic(s). For example the September 11th terrorist attacks killed around 3,025 in a US population of 285 million that had a death per million rate of 11 people. In the Battle of Antietam in the American Civil War, around 3,600–5,000 people died in a US population of 33.2 million with a death per million rate of 110–115 people.[40] Both of these events had extremely high numbers of deaths, but in order to grasp the significance and the magnitude of the events you need to compare the statistics to other events and to ask how the deaths were calculated (and if they include individuals who may have died later as a result of the event, either by wounds, suicides, or diseases). Further, you must always question the source and purpose of your data. Sometimes the reporters or collectors of a statistic have a specific underlying philosophy or bias and are using that piece of data to cause alarm and incite action.

Questions to Evaluate Data

Asking questions of your data will help you evaluate its reliability and useability.[41]

1. What was the purpose of the collection? If you use the data differently than the original collectors, could the data contain unanticipated biases or omissions that skew your research?

2. Who collected/created the data? How are the collectors in a position to know about the data? When was it collected? Sometimes data is not collected with an objective purpose in mind, rather a desire to highlight a problem perceived by the collector. Also sometimes a specific objective skews the data because the collector is unable to collect data from all sides of an issue.

3. How was the data collected and the statistic created? Even if you do not understand or even know the methodology, you need to have a sense of

the source of the data and how it was compiled. Sometimes the collectors may have been unreliable, such as poorly paid British clerks collecting statistics on colonial India or certain populations excluded because they were marginalized in society (e.g., Jews).

4. What bias can be attributed to the time in which the data was collected? For instance, differentiating between races today does not have the assumptions of past generations of racial inferiority.

5. What data is missing? Watch for data that is selective. Is a population left out, perhaps because of race or gender, or is there an alternative set of data that might change your perception? For instance, if auto accidents are the leading cause of deaths in young people, what are alternative causes of death?

6. Thinking about a single number or several numbers:

   • Is the number too big (could the decimal point be misplaced)?

   • Does the number seem plausible considering those benchmark numbers you know?

   • Can this actually be measured? Is this a meaningful number?

7. Is the result expressed in a way that is illogical or seemingly intent on deception? For instance, 11½ days equals 1 million seconds?

Data Problems: Signs That Something is Wrong

Watch for these particular problems with data and statistics,[42] especially those that have been filtered or reported by a second source, for instance, in a newspaper story and not the original published report or table:

1. Large numbers and rounded numbers. For instance, rounding up to 300 million from 297 million is a 3 million difference, unlike rounding up from 297 to 300. Also watch for "loaded" words such as greatest, worst, leading cause, epidemic.

2. Poor definition of what is being counted. If the problem is defined too broadly, for instance, does number of rapes include actual, attempted, or broader definitions of groping or touching? Does homelessness include those living with relatives?

3. Weak sample both in size and variety. Is the sample statistically significant and representative? For instance the Kinsey Report, *Sexual Behavior of the Human Male* (1948) and *Sexual Behavior of the Human Female* (1953),

reported that the numbers of sexual encounters outside of marriage were significant, but the pool of subjects was overwhelmingly college educated and contained more homosexuals than a truly random and representative general population. The Kinsey Report did not presuppose any findings and did intend to be unbiased, but inadvertently, through the studies' methodology, erroneous results may have been generated.

4. Inappropriate comparisons. For instance, the United States counts lawyers as those who pass the bar, but in Japan those who are not licensed, but have a degree can work for corporations.

5. Portrayal of a small number or shocking instance as common or average or indicative of a trend.

6. Change of rate and significance over time. Using rates and percentages can be misleading, for instance, a 100% increase for a population of 200 is quite different than a 100% increase for a population of 2 million. Economists account for this disparity over time by presenting time series data in "constant dollars," often represented by the phrase: "in 1970 dollars."

7. Wording and order of survey questions may be misleading. For example, if a majority of respondents agree that abortion is acceptable to save a mother's life, does that translate into a majority supporting legalized abortion?

8. Graphs (pie charts, bar graphs, line graphs) that visually represent data, can distort your sense of significance. Watch the scale or numbers on the access. A wide spread of numbers may create short bars in the graph and make a significant problem look insignificant because of the size of the bar on the graph.

Datasets: Doing Your Own Thing

You may want to put your own data together instead of relying on a preformatted table. There are many sources of online data, but many will only provide statistics and data for about the last 20 years. The Minnesota Population Center has various sets of data for various years in the *IPUMS (Integrated Public Use Microdata Series, http://www.ipums.org/)* collections. The free data requires a registration and reliably covers 1960 to the present with some datasets going back into the late eighteenth century. *ICPSR (Interuniversity Consortium for Political and Social Research*, http://www.icpsr.umich.

edu/icpsrweb/ICPSR/) at the University of Michigan is a large gateway to datasets collected by many academic researchers and research organizations, including universities. Historical datasets include: *Time Series Data for Chicago, 1840–1973, Slave Sales and Appraisals, 1775–1865,* and *Internal Colonialism Study: National Integration in the British Isles, 1851–1966.* Use of *ICPSR* data requires either a membership by your university or a purchase of a dataset, although some data is freely downloadable. The Cross-National Time-Series Data Archive (http://www.databanksinternational.com/) has some data for various countries from about 1815. Global Financial Data (http://www.globalfinancialdata.com/index.html) also has historical statistics, but you must be a subscriber. Sources like the Historical Census Browser at the University of Virginia http://mapserver.lib.virginia.edu/ are free. Consult with your librarian about what raw data sources might exist and what fee-based resources you have access to.

The more complex and the more data and statistics you use, the more important it is that you are certain that you are counting properly and expressing significant numbers. Conscientious historians have tried to legitimately discuss the significance of some statistics they have gathered only to find out that the conclusions they drew are weakened by the data they have. You may decide you want to use large datasets to custom create your own variables. Before embarking on creating your own data, you will want to consult with your professor or teacher to make sure you are defining your variables and their relationships effectively. Many college and university libraries also have a data librarian that has access to larger sets of data and can help you run searches and set up results.

SELECTED RESOURCES

Encyclopedias and Background Information

Statistics: A Very Short Introduction. David J. Hand. New York: Oxford University Press, 2008. Nice, broad overview of terms and processes. Not necessarily historical.

Polling America: An Encyclopedia of Public Opinion. Samuel J. Best and Benjamin Radcliff, eds. Westport, CT: Greenwood Press, 2005. Good for modern-day definitions and processes.

The Dimensions of the Past: Materials, Problems, and Opportunities for Quantitative Work in History. Val R. Lorwin and Jacob M. Price. New Haven: Yale University Press, 1972. Dated, but useful to identify statistics in other countries outside of the United States.

Understanding Statistics

Making History Count: A Primer in Quantitative Methods for Historians. Charles H. Feinstein and Mark Thomas. New York: Cambridge University Press, 2002. *History by Numbers: An Introduction to Quantitative Approaches.* Pat Hudson. New York: Oxford University Press, 2000. Two hardcore "how to" guides for historians who generally do not have a quantitative background. *A Guide to Quantitative History.* R. Darcy, and Richard C. Rohrs. Westport, CT: Praeger, 1995.

Collections of General Statistics/Statistical Abstracts

International Historical Statistics: Africa, Asia, and Oceana 1750–2005. 6th ed. B. R. Mitchell. New York: Palgrave Macmillan, 2003.
International Historical Statistics: The Americas 1750–2005. 6th ed. B. R. Mitchell. New York: Palgrave Macmillan, 2003.
International Historical Statistics: Europe 1750–2005. 6th ed. B. R. Mitchell. New York: Palgrave Macmillan, 2007.
Handbook of Historical Statistics (series). Boston: G. K. Hall, dates vary. Part of the international historical statistics series. A single volume is devoted to one country or region. Primarily nineteenth and twentieth century. Search by the series name.
Statistical Abstract of the United States. Washington, DC: Government Printing Office, 1879– . Annual. Vols. for 1878–1902 issued by the Bureau of Statistics, Dept. of the Treasury; 1903–1911 by the Bureau of Statistics, Dept. of Commerce and Labor; 1912–1937 by the Bureau of Foreign and Domestic Commerce 1938, the Bureau of the Census. http:// http://www.census.gov/compendia/statab/past_years.html (accessed December 28, 2011). The last edition of the *Statistical Abstract* will be published in 2012.
United States Historical Census Data Browser. Online. Available: http://mapserver.lib.virginia.edu/ (accessed December 4, 2011).
Historical Statistics of the States of the United States: Two Centuries of the Census, 1790–1990. Compiled by Donald B. Dodd. Westport, CT: Greenwood, 1993.
Historical Statistics of the United States, Millennial Edition Colonial Times to the Present. New York: Cambridge University Press, 2006. (Also available electronically by subscription.)
Historical Statistics of the South, 1790–1970. Donald B. Dodd and Wynelle S. Dodd. Tuscaloosa: University of Alabama Press, 1973. Some statistics are from state sources.

Abstract of British Historical Statistics. B. R. Mitchell. Cambridge: University Press, 1962.

Second Abstract of British Historical Statistics. B. R. Mitchell and H. G. Jones. Cambridge: Cambridge University Press, 1971.

Annual Abstract of Statistics. London: HMSO, 1840– . Formerly, *Statistical Abstract for the United Kingdom.*

A Vision of Britain through Time. See the Census Section for statistics. http://www.visionofbritain.org.uk/index.jsp (accessed December 4, 2011).

Historical Statistics of Canada. 2d ed. F. H. Leacy, ed. Ottawa: Statistics Canada, 1983. Also online: http://www.statcan.gc.ca/start-debut-eng.html (accessed December 4, 2011).

Historical Statistics of Canada. M. C. Urquhart, ed. Cambridge, England: Cambridge University Press, 1965. Wages, government financials, agricultural production. Primarily twentieth century.

Historical Statistics of Japan. Tokyo: Nikon Tokei Kyokai (Japan Statistical Association), 2006. 5 vols. Also online http://www.stat.go.jp/english/data/chouki/index.htm (accessed December 4, 2011).

Russia and Eurasia Facts and Figures Annual. Gulf Breeze, FL: Academic International Press, 1993– . Annual. Formerly *USSR Facts and Figures Annual.*

East European and Soviet Data Handbook: Political, Social and Developmental Indicators 1945–1975. Paul S. Shoup. New York: Columbia University Press, 1981.

Electronic Repository of Russian Historical Statistics. Eighteenth to twenty-first centuries, forthcoming. http://www.nes.ru/en/science/russiastats (accessed December 4, 2011).

Annuaire Statistique de la France. Paris: Institut National de la Statistique et des Etudes Economiques, 1878– . Annual.

Statistisches Jahrbuch...für die Bundesrepublik Deutschland. Stuttgart: W. Kohlhammer, 1880– . Earlier titles include: *Statistisches Jahrbuch für das Deutsche Reich* and *Statistisches Jahrbuch der Deutschen Demokratischen Republik.* Statistics for Germany.

China Facts and Figures Annual. Gulf Breeze, FL: Academic International Press, 1978– . Annual.

Statistical Abstract of Latin America 1956–2002. University of California, Los Angeles, and UCLA Latin American Center. Los Angeles: University of California at Los Angeles.

Montevideo-Oxford Latin American Economic History Database 1900– . Database contains basic demographic and economic statistics. http://oxlad.qeh.ox.ac.uk/search.php (accessed November 25, 2011).

African Statistical Yearbook. Annuaire Statistique pour L'Afrique. United Nations. [Addis Ababa]: Economic Commission for Africa, United Nations, 1974– .

Statistical Yearbook for Asia and the Far East. Annuaire Statistique pour L'Asie Et L'Extrême-Orient. United Nations. Bangkok: Economic Commission for

Asia and the Far East, 1968– . Later title, *Statistical Yearbook for Asia and the Pacific.*

Social Explorer 1790– . http://www.socialexplorer.com/ (accessed December 4, 2011). List of free historical websites for many European countries.

Links to British Historical Data from Oxford University. http://historyatox.wordpress.com/2011/05/09/delicious110509/. (accessed December 4, 2011). See the free list toward the bottom of the site.

Digital South Asia Library. http://dsal.uchicago.edu/statistics/ (accessed December 4, 2011). Mostly statistics from British India.

Statistical Yearbook of the League of Nations. Geneva, Switzerland: Economic Intelligence Service, League of Nations, 1931–1944. Basic social and economic statistics of member nations. Lists sources of information.

Statistical yearbook = Annuaire statistique. New York [etc.]: United Nations, 1948– . Title varies. Compilation of general statistics. Current issues available online at: http://unstats.un.org/unsd/syb/default.htm (accessed December 28, 2011).

Cross-National Time-Series Data Archive. http://www.databanksinternational.com/ (accessed December 28, 2011). Annual data for countries since about 1815.

Fedstats. http://www.fedstats.gov/ (accessed December 28, 2011). List of US government agencies and the statistics they produce.

Almanacs and Yearbooks

A Topical Index of Early U.S. Almanacs, 1776–1800. Robert K. Dodge, comp. Westport, CT: Greenwood Press, 1997. Index by topic within year. Nice bibliography of almanacs as well.

The World Almanac and Book of Facts. New York: Press Pub. Co. (The New York World), 1923– .

The Statesman's Year-book/New Statesman's Yearbook. London: Palgrave, 1864– . British.

An Almanack for the Year of Our Lord. London: J. Whitaker, 1869– . Commonly referred to as *Whitaker's Almanac.* British.

The Farmers' Almanac, for the Year of… various publishers, 1800s– .

Annual Register (varies: *The Annual Register of World Events, Cobbett's Annual Register, The Annual Register: A Review of Public Events at Home and Abroad for the Year…*) 1758– . Annual information about Britain and the world. Good for basic statistics on many places in the world, some of which no longer exist. The Bodleian Library has some of the early volumes online (http://www.bodley.ox.ac.uk/cgi-bin/ilej/pbrowse.pl?item=title&id=ILEJ.5.&title=), as well as the Hathi Trust collection (http://catalog.hathitrust.org/Record/009795767). Some volumes are available in the database, *Early English Books Online,* A subscription database of the Annual Register is from ProQuest/Chadwick Healy. Check with your library

Economic, Financial, and Commercial Statistics

Two Thousand Years of Economic Statistics: World Population, GDP and PPP.
Aleksandr V. Avakov. New York: Algora Pub, 2010.

Measuring Worth. http://www.measuringworth.com/ (accessed December 4, 2011).

Current Value of Old Money. http://projects.exeter.ac.uk/RDavies/arian/current/
howmuch.html (accessed December 4, 2011). Links to a number of historical
money sites and calculators.

Value of a Dollar: Colonial Era to the Civil War 1600–1865. Scott Derks and Tony
Smith. Millerton, NY: Grey House Publishing, 2005.

The Value of a Dollar: Prices and Incomes in the United States, 1860–2009. 4th ed.
Scott Derks. Amenia, NY: Grey House Pub, 2009. (Also part of the Gale Virtual
Reference Library.)

How Much Is It Worth Today? Online. http://eh.net/hmit/ (accessed December 4,
2011).

Value of a Pound: Prices and Incomes in Britain 1900–1993. Oksana Newman and
Allan Foster. New York: Gale Research, 1995.

How Much is that in Real Money?: A Historical Commodity Price Index... 2nd rev.
and enl. ed., John J. McCusker. Worcester, MA: American Antiquarian Society,
2001. Covers 1865–2000.

Money and Exchange in Europe and America, 1600–1775: A Handbook. John
McCusker. Chapel Hill: University of North Carolina Press and the Institute
of Early American History and Culture, 1978. Tables by state or country (e.g.,
Barbados) or city (e.g., Paris). Introduction to currency, coinage, and exchange
for each place.

Handbook of Medieval Exchange. Peter Spufford. London: Royal Historical Society,
1986. Discusses currencies of Europe with values by year, as available. Begins
in twelfth century.

Prices and Wages in England from the Twelfth to the Nineteenth Century. 2 vols.
New York: Longmans, Green, 1939. Analysis and tables of purchases/prices of
goods.

Recherches et documents sur L'histoire des prix en France de 1500 à 1800. Henri
Hauser. Paris: Les Presses Modemes, 1936.

EH.net. Economic History Association. https://eh.net/ (accessed December 4, 2011).
Collections of economic history information. See especially the databases section.

Medieval and Early Modern Databank. http://www2.scc.rutgers.edu/memdb/
(accessed December 4, 2011).

Wholesale Commodity Prices in the United States, 1700–1861. Arthur Harrison Cole.
Cambridge, MA: Harvard University and the International Scientific Committee
on Price History, 1938. Volume 1, by year, then commodity and place. Volume 2
provides an overview and analysis by place.

Wholesale Prices for 213 Years, 1720–1932. G. F. Warren and F. A. Pearson. Ithaca,
NY: Cornell University, 1932.

OECD historical statistics = Statistiques rétrospectives de l'OCDE. Paris: OECD, 1999. Covering 1960–1997. Organisation for Economic Co-operation and Development includes comparative economic statistics for most "free market" nations.

Worldbank Financial Data. 1960– . http://databank.worldbank.org/ (accessed December 28, 2011). Basic data from countries around the world.

International Financial Statistics. Washington, DC: International Monetary Fund, 1945– . Basic data from countries around the world.

Global Financial Database. http://www.globalfinancialdata.com/index.html (accessed December 28, 2011). Requires a subscription. Financial data from the twelfth century to the present.

General Demographics, Social Characteristics

American Consumer Series. Ithaca, NY: New Strategist Publications, various dates and editions. Includes such titles as *American Attitudes, Official Guides to the Generations, Racial and Ethnic Diversity.* Most statistics are from the 1970s forward.

Yearbook of Labour Statistics. Geneva: International Labor Organization, 1935– . Data on worldwide unemployment, wages, strikes, and so on.

Statistical yearbook = Annuaire statistique. Unesco. Paris: Unesco, 1963. Also online: http://www.uis.unesco.org/Pages/default.aspx (accessed December 5, 2011).

World Military and Social Expenditures. Ruth Leger Sivard. Leesburg, VA: WMSE Publications, 1974– . World Military Expenditures and Arms Transfers.

SIPRI Yearbook: World Armaments and Disarmament. Stockholm International Peace Research Institute. Stockholm: Almquist & Wiksell, 1968– . Online since 1988: http://www.sipri.org/research/armaments/milex/milex_database (accessed December 5, 2011).

Historical Statistics of Black America. Jessie Carney Smith and Carrell Horton. New York: Gale Research, 1995.

Nations within a Nation: Historical Statistics of American Indians. Paul Stuart. New York: Greenwood Press, 1987.

Demographic yearbook. Annuaire démographique. United Nations. New York: Dept. of Economic and Social Affairs, Statistical Office, United Nations, 1948– . Also online: http://unstats.un.org/unsd/demographic/products/dyb/dyb2.htm (accessed December 5, 2011).

State, Economy and Society in Western Europe, 1815–1975: A Data Handbook in Two Volumes. Peter Flora and James Alber, et al. Chicago: St James Press, 1983–1987.

China Social Statistics. William T. Liu, ed. China Statistics Series. Household expenditures, education levels, health and crime data, and so on. Coverage varies according to topic, some back into the late 1940s. Part of a series.

The European Population since 1945. Franz Rothenbacher. New York: Palgrave Macmillan, 2005.

Montevideo-Oxford Latin American Economic History Database (1900–2000). Fee based. http://oxlad.qeh.ox.ac.uk/ (accessed December 5, 2011).

Slave Movement during the Eighteenth and Nineteenth Centuries. http://www.disc.wisc.edu/slavedata/ (accessed December 5, 2011).

Censuses

Many of the general abstracts listed above rely on census data for many of their tables of statistics. The sources below are devoted wholly to census statistics and focus on the United States and Great Britain. Many other countries will have similar print and online sources. Since a government generally conducts the census, see also the bibliography sources below on government sources. For background on the United States Census, see *Encyclopedia of the U.S. Census*, Margo J. Anderson (Washington, DC: CQ Press, 2000).

National Historical Geographic Information System. https://www.nhgis.org/ (accessed December 5, 2011). Map historic US census data.

Vision of Britain through Time. http://www.visionofbritain.org.uk/ (accessed December 5, 2011).

Census Records in the National Archives (Britain). http://www.nationalarchives.gov.uk/records/census-records.htm (accessed December 5, 2011). Most results require a subscription.

Online Historical Census Reports. http://www.histpop.org/ (accessed December 5, 2011).

Canadian Century Research Infrastructure. http://www.canada.uottawa.ca/ccri/CCRI/index.htm (accessed December 5, 2011).

Census Reports of Great Britain. Interdepartmental Committee on Social and Economic Research. Guides to Official Sources, No. 2. London: His Majesty's Stationary Office, 1951. A guide to what was asked and what reports resulted for the censuses between 1801 and 1931.

The Handbook of National Population Censuses: Latin America and the Caribbean, North America, and Oceania. Doreen S. Goyer and Eliane Domschke. Westport, CT: Greenwood Press, 1983.

The Handbook of National Population Censuses: Europe. Doreen S. Goyer and Gera E. Draaijer. New York: Greenwood Press, 1992.

The Handbook of National Population Censuses: Africa and Asia. Eliane Domschke and Doreen S. Goyer. New York: Greenwood Press, 1986. Three guides to finding historic censuses of other countries.

Polls/Public Opinion

For a fuller list of potential sources, see Molly Gastinger, University of Pennsylvania Libraries guide (http://gethelp.library.upenn.edu/guides/polisci/polls.html); Michael Engle, Cornell University Libraries guide (http://

olinuris.library.cornell.edu/ref/pollres.html), and Princeton University's *Public Opinion Polls for Historians* guide (http://libguides.princeton.edu/content. php?pid=265323) (accessed December 2, 2011). A nice list of organizations in other countries exists at the end of the *Wikipedia* article on Opinion Polls (http://en.wikipedia.org/wiki/Opinion_poll). Most of these sites have relatively current data.

The Gallup Poll Cumulative Index: Public Opinion, 1935–1997. Alex M. Gallup. Wilmington, DE: Scholarly Resources, Inc., 1999. Also on CD-Rom.

The Gallup Poll Cumulative Index: Public Opinion, 1998–2007. Alex M. Gallup. Lanham, MD: Roman and Littlefield, 2008. Subject index to printed set of Gallup polls.

Index to International Public Opinion: France 1939, 1944–1975. George H. Gallup. New York: Random House, 1976.

Gallup International Public Opinion Polls: Great Britain, 1937–1975. George H. Gallup. New York: Random House, 1976. These two sources reprint poll questions and results from two major European countries.

British Political Opinion, 1937–2000: The Gallup Polls. Anthony King and Robert J. Wybrow. London: Politico's, 2001.

British opinion polls, 1960–1988: A Comprehensive Subject and Names Index of the Complete Range of Surveys and Opinion Polls by Gallup, NOP, MORI, and Harris in Great Britain, 1960–1988. David Tyler, ed. and comp. Reading, Berkshire: Research Publications, 1990. Index to the micro collection of British Opinion Polls.

Mass Observation Archive [microform]: Papers from the Mass-Observation Archive at the University of Sussex. Adam Matthew. Collection is online and is by subscription. For contents, see the online guide: http://www.ampltd.co.uk/digital_guides/m.aspx (accessed December 3, 2011). Primarily twentieth century material, but other centuries as well.

American Public Opinion Index. Louisville, KY: Opinion Research Service, 1981–2000. Also in microform. Index to polls conducted by various organizations.

Public Opinion: A Bibliography with Indexes. William A. Blade. New York: Nova Science Publishers, 2002. Bibliography of published works with public opinion data included. Coverage is heavily United States and mid-twentieth century to the present, but references to nineteenth century and early twentieth century studies are included.

NORC Bibliography of Publications, 1941–1991: A Fifty Year Cumulation. Patrick Bova and Michael Preston Worley. Chicago: National Opinion Research Center, University of Chicago, 1991. The National Opinion Research Center's list of publications and studies.

Index to International Public Opinion. Survey Research Consultants International, Inc. New York: Greenwood, 1981–1999. Prints the actual question from the poll and the results. Includes Western Europe, India, Japan, and the United States.

Public Opinion: A Bibliography with Indexes. William A. Blade, ed. New York: Nova Science Publishers, Inc., 2002. References works that contain public opinion data. Most sources are late twentieth century, but would refer to sources that include much older data.

Public Opinion Quarterly. American Association for Public Opinion Research, Princeton University, Woodrow Wilson School of Public and International Affairs, and Columbia University. Oxford, UK: Oxford University Press, 1937–.

Washington Post Poll Vault. 1988–. http://www.washingtonpost.com/wp-srv/politics/polls/vault/vault.htm (accessed December 2, 2011). Searching is difficult, but contains both the questions and results.

Polling the Nations. 1986–. Subscription Database. Polls from many nations, including the United States and individual states.

ipoll Databank. Roper Public Opinion Center. 1935–. Fee based. http://www.ropercenter.uconn.edu/data_access/ipoll/ipoll.html#.TtzxLErk3ZM (accessed December 2, 2011). Database of opinion polls from the major polling organizations.

See also the websites of the major polling centers, some of which have "historical" (about the last 30 years) data and larger datasets:

Gallup Organization. http://www.gallup.com
Roper Center. http://www.ropercenter.uconn.edu/
Pew Research Center. http://people-press.org/
Polling Report. http://www.pollingreport.com/
Harris Interactive. http://www.harrisinteractive.com/
International Communications Research. http://www.icrsurvey.com/
Mason-Dixon Polling & Research. http://www.mason-dixon.com/
Opinion Dynamics. http://www.opiniondynamics.com/
Princeton Survey Research Associates. http://www.psrai.com/

Market Research

Market Research Agencies: A Guide to Publications and Activities Relating to Domestic Marketing. United States. Washington, DC: United States Government Printing Office, 1926–1950 [with some gaps]. (Later eds. published with title *Market Research Sources.*) Bibliography with summaries of public and private marketing investigations. Some will be government documents (both federal and state) and some will be publications by a private agency. Part of the Domestic Commerce Series, which provides all kinds of industry information.

Research on Consumer Reactions. Lincoln H. Clark. New York: Harper, 1958. Volume 3, chapter 12 has an extensive bibliography of consumer behavior research reports from the 1940s and 1950s United States. The four volumes of the set generally give historical information about early to mid-twentieth century consumer attitudes.

Fairchild Publications. Published a series of industry guides to consumer preferences from sometime in the 1960s. Date varies according to the industry (examples include toiletries, women's and children's apparel, etc.) Search by the word
"Fairchild" in your online catalog and *WorldCat.*

Major Social Surveys

Bibliographies of Published Social Surveys

*A Bibliography of Social Surveys; Reports of Fact-Finding Studies Made As a Basis
for Social Action; Arranged by Subjects and Localities; Reports to January
1, 1928.* Allen H. Eaton and Shelby M. Harrison. New York: Russell Sage
Foundation, 1930. Bibliography of surveys conducted prior to 1930s for topics
including jails, homelessness, cost of living, crime and criminals. International,
as well as US, sources.

The Social Survey. Zenas L. Potter. New York: Russell Sage Foundation, Department
of Surveys and Exhibits, 1915. Available online through the Hathi Trust: http://
babel.hathitrust.org/cgi/pt?id=uc1.b172170 (accessed December 27, 2011).
Similar to the source above but concentrates on US local surveys.

The Local Social Survey in Great Britain. A. F. Wells. London: George Allen &
Unwin, Ltd., 1935. Bibliography at the end identifies major social surveys either
by local or special topic.

Survey Research in the United States: Roots and Emergence, 1890–1960. Jean M.
Converse. Berkeley: University of California Press, 1987. Secondary work on the
development of surveying in the United States. Good to identify major research
studies and the published articles that would include the data analysis.

Empirical Social Research in Germany, 1848–1914. Anthony Oberschall. Paris:
Mouton, 1965. Similar to Converse above, but for Germany.

Major Published Social Surveys

*London Labour and the London Poor: The Condition and Earnings of Those That
Will Work, Cannot Work, and Will Not Work.* Henry Mayhew. London: C. Griffin
and Co, 1861.

Life and Labour of the People in London. Charles Booth, et al. London: Macmillan
and Co., Ltd.; New York, The MacMillan Co., 1902. Series I: Poverty, Series
II: Industry, Series III: Religious Influences. Sometimes published as a whole
set of 9 volumes without the series designation. Also available online through
Hathi Trust http://catalog.hathitrust.org/Record/010628263 (accessed April
29, 2011).

The New Survey of London Life & Labour. London School of Economics and
Political Science and Hubert Llewellyn Smith. London: P. S. King & Son, 1930.
Follow up to Charles Booth's earlier survey.

The Statistical Account of Scotland: Drawn Up from the Communications of the Ministers of the Different Parishes. John Sinclair. Edinburgh: W. Creech, 1791. Also available online at: http://stat-acc-scot.edina.ac.uk/sas/sas.asp?action=public (accessed December 2, 2011).

Hull-House Maps and Papers, A Presentation of Nationalities and Wages in a Congested District of Chicago, Together with Comments and Essays on Problems Growing Out of the Social Conditions. New York: T.Y. Crowell, 1895. Also available online through Hathi Trust http://catalog.hathitrust.org/Record/001133285 / (accessed December 2, 2011).

The Philadelphia Negro: A Social Study. W. E. B. Du Bois. Philadelphia: Published for the University, 1899.

Livelihood and Poverty: A Study in the Economic Conditions of Working-class Households in Northampton, Warrington, Stanley and Reading. A. L. Bowley and A. R. Burnett-Hurst. London: G. Bell and Sons, Ltd., 1915.

Studies in Social Psychology in World War II. Samuel A. Stouffer, et al. Princeton, NJ: Princeton University Press, 1949. Major survey of the lives of the American soldier, including adjustment to army life, effects of instructional films, negro soldiers, postwar adjustment, and effects of combat.

Charities and The Commons. January–March 1909. Published 35 articles about social conditions in Pittsburgh.

Bibliographies and Indexes for Statistics

Statistics Sources: A Subject Guide to Data on Industrial Business, Social Educational, Financial and Other Topics for the United States and Internationally. Paul Wasserman et al. Detroit, MI: Gale, 1962– . Indexes statistics in other published sources.

The History of Statistics: Their Development and Progress in Many Countries. John Koren, ed. New York: The American Statistical Association and The Macmillan Company of New York, 1918. Dated. However, a reasonable overview by country of sources and collection methods of governmental statistics, especially census data.

Statistical Sources for Social Research on Western Europe, 1945–1995: A Guide to Social Statistics. Franz Rothenbacher. Europe in Comparison: A Series of Guidebooks for the Social Sciences, Vol. 6. Opladen: Leske and Budrich, 1998. Bibliography by type of publication or statistic (e.g., international publications, abstracts) and by country.

Bibliography of Official Statistical Yearbooks and Bulletins. Gloria Westfall. Alexandria, VA: Chadwyck-Healy, Inc., 1986.

Guide to Official Publications of Foreign Countries. Susan I. Jover, Bethesda, MD: Congressional Information Service, 1997. Country by country listing.

A Retrospective Bibliography of American Demographic History from Colonial Times to 1983. David R. Gerhan and Robert V. Wells. New York: Greenwood Press, 1989.

Bibliography of American Demographic History: The Literature from 1984 to 1994. David R. Gerhan, Westport, CT: Greenwood Press, 1995. These two books cite published studies that use historical statistics. *Demography from Scanty Evidence: Central Africa in the Colonial Era.* Bruce Fetter. Boulder, CO: L. Rienner Publishers, 1990. Dated articles, but good discussion using hard to find statistical resources for Africa.

OffStats. University of Auckland. http://www.offstats.auckland.ac.nz/ (accessed December 28, 2011). Finder for official statistics on the Internet. Many will not be historical.

Sources of Non-official UK Statistics. 6th ed. David Mort. Burlington, VT: Gower, 2006. Bibliography of sources.

Finding and Using Datasets

Below is a list of potential sources of datasets of use to historians. Generally datasets tend to be more current, within the last 10–20 years. These sources have at least some historical data included. For a more extensive guide for datasets, see Kristen Partio's guide, Carleton College (http://apps.carleton.edu/campus/library/help/help/liaisons/kpartlo/statsdbs/) and Jen Darragh's guide, Johns Hopkins University (http://guides.library.jhu.edu/content.php?pid=62430&sid=459596) (accessed December 4, 2011).

International Institute of Social History (IISH) List of Datafiles of Historical Prices and Wages. http://primary-sources.eui.eu/other-portals/iish-list-datafiles-historical-prices-and-wages (accessed December 4, 2011). For Europe.

Resources for Economists on the Internet. http://rfe.org/showCat.php?cat_id=6 (accessed December 4, 2011).

European Social Survey. http://www.europeansocialsurvey.org/ (accessed December 4, 2011). Mostly more recent information.

ICPSR (Interuniversity Consortium for Political and Social Research). http://www.icpsr.umich.edu/icpsrweb/ICPSR/ (accessed December 4, 2011). Consortium of over 700 research organizations and institutions that contribute to a data archive. Some historical datasets are included.

IPUMS (Integrated Public Use Microdata Series). http://www.ipums.org/ (accessed December 4, 2011) Some historical US and international datasets.

General Social Survey. http://ww3.norc.org/GSS+Website (accessed December 4, 2011) To find the link to the website, it is easier to do a Internet search on the words "general social survey".

Cross National Time Series Archive. http://www.databanksinternational.com/ (accessed December 4, 2011). Annual data for countries from 1815 to the present, based on the *Statesman's Yearbook*. Fee based.

Global Finance Data. http://www.globalfinancialdata.com/ (accessed December 4, 2011). Data reaches back into the eighteenth century. Fee based.

UK Data Archives. http://www.data-archive.ac.uk/ (accessed December 4, 2011). Collection of datasets, many historical, most freely available. Site is confusing.

UK Datasets. http://www.nationalarchives.gov.uk/documentsonline/datasets.asp (accessed December 4, 2011).

Eurobarometer. Public Opinion Analysis Sector of the European Commission. 1973– . http://ec.europa.eu/public_opinion/index_en.htm (access December 28, 2011). Public opinion data.

FOR FURTHER READING

Best, Joel. *Damned Lies and Statistics: Untangling Numbers from the Media, Politicians, and Activists.* Berkeley: University of California Press, 2001.

Best, Joel. *More Damned Lies and Statistics: How Numbers Confuse Public Issues.* Berkeley: University of California Press, 2004.

Best, Joel. *Stat-Spotting: A Field Guide to Identifying Dubious Data.* Berkeley: University of California Press, 2008.

These three books by Best are full of examples that are understandable by anyone.

Bulmer, Martin, Kevin Bales, and Kathryn Kish Sklar. *The Social Survey in Historical Perspective, 1880–1940.* Cambridge: Cambridge University Press, 1991.

Cohen, I. Bernard. *The Triumph of Numbers: How Counting Shaped Modern Life.* New York: W. W. Norton & Co., 2005.

Cohen, Patricia Cline. *A Calculating People: The Spread of Numeracy in Early America.* Chicago: University of Chicago Press, 1982.

Cullen, Michael. *The Statistical Movement in Early Victorian Britain: The Foundations of Empirical Social Research.* Hassocks: Harvester Press, 1975.

Herbst, Susan. *Numbered Voices: How Opinion Polling Has Shaped American Politics.* Chicago: University of Chicago Press, 1993.

Kellam, Lynda M., and Katharin Peter. *Numeric Data Services and Sources for the General Reference Librarian.* Oxford: Chandos Publishing, 2011.

Porter, Theodore M. *The Rise of Statistical Thinking 1820–1900.* Princeton, NJ: Princeton University Press, 1986.

Rosenbloom, Joshua L. *Quantitative Economic History: The Good of Counting.* London: Routledge, 2008.

Zuberi, Tukufu. *Thicker Than Blood: How Racial Statistics Lie.* Minneapolis, MN: University of Minnesota Press, 2001. Useful for understanding how to read historical statistics based on race. Race as a social construct affects how racial statistics are interpreted.

Case Study—Contextualizing Statistics

The data listed in Table 140 (fig. 10.2) raises a number of questions about child and immigrant labor and how practices differed by region.

1. Look at the data in the table (fig. 10.2) and make some associations and assessments. For example, foreign-born white male children

No. 140.—MALE POPULATION 10 TO 15 YEARS OF AGE EMPLOYED AS BREADWINNERS: NUMBER AND PERCENTAGE, ETC.—Continued.

State or Territory.	Foreign-born white.						Negro, Indian, and Mongolian.						
	Total males 10 to 15 years of age.	In all occupations.		In agricultural pursuits.		In all other occupations.		Total males 10 to 15 years of age.	In all occupations.		In agricultural pursuits.		In all other occupations.
		Number.	Per cent.	Number.	Per cent.	Number.	Per cent.		Number.	Per cent.	Number.	Per cent.	Number.	Per cent.
Alabama	268	90	33.6	13	4.9	77	28.7	68,282	41,469	65.5	35,687	56.3	5,832	9.2
Arizona	582	140	24.1	38	6.5	102	17.5	2,018	746	37.0	701	34.7	45	2.2
Arkansas	210	79	37.6	63	30.0	16	7.6	27,394	15,890	58.0	14,443	52.7	1,447	5.3
California	3,455	700	20.4	129	3.8	571	16.6	2,055	420	20.4	109	5.3	311	15.1
Colorado	1,328	235	17.7	41	3.1	194	14.6	533	31	5.8	5	.9	26	4.9
Connecticut	5,183	1,727	33.3	99	1.9	1,628	31.4	693	96	13.9	32	4.6	64	9.2
Delaware	251	97	38.6	11	4.4	86	34.3	2,061	677	32.8	470	22.8	207	10.0
District of Columbia	205	55	26.8			55	26.8	4,130	548	13.3	10	.2	538	13.0
Florida	527	126	23.9	12	2.3	114	21.6	18,441	5,778	37.4	4,037	26.1	1,741	11.3
Georgia	238	64	26.9	7	2.9	57	23.9	79,473	43,340	54.5	35,270	44.4	8,070	10.2
Idaho	311	56	18.0	39	12.5	17	5.5	222	30	13.5	*20	9.0	10	4.5
Illinois	17,367	5,036	29.0	639	3.7	4,397	25.3	4,261	849	19.9	330	7.7	519	12.2
Indiana	1,765	451	25.6	93	5.3	358	20.3	3,390	505	14.9	174	5.1	331	9.8
Indian Territory	111	33	29.7	5	4.5	28	25.2	7,042	2,402	34.1	2,164	30.7	238	3.4
Iowa	3,898	1,300	32.5	951	23.8	349	8.7	794	150	18.9	18	2.3	132	16.6
Kansas	1,673	497	29.7	317	18.9	180	10.8	3,881	511	13.2	221	5.7	290	7.5
Kentucky	385	104	27.0	15	3.9	89	23.1	19,761	6,566	33.2	3,968	20.1	2,598	13.1
Louisiana	1,329	504	37.9	330	24.8	174	13.1	48,701	24,983	51.3	21,107	43.3	3,876	8.0
Maine	3,055	1,013	33.2	91	3.0	922	30.2	105	6	5.7	1	1.0	5	4.8
Maryland	1,901	645	33.9	87	4.6	558	29.4	15,610	4,591	29.4	2,568	16.5	2,023	13.0
Massachusetts	19,118	5,067	26.5	142	.7	4,925	25.8	1,296	131	10.1	20	1.5	111	8.6
Michigan	10,981	2,299	20.9	687	6.3	1,612	14.7	1,351	167	12.4	68	5.0	99	7.3
Minnesota	8,355	1,987	23.8	1,313	15.7	674	8.1	827	137	16.6	39	4.7	98	11.9
Mississippi	105	41	39.0	19	18.1	22	21.0	70,969	42,163	59.4	38,430	54.2	3,733	5.3
Missouri	2,334	762	32.6	133	5.7	629	26.9	10,326	2,469	23.9	1,167	11.3	1,302	12.6
Montana	846	114	13.5	27	3.2	87	10.3	812	60	7.4	13	1.6	47	5.8
Nebraska	2,776	760	27.4	561	20.2	199	7.2	564	48	8.5	7	1.2	41	7.3
Nevada	51	15	(¹)	11	(¹)	4	(¹)	332	44	13.3	25	7.5	19	5.7
New Hampshire	2,970	1,030	34.7	37	1.2	993	33.4	36	7	(¹)	1	(¹)	6	(¹)
New Jersey	9,055	2,937	32.4	121	1.3	2,816	31.1	3,090	568	18.4	194	6.3	374	12.1
New Mexico	337	85	25.2	23	6.8	62	18.4	1,122	335	29.9	312	27.8	23	2.0
New York	42,343	10,606	25.2	387	.9	10,269	24.3	4,053	698	17.2	99	2.4	599	14.8
North Carolina	84	28	(¹)	11	(¹)	17	(¹)	48,670	28,997	59.6	23,137	47.5	5,860	12.0
North Dakota	3,347	797	23.8	690	20.6	107	3.2	491	32	6.5	30	6.1	2	.4
Ohio	6,769	1,593	23.5	127	1.9	1,466	21.7	5,386	695	12.9	211	3.9	484	9.0
Oklahoma	295	85	28.8	72	24.4	13	4.4	1,252	452	20.1	402	17.9	50	2.2
Oregon	829	145	17.5	63	7.6	82	9.9	490	80	16.3	12	2.4	68	13.9
Pennsylvania	20,659	9,068	43.9	153	.7	8,915	43.2	7,092	1,277	18.0	231	3.3	1,046	14.7
Rhode Island	4,049	1,781	44.0	*52	1.3	1,729	42.7	393	45	11.5	8	2.0	37	9.4
South Carolina	*68	18	(¹)	4	(¹)	14	(¹)	63,703	37,791	59.3	33,165	52.1	4,626	7.3
South Dakota	1,802	615	34.1	553	30.7	62	3.4	1,182	28	2.4	27	2.3	1	.1
Tennessee	285	74	26.0	21	7.4	53	18.6	35,419	16,498	46.6	12,216	34.5	4,282	12.1
Texas	5,132	1,802	35.0	1,114	21.6	688	13.4	48,746	19,648	40.3	17,085	35.0	2,563	5.3
Utah	844	158	18.7	61	7.2	97	11.5	176	21	11.9	9	5.1	12	6.8
Vermont	1,132	239	21.1	67	5.9	172	15.2	50	8	(¹)	2	(¹)	6	(¹)
Virginia	311	91	29.3	23	7.1	68	22.2	50,805	19,973	39.3	12,599	24.8	7,374	14.5
Washington	1,682	261	15.5	90	5.4	171	10.2	800	196	24.6	82	10.3	114	14.3
West Virginia	353	157	44.5	13	3.7	144	40.8	2,483	785	31.6	193	7.8	592	23.8
Wisconsin	8,378	2,565	30.6	950	11.3	1,615	19.3	697	72	10.3	18	2.6	54	7.7
Wyoming	205	54	26.3	14	6.8	40	19.5	134	14	10.4	1	.7	13	9.7
Total	199,635	58,236	29.2	10,518	5.3	47,718	23.9	664,594	323,027	48.6	261,088	39.3	61,939	9.3
*Geographical divisions.*²													
North Atlantic	107,564	33,518	31.2	1,149	1.1	32,369	30.1	16,808	2,836	16.9	588	3.5	2,248	13.4
South Atlantic	3,938	1,281	32.5	167	4.2	1,114	28.3	282,976	142,480	50.5	111,449	39.5	31,031	11.0
North Central	69,545	18,662	26.8	7,014	10.1	11,648	16.7	33,150	5,663	17.1	2,310	7.0	3,353	10.1
South Central	8,140	2,812	34.5	1,652	20.3	1,160	14.3	323,566	170,071	52.6	145,452	45.0	24,619	7.6
Western	10,448	1,963	18.8	536	5.1	1,427	13.7	8,694	1,977	22.7	1,289	14.8	688	7.9

¹ Per cent not shown where base is less than 100.   ² For States and Territories included in each division see note 5, p. 43.

Fig. 10.2. "No. 140. Male Population 10–15 Years of Age Employed as Breadwinners," *Statistical Abstract of the United States 1910*, 33rd ed. (Washington, DC: Government Printing Office, 1911).

were more likely to work in an occupation other than agricultural pursuits (5.3% in agriculture, 23.9% in other occupations) than Negro, Indian, and Mongolian children (39.9% in agriculture, 9.3% in other occupations). However this pattern does not hold true in Minnesota where foreign-born white male children were more likely to work in agricultural pursuits than in other occupations (15.7% in agriculture, 8.1% in other occupations). Negro, Indian, and Mongolian children in Minnesota were more likely to work in occupations other than agricultural (4.7% in in agriculture, 11.9% in other occupations). To discuss the differences you need to look at immigration patterns (more statistics) and local economies (urban, rural, and agricultural). Note that this table lists statistics for "breadwinners," which means these children were not just helping out on the family farm with their parents. Think about what other statistics might be comparable or provide perspective for this data.

2.   Look in several *Statistical Abstracts* of the United States around 1910 for statistics on immigrants by location and age. You may also want to look for common occupations by state, as well as overall demographics about the population. Who were the foreign-born population and how do they compare to the population as a whole?

3.   Look for secondary sources on the history of child labor and the history of agriculture in the United States. For example:

Hindman, Hugh D. *Child Labor: An American History*. Armonk, NY: M.
   E. Sharpe, 2002.
Marten, James Alan. *Childhood and Child Welfare in the Progressive
   Era: A Brief History with Documents*. New York, NY: Bedford/St.
   Martins, 2004.

Consider race:

Schwalm, Leslie A. *Emancipation's Diaspora: Race and Reconstruction
   in the Upper Midwest*. Chapel Hill: University of North Carolina
   Press, 2009.
Fuller, Sherri Gebert. *Chinese in Minnesota*. St. Paul: Minnesota
   Historical Society Press, 2004.
Taylor, David Vassar. *African Americans in Minnesota*. St. Paul, MN:
   Minnesota Historical Society Press, 2002.

and a general history of Minnesota:

Lass, William E. Minnesota: A History. 2nd ed. New York: W.W Norton,
   2000

4. Look for related primary sources. For instance, a collection of documents:

Bremner, Robert H. *Children and Youth in America: A Documentary History*. Cambridge, MA: Harvard University Press, 1970.

Explore some of the primary sources and search techniques in chapter 6. Try to locate a diary of an immigrant or a farmer or a reminiscence of a former child laborer.

NOTES

1. "Table 121. Deaths by Age and Selected Causes: 2007," *Statistical Abstract of the United States 2012*, 131st ed. (Washington, DC: Government Printing Office, 2012); "Table 859. Corn—Acreage, Production, and Value by Leading States 2008–2010," *Statistical Abstract of the United States 2012*, 131st ed. (Washington, DC: Government Printing Office, 2012).

2. "Table 495. Federal Individual Income Tax—Current Income Equivalent to 2000 Constant Income for Selected Income Groups: 2000–2010," *Statistical Abstract of the United States 2012*, 131st ed. (Washington, DC: Government Printing Office, 2012); NA, "Ice Cream Preferences Differ by Gender," *Progressive Grocer*, June 10, 2009. http://www.progressivegrocer.com/top-story-ice_cream_preferences_differ_by_gender-18933.html (accessed April 29, 2011).

3. I. Bernard Cohen, *The Triumph of Numbers: How Counting Shaped Modern Life* (New York: W. W. Norton, 2006), 51–53; Michael J. Cullen, *The Statistical Movement in Early Victorian Britain: The Foundations of Empirical Social Research* (New York: Barnes & Noble, 1975), 19; Eileen Janes Yeo, "The Social Survey in Social Perspective, 1830–1930," in Martin Bulmer, Kevin Bales, and Kathryn Kish Sklar, *The Social Survey in Historical Perspective, 1880–1940* (Cambridge: Cambridge University Press, 1991), 49–51.

4. Cohen, *Triumph of Numbers*, 47–48.

5. Ibid., 51–53.

6. Ibid., 101–105; Cullen, *Statistical Movement in Early Victorian Britain*, 15.

7. Cohen, *Triumph of Numbers*, 100.

8. Ibid., 73–75, 90–92.

9. Ibid., 117.

10. Ibid., 114. For example, *Recherches Statistiques* and the *New England Almanac*.

11. Cohen, *Triumph of Numbers*, 147–151.

12. Martin Bulmer, "The Social Survey in Historical Perspective," in *The Social Survey in Historical Perspective, 1880–1940*, ed. Martin Bulmer, Kevin Bales, and Kathryn Kish Sklar (Cambridge: Cambridge University Press, 1991), 1–2.

13. Martin Bulmer, "W. E. B. Du Bois as a Social Investigator: The Philadelphia Negro, 1899," in *The Social Survey in Historical Perspective, 1880–1940*, ed. Martin Bulmer, Kevin Bales, and Kathryn Kish Sklar (Cambridge: Cambridge University Press, 1991), 170–188; Tukufu Zuberi, *Thicker Than Blood: How Racial Statistics Lie* (Minneapolis: University of Minnesota Press, 2001), 82–83, 86–88.

14. Steven R. Cohen, "The Pittsburg Survey and the Social Survey Movement: A Sociological Road Not Taken," in *The Social Survey in Historical Perspective, 1880–1940*, ed. Martin Bulmer, Kevin Bales, and Kathryn Kish Sklar (Cambridge: Cambridge University Press, 1991), 245–268; *Charities and the Commons*, January–March 1909, 517.

15. E. P. Hennock, "Concepts of Poverty in British Social Surveys from Charles Booth to Arthur Bowley," in *The Social Survey in Historical Perspective, 1880–1940*, ed. Martin Bulmer, Kevin Bales, and Kathryn Kish Sklar (Cambridge: Cambridge University Press, 1991), 201.

16. Irmela Gorges, "The Social Survey in Germany before 1933," in *The Social Survey in Historical Perspective, 1880–1940*, ed. Martin Bulmer, Kevin Bales, and Kathryn Kish Sklar (Cambridge: Cambridge University Press, 1991), 328.

17. Alain Desrosières, "The Part in Relation to the Whole: How to Generalise? The Prehistory of Representative Sampling," in *The Social Survey in Historical Perspective, 1880–1940*, ed. Martin Bulmer, Kevin Bales, and Kathryn Kish Sklar (Cambridge: Cambridge University Press, 1991), 238–239.

18. Pat Hudson, *History by Numbers: An Introduction to Quantitative Approaches* (London: Arnold, 2000), 7–8, 54–55.

19. Ibid., 8–9; Darrell Huff, *How to Lie with Statistics* (New York: Norton, 1993), 90.

20. Hudson, *History by Numbers*, 9–10, 109–110.

21. Ibid., 10, 169–170.

22. Ibid., 11.

23. Ibid., 11–12, 20.

24. Patricia Cline Cohen, *A Calculating People: The Spread of Numeracy in Early America* (Chicago: University of Chicago Press, 1982), 36.

25. Cohen, *Triumph of Numbers*, 96–97.

26. Robert V. Wells, "Colonial Censuses," in *Encyclopedia of the U.S. Census*, ed. Margo J. Anderson (Washington, DC: CQ Press, 2000).

27. Cohen, *A Calculating People*, 214–215.

28. Bulmer, "The Social Survey in Historical Perspective," 5.

29. Ibid., 1–2, 9–12.

30. Zuberi, *Thicker Than Blood*, 82–83.

31. Susan Herbst, *Numbered Voices: How Opinion Polling has Shaped American Politics* (Chicago: University of Chicago Press, 1993), 51–53; Anthony Oberschall, "The Historical Roots of Public Opinion Research," in *The SAGE Handbook of Public Opinion Research*, ed. Wolfgang Donsbach and Michael W. Traugott (Los Angeles: SAGE Publishers, 2008), 84.

32. Herbst, *Numbered Voices*, 69–70, 81; Buchanan/Fremont straw poll reported in *Chicago Tribune*, September 17, 1856, 2.

33. Oberschall, "The Historical Roots of Public Opinion Research," 87. Gallup later predicted Dewey would beat Truman. Other public opinion polls include: Fortune Survey (by Paul Cherrington and Elmer Robert), Crossley Survey, Louis Harris Survey, and Field Poll.

34. Oberschall, "The Historical Roots of Public Opinion Research," 86.

35. Charles M. Dollar and Richard J. Jensen, *Historian's Guide to Statistics: Quantitative Analysis and Historical Research* (New York: Holt, Rinehart, and Winston, 1971), 12.

36. Joel Best, *More Damned Lies and Statistics: How Numbers Confuse Public Issues* (Berkeley: University of California Press, 2004), 13.

37. *The Annual Register; or, A View of the History, Politics, and Literature for the Year…* (London: J. Dodsley, 1801), 167, 163.

38. US Bureau of the Census, "No. 138. - Population Gainfully Occupied: Adults and Children By Sex and By States and Territories, Census Year, 1900," *Statistical Abstract of the United States 1910*, 33rd ed. (Washington, DC: Government Printing Office, 1911).

39. Dollar and Jenson, *Historian's Guide to Statistics*, 9.

40. Joel Best, *Stat-Spotting: A Field Guide to Identifying Dubious Data* (Berkeley: University of California Press, 2008), 7–9, 35.

41. Hudson, *History by Numbers*, 15–16; Joel Best, *Damned Lies and Statistics: Untangling Numbers from the Media, Politicians, and Activists* (Berkeley: University of California Press, 2001), 19–20, 27–29, 115–116; Best, *More Damned Lies*, 19–20; Huff, *How to Lie with Statistics*, 123–142; John Tosh, *The Pursuit of History: Aims, Methods, and New Directions in the Study of Modern History*, 4th ed. (London: Longman, 2006), 276; Best, *Stat-Spotting*, 75–76, 103; John Allen Paulos, *Innumeracy: Mathematical Illiteracy and Its Consequences*. (New York: Hill and Wang, 1988), 10.

42. Best, *Damned Lies and Statistics*, 19–20, 37, 39–40, 43, 46–48, 88–90, 97–116; Best, *Stat-Spotting*, 30–33, 38.

Presenting Your Research: Traditional Research Paper, Presentation, Poster, or Website?

11

WHAT YOU WILL LEARN IN THIS CHAPTER

- the differences between a research paper, a website, an oral presentation, or poster session in presenting your research
- basics of writing a historical research paper
- basics of creating a slide presentation
- basics of designing a scholarly website
- basics of designing a poster

In the past, the predominant format for presenting your research was the research paper. While the research paper is still the standard choice, websites, slide presentations, and posters offer additional ways to enhance the presentation of your research. These formats serve different purposes and should not be used interchangeably. While you would not confuse a slide presentation with a website or a research paper, sometimes it is tempting to take one format and transform it into another. Ultimately, your professor or teacher determines the requirements of your project. But when you do have a choice of format, you will need to use your chosen format effectively, according to its strengths, so that your research and argument will become clear to your audience.

A research paper directs your argument to a very focused conclusion. Heavily reliant on text, it clearly lays out your evidence for your audience to follow in a linear manner. While you may have some illustrations in the form of charts or photographs, the focus is on the text, the narrative, and the argument. Papers are best for research topics that require the presentation of evidence with large amounts of footnotes and a directed analytical conclusion.

Websites allow for a different arrangement of text and graphics, greater freedom for the reader or the audience, as well as incorporation of material that the stricter, linear form of an essay makes more difficult. For instance, succinct textual analysis contained in a website can be linked to enhanced (enlarged, translated, etc.) primary source documents and images. Websites can be useful in presenting historical collections of materials, especially when you have a wealth of exemplary primary source materials that can be hyperlinked. While you will find papers posted on the Internet, good web scholarship and publishing is more than putting online a written paper with hyperlinks available or collecting and organizing primary sources. Web scholarship combines the analysis of a paper with the multimedia capabilities of the Internet to transcend the limitations of the written page.

Besides writing papers and creating websites, you might be asked to present your research orally or visually to your fellow classmates, just as professors and academics present research findings at conferences. Using *PowerPoint*, or other presentation software, you can produce and organize a series of slides for your audience to follow the key points of your verbal presentation. You may also be asked to visually present your findings in a poster. Instead of a progression of slides, you must put all of your information on one large canvas that is visible from a distance. Just as a website should not be used in the same way as a traditional research paper, putting the complete text of a paper or a series of *PowerPoint* slides on the web is a misuse of that medium. Knowing how to use each medium for conveying research effectively will result in a stronger and more creative project, no matter which one your professor requires. Regardless of format, solid interpretation, synthesis, analysis, citation of sources, and discourse are contained in all good historical scholarship.

Creating a Research Paper

Writing Style

Writing a research paper is by far the most common method of presenting undergraduate research in the humanities. A research paper is most effective when you are presenting your argument in a linear fashion, have few images or other multimedia materials to link to the text, and are guiding the reader to your conclusion. Numerous guides, both printed and on the Internet, give detailed instruction on how to organize and construct a research paper. See, for example, Patrick Rael's *Reading, Writing, and Researching for History: A Guide for College Students* (http://www.bowdoin.edu/WritingGuides/), especially its section on designing a research paper; William Kelleher Storey's *Writing History: A Guide for Students*, for its chapters on how to formulate a thesis, write text, and build sentences into an argument; and Donald Hall and Sven Birerts, *Writing Well*, on writing a research paper. Each of these guides explains historical writing, and scholarly writing in general, in a different manner.[1] Rael's guide is excellent and online. At least one of the others should be available in your library if you wish to consult them for more in-depth instruction beyond what is provided here. Remember, as noted in chapter 1, the *Chicago Manual of Style* is the authority on grammar and language for historians.

Chapter 1 also discussed creating a preliminary outline for your research, dividing your topic into related, manageable ideas to help you organize your thoughts. It would be surprising if, now as you are ready to compose, your original organization remained intact. Before you begin to write, assess your intended argument, line up your evidence, and look at its logical flow with your intended interpretation. This will help you organize your sections and paragraphs, as well as make sure you emphasize the most important parts of your argument.

You can choose to write your research paper in two basic styles common to history writers. William Kelleher Storey in *Writing History*, defines these two styles as follows:[2]

- *Analytical.* The analytical style makes a comparison around a concept or idea: for instance, examining how the discovery of moveable type and the printing press affected literacy among the gentry and less wealthy classes. The focus is on how the concept or ideas developed and influenced the participants (including individuals, nations, or institutions) and what led to a change in the environment (in this case, literacy).

- *Narrative.* The narrative style tells a story, what happened historically, often in chronological order. This usually centers on a person, place, event, or era. The topic can be as large as the history of the Roman Empire or something more manageable such as the Jesuits' attempts at converting the Guarani Indians in Paraguay to Christianity in the seventeenth and eighteenth centuries.

Narrative is the more common style. It is often used in political and intellectual history, while the analytical style is common in cultural and economic history.[3] No matter which style you decide to use, you will still have to present your argument logically, indicating to the reader why your evidence is significant and an important contribution to the scholarship already surrounding the topic.

Formulating an Argument

While you have already formulated your thesis and your argument with your professor, you must be cautious about how you carry out that argument. Indeed, you are supposed to present your educated opinion and analysis based on your evidence, but you should avoid deliberately incorporating your own personal biases and judgments into your research. As you think about your paper, consider the three voices in your argument: you, as the author, your readers/audience, and your sources.[4] True scholarship considers all opinions, including those critical and counter to your conclusion.[5] If you ignore other historians' works and primary source evidence that counter your conclusion, your argument is weakened. Good scholarship incorporates them and addresses how and why your argument differs.

It is all too easy to fall into fallacies and false conclusions. As you write, make sure that your argument makes logical sense. Do not make universal generalizations with such words as "all" or "every." Do use such words as "many," "most," and "some." Be careful about creating dichotomies in your thesis that leave no option for other choices. For example, Charles McDougald's title, *The Marcos File: Was He a Philippine Hero or Corrupt Tyrant?*, leaves little room for analyzing the complexities of Ferdinand Marcos's reign.[6] Be sure that your statistical data reflect your topic and that the data that you are presenting are really quantifiable and measurable. Watch for false data. Be careful about classifying individuals into groups and making broad statements about how those groups behave. For instance, not all African Americans or nobility or Muslims or Russian soldiers in the Russian Revolution or any other group you may choose to categorize and characterize necessarily behaved as a unified group or had no unique characteristics. Be careful of extrapolating or ascribing the behavior or motivations of one individual to the whole group. Watch that your modern-day understanding of the world does not lead you to make assumptions about what individuals and societies knew in another time. This could lead to a misinterpretation of primary source materials. Finally, be careful not to overemphasize one piece of evidence over another. Rather, consider all of your evidence and its importance as a whole. Relying heavily on one piece of evidence could cause you to misinterpret its meaning. These problems of argument and many more are discussed in great detail and in complex philosophical terms in David Hackett Fischer's *Historians' Fallacies: Toward a Logic of Historical Thought.*[7]

Paper Construction

Once you have decided on a style and the divisions or outline of your paper, you need to think about the construction of tight paragraphs and the flow of your ideas. A typical eight- to ten-page paper begins with an introduction, outlining your argument and thesis, followed by a series of logical paragraphs that correspond to and support your introduction and thesis, and ending with a conclusion that draws together the evidence, pointing out why the argument in the introduction is valid and credible. The conclusion should be more than a summary of your points and should not present new evidence or information. Historian, Jim Cullen, suggests two ways of concluding your paper. Bring your evidence to a broad view. Why does it matter? Or, think of the conclusion as containing "the motive." State in direct and explicit terms what you have been suggesting throughout your work.[8] Jim Cullen sums up the process, "In a truly analytic essay, the introduction doesn't tell, it asks. And the body doesn't either; it shows. The conclusion does to some degree sum up, but the goal now is to extend—so suggest the broader implications of the argument you've been making."[9] The introduction and conclusion need not be restricted to a single paragraph each, nor must they be written in order as you progress through the paper. You may begin with a vague, single-paragraph introduction with a fairly strong, single-sentence argument. By the time you have concluded the first draft, your introduction may be clearer to you and you will be able to return and lay out in an expanded introduction the purpose and thesis of your paper. Remember that you should write more than one draft of a paper. How many drafts will you go through? There is no magic number, but always more than one and probably more than you imagine. Scholarship is as much thinking, organizing, and presenting your collection of knowledge and evidence as it is the actual gathering of the sources. While you need a solid foundation of evidence, evidence alone will not "create" a quality paper. You need time to make connections. Write a first draft, put it away for a couple of days, and revise it after you have had some additional time to think about the connections you have made. Finally, let someone else read it (perhaps someone at a writing center on campus) and then revise it at least one more time. Your grade, as well as your comprehension of the subject, will be reflected in this process.

Ebb and Flow of Paragraphs

Connected together, your paragraphs fortify and build your argument. Below are some tips on creating effective paragraphs and sentences and on joining them together to create a flowing paper. These tips are fairly standard and not exclusively for historians; many can be applied to all scholarly writing.

- Begin each paragraph with a strong topic sentence, indicating what the paragraph is about. The rest of the paragraph should support and elaborate on this piece of your evidence with supporting details. The topic sentence should always need explaining. Avoid factual statements unless really necessary or appropriate. Generally, stick with one idea per paragraph. Think of your paragraph as a box and as a collection of related ideas that you will organize.[10]

- Create transitions between paragraphs. Do not make your readers feel as if they are on a roller coaster as you switch between topic sentences. Your paragraphs should be related because you are building an argument. Make your reader understand why and how all of your ideas connect. If you need to make an abrupt shift, consider a section heading.

- Write in the third person. Generally avoid using the pronoun "I." As the writer of the text, it is assumed that you are the source of the opinions and arguments that are not documented by footnotes. Remember that presenting others' ideas as your own is plagiarism.

- Do not use contractions.

- Avoid personal bias in your analysis. You have an argument, but becoming judgmental and letting your personal viewpoints color your assessment weakens your credibility.[11]

- Watch your verb tenses. Historians are permitted to use past tense since they are writing about the past, unlike most other scholarly disciplines. This can cause you to inadvertently shift between present and past tenses.[12]

These are only a few tips. Your professor or teacher will suggest others, as well as have more guidelines that he or she wishes you to follow. Writing well is important for conveying your ideas to your reader. Writing well means good sentence structure and formation, smooth flow of text, a tight argument that avoids common fallacies, and backing your research with primary and secondary sources. See the For Further Reading section at the end of this chapter for full-length guides to writing and composition. Make use of your writing center on campus. No matter how well you have performed your research by gathering sources, if your readers cannot understand the argument, your ideas will be lost. The same is true whether you are writing a research paper or presenting your research orally.

Oral, Slide, and Poster Presentations

Oral presentations require you to summarize your findings and evidence in a succinct and outline form in a set time frame. Unlike a paper, which values narrative and prose style, an oral presentation consists of points of interest that reflect topics but not detailed analyses of those topics. Slide presentation software, such as *Microsoft PowerPoint* is a commonly used to illustrate the significant talking points. Effective slide presentations highlight the key points on slides to which you will verbally *add* information and analysis.[13]

Remember that the purpose of a slide presentation is to provide an organizational framework for you, the speaker, to guide your audience through your research. It is not meant to contain all of the information you have gathered. Edward Tufte coined the term "phluff" in his diatribe against the misuses of *PowerPoint, The Cognitive Style of PowerPoint*.[14] Phluff, according to Tufte, is overpowering graphics and words that call more attention to the format of your presentation than to its content. So select a background that visually enhances but does not overshadow the data or text you wish to present. Animation and sound can also distract the audience from your message. Remember to keep the information at the center and not the bells and whistles of *PowerPoint*. Unable to control the pace of your lecture or the quantity of information presented, your audience can become bored, distracted, confused, and frustrated. Tufte warns, "Designer formats will not salvage weak content. . . . Audience boredom is usually a content failure not a decoration failure."[15] This is true not just for an oral presentation but for all methods of presenting your research. Used ineffectively, it can transform a learned presentation into an endless and uninteresting talk, and it can either dilute or totally destroy the flow of your argument and communication with your listeners.

Here are some "dos" and "don'ts" when creating an oral presentation:[16]

- Provide a few statistics on a single slide. If you need to give your audience a chart or a significant quantity of facts or figures, provide them with a handout. Hold these supplemental materials until your audience needs them or until the end of the presentation, otherwise the audience may pay more attention to your handouts than to your presentation.

- On the slides, make bulleted lists clear and simple in their organization and hierarchy. Complex lists and elaborate hierarchies visually confuse an audience and make it very difficult for them to make sense of the information presented. Complicated ideas should be verbally explained.

- Never read slides aloud verbatim. Let the audience read the material for themselves. In fact, seldom read anything to your audience that you display on the screen.

- Use the technology embedded in your slides to enhance your presentation. Launching a webpage from a slide is useful to incorporate examples into your presentation. But just because your presentation software has the capability of launching webpages from embedded links does not mean you can repackage your presentation into a website.

- Use visuals. This is what enlivens a talk.

- Use repetition, parallelism and climatic order in your oral presentation. Repeat the important phrases you want your audience to remember and to recognize as important and central to your argument. If you create parallel points, constructing those points in parallel language and form, your audience can create a mental list of your points. Finally a climax, brings everything to the point you are making.

- Practice (and practice and practice) your presentation. Time your presentation. If you go over or if it is too long, your audience can become bored or even hostile. You have a responsibility to keep to the time allotted.

- Know your audience and their level of understanding. Speaking above or below your audience may cause them to become bored or angry, and certainly not give you any of their attention.

For an interesting illustration and parody of *PowerPoint* misused to its extreme, see Peter Norvig's *PowerPoint* presentation of Abraham Lincoln's Gettysburg Address (fig. 11.1).[17] This is a prime example of how

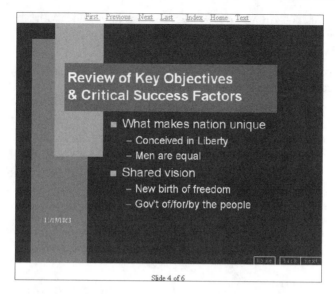

Figure 11.1. One of the slides from Peter Norvig's *PowerPoint* rendition of Abraham Lincoln's Gettysburg Address. This is both a silly and a serious example of a *PowerPoint* (.ppt) presentation. Seriously, Norvig in the persona of Lincoln has not attempted to put every word of the speech on this or the other series of slides illustrating the famous speech. On the silly side, a .ppt presentation cannot reflect the oratorical skill of Lincoln or convey the emotion of the speech for the speaker/orator or the thousands who have read and heard it spoken in the decades since 1863. *©Peter Norvig, used with permission.*

a *PowerPoint* slide cannot replace a good speech or adequately reflect its true content.

Some software alternatives to *PowerPoint* may help you to express your information in ways that are more interesting and engaging to your audience. These include:

- Prezzi—"A cloud based presentation software" that allows you to zoom in and out on a "canvas." http://prezi.com/ (accessed September 25, 2011).

- Pecha Kucha—20 by 20 presentation software. Twenty slides in twenty seconds. http://www.pecha-kucha.org/ (accessed September 25, 2011).

- Brainshark—Allows you to integrate *PowerPoint* slides with other forms of media, including video, audio, and still photographs. http://www.brainshark.com/ (accessed September 25, 2011).
- Jing—Make a short video of what you see on your computer screen. Excellent for showing how to do something. Choose between the free version or an upgrade for an annual fee. http://www.techsmith.com/jing.html (accessed April 28, 2012).
- Keynote—the Apple computer program for slide presentations. Requires a purchase as part of the iWork suite of software.
- *S5: A Simple Standards Based Slide Show System.* An open source alternative to *PowerPoint*, based on XHTML, CSS, and JavaScript, although as a user you do not need to know anything about these coding languages. See http://meyerweb.com/eric/tools/s5/ (accessed April 28, 2012).

Creating a Poster

You may have occasion to present your research in poster format. A poster succinctly, visually presents your question or argument and evidence on a single large one-page canvas. Often you will give a very short, informal presentation about your research and allow audience members to individually ask you questions about your findings. Creating a poster can be even more daunting than creating a slide presentation. Your audience should be able to stand back at a short distance, look at your poster, and understand the basics of your question or argument and your data or evidence. Your audience will be able to walk up to you and ask questions about your research.

How you present that research is important and somewhat different than either a paper or slide presentation. Clearly present your thesis statement. Arrange the poster with basic points of information in boxes and visually create a flow from thesis to individual topics (fig.11.2 has some examples). Because a poster is meant to be visual, do not write in sentences, but express your ideas simply with bullet points. Include other graphics, such as images, drawings or facsimiles of your primary source evidence. Remember this is meant to be a visual experience for your audience and should not contain everything you know. You are there, in person to do the explaining. Think of the poster as a guided tour.

Figure 11.2. Sample of poster layouts. Some samples of designing the flow of information on posters.

Public Presenting

While your organization of your slide presentation or poster is important, how you deliver your presentation is equally important. Historians and all researchers are often called to publicly present their research findings. In fact as discussed in chapter 1, often the public presentation of research is the preliminary step before writing a journal article or book. Some conferences allow you to actually read a paper verbatim. Others require a less formal slide presentation. You will have notes and have a set progression of topics, much like a paper, but you will explain while your audience listens. This format is much like a classroom lecture. The poster session is even more casual, one on one conversation. You may be called to present your research in any of these formats. Below is a chart to help you use the best presentation format for your research.

PAPER, PRESENTATION, POSTER, OR WEBSITE

	Paper	Presentation	Professional Poster	Website
Purpose	*Thoroughly examine part of a topic and to add a new interpretation to the historical record. Read by one person at a sitting. No direct and immediate interaction between the reader and the author.*	*Guide your remarks and general discussion of a topic. For a group to view in a single sitting.*	*Report preliminary findings or highlight a process. Generally instructs on one specific aspect of research.*	*Free flow of ideas that combine explanation and visuals. While a paper is linear, visitors to a website will jump around through the hyperlinks in the site.*
Audience	*Your professor and classmates or other scholars who are familiar with the topic.*	*Colleagues and other researchers, including your classmates. You may also be teaching a group that has no knowledge of the subject, but a need to learn your content.*	*Other practitioners and researchers interested in your topic.*	*Everyone. Even though you will target your classmates and others interested in your topic, anyone can find your website, including K–12 students.*

Arrangement and Characteristics	Linear: You present your thesis statement, followed by a discussion of the evidence, and a conclusion.	Outline form. Each slide has a topic with basic related points. Mostly text, but not meant to be read.	Single-sheet canvas. All information must be on a very large single sheet of paper. Text must be able to be read at a distance. The poster needs some sort of logical flow for an individual to be able to connect your ideas, similar to an outline in graphic form. Block text with many visuals (even if it is just colored boxes).	Sort of a combination of a paper and a poster. Visually chunk text and add lots of images or other illustrations. Intention is not to be read in a linear fashion like a research paper. Arrange top page as an overview and lower linked pages categorically.
Language	Emphasis is on the language, how you express your ideas in a clear, descriptive, analytical way. The construction of sentences and use of words is very important. Formal Language.	Very direct and sparse. Your oral presentation will fill in between your points on the slide. Do not treat this as a paper with long sentences (or even paragraphs). More formal than informal language.	Avoid lots of words. Language should be succinct and direct while descriptive. This is not a paper, but a means for someone to discover interest in your idea. More informal language than formal, but using appropriate technical terms.	Again somewhere between a paper and a poster. You can have longer descriptive and analytical portions, but they must be accompanied by some sort of visuals. Use informal language. Do not simply post a research paper on a website. If necessary, attach it as supplemental information.

Box 11.1 Historiographic Essays, Annotated Bibliographies, and Book Reviews

Writing a Historiographic Essay

Another type of paper your professor may ask you to write is a historiographic essay. Because history is based on arguments, the historiographic essay examines and compares other historians' arguments in opposition to each other. Whereas your research paper is built on both primary source evidence and other historians' interpretations, the historiographic essay concentrates only on the secondary works of historians. You will create in essay form, a commentary that interweaves the titles of works and authors with their theories. Because this essay focuses on secondary works and their themes, your topic selection and your note taking will differ from the manner of a research paper. Your topic will, of necessity, be larger and less focused, for instance, the reign of Peter the Great of Russia (1672–1725). Your topic selection is not a thesis statement, but you will examine other historians' arguments about this given time. Some historians will look at the politics of Peter and his contemporaries, while others will look at society more holistically. Your essay may also be restricted to books and journal articles (and probably exclude websites) published between certain dates, perhaps the last 10 years. You will pick the best, most cohesive 20 or so titles (or a number specified by your professor or teacher) and discuss the works. Your conclusion will talk about the credibility of each argument. For a more detailed examination with excellent examples, see chapter 5 of Anthony Brundage, *Going to the Sources: A Guide to Historical Research and Writing*, 4th ed. Wheeling, IL: Harlan Davidson, 2008.

Writing an Annotated Bibliography

A bibliography is a list of citations used in your research. An annotated bibliography provides information about those citations, usually a one- to two-sentence summary of the contents of the work in addition to the bibliographic information. A critical annotated bibliography provides a very short analysis of the work, highlighting in five to seven sentences discussing how the work fits into the available literature and it achieves its purpose or argument. Critical annotated bibliographies are sometimes used in place of a paper so that students will find, examine, and contextualize resources but will not have to take the time to structure and write an entire paper. In many ways, a critical annotated bibliography is a list of brief book reviews (but will include journal articles in the same process). You will be asking the same questions as those for a book review, but you must be even more abbreviated in your writing. Your purpose is to give the reader a critical understanding of the sources you have selected. See *Annotated Bibliographies*, University of Wisconsin Writing Center (http://www.wisc.edu/writing/Handbook/AnnotatedBibliography. html) and *How to Write an Annotated Bibliography*, University of California, Santa Cruz (http://library.ucsc.edu/ref/howto/annotated. html).

Writing a Book Review

Writing a book review is more than just summarizing the content of a book. Remember that history is a discourse or discussion of research, so you must place your book in the context of the other literature on the topic. In fact, the content of a book review is more heavily an evaluation of the quality of the research and contextualization of the historian's argument than a summary of the content of the book. The length of your review is limited, so you must get to the point and focus on the main concerns both of the author and of your critique. Many of the considerations for a book review will mirror the questions you ask to evaluate sources listed in chapter 5. However, in the case of actually writing a book review, you will elaborate more extensively on these questions and read your book with a different purpose in mind. The content of a book review should consider the following:

- What is the author's thesis and purpose?
- Has the author's background affected his or her analysis? What are his or her qualifications?
- Who is the audience, and does the author speak to that audience?
- A *brief* summary of the content.
- What does the author offer as evidence?

- How does the book fit into the existing research? Does it add anything of value, or is it a repetition of what has already been examined?
- What is missing from the author's analysis?
- Present your assessment of the successes and failures of the author's research.

You will write your review as an essay. Your professor or teacher will probably have a preferred format. If not, begin with the summary and organize your critique with specific examples of why the author is successful or unsuccessful.

- *Book Review Writing Guide*, University of Alberta Libraries. (http://guides.library.ualberta.ca/content. php?pid=54968&sid=827653) (accessed April 28, 2012)
- *Write a Book Review with Rodman Philbrick* (http://teacher. scholastic.com/writewit/bookrev/) (accessed November 20, 2011)
- *Campus Writing Program, Indiana University Writing Tutorial Services: Writing Book Reviews* (http://www.indiana.edu/~wts/ pamphlets/book_reviews.shtml) (accessed November 20, 2011)
- *Writing in History 100: The History of Western Civilization*, George Mason University, Department of History and Art History (http://chnm.gmu.edu/courses/westernciv/writing/types_of_ writing/book_reviews.html) (accessed November 20, 2011)

Websites for Historical Research

Historical and Scholarly Websites

A website can offer an alternative method of presentation for your research and argument in a way that a paper and oral presentation cannot. Much like the images of early photography, which mimicked painted portraits, many scholarly websites are text-heavy and appear to be either illustrated papers, nicely organized collections of primary sources, or encyclopedic websites with little or no analysis. These uses do have considerable value as they make scholarship and resources available to a wider audience, as well as preserve historic resources, but they hardly use the special attributes of the web to its fullest.

Website Design: How to Begin

Today's culture promotes a multimedia approach that allows the viewer to construct his or her own means of understanding your analysis. The print newspaper *USA Today* provides a common example of how the hypertext format has invaded our lives even in resources that are not electronic. Information is presented in small paragraphs and short sections, while stories are much less linear in nature than they are in other newspapers. Additionally, the language of its headlines and the "navigation" between sections suggest a website motif.[18] Much of what is created for the Internet is still modeled on print formats, even though electronic resources have functions that allow them to transcend the confines of print. The integrated use of graphics and text with hyperlinks provides a multilayered set of arguments and evidence for a diverse audience. That audience, while reading and drawing conclusions, also participates in the interpretation process as individuals can make different decisions about which path of information to follow and in what order.[19]

The guidelines presented here will teach you how to lay out the kind of website that might be assigned as a project for one of your history courses. What you will not find here are instructions on how to write code in HTML, XHTML, XML, or any other version of markup language. There are a number of WYSIWYG ("what you see is what you get") programs that will allow you to build interesting websites very simply. Using them is like word processing, only you are creating a document that will be transferred to the web. One recommended software program is *Adobe Dreamweaver*. Some scholars have been using blogging software, such as *Wordpress* (http://wordpress.org/), to create simple websites.

While these two programs will perform the HTML coding, they will not design the layers and complexities of your site. Called "information architecture," the design and layout of the entire site is important for your visitors and your focus or argument. Architecture in this sense is not the programming of the website but, rather, how it is laid out, labeled, and organized, as well as how visitors will navigate through it. Just as a paper has an outline, so too a website has a framework. Right at the beginning is where your web project takes a different shape from a research paper. The quality of the content stays the same, but the new multilayered and multidimensional format will radically alter your method and style of presentation. Many of the recommendations about information architecture in this chapter are derived from several seminal books. For more in-depth information, see Patrick J. Lynch and Sarah Horton's *Web Style Guide*, Louis Rosenfeld and Peter Morville's

Information Architecture for the World Wide Web, and Steve Krug's *Don't Make Me Think: A Common Sense Approach to Web Usability*. These books were written for commercial website design, so while their principles are sound, you must adapt them for academic purposes. In *Digital History: A Guide to Gathering, Preserving, and Presenting the Past on the Web*, Daniel J. Cohen and Roy Rosenzweig take many of these principles and apply them to historical web production.[20] To begin, think about your audience and your purpose and then adapt these design principles to the analytical properties of historical research and writing with the unique multimedia capabilities of the web.

Preplanning: The Major Considerations

As you begin to plan your website, both the main (or home) page and the subsequent (or under) pages, there are some important considerations to keep in mind:

- *Audience.* Think about who the visitors to your website might be. Certainly, your professor and your classmates, all of whom will probably have some knowledge of your topic, are part of the audience. Remember that the Internet is public and many individuals will use your site. State your website's purpose and content clearly up front. Consider how your audience will associate ideas and concepts and then decide how best to present various pages and levels of information. Be aware of some common assumptions about web audiences:
  - They are easily lost and need directions.[21]
  - Viewers will scan any section of a page to decide where to begin.
  - Readers read 25% slower online than in print.[22]
  - Web readers are more active in their reading.[23] More than just questioning your analysis, they will look for links that will supply concrete examples of your ideas.
  - Web users choose to read different types of materials on the web (generally, bits of information, such as encyclopedic facts) versus reading longer works in print.[24]
  - Your visitors also seek information in a variety of ways. Designing multiple access points to meet the needs of these kinds of users will help you plan your general layout.

- *General layout.* Think about your layout in several ways, depending on the complexity and depth of your project. You should sketch out your ideas on a piece, or several pieces, of paper (Post-it® notes or index cards work well), thinking about the content of the top layer/page and the content of the subsequent, underneath layers/pages. Think about how the breadth and depth of your website relate. Is your site more cohesive, with more categories linked from the top/homepage and less information? Will your page seem more logical with fewer categories on the top/homepage but more under pages? If your site's navigation is poor, your visitors may not even be able to find their way backward. More about navigation design is below.

▪ *Site organization.* Having an organizational scheme will keep your website cohesive. Think about what you want the viewer to understand most: time (chronology), place (geography), or people (an author, ethnic groups, etc.) Here are some common types that may be useful.[25]

   • *Alphabetical* (list of topics by title, regardless of how they are associated or any ranking of value)

   • *Chronologically* (date, century)

   • *Geographical* (Region or country)

   • *Topical* (subject)

   • *Audience* (a section for K–12 teachers, etc.)

Most websites do not employ a single organizational scheme. You will probably want to use multiple techniques to connect with the different ways your visitors will look for information, as well as the different modes in which your material is best organized, synthesized, and expressed.

▪ *Page layout.* When organizing a single page, web designer Steve Krug suggests that you imagine dividing that page into zones or boxes. The more important the information is, the higher on the page and the more strategically positioned it should be.[26] Think of how a newspaper zones information into areas, boxes text, and enlarges and changes fonts. Information "above the fold" on a newspaper and on the first screen of a webpage not only receives the most attention but also tells the visitor what is most important.

Navigation

Once you decide on an overall organizational scheme, you need to decide how the information on your website interrelates. When writing a paper or a book, you create sections, paragraphs, and chapters. Through this flow and interconnectedness the text will contain sections of information. When organizing your website, create general categories under which points, or "chunks," of evidence can be organized.[27]

- *Make your navigation "persistent and consistent."* Put the same buttons for navigation on every page and in the same spot, and use the same words.

- *Keep the quantity of buttons or links to an appropriate number.* Generally, humans remember ideas in groups of seven.[28] A large list of categories on your homepage will hopelessly confuse your visitor.

- *Make your clickable links, or hyperlinks, obvious.* They should either appear in a different color of text or be underlined.

- *Leave a "breadcrumb trail."* Your visitor must be able to find a way back through the page(s) from where she or he came. Provide a trail (e.g., "Women in Science.France.Chemists.") so your visitor can click on any spot.

What Every Good Website Must Have

Once you have established your navigation and layout, there are other content issues to address. Chapters 5 and 7 describe how to evaluate sources. Just as sources must be evaluated for research, many of the same considerations are essential in website construction so that visitors can evaluate the information provided.

- *Biographical information about the author.* State who you are and your qualifications. It may be as simple as saying you are a history student and naming your school. Your audience will use this information to determine your information's credibility, as well as your perspective.

- *Statement of purpose.* Understanding the intent of the site assists the visitor in placing it in the context of similar sites. False expectations about a site can cause visitors to be disappointed in its content and dismiss the evidence offered.

- *Mail link to send questions.* Your visitors need to be able to contact you for everything from broken links to philosophical disagreements. Remember, part of historical research is discussion. The Internet, unlike a research paper, makes this kind of discourse not only possible but also easy and immediate.

▪ *Last updated date.* Currency of information for historians is not as critical a consideration as the latest medical discoveries for physicians. However, visitors want to know you maintain the links and the content on your site.

▪ *A title.* Display it on the front, usually top, of each page so that your visitors will know where they are and what they are looking at.

While navigation and structure (or information architecture) are crucial to your website, the text of a website is, of course, important. Even though the Internet is a visual, multimedia-driven medium, text is still an essential part of a website, especially for an academic one. However, writing for an Internet audience, even an academic audience, is very different from writing a formal paper.

Writing Text for the Web

Formal historical paper writing values text that is expressive and that flows, has connections and transitions between paragraphs, and draws the reader to a conclusion. For the web, you must change your style of presentation without sacrificing the critical analysis and discussion expected in a research project.[29] Large blocks of flowing text are visually distracting on a webpage. Create chunks of bulleted pieces of succinct text. Remember that, unlike a book or journal article, your website will not be read "from cover to cover." Text that goes on for more than four screens will not be read.[30] Make sure you stay with your topic and do not go off on a tangent; be succinct with your words and descriptions.

In *Hot Text*, Jonathan and Lisa Price, professional web developers and technical writers, offer the following six guidelines for writing website text:[31]

▪ "*Shorten text.*" Do not repeat or summarize points as you would in a research paper. Be careful not to be so succinct as to make your ideas ambiguous. Use graphics to illustrate your ideas.

▪ "*Make text scanable.*" Use headlines and subheadings with key words that reflect meaningful ideas to your audience. Make bulleted lists that highlight the text you want noticed.

▪ *Create useable links.* Let visitors know where they are on your site, when they are connecting to another site, and what might happen when they click on your link. For example, will they hear something from their computer when another website opens? Use links within sentences sparingly but appropriately.

- *"Build chunky paragraphs."* Create one-idea paragraphs with succinct topic sentences. Know when to write a paragraph and when to bullet ideas. Do not digress from the focus of your website.

- *"Reduce cognitive burdens."* Tell visitors what they need to know in the appropriate language. Do not use ambiguous phrases. Employ clear grammar and write in the active voice. You should still use critical thinking and complex concepts; just avoid long paragraphs.

- *"Write meaningful menus."* Be precise about your navigational categories, but speak to your audience. Create a logical hierarchy of ideas that your visitors can follow.

Common Mistakes to Avoid on Websites

A few mistakes can lead your web endeavor astray. As you construct your website, keep the following in mind:

- *Too much text.* Duplicating what can be put in a printed text, such as a research paper, book, or journal article, can be deadly in a website. While a scholarly website can sustain a greater quantity of text than a commercial website, you should guard against an overabundance of text and too few multimedia elements. No one is inclined to sit at a computer screen for a long period of time and plow through dense text. Create a mix of text and graphics. Bullet text as appropriate.

- *Too few graphics.* Integration of multimedia into your analysis is one of the main reasons for using a website in the first place. Be sure, however, that your website also incorporates insight and analysis. There is no standard framework for including these analytical components. This is where your creativity and scholarship converge.

- *Too many graphics or too fancy or complicated a layout.* If your page is too full of images and the latest technological innovations, it becomes hard to see your discussion, analysis, and research. Just because you can include all of this technology, does not mean you should. Technology should enhance your visitors' understanding of the information you present, not hinder their learning. Using animation in your graphics may be cute, but if it does not add to your interpretation, it will annoy some of your visitors and distract from the overall

---

Box 11.2 Blogs and Wikis

Blogs and wikis are other possible ways to present your research and or begin scholarly discourse. Opinion blogs differ from research blogs. Opinion blogs offer the owner's opinion about various topics, usually around a broad subject. Research blogs often present research ideas and invite scholars to comment on that research's development. Research blogs often act as a conduit of information of interest to scholars working on the same topic as the blog. *Wordpress* (http://wordpress.com/) or *Blogger* (http://blogger.com) are two common pieces of free blogging software and easy to learn.

Wikis allow an individual or an entire class to create an online encyclopedia with entries on specific focused topics. The nature of wikis (like Wikipedia) allows a group to edit entries and engage in group research. Software like *Pbworks* (http://pbworks.com/) will allow you to create your own simple wiki. Many class courseware packages also have blogs and wiki sections which allow creation of these types of resources.

---

navigation. A webpage with too many graphics may take too long to load for some visitors. Remember, Internet visitors have extremely short attention spans, and they will leave your page before they get any information if your page does not load quickly.

- *Too hierarchical or too deep.* Do not make too many layers from the initial page. It will be difficult for visitors to find their way back and to change course. Your pages should always provide a good sense of where the visitor is in the site. Keep your navigation clean and consistent. Include in your navigation bar a one-click button back to the homepage.

- *Too little substance.* Remember that your research should add something to the existing body of known research, not just regurgitate known theories and facts. This, of course, should be true of a research paper or slide presentation as well.

- *"Scope creep."* Lynch and Horton in *Web Style Guide* coined this phrase for websites that add features and functions that are not central to the idea, diluting their focus.[32] It can be tempting to include information on a website because you enjoy the technology, for instance, creating a virtual tour or scanning in many primary documents. Make sure that the virtual tour enhances your argument and is not just for play and that the extra documents are focused on your topic and do not lead the visitor into some digression.

Case Study—A Student Paper: "Americans and the Bomb"

While this chapter has discussed a variety of methods of presenting your research, the research paper is still the standard method of presenting your findings. Below is an actual paper written by Matt Edward for History 206: Introduction to Historical Inquiry at Miami University of Ohio (and used with permission). Look at the annotations in the text and watch how he has developed his topic. Look at the sources he has used. The number of primary sources (eleven) exceeds the number of secondary sources (five). The types of secondary sources used are four books and one journal article. The types of primary sources mix newspapers (four articles), magazines (three), journal articles of the age (two), and online copies of Truman's papers (two). Students are often concerned about how many sources they should have for a 10-page paper, and professors may specify a number and kind (books, journal articles, primary sources). You can see in this case there are about 16 sources which might seem like a lot. There is no recommended number of sources, but you do not want to rely on a single secondary source for most of your interpretive information. In this case, the author has four different authors (two books have the same author), so there are a variety of interpretations. The primary sources are not long, but very specific. Some sources discuss the political and public face of the Atomic Bomb with statements from President Harry Truman and articles from such newspapers as the *New York Times* and the *Washington Post*. These sources are balanced with an article written by Albert Einstein, who has a social-scientific view of the significance of the bomb. As you integrate sources into your thesis remember to look for a variety of perspectives in both primary and secondary sources. Make sure the sources address your thesis.

| Matt Edwards
HST 206
12/2/2011 | Paper begins with the basic information about the creator and the topic. List your name, class, date, and title. Some professors may want a title page with this information on it. |

Americans and the Bomb

Introduction ◄——— Section Heading

The atom bomb, first dropped on the Japanese city of Hiroshima on August 6, 1945, came to be one of the defining symbols of the 20th century. In a matter of mere seconds, warfare was transformed from a strategic contest between armies of men and machines into a dehumanized "push-button" reality in which offense perpetually trumped defense.[1] This new type of atomic warfare was central during the Cold War and came to be a major concern to people around the world. The bomb also had a profound effect on science. The atom bomb prominently displayed the power and applicability of atomic research, which would lead to major developments in fields other than ballistics, most notably energy. The effects of the atom bomb on global politics and international relations were also profound. The bomb forever changed the definition of power and prompted a dramatic shift in diplomatic strategy on behalf of those states with a stake in the international system, most notably the two "superpowers". Ironically, the use of the atomic bomb on Japan had a potentially positive effect on global politics in that it prompted scientists and policymakers alike to call for a new era of international cooperation and global governance in order to ensure the survival of the planet.[2] However, these calls were to go unheeded as world leaders would succumb to the polarization and brinksmanship wrought by the bomb and manifested so plainly during the Cold War.

> Sets the context, the significance of the topic. This is why this topic matters.

> Draws together these significant issues. Suggests a relationship and results (the Cold War).

---

[1] Hanson Baldwin, "The Atom Bomb and Future War," *Life*, August 20, 1945.

[2] Albert Einstein, "Dr. Einstein on the Atomic Bomb," *Reader's Digest*, December 1945, 7.

Much has been written about the lasting effects of the

Focus. Picked a manageable topic.

atomic bomb on world history. While these effects are undoubtedly significant and deserve attention, the focus of this paper will be on the initial reactions of the American public to the use of the atomic bomb on Japan. The central question upon which this paper is based is: How did Americans react to the dropping of the atomic bomb on Hiroshima and Nagasaki? The answer to this

Good introductions ask a question and suggest why that question matters to the future, or shaped the future.

question is significant because it will allow historians to better understand American attitudes towards science, war, and the value of human life at the dawn of the atomic era. The answer will also shed light on the American psyche in the aftermath of WWII and American attitudes towards the future

at the dawn of the atomic era. In my efforts to answer this question, I will rely on primary sources from the year 1945, particularly articles in newspapers, periodicals, and public statements from policymakers. While it is impossible to identify a single reaction attributable to such a heterogeneous

Again, a manageable topic. A significant year, several types of primary sources.

entity as "the American public," my research has indicated that there were three basic emotions which best capture the sentiment of the whole: shock, fear, and, to a lesser extent, a sense of righteousness. This paper will be devoted to expanding upon my findings and providing a basic rationale for these reactions.

Sets up the divisions of the essay in the introduction.

Shock ⬅—— *Section Heading: first point*

The term which best encapsulates the initial response of the American public to the dropping of the atomic bomb on Hiroshima is shock. In order to understand this reaction and its causes, one must analyze the earliest pieces of information available for public consumption. In the case of the atomic bombing of Hiroshima, the most significant piece of information with the greatest immediate impact on press reports and, subsequently, on public understanding of the

Sets up primary evidence. Who and what the evidence is.

event, was Harry Truman's address to the nation. Given sixteen hours after the bombing on August 6, 1945, President Truman's address offered a shocking description of the bomb's destructive capabilities which had a profound impact on many Americans.[3] Suddenly Americans were forced to contend with the reality of a bomb

> *Ties the primary source to a secondary source. See notes.*

which had "more power than 20,000 tons of T.N.T" and was the most powerful bomb ever deployed in the course of human history.[4]

The shock demonstrated by the American public at the unveiling of the atomic bomb is encapsulated in a number of articles from newspapers and periodicals published shortly after the bombing of Hiroshima. The author of a *Washington Post* article published only a day after the dropping of the atomic bomb on Hiroshima states, "It is probably correct to say that most Americans received this news [revelations of the atomic bomb] not with exultation but with a kind of bewildered awe."[5] Cognizant of President Truman's announcement of the devastating power of the bomb but unaware of the human toll the attack exacted upon Japan, the author of this article also underscored the fact that prior to Truman's announcement, Americans were unaware of the bomb's existence. According to the author, the shock expressed by the American people could at least partially be attributed to the fact that the forces underlying the power of the bomb were previously only conceived of in the realm of science fiction and pulp magazines.[6] Indeed, Allan Winkler argues that the government went to great lengths in order to keep the Manhattan project, the research project which culminated in the development of the atomic bomb, completely unknown to the general public.[7] As a result of this secrecy, Winkler concludes that, to the American

---

[3] Harry S. Truman, "Statement by the President Announcing the Use of the A-Bomb at Hiroshima," August 6, 1945. Online by Gerhard Peters and John T. Woolley, *The American Presidency Project.* http://www.presidency.ucsb.edu/ws/?pid=12169; For a discussion of public reaction to Truman's address, see Paul Boyer, Fallout (Columbus: Ohio State University Press, 1998), 6.

[4] Truman, " Statement by the President Announcing the Use of the A-Bomb at Hiroshima."

[5] "The Haunted Wood," The Washington Post, August 7, 1945, http://proquest.umi.com.proxy.lib.muohio.edu/pqdweb?index=1&did=214510812&SrchMode=1&sid=4&Fmt=10&VInst=PROD&VType=PQD&RQT=309&VName=HNP&TS=1322934582&clientId=26867 (accessed December 3, 2011).

[6] Ibid.

[7] Allan Winkler, *Life Under a Cloud* (New York: Oxford University Press, 1993), 25.

public, the news of the dropping of the atomic bomb on Hiroshima came as a "tremendous surprise."[8]

While the existence of such a destructive weapon as the atomic bomb and the apparent (but not yet wholly evident) devastation it wrought on Japan undoubtedly came as a surprise to the American public, many Americans were stunned by the bomb's nearly instant impact on daily life. In an article published in the *New York Times* approximately a week after the attack on Hiroshima, Anne O'Hare McCormick proposed that Americans were shocked by the radical change in their own perceptions of security instigated by the bomb.

> *Mentions the primary source in the text because it is important for the reader to know the source in this case*

O'Hare McCormick wrote, "Perhaps it is the shock of the atomic bomb, which has made him [the American] feel more powerful and at the same time more vulnerable—at the mercy of forces that cannot be held."[9] The sentiment expressed in this article indicates that

> *Adds context to the quote to make it understandable.*

even a few days after knowledge of the atomic bomb was made public and American victory was declared in the Pacific, Americans were aware of a vague yet powerful transformation in their own lives and sense of American security. The shocking power of the atomic bomb had a profound effect on the American psyche. According to Paul Boyer, "From the earliest moments, the American people recognized that things would never be the same again."[10]

Fear ◄——— Section heading: second point

> *Summary of ideas of the first point (and next page).*

While the nation was still coming to grips with the dawning of the atomic age, a very real fear began to develop which would linger in the collective conscious of the United States for years to come. This fear may be broadly defined as the fear

> *Transition between first and second point.*

---

8 Ibid.

9 Anne O'Hare McCormick, "The American Mood on the Eve of Victory," *The New York Times*, August 13, 1945, http://proquest.umi.com.proxy.lib.muohio.edu/pqdweb?index=2&did=88277753&SrchMode=1&sid=1&Fmt=10&VInst=PROD&VType=PQD&RQT=309&VName=HNP&TS=1322941789&clientId=26867 (accessed December 3, 2011).

10 Paul Boyer, *By the Bomb's Early Light* (New York: Pantheon Books, 1985), 4.

> First person is acceptable in this case. ➡

of the destructive capability of the atomic bomb and the cruel science that created it. However, my research has shown that within this broader fear, two strands may be distinguished. First, the American public was terrified of the prospect that the atomic bomb might be used in an attack on a city in the United States. The second strand of fear was the fear that atomic weaponry would destroy the world and humanity with it. This second fear, more abstract and distant than the first, was nevertheless very real and resonated in popular discourse in the United States throughout the Cold War.

The fear held by the American public that atomic weaponry might be used against the United States was prompted largely by the vague reports of the bomb's devastating power in tandem with the flurry of complex scientific information released to the public in the wake of the attack ⬅ *Idea touched on in the introduction.*

on Hiroshima. In news reports, Americans were informed of Japanese cities destroyed by blasts the likes of which had never been seen in the history of the universe.[11] As more information became available about the nature of these atomic weapons, Americans were exposed to the science behind the bombs, which served to further unsettle the population. The force of the atomic bombs was often described in galactic terms. For example, one report noted that the energy released by the atomic bomb dropped on Hiroshima had no precedent in this universe, not even on the surface of the sun.[12] In his announcement of the dropping of the atomic bomb, President Truman described the event as "a harnessing of the basic power of the universe.[13] Compounding the unsettling effect of this information was the fact that news stories from the period directly after the bombing of Hiroshima were generally vague in their discussions of the human toll exacted by the bomb on the Japanese. Christine Hong argues that ⬅ *Note the connection of a secondary source argument with a primary source example.*

the presentation of information about the effects of the atomic bomb without specific reference to the death of Japanese civilians made it easier for Americans to conceptualize the devastation of the bomb without

---

[11] John O'Neill, "The Blasts that Shook the World," *Reader's Digest*, October 1945, 8.

[12] Ibid.

[13] Truman, "Statement by the President Announcing the Use of the A-Bomb at Hiroshima."

instigating feelings of guilt.[14] This distinction made it easier for Americans to imagine the effects of the atomic bomb on their own cities, a fear "that would be the constant companion of Americans for the rest of their lives, and of millions not yet born in 1945."[15] A demonstration of this point is presented in an article in the *New York-Herald Tribune*, in which the author states, "[One] forgets the effect on Japan… as one senses the foundations of one's own universe trembling."[16]

The second fear expressed by the American public was the fear that atomic weapons might one day destroy the world. This fear, demonstrated in a number of periodicals almost immediately after the bombing of Hiroshima, represented a natural extension of the primary fear of national destruction. John O'Neill, writing in 1945, encapsulated this fear among the American public when he asserted that "there has been fearful speculation that man might blow up the earth through his bungling experiments with the release of atomic energy."[17] O'Neill seemed skeptical of this possibility, but his observation demonstrates the far ranging insecurity which pervaded American society and came to shape international relations.

An interesting result of the use of the atomic bomb on Japan was the transformative effect it had on international relations. In the months after the bomb was dropped and World War Two was brought to a close, many in the United States began calling for a renewed focus on peace in

> *Idea touched on in the introduction.*

international relations. Indeed, a writer for the *Washington Post* argued in 1945 that, "it is possible at this point to draw only one conclusion, namely, that if the peoples of the world cannot now live in unity and peace, they will presently not live at all."[18] According to Boyer, this "primal fear of extinction" was pervasive throughout the United States and was one of the hallmarks of the initial American response to the dropping of the atomic bomb.[19]

---

[14] Christine Hong, "Flashforward Democracy: American Exceptionalism and the Atomic Bomb in Barefoot Gen," *Comparative Literature Studies* 46, no. I (2009): 125.

[15] Boyer, *By the Bomb's Early Light*, 5.

[16] "The Atomic Bomb," *New York Herald Tribune*, August 7, 1945, 2, quoted in Paul Boyer, *By the Bomb's Early Light* (New York: Pantheon Books, 1985), 6.

[17] O'Neill, 8.

[18] "The Haunted Wood," 6

[19] Boyer, *By the Bomb's Early Light*, 15.

Righteousness ◄————— Section heading: third point

The third major reaction of the American public to the news of the dropping of the atomic bomb on Japan was a sense that the action, no matter how devastating, was justified. This sense of righteousness had its roots in a number of sources ranging from a sense of revenge for the Japanese attack on Pearl Harbor to the belief, ardently propagated by the Truman administration, that the only alternative to the use of the atomic bomb was a costly invasion of Japan. This last point proved to be particularly persuasive in part because of the political efforts of the Truman administration but also because of the war weariness of the American citizens.[20] Nevertheless, the sense of righteousness which existed across the country in the wake of the dropping of the atomic bomb is a major theme in the greater reaction of the American public.

According to polling conducted in September of 1945, 69 percent of respondents viewed the dropping of the atomic bomb on Japan as "a good thing."[21] Historians disagree as to what contributed to this favorable opinion held by the American public, but the impetus undoubtedly lies in the information that was made available to the public in the aftermath of the bombing of Hiroshima. For example, J. Samuel Walker argues that the generally favorable response of the American public to the atomic bomb can be attributed to the popularly held perception that the only alternative to using the atomic bomb was an invasion of the Japanese mainland.[22] Indeed from the first announcement of the use of the atomic bomb, the Truman administration clearly attempted to establish a link of causality from the atomic bombing of Hiroshima to the imminent end of the war. In his address, Truman stated that, "we are now prepared to obliterate more rapidly and completely every productive enterprise the Japanese have above ground in

---

[20] Peter N. Kirstein, "Hiroshima and Spinning the Atom: America, Britain, and Canada Proclaim the Nuclear Age, 6 August 1945," *The Historian* (2009): 18, https://proxy.lib.muohio.edu/login?source=ebsco&url=http://search.ebscohost.com.proxy.lib.muohio.edu/login.aspx?direct=true&db=a9h&AN=45694253&site=ehost-live (accessed December 2, 2011).

[21] Lillian Wald Kay, "Public Opinion and the Atom," *Journal of Educational Sociology* 22 (January 1949): 357, quoted in Paul Boyer, *By the Bomb's Early Light*, 22.

[22] J. Samuel Walker, *Prompt & Utter Destruction: Truman and the Use of Atomic Bombs Against Japan* (Chapel Hill: University of North Carolina Press, 1997), 5.

any city."[23] Truman went on to state, "If they [the Japanese] do not now accept our terms they may expect a rain of ruin from the air, the like of which has never been seen on this earth."[24] These statements

> Adds clarity to quote.

were widely disseminated to the American public and, when the war ended, helped to establish a link between the use of the atomic bomb and the cessation of hostilities.

In *Life Under a Cloud*, Allan Winkler asserts that there was a concerted effort among policymakers and scientists to manipulate the reaction of the American public to the use of the atomic bomb in order to create a more favorable environment to continue atomic research and deflect attention from the actual use of the bomb on Japan.[25] One component of this effort was the deliberate linking of the atomic bombing of Hiroshima to the bombing of Pearl Harbor by the Japanese. In his announcement of the atomic bomb, President Truman reminded Americans of the devastation wrought by the Japanese on the United States at Pearl Harbor in an obvious attempt to justify the use of the bomb to end the war.[26] Statements such as these were reprinted in many newspapers and periodicals and undoubtedly had an impact on the way in which Americans reacted to the bombing.[27]

> Look at the information in the footnote. The footnote gives more information that is too bulky and irrelevant to be included in the essay text.

A more revealing example may be found in a letter written by President Truman in response to a critic of his decision to use the atomic bomb. Truman writes, "Nobody is more disturbed over the use of Atomic bombs than I am but I was greatly disturbed over the

---

[23] Truman, "Statement by the President Announcing the Use of the A-Bomb at Hiroshima."

[24] Ibid.

25 Winkler, 8.

26 Truman, "Statement by the President Announcing the Use of the A-Bomb at Hiroshima."

[27] For examples of these statements being cited in contemporary periodicals, see "The Haunted Wood"; Arthur Henning, "Power of the Universe Tapped to Create New Missile," *Chicago Daily Tribune*, August 7, 1945, http://search.proquest.com.proxy.lib.muohio.edu/hnpchicagotribune/docview/177141348/133707766FF47048936/2?accountid=12434 (accessed December 4, 2011).

unwarranted attack by the Japanese on Pearl Harbor."[28] These sorts of linkages are placed into context by Paul Boyer, who writes, "To be sure, the immediate reaction was also influenced by the fact that for nearly four years Japan had been the hated, treacherous enemy. Vengeance was on many minds."[29]

Conclusion

> Section heading: this is the summation/restatement of the question and the reason behind the essay.

The use of the atomic bomb on Japan was a watershed event in the course of world history. Much has been written about the lasting effects of atomic weapons on warfare, international relations, and global politics, but there is a comparative dearth of material that focuses exclusively on the reactions of the American public to the atomic bomb. While it is diffi-

> Contextualizes the conclusion with other researchers and states why this research is distinct and important.

cult to characterize the reaction of "the American public," my research has shown that three main themes are present in the newspapers and periodicals of 1945 which help historians to understand the American response. One theme was that of a sense of shock at the very existence of a bomb which could destroy an entire city in the blink of an eye.

> Reiteration of the three major points (shock, fear, righteousness) and succinctly how these points relate to the American understanding of the Bomb.

The second major theme was a widespread fear that the bomb may one day be used to level a city in the United States, or even may one day destroy humanity. The third major theme of the reaction of the American public was the sense that the Japanese had such an attack coming to them. As the vast majority of Americans had little firsthand knowledge of the atomic bomb due to the secrecy of the Manhattan Project, the media and public officials had a profound impact on the shaping of American public opinion on the

---

[28] Harry Truman to Samuel M. Calvert, August 11, 1945, Official File, Papers of Harry S. Truman, Harry S. Truman Library and Museum, http://www.trumanlibrary.org/flip_books/index.php?tldate=1945–08-09&groupid=3705&titleid=&pagenumber=1&collectionid=ihow (accessed December 4, 2011).

[29] Boyer, *By the Bomb's Early Light*, 12.

atomic bomb. As one studies the news reports and articles written about the atomic bomb in the year 1945, one is struck by the total lack of information pertaining to the specific toll exacted upon the Japanese people.[30] Deprived of this information and bombarded with vague descriptions of the bomb's terrifying power and the justifications of the Truman administration, the American public was broadly unconcerned with the humanitarian cost of the atomic bomb and looked toward the future with a dread known only to those who were present at the dawn of the atomic age.

Ties to future—why this essay matters.

[30] For an explanation of this phenomenon, see Christine Hong, "Flashforward Democracy: American Exceptionalism and the Atomic Bomb in Barefoot Gen," *Comparative Literature Studies* 46, no. I (2009): 125.

FOR FURTHER READING

Cohen, Daniel J., and Roy Rosenzweig. *Digital History: A Guide to Gathering, Preserving, and Presenting the Past on the Web.* Philadelphia: University of Pennsylvania Press, 2006. http://chnm.gmu.edu/digitalhistory/ (accessed December 30, 2011).

Hammerich, Irene, and Claire Harrison. *Developing Online Content: The Principles of Writing and Editing for the Web.* New York: John Wiley & Sons, 2002. This text is especially useful for creating text for a more academic website, instead of a commercial one. It pays a great deal of attention to how to focus and tightly write your text, just as you would for a research paper. Excellent source.

Holmes, Merlyn. *Web Usability and Navigation: A Beginner's Guide.* Berkeley: McGraw-Hill/Osborne, 2002. This source discusses page layout and provides lots of examples of usability tests. This will help you with navigation issues rather than text development.

Jakob, Nielsen. *useit.com.* http://www.useit.com/ (accessed December 30, 2011). Website dedicated to usable information technology. See especially his *Alertbox* columns.

Krug, Steve. *Don't Make Me Think!: A Common Sense Approach to Web Usability.* Indianapolis: New Riders Publishing, 2000. Sensible, positive approach to organizing a website. One of the best books to read. Includes chapters on how to evaluate the usability of your own website.

Lynch, Patrick J., and Sarah Horton. *Web Style Guide*. 2d ed. New Haven: Yale University Press, 2001. http://www.webstyleguide.com/index.html. Aimed at scientists, this is an excellent guide to website construction. Particularly useful for inclusion of images.

Nicol, Adelheid A. M., and Penny M. Pexman. *Displaying Your Findings: A Practical Guide for Creating Figures, Posters, and Presentations*. Washington, DC: American Psychological Association, 2010.

Price, Jonathan, and Lisa Price. *Hot Text: Web Writing that Works*. Indianapolis: New Riders Publishers, 2002. Step-by-step guide to designing, writing, and placing text. Excellent tips on how to refine and target your audience.

Reiss, Eric L. *Practical Information Architecture: A Hands-on Approach to Structuring Successful Websites*. New York: Addison Wesley, 2000. Alternative guide to the others listed here.

Rosenfeld, Louis, and Peter Morville. *Information Architecture for the World Wide Web*. 2d ed. Sebastapol, CA: O'Reilly & Associates, 2002. The best, most comprehensive source for information architecture. Readable. This is the place to begin!

Veen, Jeffrey. *The Art and Science of Web Design*. Indianapolis: New Riders, 2001. More technical than most guides in terms of the mechanics of creating websites. Integrates the technical with information architecture issues.

Webmonkey. http://www.webmonkey.com (accessed December 30, 2011). Website with tips on design and programming tips.

Williams, Robin. *The Non-Designers Design Book*. Berkeley: Peachpit Press, 2010. Graphic and visual discussion of page layout, whether for the web or for a more traditional paper layout. Discusses such issues as font choices, sizes of fonts and graphics, and image vs. text placement on a page.

Wong, Dona M. *The Wall Street Journal Guide to Information Graphics: The Dos and Don'ts of Presenting Data, Facts, and Figures*. New York: W. W. Norton & Co., 2010.

NOTES

1. Patrick Rael, *Reading, Writing, and Researching for History: A Guide for College Students* (Brunswick, ME: Bowdoin College, 2004), http://www.bowdoin.edu/WritingGuides/ (accessed September 15, 2011); William Kelleher Storey, *Writing History: A Guide for Students*, 3d ed. (New York: Oxford University Press, 2009); Donald Hall and Sven Birkerts, *Writing Well*, 9th ed. (New York: Longman, 2007).

2. William Kelleher Storey, *Writing History: A Guide for Students,* 2d ed. (New York: Oxford University Press, 2004), 61–65, 81–86.

3. Ibid., 81.

4. Jim Cullen, *Essaying the Past: How to Read, Write, and Think about History* (Malden, MA: Wiley/Blackwell, 2009), 122.

5. Storey has a nice discussion of including counterarguments on pages 84–86 in the 3d edition.

6. Charles C. McDougald, *The Marcos File: Was He a Philippine Hero or Corrupt Tyrant?* (San Francisco: San Francisco Publishers, 1987).

7. David Hackett Fischer, *Historians' Fallacies: Toward a Logic of Historical Thought* (New York: Harper and Row, 1970).

8. Hal and Birkerts, *Writing Well*, 57; and Cullen, *Essaying the Past*, 117–120.

9. Cullen, *Essaying the Past*, 116–117.

10. Cullen, *Essaying the Past*, 95; and Hal and Birkerts, *Writing Well*, 61.

11. Storey, *Writing History*, 2d ed. 74.

12. Ibid., 88.

13. Jamie McKenzie, "Scoring Power Points," *From Now On: The Educational Technology Journal* 10 (Sept. 2000), http://www.fno.org/sept00/powerpoints. html (accessed December 2, 2011); Trevor Shaw, "Dodging the Bullets: The Danger of Reductionism in PowerPoint Presentations," *Multimedia Schools* 10 (Nov. 2003): 46

14. Edward R. Tufte, *The Cognitive Style of Power Point* (Cheshire, CT: Graphics Press, 2003).

15. Ibid., 24.

16. Ibid., 22–25; and Andrea A. Lunsford and John J. Ruszkiewicz, *Everything's an Argument* (Boston: Bedford/St. Martins, 2010), 466–485.

17. Peter Norvig, *The Gettysburg PowerPoint Presentation*, http://www.norvig. com/Gettysburg/ (accessed September 25, 2011).

18. Jay David Bolter, *Writing Space: Computers, Hypertext, and the Remediation of Print*, 2d ed. (Mahwah, NJ: Lawrence Erlbaum Associates, 2001), 51.

19. Ibid., 68.

20. Patrick J. Lynch and Sarah Horton, *Web Style Guide,* 3d ed. http://webstyle-guide.com/wsg3/index.html/ (accessed September 25, 2011); Louis Rosenfeld and Peter Morville, *Information Architecture for the World Wide Web*, 3d ed. (Sebastopol, CA: O'Reilly, 2006); Steve Krug, *Don't Make Me Think: A Common Sense Approach to Web Usability,* 2d ed. (Berkeley, CA: New Riders, 2006); Daniel J. Cohen and Roy Rosenzweig, *Digital History: A Guide to Gathering, Preserving, and Presenting the Past on the Web* (Philadelphia: University of Pennsylvania Press, 2006).

21. Michael Gold, *Best Practices for Your Website. Making Your Website Work for Your User*, Steve Kantola, prod. Mill Valley. Kantola Productions, Stanford Video, 2003, videocassette, 46 min.

22. Jakob Nielsen, *Designing Web Usability: The Practice of Simplicity* (Indianapolis: New Riders, 2000), 106.

23. Jonathan Price and Lisa Price, *Hot Text: Web Writing that Works* (Indianapolis: New Riders, 2002), xiii.

24. Judy Gregory, "Writing for the Web Versus Writing for Print: Are They Really so Different?" *Technical Communication* 51 (May 2004): 278.

25. Rosenfeld and Morville, *Information Architecture,* 56–64.

26. Krug, *Don't Make Me Think,* 31–39.

27. These navigation rules, common to most websites, are a summary of information presented by both Krug and Rosenfeld and Morville.

28. Ibid.

29. Many ideas and suggestions in this section come from Lynch and Horton's *Web Style Guide*, Editorial Style (http://webstyleguide.com/wsg3/index.html) (accessed December 2, 2011). See also Constance Hale, ed., *Wired Style: Principles of English Usage in the Digital Age* (San Francisco: HardWired, 1996); Price and Price, *Hot Text*; Gregory, "Writing for the Web," 276–285.

30. Lynch and Horton, "Page Design," in *Web Style Guide* (http://webstyleguide.com/wsg3/index.html) (accessed December 2, 2011).

31. Price and Price, *Hot Text*, 84–269.

32. Lynch and Horton, "Process," in *Web Style Guide*.

Index